MOST REQUESTED RECIPES

Taste of Home

TASTE OF HOME BOOKS • RDA ENTHUSIAST BRANDS, LLC • MILWAUKEE, WI

123

130

RECIPES YOU'LL KEEP FOREVER

Every great cook has that special collection of recipe all-stars. You know the ones. The keepers smudged and annotated with Mom's handwritten notes for getting it *just right*. Instagram-worthy dishes that have friends and followers liking, clicking, pinning and gushing with accolades.

You don't have to look far to find these kinds of recipes and more because they're all right here in one convenient cookbook. Now in its 7th edition, ***Taste of Home Most Requested Recipes*** showcases 378 first-rate favorites to create unforgettable meals from start to finish.

Each dish was reviewed and approved by experts in the *Taste of Home* Test Kitchen, so you know everything will turn out amazing. And because these are the classics today's cooks are setting on their own tables, you can rest assured they're going to be hits with your family and friends, too.

Step-by-step instructions and vibrant full-color photos make it easy to cook with confidence. With dozens of helpful kitchen tips and tricks and first-person reader reviews, you'll know why a recipe is ranked as one of the best.

And when life gets busy, refer to these handy at-a-glance icons to make the most of your time in the kitchen.

These quick-to-fix recipes are table ready in 30 minutes or less.

5i These dishes require no more than five items (not counting water, oil, salt, pepper and optional ingredients). What could be easier?

Winners and runners-up in one of our *Taste of Home* recipe contests.

You and your family deserve the best, so what are you waiting for? Whether you need a showstopper for a potluck, a sweet treat for a birthday party or a fresh twist on an old dinnertime fave, you're guaranteed to find a winner in ***Taste of Home Most Requested Recipes!***

1610 N. 2nd St., Suite 102, Milwaukee WI 53212-3906

Visit: *tasteofhome.com* for other *Taste of Home* books and products.

International Standard Book Numbers:
D 978-1-61765-881-5
U 978-1-61765-882-2
International Standard Serial Number: 2166-0522
Component Numbers:
D 119200032H
U 119200034H

Deputy Editor: Mark Hagen
Senior Art Director: Raeann Thompson
Editor: Amy Glander

Senior Designer: Courtney Lovetere
Designer: Jazmin Delgado
Copy Editor: Amy Rabideau Silvers

Cover Photography Photographer: Jim Wieland
Set Stylist: Stacey Genaw
Food Stylist: Josh Rink

Pictured on front cover: Cheese-Stuffed Shells, p. 103

Pictured on title page: Buttermilk Cake with Cider Icing, p. 179

Pictured on back cover: Spinach Salad with Tortellini & Roasted Onions, p. 65; Spiced Devil's Food Cake, p. 169; Can-Can Chicken, p. 97

Printed in U.S.A.
1 3 5 7 9 10 8 6 4 2

92

207

18

37

TABLE OF CONTENTS

82

To find a recipe: tasteofhome.com
To submit a recipe: tasteofhome.com/submit
To find out about other *Taste of Home* products: shoptasteofhome.com

LIKE US facebook.com/tasteofhome

TWEET US twitter.com/tasteofhome

Appetizers, Snacks & Beverages

What's a party without a stellar lineup of savory noshes and finger foods you can pop in your mouth? Here are our top picks to make your celebration shine.

APPLE-GOUDA PIGS IN A BLANKET

Every New Year's I used to make beef and cheddar pigs in a blanket. Then one year I decided to switch it up with apple and Gouda for an even better flavor combination.
—Megan Weiss, Menomonie, WI

Takes: 30 min. • **Makes:** 2 dozen

- **1 tube (8 oz.) refrigerated crescent rolls**
- **1 small apple, peeled and cut into 24 thin slices**
- **6 thin slices Gouda cheese, quartered**
- **24 miniature smoked sausages**
- **Honey mustard salad dressing, optional**

1. Preheat oven to 375°. Unroll the crescent dough and separate into eight triangles; cut each lengthwise into three thin triangles. On the wide end of each triangle, place one slice apple, one folded piece of Gouda cheese and one sausage; roll up tightly.
2. Place 1 in. apart on parchment-lined baking sheets, point side down. Bake until golden brown, 10-12 minutes. If desired, serve with honey mustard dressing.
1 APPETIZER: 82 cal., 6g fat (2g sat. fat), 11mg chol., 203mg sod., 5g carb. (1g sugars, 0 fiber), 3g pro.

DID YOU KNOW?
Gouda is a semi-firm creamy yellow Dutch cheese that can be mild or pungent in flavor. It is usually found wrapped in a red wax rind and often served as a dessert cheese with fruit, on sandwiches, with wine or on cheese platters. You can also purchase it in a block or pre-sliced.

5i

TIPSY ICED COFFEE

My family loves this frozen coffee with amaretto and whipped cream. Serve it at brunch or as an after-dinner treat.
—Sonya Labbe, West Hollywood, CA

Prep: 10 min. + freezing • **Makes:** 8 servings

- **4 cups strong brewed coffee**
- **½ cup amaretto**
- **¼ cup plus 3 Tbsp. sugar, divided**
- **⅔ cup heavy whipping cream**

1. In a large bowl, whisk coffee, amaretto and ¼ cup sugar. Cool to room temperature.
2. Transfer to an 8-in. square dish. Freeze 1 hour. Stir with a fork. Freeze 2-3 hours longer or until completely frozen, stirring every 30 minutes.
3. Meanwhile, in a small bowl, beat cream until it begins to thicken. Add remaining 3 Tbsp. sugar; beat until stiff peaks form. Cover and refrigerate until serving.
4. To serve, stir mixture with a fork; spoon into glasses. Top with whipped cream. Serve immediately.
NOTE: Not sure which brand of coffee to buy? Visit *www.tasteofhome.com/article/coffee-brands-taste-test/* to view the brands our editors and the *Taste of Home* Test Kitchen recommend.
1 CUP WITH 2 TBSP. WHIPPED CREAM: 165 cal., 7g fat (5g sat. fat), 23mg chol., 7mg sod., 17g carb. (17g sugars, 0 fiber), 1g pro.

VEGGIE RANCH TORTILLA PINWHEELS

These bite-sized appetizers are a hit wherever I take them. They're easy to make ahead of time and pair well with other party classics.
—Lori Kostecki, Wausau, WI

Takes: 25 min. • **Makes:** about 5 dozen

- **2 pkg. (8 oz. each) cream cheese, softened**
- **1 envelope ranch salad dressing mix**
- **5 green onions, chopped**
- **1 can (4 oz.) chopped green chiles, drained**
- **1 can (3.8 oz.) sliced ripe olives, drained**
- **1 celery rib, chopped**
- **¼ cup chopped sweet red pepper**
- **2 to 3 Tbsp. real bacon bits**
- **8 flour tortillas (10 in.)**

In a small bowl, beat cream cheese and dressing mix until blended. Beat in the onions, green chiles, olives, celery, red pepper and bacon. Spread over tortillas. Roll up. Cut each into 1-in. slices. Refrigerate leftovers.
1 PIECE: 58 cal., 3g fat (2g sat. fat), 8mg chol., 188mg sod., 5g carb. (0 sugars, 1g fiber), 1g pro.

PINEAPPLE CHEESE BALL

Pineapple lends a sweet and fruity tang to this fun and tasty cheese ball. You can form the mixture into one large ball or make two smaller balls—one to serve before a meal and one to take to an event.
—Anne Halfhill, Sunbury, OH

Prep: 20 min. + chilling
Makes: 1 cheese ball (24 servings)

- **2 pkg. (8 oz. each) cream cheese, softened**
- **1 can (8 oz.) unsweetened crushed pineapple, drained**
- **¼ cup finely chopped green pepper**
- **2 Tbsp. finely chopped onion**
- **2 tsp. seasoned salt**
- **1½ cups finely chopped walnuts**
- **Assorted crackers**

In a small mixing bowl, beat the cream cheese, pineapple, green pepper, onion and seasoned salt until blended. Cover and refrigerate for 30 minutes. Shape mixture into a ball; roll in walnuts. Cover and refrigerate overnight. Serve with crackers.
2 TBSP.: 87 cal., 8g fat (2g sat. fat), 10mg chol., 155mg sod., 3g carb. (1g sugars, 1g fiber), 3g pro.

PARMESAN-PRETZEL CRISPS

Here's a speedy snack to include on your next party menu. I usually have the ingredients on hand, and it is so easy to make.

—Pauline Porterfield, Roxboro, NC

Prep: 10 min. • **Bake:** 10 min./batch
Makes: about 3 dozen

- **1½ cups shredded Parmesan cheese**
- **¼ cup finely crushed pretzels**
- **⅛ tsp. crushed red pepper flakes**
- **Pizza sauce and sliced fresh basil, optional**

1. Preheat oven to 350°. Toss together the cheese, pretzels and red pepper flakes. Place 2 tsp. mixture in each greased nonstick mini muffin cup.

2. Bake until golden brown, 10-15 minutes. If desired, serve with pizza sauce and basil.

1 CRISP: 16 cal., 1g fat (1g sat. fat), 2mg chol., 66mg sod., 1g carb. (0 sugars, 0 fiber), 1g pro.

PEPPERONI ROLL-UPS

This fast appetizer recipe goes over big at my house. Each bite has gooey, melted cheese and classic pizza flavor. Try serving them with pizza sauce for dipping.

—Debra Purcell, Safford, AZ

Takes: 20 min. • **Makes:** 8 appetizers

- **1 tube (8 oz.) refrigerated crescent rolls**
- **16 slices pepperoni, cut into quarters**
- **2 pieces string cheese (1 oz. each), cut into quarters**
- **¾ tsp. Italian seasoning, divided**
- **¼ tsp. garlic salt**

1. Unroll crescent dough; separate into eight triangles. Place eight pepperoni pieces on each. Place a piece of cheese on the short side of each triangle; sprinkle with ½ tsp. Italian seasoning. Roll up each, starting with the short side; pinch seams to seal. Sprinkle with garlic salt and remaining Italian seasoning.

2. Place 2 in. apart on a greased baking sheet. Bake at 375° for 10-12 minutes or until golden brown. Serve warm.

2 ROLL-UPS: 282 cal., 17g fat (5g sat. fat), 12mg chol., 766mg sod., 22g carb. (4g sugars, 0 fiber), 7g pro.

OLIVE-ONION CHEESE BREAD

This will have your guests reaching for more. The cheese, onions, and olives make this bread a delicious and flavorful appetizer.

—Amy Daniels, Brodhead, WI

Takes: 30 min. • **Makes:** 16 servings

- **4 cups shredded part-skim mozzarella cheese**
- **1 cup butter, softened**
- **1 cup mayonnaise**
- **8 green onions, thinly sliced**
- **1 can (8 oz.) mushroom stems and pieces, drained and chopped**
- **1 can (4¼ oz.) chopped ripe olives**
- **1 loaf (1 lb.) unsliced French bread**

1. In a large bowl, combine the first six ingredients. Cut bread in half lengthwise; place on an ungreased baking sheet. Spread with cheese mixture.

2. Bake at 350° for 15-20 minutes or until the cheese is melted. Cut each half into eight slices.

1 SLICE: 369 cal., 28g fat (12g sat. fat), 51mg chol., 590mg sod., 18g carb. (2g sugars, 1g fiber), 11g pro.

PARTY PESTO PINWHEELS

I took a few of my favorite recipes and combined them into these delicious hors d'oeuvres. The colorful spirals come together easily, thanks to refrigerated crescent roll dough, prepared pesto sauce and a jar of roasted red peppers.

—Kathleen Farrell, Rochester, NY

Takes: 30 min. • **Makes:** 20 pinwheels

- **1 tube (8 oz.) refrigerated crescent rolls**
- **⅓ cup prepared pesto sauce**
- **¼ cup roasted sweet red peppers, drained and chopped**
- **¼ cup grated Parmesan cheese**
- **1 cup pizza sauce, warmed**

1. Unroll crescent dough into two long rectangles; seal seams and perforations. Spread each with pesto; sprinkle with red peppers and cheese.

2. Roll each up jelly-roll style, starting with a short side. With a sharp knife, cut each roll into 10 slices. Place cut side down 2 in. apart on two ungreased baking sheets.

3. Bake at 400° for 8-10 minutes or until golden brown. Serve warm with pizza sauce.

1 PINWHEEL: 76 cal., 5g fat (1g sat. fat), 2mg chol., 201mg sod., 6g carb. (2g sugars, 0 fiber), 2g pro.

CHEDDAR-BACON DIP

Both children and adults enjoy this dip. I like it, too—it's so quick and easy to prepare. I make it for birthday parties, holiday gatherings and other special occasions.

—Carol Werkman, Neerlandia, AB

Prep: 15 min. + chilling • **Makes:** 12 servings

- **1 pkg. (8 oz.) cream cheese, softened**
- **1 cup sour cream**
- **5 green onions, thinly sliced**
- **4 medium tomatoes, chopped**
- **1 large green pepper, chopped**
- **1 jar (16 oz.) taco sauce**
- **2 cups shredded cheddar cheese**
- **1 lb. sliced bacon, cooked and crumbled**
- **Tortilla or nacho tortilla chips**

1. In a bowl, beat cream cheese and sour cream until smooth. Spread in an ungreased 13x9-in. dish or on a 12-in. plate. Combine onions, tomatoes and green pepper; sprinkle over the cream cheese layer.

2. Pour taco sauce over the vegetables. Sprinkle with cheddar cheese. Refrigerate. Just before serving, sprinkle with bacon. Serve with chips.

1 SERVING: 277 cal., 22g fat (13g sat. fat), 65mg chol., 590mg sod., 9g carb. (5g sugars, 2g fiber), 11g pro.

WARM CRAB & SPINACH DIP

In Maryland, we stayed at a hotel that sent guests home with a crab dip recipe and a spice packet. The dip was so good I created my own homemade version that rekindles memories of that trip.

—Kristina Wenner, Jamison, PA

Prep: 20 min. • **Cook:** 15 min.
Makes: 4½ cups

- 2 **Tbsp. olive oil**
- ⅓ **cup finely chopped sweet onion**
- 2 **garlic cloves, minced**
- 1 **pkg. (8 oz.) softened cream cheese, cubed**
- 1 **pkg. (5.2 oz.) Boursin garlic and fine herbs cheese**
- ¼ **cup 2% milk**
- ¼ **cup half-and-half cream**
- ¼ **cup white wine or chicken broth**
- 1 **Tbsp. seafood seasoning**
- 2 **tsp. Worcestershire sauce**
- 1 **tsp. Louisiana-style hot sauce**
- ⅛ **tsp. crushed red pepper flakes, optional**
- 2 **cans (6 oz. each) lump crabmeat, drained and picked over**
- 1 **pkg. (10 oz.) frozen chopped spinach, thawed and squeezed dry**
- 2 **cups shredded cheddar cheese**
- **Blue tortilla chips**

1. In a large nonstick skillet, heat oil over medium heat. Add onion and garlic; cook 3 minutes. Stir in cream cheese and Boursin until melted. Add milk, cream and wine, stirring constantly.

2. Add seafood seasoning, Worcestershire, hot sauce and red pepper flakes. Stir in crab, spinach and cheddar cheese until cheese melts and mixture is bubbly. Serve warm with blue tortilla chips.

¼ CUP: 170 cal., 14g fat (8g sat. fat), 55mg chol., 421mg sod., 2g carb. (1g sugars, 1g fiber), 9g pro.

APPETIZER ROLL-UPS

Cream cheese and a variety of vegetables and herbs turn everyday deli cold cuts into a fancy and filling appetizer. It makes for a pretty party platter, but don't expect your arrangement to stay complete for long once this snack is served.

—Marcella Funk, Salem, OR

Prep: 20 min. + chilling • **Makes:** 6 dozen

ROAST BEEF ROLL-UPS

- 4 **oz. cream cheese, softened**
- ¼ **cup minced fresh cilantro**
- 2 **to 3 Tbsp. minced banana peppers**
- 1 **garlic clove, minced**
- ½ **lb. thinly sliced cooked roast beef**

HAM AND TURKEY ROLL-UPS

- 12 **oz. cream cheese, softened**
- ½ **cup shredded carrot**
- ½ **cup shredded zucchini**
- 4 **tsp. dill weed**
- ½ **lb. thinly sliced fully cooked ham**
- ½ **lb. thinly sliced cooked turkey**

1. In a small bowl, combine the cream cheese, cilantro, peppers and garlic. Spread about 2 Tbsp. on each slice of beef. Roll up tightly and wrap in plastic.

2. For ham and turkey rolls, in another bowl, combine the cream cheese, carrot, zucchini and dill. Spread about 2 Tbsp. on each slice of ham and turkey. Roll up tightly; wrap in plastic. Refrigerate overnight. Slice the roll-ups into 1½-in. pieces.

1 HAM OR TURKEY ROLL-UP: 41 cal., 3g fat (2g sat. fat), 15mg chol., 93mg sod., 1g carb (0 sugars, 0 fiber), 3g pro.

1 BEEF ROLL-UP: 28 cal., 2g fat (1g sat. fat), 10mg chol., 68mg sod., 1g carb. (0 sugars, 0 fiber), 2g pro.

READER REVIEW

"These are great to throw together if unexpected guests visit. It's filling and it always presents so nicely on a serving plate. I've also used these as a snack when the kids come home from school. So handy to pick up and go!"

KARENDYC, TASTEOFHOME.COM

TZATZIKI SHRIMP CUCUMBER ROUNDS

I created this recipe with what I had on hand one night, and now it's one of my husband's favorites. The bacon-wrapped shrimp, garlicky sauce and burst of cool cuke flavor make these irresistible.
—*Shannon Rose Trelease, East Hampton, NY*

Prep: 25 min. • **Cook:** 10 min./batch
Makes: 2 dozen

- **¼ cup reduced-fat plain yogurt**
- **2 Tbsp. finely chopped peeled cucumber**
- **⅛ tsp. garlic salt**
- **⅛ tsp. dill weed**
- **6 bacon strips**
- **24 uncooked shrimp (31-40 per lb.), peeled and deveined**
- **1 to 2 Tbsp. canola oil**
- **2 medium cucumbers, cut into ¼-in. slices**

1. In a small bowl, combine plain yogurt, chopped cucumber, garlic salt and dill; set aside.
2. Cut each bacon strip in half widthwise and then lengthwise. Wrap a piece of bacon around each shrimp. Secure with toothpicks.
3. In a nonstick skillet, heat oil over medium heat; cook shrimp in batches for 3-4 minutes on each side or until bacon is crisp.
4. Spoon a rounded ½ tsp. yogurt sauce onto each cucumber slice; top with shrimp.
1 APPETIZER: 30 cal., 2g fat (0 sat. fat), 18mg chol., 64mg sod., 1g carb. (0 sugars, 0 fiber), 3g pro.

READER REVIEW

"So simple, delicious and elegant. I brought these to a holiday function and everyone loved them!"

CINDIAK, TASTEOFHOME.COM

PEPPERED MEATBALLS

Plenty of ground pepper is the secret to these saucy meatballs. Enjoy them as an appetizer or serve them over noodles for a main dish.

—Darla Schroeder, Stanley, ND

Prep: 35 min. • **Cook:** 2 hours
Makes: 1½ dozen

- ½ **cup sour cream**
- 2 **tsp. grated Parmesan or Romano cheese**
- 2 **to 3 tsp. pepper**
- 1 **tsp. salt**
- 1 **tsp. dry bread crumbs**
- ½ **tsp. garlic powder**
- 1½ **lbs. ground beef**

SAUCE

- 1 **can (10¾ oz.) condensed cream of mushroom soup, undiluted**
- 1 **cup sour cream**
- 2 **tsp. dill weed**
- ½ **tsp. sugar**
- ½ **tsp. pepper**
- ¼ **tsp. garlic powder**

1. In a large bowl, combine sour cream and cheese. Add the pepper, salt, bread crumbs and garlic powder. Crumble meat over mixture and mix well. Shape into 1-in. balls.
2. Place meatballs on a greased rack in a shallow baking pan. Bake at 350° until no longer pink, 20-25 minutes; drain.
3. Transfer to a 1½-qt. slow cooker. Combine the sauce ingredients; pour over meatballs. Cover and cook on high for 2-3 hours or until heated through.
2 EACH: 259 cal., 18g fat (9g sat. fat), 77mg chol., 565mg sod., 5g carb. (2g sugars, 0 fiber), 17g pro.

PARTY FRANKS

These tiny, tangy appetizers have broad appeal. I make them for holidays, weddings and family reunions. Make the sauce ahead for convenience and reheat with the franks before serving.

—Lucille Howell, Portland, OR

Prep: 30 min. • **Bake:** 20 min.
Makes: 16 servings

- ¾ **cup chopped onion**
- 2 **Tbsp. vegetable oil**
- 1 **cup ketchup**
- ½ **cup water**
- ½ **cup cider vinegar**
- 2 **Tbsp. sugar**
- 2 **Tbsp. Worcestershire sauce**
- 2 **Tbsp. honey**
- 2 **tsp. ground mustard**
- 2 **tsp. paprika**
- ¾ **tsp. salt**
- ¼ **tsp. pepper**
- ⅛ **tsp. hot pepper sauce**
- 1 **large lemon, sliced**
- 2½ **to 3 lbs. miniature hot dogs or smoked sausage links**

In a saucepan, saute onion in oil until tender. Stir in the next 11 ingredients. Add lemon. Bring mixture to a boil. Reduce heat; simmer, uncovered, for 20-25 minutes or until slightly thickened, stirring occasionally. Discard lemon slices. Place hot dogs in a 13x9-in. baking dish. Top with sauce. Bake, uncovered, at 350° for 18-20 minutes or until heated through. Keep warm; serve with toothpicks.
⅓ CUP: 268 cal., 21g fat (7g sat. fat), 45mg chol., 1047mg sod., 11g carb. (9g sugars, 0 fiber), 9g pro.

CRAB CAKES WITH PEANUT SAUCE

Crab cakes are a go-to on my party food list. It would be accurate to say the peanut sauce in this recipe takes the cake!
—Amber Massey, Argyle, TX

Prep: 25 min. + chilling • **Cook:** 5 min./batch
Makes: 1 dozen (⅓ cup sauce)

- ¼ **cup rice vinegar**
- 2 **Tbsp. creamy peanut butter**
- 1 **garlic clove, minced**
- 1 **tsp. brown sugar**
- 1 **tsp. olive oil**
- ¼ **tsp. ground mustard**
- **Dash cayenne pepper**

CRAB CAKES

- 1 **cup plain Greek yogurt**
- ⅔ **cup crushed saltines (about 15 crackers)**
- ¼ **cup finely chopped celery**
- ¼ **cup finely chopped roasted sweet red pepper**
- ¼ **cup minced fresh parsley**
- 2 **Tbsp. finely chopped onion**
- 1 **large egg white, lightly beaten**
- 1 **Tbsp. fresh lemon juice**
- 2 **tsp. prepared horseradish**
- ½ **tsp. paprika**
- ¼ **tsp. salt**
- 1 **lb. lump crabmeat, drained**
- 1 **Tbsp. olive oil**
- **Minced fresh chives**

1. In a small bowl, whisk the first seven ingredients until blended. Set sauce aside.
2. In a large bowl, mix the first 11 crab cake ingredients until blended. Fold in crab. Shape into twelve ½-in.-thick patties. Refrigerate, covered, 30 minutes.
3. In a large skillet, heat 1 Tbsp. olive oil over medium-high heat. Add crab cakes in batches; cook 2-3 minutes on each side or until golden brown. Sprinkle with chives; serve with sauce.
1 CRAB CAKE WITH 1 TSP. SAUCE: 114 cal., 6g fat (2g sat. fat), 49mg chol., 270mg sod., 6g carb. (2g sugars, 0 fiber), 10g pro.

TEST KITCHEN TIP
If you love the creaminess and spicy flavor of the peanut sauce in this recipe, try it on salads, spring rolls, noodle dishes, as a veggie dip, or pair it with your favorite homemade Thai dish.

CHILI-LIME CHICKEN WINGS

Who would have guessed that mixing maple syrup, chili sauce and lime juice would make chicken wings taste so good? Family and guests alike will scramble to ensure they get more than one of these utterly delicious wings—so be sure to make extras!
—Taste of Home *Test Kitchen*

Prep: 20 min. • **Cook:** 10 min./batch
Makes: 2 dozen

- 2½ **lbs. whole chicken wings**
- 1 **cup maple syrup**
- ⅔ **cup chili sauce**
- 2 **Tbsp. lime juice**
- 2 **Tbsp. Dijon mustard**
- 1 **cup all-purpose flour**
- 2 **tsp. salt**
- 2 **tsp. paprika**
- ¼ **tsp. pepper**
- **Oil for deep-fat frying**
- **Thinly sliced green onions and lime wedges, optional**

1. Cut wings into three sections; discard wing tip sections. In a large saucepan, combine the syrup, chili sauce, lime juice and mustard. Bring to a boil; cook until liquid is reduced to about 1 cup.
2. Meanwhile, in a large shallow dish, combine the flour, salt, paprika and pepper. Add wings a few at a time and toss to coat.
3. In an electric skillet or deep fryer, heat the oil to 375°. Fry wings, a few at a time, for 6-8 minutes or until no longer pink, turning once. Drain on paper towels. Transfer wings to a large bowl; add sauce mixture and toss to coat. Serve immediately, with sliced green onions and lime wedges if desired.
NOTE: Uncooked chicken wing sections (wingettes) may be substituted for whole chicken wings.
1 PIECE: 142 cal., 8g fat (1g sat. fat), 15mg chol., 198mg sod., 12g carb. (9g sugars, 0 fiber), 5g pro.

AMBER MASSEY
Argyle, TX

WAFFLE FRY NACHOS

My husband and two grown sons enjoy this riff on nachos while on camping trips. They can devour a platter in no time! The snack is also fun to make when friends come over.
—Debra Morgan, Idaho Falls, ID

Takes: 25 min. • **Makes:** 8 servings

- **1 pkg. (22 oz.) frozen waffle fries**
- **10 bacon strips, cooked and crumbled**
- **3 green onions, sliced**
- **1 can (6 oz.) sliced ripe olives, drained**
- **2 medium tomatoes, seeded and chopped**
- **⅔ cup salsa**
- **1½ cups shredded cheddar cheese**
- **1½ cups shredded Monterey Jack cheese**
- **Sour cream**

Bake fries according to package directions. Transfer to a 10-in. ovenproof skillet. Top with the bacon, onions, olives, tomatoes, salsa and cheeses. Return to the oven for 5 minutes or until cheese is melted. Serve with sour cream.

1 CUP: 370 cal., 23g fat (12g sat. fat), 48mg chol., 683mg sod., 25g carb. (3g sugars, 4g fiber), 15g pro.

ANTIPASTO BAKE

Stuffed with savory meats and cheeses, this hearty bake would satisfy an entire offensive line! It comes together quickly and bakes in under an hour, making it the perfect game-day appetizer. The all-stars in this ooey-gooey dish include salami, pepperoni, prosciutto and a flavorful assortment of cheeses—Swiss, Colby-Monterey Jack and provolone.
—Brea Barclay, Green Bay, WI

Prep: 20 min. • **Bake:** 45 min. + standing
Makes: 20 servings

- **2 tubes (8 oz. each) refrigerated crescent rolls**
- **¼ lb. thinly sliced hard salami**
- **¼ lb. thinly sliced Swiss cheese**
- **¼ lb. thinly sliced pepperoni**
- **¼ lb. thinly sliced Colby-Monterey Jack cheese**
- **¼ lb. thinly sliced prosciutto**
- **¼ lb. thinly sliced provolone cheese**
- **2 large eggs**
- **½ tsp. garlic powder**
- **½ tsp. pepper**
- **1 jar (12 oz.) roasted sweet red peppers, drained**
- **1 large egg yolk, beaten**

1. Preheat oven to 350°. Unroll one tube of crescent dough into one long rectangle; press perforations to seal. Press onto bottom and up sides of an ungreased 11x7-in. baking dish.
2. Layer the meats and cheeses on dough in the order listed. Whisk eggs and seasonings until well blended; pour into dish. Top with roasted pepper.
3. Unroll remaining tube of dough into a long rectangle; press perforations to seal. Place over the filling; pinch seams tight. Brush with beaten egg yolk; cover with foil. Bake for 30 minutes; remove foil. Bake until golden brown, 15-20 minutes. Let stand 20 minutes.

1 PIECE: 229 cal., 15g fat (7g sat. fat), 58mg chol., 662mg sod., 10g carb. (2g sugars, 0 fiber), 11g pro.

COLLEEN DELAWDER
Herndon, VA

POTATO CHIP CHICKEN STRIPS

Here's a fast and tasty change of pace from typical fried chicken.
—Judith LaBrozzi, Canton, OH

Prep: 20 min. • **Bake:** 20 min.
Makes: 10 servings

- **1 cup sour cream**
- **⅛ tsp. garlic salt**
- **⅛ tsp. onion salt**
- **⅛ tsp. paprika**
- **1 pkg. (12 oz.) potato chips, crushed**
- **2 lbs. boneless skinless chicken breasts, cut into 1-in. strips**
- **¼ cup butter, melted**
- **Salsa, barbecue sauce or sweet-and-sour sauce**

1. In a shallow bowl, combine sour cream and seasonings. Place crushed potato chips in another shallow bowl. Dip chicken strips in sour cream mixture, then coat with potato chips. Place in a greased 15x10x1-in. baking pan. Drizzle with butter.
2. Bake at 400° for 20-22 minutes or until chicken is no longer pink. Serve with salsa or sauce.
FREEZE OPTION: Transfer cooled chicken strips to an airtight container; freeze. To use, reheat chicken strips in a greased 15x10x1-in. baking pan in a preheated 400° oven until crisp and heated through.
1 SERVING: 625 cal., 37g fat (15g sat. fat), 129mg chol., 664mg sod., 31g carb. (1g sugars, 2g fiber), 36g pro.

PEACHY JALAPENO GUACAMOLE

Fresh jalapenos and summer-ripe peaches give this creamy guacamole so much flavor. It's got a little kick, but I love that it's not so spicy it burns off my taste buds!
—Colleen Delawder, Herndon, VA

Takes: 15 min. • **Makes:** 1½ cups

- **2 medium ripe avocados, peeled and cubed**
- **2 Tbsp. lime juice**
- **½ tsp. kosher salt**
- **½ tsp. ground cumin**
- **¼ tsp. pepper**
- **1 medium peach, peeled and finely chopped**
- **1 jalapeno pepper, seeded and minced**
- **2 Tbsp. finely chopped red onion**
- **Tortilla chips**

Mash avocados with lime juice, salt, cumin and pepper. Gently stir in peach, jalapeno and red onion. Serve with tortilla chips.
¼ CUP: 90 cal., 7g fat (1g sat. fat), 0 chol., 164mg sod., 7g carb. (2g sugars, 4g fiber), 1g pro. **DIABETIC EXCHANGES:** 1 fat, ½ starch.

TEST KITCHEN TIP
This guacamole is excellent with tortilla chips but also complements grilled chicken or fish. Leave the seeds in the jalapeno pepper if you like a little extra heat.

OYSTER CHEESE APPETIZER LOG

Every winter, I make lots of cheese logs and freeze them for when I'm expecting company or need a special appetizer to bring to a party or potluck. In this recipe, the blend of smoked oysters, chili powder, walnuts and cream cheese is out of this world. Serve with wheat, sesame or your favorite fancy crackers.
—William Tracy, Jerseyville, IL

Takes: 20 min.
Makes: 2 logs (16 servings each)

- **3 pkg. (8 oz. each) cream cheese, softened**
- **2 Tbsp. steak sauce**
- **¼ cup Miracle Whip**
- **1 garlic clove, peeled and minced, or 1 tsp. garlic powder**
- **1 small onion, finely chopped**
- **2 cans (3¾ oz. each) smoked oysters, well-drained and chopped**
- **3 cups chopped pecans, divided**
- **3 Tbsp. chili powder**
- **Minced fresh parsley**

In mixer bowl, combine the cream cheese, steak sauce, Miracle Whip, garlic and onion. Stir in oysters and 1 cup of pecans. Shape into two 9-in. logs. Roll logs in mixture of chili powder, remaining pecans and parsley.
2 TBSP.: 117 cal., 12g fat (2g sat. fat), 10mg chol., 62mg sod., 3g carb. (1g sugars, 1g fiber), 2g pro.

THICK STRAWBERRY SHAKES

Cool off with this thick and rich shake that will remind you of classic malt shoppe treats!
—Kathryn Conrad, Milwaukee, WI

Takes: 5 min. • **Makes:** 2 servings

- **⅓ cup 2% milk**
- **1½ cups vanilla ice cream**
- **½ cup frozen unsweetened strawberries**
- **1 Tbsp. strawberry preserves**

In a blender, combine all ingredients; cover and process until smooth. Pour into chilled glasses; serve immediately.
1 CUP: 257 cal., 12g fat (7g sat. fat), 47mg chol., 100mg sod., 35g carb. (28g sugars, 1g fiber), 5g pro.

WARM BROCCOLI CHEESE DIP

I bring this cheesy hot dip to all our family gatherings. Everyone loves the crunchy broccoli and the zip from the jalapeno pepper.
—Barbara Maiol, Conyers, GA

Prep: 15 min.
Cook: 2½ hours
Makes: 22 servings (5½ cups)

- **2 jars (8 oz. each) process cheese sauce**
- **1 can (10¾ oz.) condensed cream of chicken soup, undiluted**
- **3 cups frozen chopped broccoli, thawed and drained**
- **½ lb. fresh mushrooms, chopped**
- **2 Tbsp. chopped seeded jalapeno pepper**
- **Assorted fresh vegetables**

In a 1½-qt. slow cooker, combine cheese sauce and soup. Cover and cook on low for 30 minutes or until cheese is melted, stirring occasionally. Stir in the broccoli, mushrooms and jalapeno. Cover and cook on low until vegetables are tender, 2-3 hours. Serve with assorted fresh vegetables.

NOTE: Wear disposable gloves when cutting hot peppers; the oils can burn skin. Avoid touching your face.

¼ CUP: 47 cal., 3g fat (2g sat. fat), 7mg chol., 277mg sod., 3g carb. (1g sugars, 1g fiber), 2g pro.

5i

SUNNY ORANGE LEMONADE

Here's a beverage that will really hit the spot. I use tree-ripened oranges and lemons that are so abundant here in Florida. Filled with tangy goodness, this lemonade will quench your thirst any time of year!
—Martha Schwartz, Sarasota, FL

Prep: 5 min. • **Cook:** 15 min. + chilling
Makes: 6 servings

- **4¼ cups water, divided**
- **1 cup sugar**
- **¾ cup lemon juice (about 4 lemons)**
- **¾ cup orange juice (about 3 oranges)**
- **2 tsp. grated lemon zest**
- **1 tsp. grated orange zest**
- **Ice cubes**
- **Lemon slices, optional**

1. In a small saucepan, bring 1¼ cups water and sugar to a boil. Reduce heat. Simmer for 10 minutes; cool.
2. Transfer to a pitcher; add lemon and orange juices and zests. Cover and refrigerate for at least 1 hour.
3. Stir in the remaining water. Serve over ice. Garnish with lemon if desired.

1 CUP: 151 cal., 0 fat (0 sat. fat), 0 chol., 1mg sod., 39g carb. (37g sugars, 0 fiber), 0 pro.

VEGGIE HAM CRESCENT WREATH

Impress your guests with the look and flavor of this pretty crescent roll appetizer. The pineapple cream cheese adds a special touch.
—Dixie Lundquist, Chandler, AZ

Prep: 20 min. • **Bake:** 15 min. + cooling
Makes: 16 appetizers

- **2 tubes (8 oz. each) refrigerated crescent rolls**
- **½ cup spreadable pineapple cream cheese**
- **⅓ cup diced fully cooked ham**
- **¼ cup finely chopped sweet yellow pepper**
- **¼ cup finely chopped green pepper**
- **½ cup chopped fresh broccoli florets**
- **6 grape tomatoes, quartered**
- **1 Tbsp. chopped red onion**

1. Remove crescent dough from tubes (do not unroll). Cut each roll into eight slices. Arrange in an 11-in. circle on an ungreased 14-in. pizza pan.
2. Bake at 375° for 15-20 minutes or until golden brown. Cool for 5 minutes before carefully removing to a serving platter; cool completely.
3. Spread cream cheese over wreath; top with ham, peppers, broccoli, tomatoes and onion. Store in the refrigerator.

1 SERVING: 142 cal., 8g fat (3g sat. fat), 9mg chol., 290mg sod., 13g carb. (3g sugars, 0 fiber), 3g pro.

STRAWBERRY WATERMELON SLUSH

After a long, hot day, we like to relax on the back porch with glasses of this fruity slush. Strawberries and watermelon blend with lemon juice and sugar for an icy treat that's an instant refresher.

—Patty Howse, Great Falls, MT

Takes: 10 min. • **Makes:** 4 servings

- ⅓ **cup lemon juice**
- ⅓ **cup sugar**
- 2 **cups cubed seedless watermelon**
- 2 **cups fresh strawberries, halved**
- 2 **cups ice cubes**

Place first four ingredients in a blender; cover and process until smooth. Add ice; process, covered, until slushy. Serve immediately.

1¼ CUPS: 112 cal., 0 fat (0 sat. fat), 0 chol., 4mg sod., 30g carb. (27g sugars, 2g fiber), 1g pro.

OLIVE ZUCCHINI SPREAD

Zucchini lovers won't be able to get enough of this spread. Slather it on bread, crackers and veggies for your next casual get-together.

—GaleLynn Peterson, Long Beach, CA

Prep: 20 min. + chilling
Makes: 48 servings (6 cups)

- 2 **pkg. (8 oz. each) reduced-fat cream cheese**
- 3 **cups shredded zucchini**
- 1 **jar (7½ oz.) marinated artichoke hearts, drained and finely chopped**
- ¼ **cup pimiento-stuffed olives, chopped**
- 1 **can (4¼ oz.) chopped ripe olives**
- 8 **garlic cloves, minced**
- 3 **Tbsp. chopped red onion**
- 2 **Tbsp. minced fresh cilantro**
- 2 **Tbsp. lime juice**
- 2 **Tbsp. olive oil**
- 1 **green onion, chopped**
- 1 **French bread baguette, sliced**

1. In a large mixing bowl, combine the first 11 ingredients; beat until blended.

2. Transfer to a serving bowl; cover and chill for at least 4 hours or overnight. Serve with baguette slices.

2 TBSP. SPREAD: 43 cal., 4g fat (2g sat. fat), 7mg chol., 93mg sod., 2g carb. (1g sugars, 0 fiber), 1g pro. **DIABETIC EXCHANGES:** 1 fat.

WASABI CRAB CAKES

With wasabi in both the crab cakes and the dipping sauce, this festive appetizer brings its own heat to a party.
—Marie Rizzio, Interlochen, MI

Prep: 35 min. • **Bake:** 15 min.
Makes: 2 dozen (½ cup sauce)

- **1 medium sweet red pepper, finely chopped**
- **1 celery rib, finely chopped**
- **⅓ cup plus ½ cup dry bread crumbs, divided**
- **3 green onions, finely chopped**
- **2 large egg whites**
- **3 Tbsp. fat-free mayonnaise**
- **¼ tsp. prepared wasabi**
- **1½ cups lump crabmeat, drained**
- **Cooking spray**

SAUCE

- **1 celery rib, finely chopped**
- **⅓ cup fat-free mayonnaise**
- **1 green onion, finely chopped**
- **1 Tbsp. sweet pickle relish**
- **½ tsp. prepared wasabi**

1. Preheat oven to 425°. Combine red pepper, celery, ⅓ cup bread crumbs, green onions, egg whites, mayonnaise and wasabi. Fold in the crabmeat.
2. Place remaining bread crumbs in a shallow bowl. Drop a heaping tablespoonful crab mixture into crumbs. Gently coat and shape into a ¾-in.-thick patty; place on a baking sheet coated with cooking spray. Repeat with remaining mixture.
3. Spritz crab cakes with cooking spray. Bake until golden brown, 15-18 minutes, turning once. Meanwhile, combine sauce ingredients. Serve with crab cakes.

1 CRAB CAKE WITH 1 TSP. SAUCE: 31 cal., 1g fat (0 sat. fat), 8mg chol., 148mg sod., 4g carb. (1g sugars, 1g fiber), 2g pro.

SAUSAGE QUICHE SQUARES

Having worked in catering, I appreciate all kinds of interesting finger foods that serve a crowd. I'm often asked to bring this appetizer to parties and potlucks. Each square is like a zippy, crustless quiche.
—Linda Wheeler, Middleburg, FL

Prep: 15 min. • **Bake:** 20 min. + cooling
Makes: about 8 dozen

- **1 lb. bulk pork sausage**
- **1 cup shredded cheddar cheese**
- **1 cup shredded Monterey Jack cheese**
- **½ cup finely chopped onion**
- **1 can (4 oz.) chopped green chiles**
- **1 Tbsp. minced jalapeno pepper, optional**
- **10 large eggs**
- **1 tsp. chili powder**
- **1 tsp. ground cumin**
- **1 tsp. salt**
- **½ tsp. garlic powder**
- **½ tsp. pepper**

1. In a large skillet, cook the sausage until no longer pink; drain. Place in a greased 13x9-in. baking dish. Layer with cheeses, onion, chiles and jalapeno if desired. In a bowl, beat eggs and seasonings. Pour over cheese.
2. Bake, uncovered, at 375° for 18-22 minutes or until a knife inserted in the center comes out clean. Cool for 10 minutes; cut into 1-in. squares.

NOTE: Wear disposable gloves when cutting hot peppers; the oils can burn skin. Avoid touching your face.

3 SQUARES: 29 cal., 2g fat (1g sat. fat), 24mg chol., 81mg sod., 0g carb. (1g sugars, 0 fiber), 2g pro.

APRICOT KIELBASA SLICES

These satisfying sausage bites are coated in a thick sauce with just the right amount of sweetness. You'll love 'em!

—Barbara McCalley, Allison Park, PA

Takes: 15 min.
Makes: 12 servings

- **1 lb. fully cooked kielbasa or Polish sausage, cut into ¼-in. slices**
- **1 jar (12 oz.) apricot preserves**
- **2 Tbsp. lemon juice**
- **2 tsp. Dijon mustard**
- **¼ tsp. ground ginger**

1. In a large cast-iron skillet, cook and stir sausage until browned. Remove from pan; discard drippings.

2. Add remaining ingredients to skillet; cook and stir over low heat until heated through, 2-3 minutes. Stir in sausage; heat through.

¼ CUP: 47 cal., 3g fat (1g sat. fat), 6mg chol., 110mg sod., 5g carb. (4g sugars, 0 fiber), 1g pro.

NACHO SALSA DIP

This zesty dip is great for any get-together, and because it's made in the slow cooker, I have more time to spend with my guests.

—Sally Hull, Homestead, FL

Prep: 15 min. • **Cook:** 3 hours • **Makes:** 7 cups

- **1 lb. ground beef**
- **⅓ cup chopped onion**
- **2 lbs. process cheese (Velveeta), cubed**
- **1 jar (16 oz.) chunky salsa**
- **¼ tsp. garlic powder**
- **Tortilla chips or cubed French bread**

1. In a large skillet, cook beef and onion over medium heat until meat is no longer pink; drain well.

2. Transfer to a greased 3-qt. slow cooker; stir in the cheese, salsa and garlic powder. Cover and cook on low for 3-4 hours or until heated through. Stir; serve warm with tortilla chips or cubed bread.

¼ CUP: 143 cal., 10g fat (6g sat. fat), 36mg chol., 484mg sod., 4g carb. (3g sugars, 0 fiber), 9g pro.

RICOTTA PUFFS

Roasted red peppers and ricotta cheese give these pastry puffs delicious flavor, while parsley and oregano add a little spark.

—Maria Regakis, Saugus, MA

Prep: 20 min. • **Bake:** 15 min.
Makes: 1½ dozen

- **1 pkg. (17¼ oz.) frozen puff pastry, thawed**
- **½ cup ricotta cheese**
- **½ cup roasted sweet red peppers, drained and chopped**
- **3 Tbsp. grated Romano or Parmesan cheese, divided**
- **1 Tbsp. minced fresh parsley**
- **1 tsp. dried oregano, crushed**
- **½ tsp. pepper**
- **1 tsp. 2% milk**

1. Preheat oven to 400°. On a lightly floured surface, unfold puff pastry. Cut each sheet into nine squares. Mix ricotta cheese, red peppers, 2 Tbsp. Romano cheese, parsley, oregano and pepper.

2. Brush the pastry edges with milk; place 2 rounded teaspoonfuls of cheese mixture in center of each square. Fold edges of pastry over filling, forming a rectangle; seal edges with a fork. Cut slits in pastry; brush with milk. Sprinkle with remaining Romano cheese.

3. Place pastries 2 in. apart on lightly greased baking sheets. Bake until golden brown, 15-20 minutes. Remove to wire racks. Serve warm. Refrigerate leftovers.

1 PUFF: 150 cal., 8g fat (2g sat. fat), 4mg chol., 140mg sod., 16g carb. (1g sugars, 2g fiber), 3g pro.

MARIA REGAKIS
Saugus, MA

SALMON MOUSSE CUPS

These tempting little tarts are perfect for parties. They disappear at an astonishing speed, so I usually double or triple the recipe. The salmon-cream cheese filling and flaky crust will melt in your mouth.
—Fran Rowland, Phoenix, AZ

Prep: 25 min. + chilling
Bake: 10 min. + cooling • **Makes:** 2 dozen

- 3 **oz. cream cheese, softened**
- ½ **cup butter, softened**
- 1 **cup all-purpose flour**

FILLING

- 1 **pkg. (8 oz.) cream cheese, softened**
- 1 **cup fully cooked salmon chunks or 1 can (7½ oz.) salmon, drained, bones and skin removed**
- 2 **Tbsp. chicken broth**
- 2 **Tbsp. sour cream**
- 1 **Tbsp. finely chopped onion**
- 1 **tsp. lemon juice**
- ½ **tsp. salt**
- 2 **Tbsp. minced fresh dill**

1. In a small bowl, beat the cream cheese and butter until smooth. Add the flour and mix well. Shape into 24 balls; press onto the bottoms and up the sides of greased miniature muffin cups.
2. Bake at 350° for 10-15 minutes or until golden brown. Cool for 5 minutes before removing from muffin pans to wire racks to cool completely.
3. For filling, in a large bowl, beat cream cheese until smooth. Add the salmon, broth, sour cream, onion, lemon juice and salt until blended. Spoon into the shells. Refrigerate for at least 2 hours. Sprinkle with dill.
2 CUPS: 228 cal., 18g fat (11g sat. fat), 58mg chol., 359mg sod., 9g carb. (1g sugars, 0 fiber), 7g pro.

PEANUTTY CHICKEN WINGS

Mild peanut and curry flavors create the tasty sauce for these wings. I doubled the recipe, and it's a good thing I did. Make these for yourself and find out why!
—Kristen Proulx, Canton, NY

Prep: 10 min. + chilling • **Bake:** 35 min.
Makes: 8 servings

- ½ **cup creamy peanut butter**
- ⅓ **cup honey**
- ¼ **cup soy sauce**
- 3 **Tbsp. canola oil**
- 1 **garlic clove, minced**
- 1 **tsp. curry powder**
- 2½ **lbs. chicken wings**

1. In a large bowl, combine the peanut butter, honey, soy sauce, oil, garlic and curry powder until blended. Cut chicken wings into three sections; discard wing tips. Add the wings to peanut butter mixture; stir to coat. Cover and refrigerate for 2 hours.
2. Transfer to an ungreased 13x9-in. baking dish. Bake, uncovered, at 375° until chicken juices run clear, 35-45 minutes.
1 SERVING: 347 cal., 24g fat (5g sat. fat), 46mg chol., 580mg sod., 15g carb. (12g sugars, 1g fiber), 20g pro.

VANILLA ALMOND HOT COCOA

Treat family and friends to this rich homemade hot cocoa at your next holiday gathering. It will warm even the coldest winter's chill.
—Vicki Holloway, Joelton, TN

Takes: 15 min. • **Makes:** 10 servings (2½ qt.)

- **1 cup sugar**
- **⅔ cup baking cocoa**
- **¼ tsp. salt**
- **8 cups 2% milk**
- **⅔ cup water**
- **2 tsp. vanilla extract**
- **½ tsp. almond extract**
- **Miniature marshmallows, optional**

In a large saucepan, combine the sugar, cocoa and salt. Stir in milk and water. Cook and stir over medium heat until heated through. Remove from the heat; stir in extracts. Serve in mugs with marshmallows if desired.
1 CUP: 195 cal., 4g fat (2g sat. fat), 16mg chol., 151mg sod., 33g carb. (30g sugars, 1g fiber), 8g pro.

CHEESEBURGER MINI MUFFINS

I invented these cute little muffins to enjoy cheeseburger flavor without the drive-thru. They make terrific party fare. I often freeze a batch and reheat as many as I need.
—Teresa Kraus, Cortez, CO

Prep: 20 min. • **Bake:** 15 min./batch
Makes: 5 dozen

- **½ lb. ground beef**
- **1 small onion, finely chopped**
- **2½ cups all-purpose flour**
- **1 Tbsp. sugar**
- **2 tsp. baking powder**
- **1 tsp. salt**
- **¾ cup ketchup**
- **¾ cup whole milk**
- **½ cup butter, melted**
- **2 large eggs**
- **1 tsp. prepared mustard**
- **2 cups shredded cheddar cheese**

1. In a large skillet, cook beef and onion over medium heat until meat is no longer pink; drain.
2. In a small bowl, combine flour, sugar, baking powder and salt. In another bowl, combine ketchup, milk, butter, eggs and mustard; stir into the dry ingredients just until moistened. Fold in the beef mixture and cheese.
3. Fill greased mini muffin cups three-fourths full. Bake at 425° for 15-18 minutes or until a toothpick comes out clean. Cool for 5 minutes before removing from pans to wire racks. Serve warm. Refrigerate leftovers.
NOTE: Muffins may be baked in standard muffin cups for 20-25 minutes; recipe makes 2 dozen.
1 MINI MUFFIN: 62 cal., 3g fat (2g sat. fat), 16mg chol., 137mg sod., 5g carb. (1g sugars, 0 fiber), 2g pro.

TEST KITCHEN TIP
These muffins also cook up tasty with ground pork or ground turkey. Use sharp cheddar cheese for the most flavor.

Breakfast & Brunch

Looking for a special way to jump-start the day? These tempting eye-openers will keep everyone full and satisfied all morning.

COURTNEY STULTZ
Weir, KS

HEARTY SAUSAGE & SWEET POTATOES

Sweet potatoes with sausage and sage make a happy dish. I get a lot of recipe requests when I serve this down-home hash.
—*Courtney Stultz, Weir, KS*

Prep: 20 min. • **Cook:** 25 min.
Makes: 6 servings

- **2 large sweet potatoes, peeled and cut into ½-in. pieces.**
- **2 Tbsp. olive oil, divided**
- **½ tsp. salt**
- **1 lb. bulk pork sausage**
- **1 large tart apple, peeled and chopped**
- **1 large carrot, cut into ½-in. pieces**
- **½ tsp. dried sage leaves**
- **½ tsp. ground cinnamon**
- **½ tsp. pepper**
- **⅛ tsp. pumpkin pie spice**

1. In a large microwave-safe bowl, combine potatoes, 1 Tbsp. oil and salt. Microwave, covered, on high for 6-8 minutes or until tender, stirring every 2 minutes.
2. Meanwhile, in a large skillet, cook sausage over medium heat 6-8 minutes or until no longer pink, breaking into crumbles; remove with a slotted spoon.
3. In same skillet, heat remaining oil over medium-low heat. Add apple and carrot; cook, covered, 5-7 minutes or until carrot is just tender, stirring occasionally. Return sausage to pan. Stir in the potatoes and seasonings; cook, covered, 10-12 minutes or until carrot is tender.
1 CUP: 409 cal., 25g fat (7g sat. fat), 51mg chol., 793mg sod., 34g carb. (15g sugars, 4g fiber), 12g pro.

5i

PECAN BACON

Crispy, sweet bacon dresses up any breakfast. When my girls see this on the table, they know they're in for a treat. The big flavor punch may just surprise you.
—Catherine Goza, Charlotte, NC

Prep: 10 min. • **Bake:** 30 min.
Makes: 6 servings

12 bacon strips
¼ cup packed brown sugar
¼ cup finely chopped pecans
⅛ tsp. ground cinnamon
⅛ tsp. pepper

1. Preheat oven to 375°. Place bacon in a single layer in a foil-lined 15x10x1-in. baking pan. Bake until lightly browned, 16-18 minutes.
2. Remove bacon from pan. Discard drippings from pan, wiping clean if necessary.
3. In a shallow bowl, mix the remaining ingredients. Dip both sides of bacon in brown sugar mixture, patting to help coating adhere; return to pan.
4. Bake 8-10 minutes longer or until bacon is caramelized. Remove immediately from pan.
2 BACON STRIPS: 283 cal., 25g fat (8g sat. fat), 37mg chol., 373mg sod., 8g carb. (7g sugars, 0 fiber), 7g pro.

HASH BROWN EGG BRUNCH

Slow cookers aren't just for making dinner. I make this often if we're having company overnight. I can prep it the night before and when we all get up in the morning, breakfast is waiting.
—Barb Keith, Eau Claire, WI

Prep: 20 min. • **Cook:** 4 hours
Makes: 10 servings

1 pkg. (30 oz.) frozen shredded hash brown potatoes, thawed
1 lb. bacon strips, cooked and crumbled
1 medium onion, chopped
1 medium green pepper, chopped
1½ cups shredded cheddar cheese
12 large eggs
1 cup 2% milk
½ tsp. salt
½ tsp. pepper

1. In a greased 5-qt. slow cooker, layer a third of each of the following: potatoes, bacon, onion, green pepper and cheese. Repeat layers twice. In a large bowl, whisk eggs, milk, salt and pepper; pour over layers.
2. Cook, covered, on high for 30 minutes. Reduce heat to low; cook, covered, until a thermometer reads 160°, 3½ to 4 hours.
1 CUP: 315 cal., 17g fat (8g sat. fat), 289mg chol., 589mg sod., 20g carb. (3g sugars, 2g fiber), 20g pro.

CORNMEAL PANCAKES

I like to joke that these pancakes are so light, you have to hold them down! When we have a chance, we'll make them with freshly ground cornmeal bought at local festivals.
—Betty Claycomb, Alverton, PA

Takes: 30 min. • **Makes:** 6 servings

- **1⅓ cups all-purpose flour**
- **⅔ cup cornmeal**
- **2 Tbsp. sugar**
- **4 tsp. baking powder**
- **1 tsp. salt**
- **2 large eggs**
- **1⅓ cups 2% milk**
- **¼ cup canola oil**
- **Pancake syrup**

Combine the first five ingredients. In another bowl, whisk eggs, milk and oil; stir into dry ingredients just until moistened. Pour batter by ¼ cupfuls onto a lightly greased hot griddle. Turn when bubbles on top begin to pop; cook until second side is golden brown. Serve with pancake syrup.

2 PANCAKES: 321 cal., 13g fat (2g sat. fat), 67mg chol., 709mg sod., 42g carb. (7g sugars, 1g fiber), 8g pro.

CRANBERRY-ORANGE VARIATION: Stir ¾ cup chopped fresh cranberries and 1 tsp. orange zest into prepared batter.

BLUEBERRY-LEMON VARIATION: Stir ¾ cup fresh blueberries and 1 tsp. lemon zest into prepared batter.

BACON VARIATION: Stir 4-6 cooked and crumbled bacon strips into prepared batter.

TEST KITCHEN TIP

For light, fluffy pancakes, mix the batter quickly and gently (there may still be a few lumps) before pouring onto the griddle. Resist the urge to flip the pancakes multiple times. And most importantly, don't press down with a spatula or you will find yourself with a stack of gummy flapjacks. If you like variations or add-ins, but have picky eaters, mix the goodies with butter instead. Stir chopped dried fruit, citrus zest, honey or maple syrup into individual servings of softened butter before serving pancakes.

GET-UP-AND-GO GRANOLA

My family enjoys on this satisfying granola before hiking and biking and while camping. It smells delicious while baking, and you can easily make it in large batches to send in gift packages to family and friends.
—Sabrina Olson, Otsego, MN

Prep: 15 min. • **Bake:** 30 min. + cooling
Makes: 15 servings (7½ cups)

- **6 cups old-fashioned oats**
- **½ cup unblanched almonds, coarsely chopped**
- **¼ cup packed brown sugar**
- **¼ cup flaxseed**
- **¼ cup canola oil**
- **¼ cup honey**
- **1 Tbsp. maple syrup**
- **1 tsp. apple pie spice**
- **½ tsp. salt**
- **½ tsp. vanilla extract**
- **½ cup dried cranberries**
- **½ cup raisins**

1. Preheat oven to 300°. In a large bowl, combine oats, almonds, brown sugar and flax. In a microwave-safe dish, whisk oil, honey, maple syrup, pie spice and salt. Microwave on high for 30-45 seconds or until heated through, stirring once. Stir in vanilla. Pour over oat mixture; toss to coat.
2. Spread evenly in a 15x10x1-in. baking pan coated with cooking spray. Bake 30-40 minutes or until golden brown, stirring every 10 minutes. Cool completely on a wire rack. Stir in cranberries and raisins. Store in an airtight container.

½ CUP: 255 cal., 10g fat (1g sat. fat), 0 chol., 84mg sod., 40g carb. (15g sugars, 5g fiber), 7g pro.

WAFFLE MONTE CRISTOS

Here's a fun twist on the classic Monte Cristo. Adults love the sweet, smoky flavor. Kids love the waffles in place of bread. You can also make these with homemade waffles.
—Kelly Reynolds, Urbana, IL

Takes: 20 min. • **Makes:** 4 servings

- ½ **cup apricot preserves**
- 8 **frozen waffles**
- 4 **slices deli turkey**
- 4 **slices deli ham**
- 4 **slices Havarti cheese (about 3 oz.)**
- 4 **bacon strips, cooked**
- 2 **Tbsp. butter, softened**
- **Maple syrup**

1. Preheat griddle over medium heat. Spread preserves over four waffles. Layer with turkey, ham, cheese and bacon; top with remaining waffles. Lightly spread outsides of waffles with butter.

2. Place the sandwiches on griddle; cook 4-5 minutes on each side or until golden brown and heated through. Serve with syrup for dipping.

1 SANDWICH: 511 cal., 23g fat (10g sat. fat), 70mg chol., 1163mg sod., 57g carb. (22g sugars, 2g fiber), 21g pro.

HEALTH TIP: Use cooking spray instead of butter and reduce bacon and cheese by half to save 130 calories, 7 grams saturated fat and almost 300 milligrams sodium per serving.

GLUTEN-FREE PANCAKES

I have Celiac disease, so these gluten-free flapjacks are a regular in our house. My kids like them with chocolate chips and maple syrup.
—Kathy Rairigh, Milford, IN

Prep: 15 min. • **Cook:** 10 min./batch
Makes: 12 pancakes

- 1 **cup brown rice flour**
- ½ **cup potato starch**
- ½ **cup ground almonds**
- 3 **tsp. sugar**
- 3 **tsp. baking powder**
- ½ **tsp. salt**
- 2 **large eggs**
- 1 **cup fat-free milk**
- 2 **Tbsp. butter, melted**
- 1 **tsp. vanilla extract**
- ⅓ **cup miniature semisweet chocolate chips, optional**

1. In a large bowl, combine the rice flour, potato starch, almonds, sugar, baking powder and salt.

2. In another bowl, whisk eggs, milk, butter and vanilla; stir into dry ingredients just until moistened. Stir in chocolate chips if desired.

3. Pour batter by ¼ cupfuls onto a hot griddle coated with cooking spray; turn when bubbles form on top. Cook until the second side is golden brown.

NOTE: Read all ingredient labels to check for gluten content prior to use. Ingredient formulas can change, and production facilities vary among brands. If you're concerned that your brand may contain gluten, contact the food company.

2 EACH: 242 cal., 10g fat (3g sat. fat), 81mg chol., 464mg sod., 33g carb. (5g sugars, 2g fiber), 7g pro. **DIABETIC EXCHANGES:** 2 starch, 2 fat.

FRUITY CROISSANT PUFF

I got this recipe from a good friend. Sweet, tart, tender and light, it tastes like a danish.
—Myra Almer, Tuttle, ND

Prep: 10 min. + chilling • **Bake:** 45 min.
Makes: 6 servings

- **4 large croissants, cut into 1-in. cubes (about 6 cups)**
- **1½ cups mixed fresh berries**
- **1 pkg. (8 oz.) cream cheese, softened**
- **1 cup 2% milk**
- **½ cup sugar**
- **2 large eggs, room temperature**
- **1 tsp. vanilla extract**
- **Maple syrup, optional**

1. Place croissants and berries in a greased 8-in. square baking dish. In a medium bowl, beat softened cream cheese until smooth. Beat in milk, sugar, eggs and vanilla until blended; pour over croissants. Refrigerate, covered, overnight.
2. Preheat oven to 350°. Remove casserole from the refrigerator while oven heats.
3. Bake, covered, 30 minutes. Remove cover; bake until puffed and golden, 15-20 minutes, and a knife inserted in the center comes out clean. Let casserole stand 5-10 minutes before serving. If desired, serve with syrup.
1 PIECE: 429 cal., 24g fat (14g sat. fat), 132mg chol., 358mg sod., 44g carb. (27g sugars, 2g fiber), 9g pro.

GARDEN FRITTATA

I created this dish one day to use up some fresh yellow squash, zucchini and tomato. It's so easy to make because you don't have to fuss with a crust. Give it different twist by trying it with whatever veggies you have on hand.
—Catherine Michel, St. Peters, MO

Prep: 25 min. • **Bake:** 45 min. + standing
Makes: 6 servings

- **1 small yellow summer squash, thinly sliced**
- **1 small zucchini, thinly sliced**
- **1 small onion, chopped**
- **1 cup shredded part-skim mozzarella cheese**
- **1 medium tomato, sliced**
- **¼ cup crumbled feta cheese**
- **4 large eggs**
- **1 cup fat-free milk**
- **2 Tbsp. minced fresh basil**
- **1 garlic clove, minced**
- **½ tsp. salt**
- **¼ tsp. pepper**
- **¼ cup shredded Parmesan cheese**

1. In a microwave-safe bowl, combine the squash, zucchini and onion. Cover and microwave on high for 7-9 minutes or until the vegetables are tender; drain well.
2. Transfer to a 9-in. pie plate coated with cooking spray. Top with the mozzarella, tomato and feta cheese.
3. In a large bowl, whisk the eggs, milk, basil, garlic, salt and pepper; pour over the cheese and tomato layer. Sprinkle with shredded Parmesan cheese.
4. Bake, uncovered, at 375° for 45-50 minutes or until a knife inserted in the center comes out clean. Let stand for another 10 minutes before serving.
1 PIECE: 161 cal., 9g fat (4g sat. fat), 142mg chol., 494mg sod., 7g carb. (5g sugars, 1g fiber), 13g pro. **DIABETIC EXCHANGES:** 2 medium-fat meat, 1 vegetable.

COCONUT-GRANOLA YOGURT PARFAITS

Homemade granola—prepared ahead of time—makes these yogurt treats special.
—Julie Merriman, Seattle, WA

Prep: 20 min. • **Bake:** 20 min. + cooling
Makes: 8 parfaits plus 2½ cups granola

- **½ cup pomegranate juice**
- **1 Tbsp. sugar**
- **¾ tsp. lemon juice**
- **¼ cup butter, cubed**
- **¼ cup packed brown sugar**
- **½ tsp. salt**
- **½ tsp. each ground cardamom, cinnamon and allspice**
- **½ tsp. vanilla extract**
- **2 cups old-fashioned oats**
- **1 cup sweetened shredded coconut**
- **½ cup coarsely chopped cashews**
- **¼ cup dried cranberries**
- **¼ cup dark chocolate chips**

PARFAITS

- **4 cups fat-free plain Greek yogurt**
- **6 Tbsp. honey, divided**
- **1 Tbsp. grated lime zest**
- **2 Tbsp. lime juice**
- **3 cups chopped Honeycrisp apples (about 2 large)**
- **1 cup pomegranate seeds**

1. Preheat oven to 325°. In a small saucepan, combine pomegranate juice, sugar and lemon juice. Bring to a boil; cook until the liquid is reduced by half. Stir in butter and brown sugar until sugar is dissolved. Remove from heat; stir in salt, spices and vanilla.
2. In a large bowl, combine oats, coconut and cashews. Drizzle with juice mixture; toss to combine. Transfer to a greased 15x10x1-in. baking pan, spreading evenly.
3. Bake 20-25 minutes or until lightly browned, stirring halfway. Cool on a wire rack. When completely cooled, stir in cranberries and chocolate chips.
4. For parfaits, in a bowl, mix yogurt, 4 Tbsp. honey, lime zest and lime juice until blended. To serve, layer ¼ cup yogurt mixture, 2 Tbsp. granola, 3 Tbsp. chopped apple and 1 Tbsp. pomegranate seeds in each of eight parfait glass. Repeat layers. (Save remaining granola for another use; store in an airtight container.)
5. Drizzle parfaits with remaining honey. Serve immediately.

1 PARFAIT: 440 cal., 15g fat (8g sat. fat), 7mg chol., 236mg sod., 64g carb. (45g sugars, 5g fiber), 20g pro.

HERB & CHEESE SCRAMBLED EGGS

I grew up on a farm where fresh eggs and herbs were plentiful. My mother made these eggs and now I make them for my own family. Just add toast and breakfast is done!
—Patricia Nieh, Portola Valley, CA

Takes: 15 min. • **Makes:** 4 servings

- **8 large eggs**
- **½ cup 2% milk or half-and-half cream**
- **4 oz. cream cheese, softened**
- **1 Tbsp. minced fresh parsley**
- **1 Tbsp. minced chives**
- **½ tsp. minced fresh thyme**
- **⅛ to ¼ tsp. salt**
- **⅛ tsp. white pepper**
- **1 Tbsp. butter**
- **Additional minced fresh herbs**

Whisk together the first eight ingredients. In a large nonstick skillet, heat butter over medium heat. Pour in egg mixture; cook and stir until eggs are thickened and no liquid egg remains. Sprinkle with additional minced herbs.

1 SERVING: 284 cal., 23g fat (11g sat. fat), 411mg chol., 343mg sod., 4g carb. (3g sugars, 0 fiber), 15g pro.

BLUEBERRY FRUIT SMOOTHIE

If you love shakes and malts, give this thick and creamy smoothie a try. The fruit and yogurt make it nutritous way to start the day.
—Mary LaJoie, Orwell, VT

Takes: 5 min. • **Makes:** 3 servings

- **1 cup reduced-fat vanilla ice cream**
- **1 cup fresh or frozen blueberries**
- **½ cup chopped peeled fresh peaches or frozen unsweetened sliced peaches**
- **½ cup pineapple juice**
- **¼ cup vanilla yogurt**

In a blender, combine all ingredients; cover and process until smooth. Pour into chilled glasses; serve immediately.

¾ CUP: 149 cal., 2g fat (1g sat. fat), 7mg chol., 57mg sod., 30g carb. (0 sugars, 2g fiber), 3g pro. **DIABETIC EXCHANGES:** 2 fruit, ½ fat.

COUNTRY POTATO PANCAKES

These potato pancakes are so versatile. They can be a side dish for just about any meal or the main course for a light meal. Potato pancakes go particularly well with pork. We have them often at our house.
—Lydia Robotewskyj, Franklin, WI

Takes: 30 min. • **Makes:** about 24 pancakes

- **3 large potatoes (about 2 lbs.), peeled**
- **2 large eggs, lightly beaten**
- **1 Tbsp. grated onion**
- **2 Tbsp. all-purpose flour**
- **1 tsp. salt**
- **½ tsp. baking powder**
- **Vegetable oil**

1. Finely grate potatoes. Drain any liquid. Add eggs, onion, flour, salt and baking powder. In a frying pan, add oil to the depth of ⅛ in.; heat over medium-high (375°).
2. Drop batter by heaping tablespoonfuls in hot oil. Flatten into patties. Fry until golden brown, turning once. Serve immediately.

2 PANCAKES: 257 cal., 8g fat (1g sat. fat), 31mg chol., 242mg sod., 41g carb. (2g sugars, 5g fiber), 6g pro.

ZUCCHINI & GOUDA SKILLET FRITTATA

This is a version of a skillet dish that my mother-in-law, Millie, created to use up her summertime zucchini. The Gouda melts beautifully, but you can make it with Swiss or sharp cheddar, too.
—Susan Marshall, Colorado Springs, CO

Takes: 30 min. • **Makes:** 6 servings

- **6 large eggs**
- **2 Tbsp. 2% milk**
- **1 tsp. chopped fresh oregano**
- **½ tsp. salt**
- **⅛ tsp. pepper**
- **2 Tbsp. butter**
- **2 medium zucchini (7 to 8 oz. each), thinly sliced**
- **1 medium onion, chopped**
- **2 Tbsp. olive oil**
- **1 medium tomato, diced**
- **1 cup shredded Gouda cheese**
- **2 Tbsp. minced fresh basil**

1. Combine first five ingredients; set aside. In a large nonstick skillet, melt the butter over medium heat. Add zucchini and onion. Cook until tender, 6-8 minutes; remove.
2. In same skillet, heat oil over medium heat. Add egg mixture. Cook until set, gently lifting edges of cooked egg to allow liquid to run underneath. Top with zucchini mixture, diced tomato and cheese. Cover and cook until the cheese is melted, 2-3 minutes. Sprinkle minced basil on top.
1 WEDGE: 238 cal., 19g fat (8g sat. fat), 218mg chol., 462mg sod., 6g carb. (4g sugars, 1g fiber), 12g pro.

READER REVIEW

"This recipe is so full of flavor and so much good stuff. I did chop the ingredients up a bit more, but it is a keeper! I loved the Gouda in it."

BONITO15, TASTEOFHOME.COM

GREEN CHILE QUICHE SQUARES

Chiles add spark to this cheesy quiche. You can vary the flavor based on the kind of croutons you buy. I like to serve fresh fruit on the side.
—Connie Wilson, Huntington Beach, CA

Prep: 15 min. + chilling
Bake: 40 min. + standing
Makes: 12 servings

- **3 cups salad croutons**
- **4 cups shredded cheddar cheese**
- **1 can (4 oz.) chopped green chiles**
- **6 large eggs**
- **3 cups whole milk**
- **2 tsp. ground mustard**
- **1 tsp. salt**
- **¼ tsp. garlic powder**

1. Arrange croutons in a greased 13x9-in. baking dish. Sprinkle with cheese and chiles. In a bowl, beat remaining ingredients. Pour over cheese. Refrigerate, covered, 8 hours or overnight.
2. Remove dish from refrigerator 30 minutes before baking. Preheat oven to 350°. Bake, uncovered, until a knife inserted in center comes out clean, 40-45 minutes. Let stand 10 minutes before cutting.
1 PIECE: 259 cal., 17g fat (11g sat. fat), 155mg chol., 646mg sod., 11g carb. (3g sugars, 1g fiber), 14g pro.

GOLDEN BUTTERMILK WAFFLES

You'll hear nothing but cheering from family and friends when you stack up these golden waffles for breakfast! My clan regularly requests this morning mainstay.
—Kim Branges, Grand Canyon, AZ

Takes: 25 min. • **Makes:** 16 (4-in.) waffles

- **1¾ cups all-purpose flour**
- **1 tsp. baking powder**
- **1 tsp. baking soda**
- **½ tsp. salt**
- **2 large eggs**
- **2 cups buttermilk**
- **⅓ cup canola oil**
- **Sliced fresh strawberries, strawberry syrup and whipped cream, optional**

1. In a large bowl, combine the flour, baking powder, baking soda and salt. In another bowl, beat the eggs; add buttermilk and oil. Stir into dry ingredients just until combined.
2. Bake in a preheated waffle iron according to manufacturer's directions until golden brown. If desired, serve with sliced fresh strawberries, syrup and whipped cream.
2 WAFFLES: 223 cal., 11g fat (2g sat. fat), 56mg chol., 435mg sod., 24g carb. (4g sugars, 1g fiber), 6g pro.

COUNTRY-STYLE SCRAMBLED EGGS

I add extra color and flavor to ordinary scrambled eggs with green pepper, onion and red potatoes.
—Joyce Platfoot, Wapakoneta, OH

Takes: 30 min. • **Makes:** 4 servings

- **8 bacon strips, diced**
- **2 cups diced red potatoes**
- **½ cup chopped onion**
- **½ cup chopped green pepper**
- **8 large eggs**
- **¼ cup whole milk**
- **1 tsp. salt**
- **¼ tsp. pepper**
- **1 cup shredded cheddar cheese**

1. In a 9-in. cast-iron or other ovenproof skillet, cook bacon over medium heat until crisp. Using a slotted spoon, remove to paper towels to drain. Cook and stir potatoes in drippings over medium heat for 12 minutes or until tender. Add onion and green pepper. Cook and stir for another 3-4 minutes or until crisp-tender; drain. Stir in bacon.
2. In a large bowl, whisk the eggs, milk, salt and pepper; add to skillet. Cook and stir until eggs are completely set. Sprinkle with cheese; stir it in or let stand until melted.
1 SERVING: 577 cal., 45g fat (19g sat. fat), 487mg chol., 1230mg sod., 18g carb. (4g sugars, 2g fiber), 25g pro.

PEACH FRENCH TOAST

Let the aroma of baked peaches, brown sugar and cinnamon wake up your family. When you serve the tender slices of French toast, be sure to scoop up the golden syrup in the bottom of the pan and drizzle it over the top.
—Geraldine Casey, Anderson, IN

Prep: 20 min. + chilling • **Bake:** 45 min.
Makes: 6 servings

- **1 cup packed brown sugar**
- **½ cup butter, cubed**
- **2 Tbsp. water**
- **1 can (29 oz.) sliced peaches, drained**
- **12 slices day-old French bread (¾ in. thick)**
- **5 large eggs**
- **1½ cups whole milk**
- **1 Tbsp. vanilla extract**
- **Ground cinnamon**

1. In a small saucepan, bring the brown sugar, butter and water to a boil. Reduce heat; simmer for 10 minutes, stirring frequently. Pour into a greased 13x9-in. baking dish; top with peaches. Arrange bread over peaches.
2. In a large bowl, whisk the eggs, milk and vanilla; slowly pour over bread. Cover and refrigerate for 8 hours or overnight.
3. Remove from the refrigerator 30 minutes before baking. Sprinkle with cinnamon. Cover and bake at 350° for 20 minutes. Uncover; bake 25-30 minutes longer or until a knife inserted in the center of French toast comes out clean. Serve with a spoon.
2 PIECES: 547 cal., 22g fat (12g sat. fat), 202mg chol., 438mg sod., 75g carb. (56g sugars, 2g fiber), 10g pro.

CREAM CHEESE & CHIVE OMELET

The first bite of creamy filling lets you know this isn't any old omelet. Make it once, and I suspect you'll be fixing it often.
—Anne Troise, Manalapan, NJ

Takes: 15 min. • **Makes:** 2 servings

- **1 Tbsp. olive oil**
- **4 large eggs**
- **2 Tbsp. minced chives**
- **2 Tbsp. water**
- **⅛ tsp. salt**
- **⅛ tsp. pepper**
- **2 oz. cream cheese, cubed**
- **Salsa**

1. In a large nonstick skillet, heat oil over medium-high heat. Whisk the eggs, chives, water, salt and pepper. Add egg mixture to skillet (mixture should set immediately at the edges).
2. As eggs set, push cooked edges toward the center, letting the uncooked portion flow underneath. When the eggs are set, sprinkle cream cheese on one side; fold other side over filling. Slide omelet onto a plate; cut in half. Serve with salsa.
½ OMELET: 305 cal., 27g fat (10g sat. fat), 455mg chol., 374mg sod., 2g carb. (1g sugars, 0 fiber), 15g pro.

ZIPPY PRALINE BACON

We live on a lake and have many overnight guests, so I serve brunch often. I'm always looking for new and interesting recipes . My husband attended a men's brunch and came home raving over this bacon, and the hostess shared the recipe. Just be sure to make more than you think you might need—everybody wants seconds.
—Myrt Pfannkuche, Pell City, AL

Takes: 20 min. • **Makes:** 20 pieces

- **1 lb. bacon strips**
- **3 Tbsp. brown sugar**
- **1½ tsp. chili powder**
- **¼ cup finely chopped pecans**

1. Preheat oven to 425°. Arrange bacon in a single layer in two foil-lined 15x10x1-in. pans. Bake 10 minutes; carefully pour off drippings.
2. Mix brown sugar and chili powder; sprinkle over bacon. Sprinkle with chopped pecans. Bake until bacon is crisp, 5-10 minutes. Drain on paper towels.
2 SLICES: 117 cal., 8g fat (2g sat. fat), 16mg chol., 302mg sod., 5g carb. (4g sugars, 0 fiber), 6g pro.

BACON & EGG SANDWICHES

I came across this unique grilled combo when I was digging in my mom's recipe box. The crisp bacon, hard-cooked eggs and crunchy green onions make these cozy sandwiches look impressive when company drops by for lunch. Best of all, they're a snap to assemble.
—Ann Fuemmeler, Glasgow, MO

Takes: 20 min. • **Makes:** 4 servings

- ½ **cup sour cream**
- 8 **slices bread**
- 4 **green onions, chopped**
- 4 **slices process American cheese**
- 2 **hard-boiled large eggs, cut into ¼-in. slices**
- 8 **cooked bacon strips**
- 2 **Tbsp. butter, softened**

1. Spread sour cream over four bread slices; top with green onions, cheese, eggs, bacon and remaining bread. Spread outsides of sandwiches with butter.
2. Toast sandwiches until golden brown and cheese is melted, 2-3 minutes per side.
1 SANDWICH: 461 cal., 27g fat (13g sat. fat), 137mg chol., 887mg sod., 32g carb. (6g sugars, 2g fiber), 19g pro.

HAWAIIAN WAFFLES

I created this waffle recipe to recapture the memorable tropical tastes we enjoyed while visiting Hawaii.
—Darlene Brenden, Salem, OR

Takes: 30 min. • **Makes:** 16 (4-in.) waffles

- 1 **can (20 oz.) crushed pineapple, undrained**
- ½ **cup sugar**
- ½ **cup sweetened shredded coconut**
- ½ **cup light corn syrup**
- ¼ **cup pineapple juice**

WAFFLES

- 2 **cups all-purpose flour**
- 4 **tsp. baking powder**
- 1 **Tbsp. sugar**
- ½ **tsp. salt**
- 2 **large eggs, separated**
- 1 **cup whole milk**
- ¼ **cup butter, melted**
- 1 **can (8 oz.) crushed pineapple, well drained**
- ¼ **cup sweetened shredded coconut**
- ¼ **cup chopped macadamia nuts**
- **Additional chopped macadamia nuts, toasted, optional**

1. In a large saucepan, combine the first five ingredients. Bring to a boil. Reduce heat. Simmer, uncovered, until sauce begins to thicken, 12-15 minutes; set aside.
2. In a large bowl, combine the flour, baking powder, sugar and salt. Combine egg yolks, milk and butter; stir into dry ingredients just until combined. Stir in pineapple, coconut and nuts. Beat egg whites until stiff peaks form; fold into batter (batter will be thick).
3. Preheat waffle maker. Fill and bake waffles according to manufacturer's directions. Serve with pineapple sauce and additional chopped nuts if desired.
2 EACH: 446 cal., 14g fat (8g sat. fat), 73mg chol., 495mg sod., 76g carb. (43g sugars, 2g fiber), 7g pro.

WHOLE WHEAT PANCAKES

To fix a large batch of tender pancakes for my five children, I rely on this fuss-free recipe. It calls for whole wheat flour and buttermilk, which make the pancakes very filling but also very light. Serve them with hot chocolate for a breakfast that's sure to delight little ones.
—Line Walter, Wayne, PA

Takes: 25 min. • **Makes:** 20 pancakes

- **2 cups whole wheat flour**
- **½ cup toasted wheat germ**
- **1 tsp. baking soda**
- **½ tsp. salt**
- **2 large eggs**
- **3 cups buttermilk**
- **1 Tbsp. canola oil**

1. In a large bowl, combine the flour, wheat germ, baking soda and salt. In another bowl, whisk the eggs, buttermilk and oil. Stir into dry ingredients just until blended.
2. Pour batter by ¼ cupfuls onto a hot griddle coated with cooking spray; turn when bubbles form on top. Cook until the second side is golden brown.
FREEZE OPTION: Freeze cooled pancakes between layers of waxed paper in an airtight freezer container. To use, place pancakes on ungreased baking sheet, cover with foil, and reheat in a preheated 375° oven 6-10 minutes. Or, place a stack of three pancakes on a microwave-safe plate and microwave on high for 45-90 seconds or until heated through.
2 PANCAKES: 157 cal., 4g fat (1g sat. fat), 45mg chol., 335mg sod., 24g carb. (4g sugars, 4g fiber), 9g pro. **DIABETIC EXCHANGES:** 1½ starch, 1 fat.

OVERNIGHT SAUSAGE & GRITS

I love this hearty dish because it can be prepared the night before and then popped into the oven an hour before you want to eat. Enjoy it as a main course or serve it as a side with pancakes or waffles.
—Susan Ham, Cleveland, TN

Prep: 10 min. + chilling
Bake: 1 hour + standing
Makes: 12 servings

- **3 cups hot cooked grits**
- **2½ cups shredded cheddar cheese**
- **1 lb. bulk pork sausage, cooked and crumbled**
- **3 large eggs**
- **1½ cups whole milk**
- **3 Tbsp. butter, melted**
- **¼ tsp. garlic powder**

1. Mix grits, cheese and sausage. Beat eggs and milk; stir into grits. Add butter and garlic powder. Transfer to a greased 13x9-in. baking dish. Refrigerate casserole, covered, 8 hours or overnight.
2. Remove dish from refrigerator 30 minutes before baking. Preheat oven to 350°. Bake, uncovered, until a knife inserted in center comes out clean, about 1 hour. Let stand 5 minutes before cutting.
1 PIECE: 259 cal., 19g fat (10g sat. fat), 104mg chol., 491mg sod., 11g carb. (2g sugars, 0 fiber), 11g pro.

CREAMY STRAWBERRY CREPES

Wrap summer-ripe strawberries and creamy filling into these delicate crepes for an elegant brunch entree.

—Kathy Kochiss, Huntington, CT

Prep: 10 min. • **Cook:** 35 min.
Makes: 14 crepes

- **4 large eggs**
- **1 cup whole milk**
- **1 cup cold water**
- **2 Tbsp. butter, melted**
- **¼ tsp. salt**
- **2 cups all-purpose flour**
- **Additional butter**

FILLING

- **1 pkg. (8 oz.) cream cheese, softened**
- **1¼ cups confectioners' sugar**
- **1 Tbsp. lemon juice**
- **1 tsp. grated lemon zest**
- **½ tsp. vanilla extract**
- **4 cups fresh strawberries, sliced, divided**
- **1 cup heavy whipping cream, whipped**
- **Additional confectioners' sugar, optional**

1. In a large bowl, beat the eggs, milk, water, butter and salt. Add flour; beat until smooth. Cover and refrigerate for 1 hour.
2. In an 8-in. nonstick skillet, melt 1 tsp. butter; pour 2 Tbsp. batter into the center of skillet. Lift and tilt pan to evenly coat bottom.
3. Cook until top appears dry; turn and cook 15-20 seconds longer. Remove to a wire rack. Repeat with remaining batter, adding butter to skillet as needed. When cool, stack crepes with waxed paper or paper towels in between.
4. For filling, in a small bowl, beat the cream cheese, confectioners' sugar, lemon juice, zest and vanilla until smooth. Fold in 2 cups berries and the whipped cream. Spoon about ⅓ cup filling down the center of 14 crepes; roll up. Garnish with remaining berries and, if desired, confectioner's sugar. Freeze the remaining crepes, unfilled, for another use. Place waxed paper between crepes in an airtight container.
2 CREPES: 504 cal., 26g fat (15g sat. fat), 194mg chol., 275mg sod., 58g carb. (28g sugars, 3g fiber), 12g pro.

CHEESY VEGETABLE EGG DISH

I'm a cook at a Bible camp, and this is one of my most popular recipes with the youngsters. I was flattered when a 10-year-old boy asked me for the recipe so he could have his mom make it at home.

—Elsie Campbell, Dulzura, CA

Prep: 20 min. • **Bake:** 35 min.
Makes: 10 servings

- 1 **medium zucchini, diced**
- 1 **medium onion, chopped**
- 1 **can (4 oz.) mushroom stems and pieces, drained**
- ¼ **cup chopped green pepper**
- ½ **cup butter, cubed**
- ½ **cup all-purpose flour**
- 1 **tsp. baking powder**
- ½ **tsp. salt**
- 10 **large eggs, lightly beaten**
- 2 **cups 4% cottage cheese**
- 4 **cups shredded Monterey Jack cheese**

1. In a large skillet, saute the zucchini, onion, mushrooms and green pepper in butter until tender. Stir in the flour, baking powder and salt until blended.
2. In a large bowl, combine eggs and cottage cheese. Stir in the sauteed vegetables and Monterey Jack cheese.
3. Transfer to a greased 2½-qt. baking dish. Bake, uncovered, at 350° for 35-45 minutes or until a thermometer reads 160°.
1 PIECE: 407 cal., 30g fat (17g sat. fat), 287mg chol., 759mg sod., 10g carb. (4g sugars, 1g fiber), 24g pro.

MAPLE BACON FRENCH TOAST BAKE

Our family loves Sunday brunch. Each season I try to bring a little different flavor to the table. This French toast bake reminds us of fall. I use regular almond milk because I can't have dairy, but whole or 2% milk work best.

—Peggie Brott, Colorado Springs, CO

Prep: 35 min. + chilling
Bake: 50 min. + standing
Makes: 12 servings

- 8 **cups cubed bread**
- 8 **large eggs**
- 2 **cups 2% milk**
- ½ **cup packed brown sugar**
- ⅓ **cup maple syrup**
- ½ **tsp. ground cinnamon**
- 1 **lb. bacon strips, cooked and crumbled**

1. Place bread in a greased 13x9-in. baking dish. In a large bowl, whisk eggs, milk, brown sugar, syrup and cinnamon. Pour over bread. Sprinkle with bacon. Refrigerate, covered, 4 hours or overnight.
2. Remove the casserole from refrigerator 30 minutes before baking. Preheat oven to 350°. Bake, uncovered, until a knife inserted in center comes out clean, 50-60 minutes. Let stand 5-10 minutes before serving.
1 PIECE: 256 cal., 10g fat (3g sat. fat), 141mg chol., 426mg sod., 29g carb. (18g sugars, 1g fiber), 12g pro.

CLASSIC LONG JOHNS

I came across the recipe for these wonderful raised doughnuts many years ago. I remember Mom making some similar to these. You can frost them with maple or chocolate glaze, then top with chopped nuts, jimmies, toasted coconut or sprinkles.
—Ann Sorgent, Fond du Lac, WI

Prep: 30 min. + rising
Cook: 5 min./batch + cooling
Makes: 2 dozen

- **2 pkg. (¼ oz. each) active dry yeast**
- **½ cup warm water (110° to 115°)**
- **½ cup half-and-half cream**
- **¼ cup sugar**
- **¼ cup shortening**
- **1 large egg**
- **1 tsp. salt**
- **½ tsp. ground nutmeg**
- **3 to 3½ cups all-purpose flour**
- **Oil for deep-fat frying**

MAPLE FROSTING
- **¼ cup packed brown sugar**
- **2 Tbsp. butter**
- **1 Tbsp. half-and-half cream**
- **⅛ tsp. maple flavoring**
- **½ cup confectioners' sugar**

CHOCOLATE FROSTING
- **2 oz. semisweet chocolate, chopped**
- **2 Tbsp. butter**
- **½ cup confectioners' sugar**
- **2 Tbsp. boiling water**
- **1 tsp. vanilla extract**

1. In a large bowl, dissolve the yeast in warm water. Add cream, sugar, shortening, egg, salt, nutmeg and 3 cups flour. Beat until smooth. Stir in enough remaining flour to form a soft dough (dough will be sticky).
2. Turn onto a floured surface; knead until smooth and elastic, about 6-8 minutes. Place in a greased bowl, turning once to grease the top. Cover with plastic wrap; let rise in a warm place until doubled, about 1 hour.
3. Punch down dough; divide in half. Turn onto a lightly floured surface; roll each half into a 12x6-in. rectangle. Cut into twelve 3x2-in. rectangles. Place on greased baking sheets. Cover and let rise in a warm place until doubled, about 30 minutes.
4. In an electric skillet or deep fryer, heat oil to 375°. Fry long johns, a few at a time, until golden brown on both sides. Drain on paper towels.
5. For maple frosting, combine brown sugar and butter in a small saucepan. Bring to a boil, stirring to dissolve sugar. Remove from heat; stir in cream and maple flavoring. Add the confectioners' sugar; beat for 1 minute or until smooth. Frost cooled long johns.
6. For chocolate frosting, in a microwave, melt chocolate and butter; stir until smooth. Stir in the remaining ingredients. Spread over cooled long johns; let stand until set.

1 LONG JOHN: 186 cal., 9g fat (3g sat. fat), 16mg chol., 121mg sod., 22g carb. (10g sugars, 1g fiber), 3g pro.

OVERNIGHT PUMPKIN FRENCH TOAST CASSEROLE

Recipes that don't tie me to the kitchen—that's what I'm all about! I make this luscious dish the night before breakfast or brunch with guests.
—Patricia Harmon, Baden, PA

Prep: 20 min. + chilling • **Bake:** 65 min.
Makes: 12 servings

- **1 loaf (1 lb.) cinnamon-raisin bread**
- **1 pkg. (8 oz.) reduced-fat cream cheese, cut into ¾-in. cubes**
- **8 large eggs**
- **1 can (12 oz.) evaporated milk**
- **1 cup canned pumpkin**
- **⅔ cup packed brown sugar**
- **½ cup fat-free milk**
- **2 tsp. ground cinnamon**
- **¼ tsp. ground nutmeg**
- **¼ tsp. ground ginger**
- **⅛ tsp. ground cloves**
- **½ tsp. salt**
- **½ cup chopped pecans**
- **Confectioners' sugar, optional**
- **Maple syrup, warmed, optional**

1. Cut each slice of bread into quarters. Arrange half of the bread in a greased 13x9-in. baking dish; layer with cubed cream cheese and remaining bread, pressing down slightly.
2. In a large bowl, whisk eggs, evaporated milk, pumpkin, brown sugar, fat-free milk, spices and salt. Pour over top. Refrigerate, covered, overnight.
3. Preheat oven to 350°. Remove casserole from refrigerator while oven heats. Bake, covered, 40 minutes. Uncover; sprinkle with pecans. Bake, uncovered, 25-30 minutes or until lightly browned and a knife inserted in center comes out clean.
4. Let stand 5-10 minutes before serving. If desired, dust with confectioners' sugar and serve with maple syrup.

1 PIECE: 302 cal., 13g fat (6g sat. fat), 148mg chol., 342mg sod., 36g carb. (20g sugars, 4g fiber), 13g pro.

PATRICIA HARMON
Banden, PA

PECAN APPLE PANCAKES

Weekend breakfasts are a big deal here in Texas, and these sweet, well-spiced pancakes make any breakfast memorable. So put on your apron and invite the neighbors in!
—Sharon Richardson, Dallas, TX

Prep: 15 min. • **Cook:** 10 min./batch
Makes: 18 pancakes

- **2 cups all-purpose flour**
- **1 cup sugar**
- **2 tsp. baking powder**
- **1 tsp. baking soda**
- **1 tsp. ground cinnamon**
- **½ tsp. salt**
- **½ tsp. ground ginger**
- **½ tsp. ground mace**
- **½ tsp. ground cloves**
- **2 large eggs**
- **1¾ cups buttermilk**
- **3 Tbsp. canola oil**
- **1¾ cups shredded peeled apples**
- **½ cup chopped pecans**

1. In a large bowl, combine the first nine ingredients. In another bowl, whisk the eggs, buttermilk and oil until blended. Add to flour mixture; stir just until moistened. Stir in the apples and pecans.
2. Lightly grease a griddle and heat over medium-low heat. Pour batter by ¼ cupfuls onto griddle. Cook until bubbles on top begin to pop and bottoms are golden brown. Turn; cook until second side is golden brown.
1 SERVING (2 EACH): 323 cal., 11 g fat (2 g sat. fat), 49 mg chol., 425 mg sod., 50 g carb., 2 g fiber, 7g pro.

COLORFUL BRUNCH FRITTATA

A friend asked me for a special recipe that could be served at his daughter's wedding brunch. I created this 13x9-in. frittata for the occasion. It's loaded with colorful veggies and looks beautiful on a buffet.
—Kristin Arnett, Elkhorn, WI

Prep: 15 min. • **Bake:** 50 min. + standing
Makes: 12-15 servings

- **1 lb. fresh asparagus, trimmed and cut into 1-in. pieces**
- **½ lb. sliced fresh mushrooms**
- **1 medium sweet red pepper, diced**
- **1 medium sweet yellow pepper, diced**
- **1 small onion, chopped**
- **3 green onions, chopped**
- **3 Tbsp. olive oil**
- **2 garlic cloves, minced**
- **3 plum tomatoes, seeded and chopped**
- **14 large eggs, lightly beaten**
- **2 cups half-and-half cream**
- **2 cups shredded Colby-Monterey Jack cheese**
- **3 Tbsp. minced fresh parsley**
- **3 Tbsp. minced fresh basil**
- **½ tsp. salt**
- **¼ tsp. pepper**
- **½ cup shredded Parmesan cheese**

1. Preheat oven to 350°. In a large skillet, saute asparagus, mushrooms, peppers and onions in oil until tender. Add garlic; cook 1 minute longer. Add tomatoes; set aside.
2. In a large bowl, whisk the eggs, cream, Colby-Monterey Jack cheese, parsley, basil, salt and pepper; stir into vegetable mixture.
3. Pour into a greased 13x9-in. baking dish. Bake, uncovered, 45 minutes.
4. Sprinkle with the Parmesan cheese. Bake 5 minutes longer or until a knife inserted in the center comes out clean. Let stand 10 minutes before cutting.
1 PIECE: 219 cal., 16g fat (8g sat. fat), 230mg chol., 294mg sod., 6g carb. (3g sugars, 1g fiber), 12g pro.

CINNAMON-RAISIN GRANOLA BARS

I make these chewy bars for quick breakfasts and road trips. Feel free to use chocolate chips instead of raisins if you like.
—Kristina Miedema, Houghton, NY

Prep: 15 min. • **Bake:** 25 min. + cooling
Makes: 2 dozen

- **2 cups old-fashioned oats**
- **1 cup all-purpose flour**
- **1 cup golden raisins**
- **¾ cup packed brown sugar**
- **½ cup toasted wheat germ**
- **¾ tsp. ground cinnamon**
- **¾ tsp. salt**
- **1 large egg, room temperature**
- **½ cup canola oil**
- **½ cup maple syrup**
- **2 tsp. vanilla extract**

1. Preheat oven to 350°. Line a 13x9-in. baking pan with foil, letting ends extend up sides; grease foil. In a large bowl, combine the first seven ingredients. In a small bowl, combine egg, oil, maple syrup and vanilla; pour over oat mixture and mix well. (Batter will be sticky.)
2. Press into pan. Bake 25-30 minutes or until set and edges are lightly browned. Cool in pan on a wire rack. Lifting with foil, remove from pan; cut into bars.
1 BAR: 160 cal., 6g fat (1g sat. fat), 8mg chol., 80mg sod., 26g carb. (15g sugars, 1g fiber), 3g pro.

HOMEMADE BREAKFAST SAUSAGE PATTIES

Buttermilk is the secret ingredient that keeps these pork patties moist, while a blend of seasonings create a wonderful taste.
—Harvey Keeney, Mandan, ND

Prep: 30 min. • **Cook:** 10 min./batch
Makes: 20 patties

- **¾ cup buttermilk**
- **2¼ tsp. kosher salt**
- **1½ tsp. rubbed sage**
- **1½ tsp. brown sugar**
- **1½ tsp. pepper**
- **¾ tsp. dried marjoram**
- **¾ tsp. dried savory**
- **¾ tsp. cayenne pepper**
- **¼ tsp. ground nutmeg**
- **2½ lbs. ground pork**

1. In a large bowl, combine buttermilk and seasonings. Add the pork; mix lightly but thoroughly. Shape into twenty 3-in. patties.
2. In a large skillet coated with cooking spray, cook patties in batches over medium heat for 5-6 minutes per side or until a thermometer reads 160°. Remove to paper towels to drain.
FREEZE OPTION: Wrap each cooked, cooled patty; transfer to an airtight container. May be frozen for up to 3 months. To use, unwrap patties and place on a baking sheet coated with cooking spray. Bake at 350° for 15 minutes on each side or until heated through.
1 SAUSAGE PATTY: 126 cal., 8g fat (3g sat. fat), 38mg chol., 251mg sod., 1g carb. (1g sugars, 0 fiber), 11g pro.

TEST KITCHEN TIP
Try these with lean ground turkey. While the patties will be slightly more delicate to work with, they'll taste just as great!

Soups & Sandwiches

What's better than the tasty duo of soup and sandwich? Whether they're enjoyed together or served on their own, these best-loved comforts just can't be beat!

BBQ BRATS

In Wisconsin, brats are a food group! We're always looking for new ways to cook them. This easy recipe is a hit at tailgate parties or cookouts, any time of year.
—Jessica Abnet, DePere, WI

Prep: 20 min. • **Cook:** 3 hours
Makes: 10 servings

- **10 uncooked bratwurst links**
- **1 bottle (12 oz.) beer or 1½ cups chicken broth**
- **1 cup ketchup**
- **1 cup honey barbecue sauce**
- **10 hot dog buns, split**
- **Spicy brown mustard**

Grill bratwursts, covered, on an oiled rack over medium heat or broil 4 in. from heat 10 minutes, turning frequently. Transfer to a 5-qt. slow cooker. In a large bowl, mix the beer, ketchup and barbecue sauce; pour over the bratwursts. Cook, covered, on low until cooked through, 3-4 hours. Place bratwursts on buns. Serve with mustard and, if desired, cooking liquid.

1 SANDWICH: 480 cal., 27g fat (9g sat. fat), 64mg chol., 1659mg sod., 41g carb. (20g sugars, 1g fiber), 16g pro.

TEST KITCHEN TIP
Brats (bratwurst) are spicy German sausages. To keep them moist and juicy, avoid overcooking them. If they are overcooked, the casings might split, allowing the juices to escape. Avoid pricking the casings before or during cooking—this can also release the juices, causing the sausage to dry out.

WHITE BEAN SOUP WITH MEATBALLS

It tastes like it's from scratch, but my Italian-inspired soup uses lots of clever shortcuts. For a meatball in every bite, I chop them up—with an egg slicer!
—Carole Lotito, Hillsdale, NJ

Takes: 30 min. • **Makes:** 6 servings

- **2 tsp. olive oil**
- **1 medium onion, chopped**
- **2 garlic cloves, minced**
- **⅛ tsp. coarsely ground pepper**
- **12 oz. frozen fully cooked Italian meatballs (about 3 cups), thawed**
- **1 cup julienned carrots**
- **1 carton (32 oz.) reduced-sodium chicken broth**
- **1 can (15½ oz.) cannellini beans, rinsed and drained**
- **8 cups coarsely chopped escarole (1 bunch) or fresh spinach**
- **Thinly sliced fresh basil, optional**

1. In a 6-qt. stockpot, heat oil over medium heat; saute onion until tender, 3-4 minutes. Add garlic and pepper; cook and stir 1 minute.
2. Stir in meatballs, carrots and broth; bring to a boil. Reduce the heat; simmer, covered, 5 minutes. Stir in beans and escarole; return to a boil. Reduce the heat; simmer, covered, until escarole has wilted, about 10 minutes. If desired, top servings with basil.
FREEZE OPTION: Freeze cooled soup in freezer containers. To use, partially thaw in refrigerator overnight. Heat through in a saucepan, stirring occasionally.
1 CUP: 301 cal., 15g fat (6g sat. fat), 27mg chol., 1050mg sod., 26g carb. (3g sugars, 8g fiber), 19g pro.

CURRIED EGG SALAD

A curry kick gives this egg salad big appeal. We love it when the weather gets warm.
—Joyce McDowell, West Union, OH

Takes: 15 min. • **Makes:** 6 servings

- **½ cup mayonnaise**
- **½ tsp. ground curry**
- **½ tsp. honey**
- **Dash ground ginger**
- **6 hard-boiled large eggs, coarsely chopped**
- **3 green onions, sliced**
- **6 slices whole wheat bread**
- **Tomato slices and cracked pepper, optional**

Mix the first four ingredients; stir in eggs and green onions. Spread on bread. If desired, top with tomato and sprinkle with pepper.
1 OPEN-FACED SANDWICH: 273 cal., 20g fat (4g sat. fat), 188mg chol., 284mg sod., 14g carb. (2g sugars, 2g fiber), 10g pro.

TEST KITCHEN TIP
To make egg salad in almost half the time, use a pastry blender instead of a knife to chop the eggs.

TUSCAN CAULIFLOWER SOUP

A classic Tuscan soup has lots of potatoes, but I make mine the low-carb way with cauliflower. Turns out, it has a heartier flavor.
—Heather Bewley, Bemidji, MN

Takes: 30 min. • **Makes:** 8 servings (2½ qt.)

- **4 cups fresh cauliflowerets (about 14 oz.)**
- **2 cans (14½ oz. each) reduced-sodium chicken broth**
- **2 cups water**
- **2 garlic cloves, minced**
- **1 lb. bulk Italian sausage**
- **1 cup sliced fresh mushrooms**
- **1 cup heavy whipping cream**
- **¼ tsp. pepper**
- **½ lb. bacon strips, cooked and crumbled**

1. In a large saucepan, combine cauliflower, broth, water and garlic; bring mixture to a boil. Simmer, uncovered, until cauliflower is tender, 12-15 minutes.
2. Meanwhile, in a large skillet, cook sausage and mushrooms over medium heat until the sausage is no longer pink, breaking up sausage into crumbles, 6-8 minutes. Remove with a slotted spoon; drain on paper towels.
3. Add sausage and mushrooms to cauliflower mixture; return to a boil. Reduce heat; simmer, uncovered, 5 minutes. Stir in whipping cream and pepper; heat through. Serve with bacon.
1¼ CUPS: 358 cal., 30g fat (14g sat. fat), 91mg chol., 941mg sod., 7g carb. (4g sugars, 1g fiber), 17g pro.

BALSAMIC BEEF HOAGIES

All my boys (big and small) like sandwiches, and balsamic beef is a welcome change from pulled barbecue chicken. If we have leftovers, we enjoy them in quesadillas, on pizza or with rice. You can find more family-friendly recipes at my blog, *theseasonedmom.com*.
—Blair Lonergan, Rochelle, VA

Prep: 25 min. • **Cook:** 5 hours
Makes: 8 servings

- **1 cup beef broth**
- **½ cup balsamic vinegar**
- **2 Tbsp. brown sugar**
- **2 Tbsp. Worcestershire sauce**
- **4 garlic cloves, minced**
- **1 boneless beef chuck roast (2 lbs.)**

SANDWICHES

- **½ cup mayonnaise**
- **8 hoagie buns, split and toasted**
- **4 medium tomatoes, sliced**
- **½ cup thinly sliced fresh basil**

1. In a small bowl, mix the first five ingredients. Place chuck roast in a 4- or 5-qt. slow cooker. Pour broth mixture over top. Cook, covered, on low until meat is tender, 5-6 hours.
2. Remove roast; shred beef with two forks. Skim fat from cooking juices. Return beef and cooking juices to slow cooker; heat through.
3. Spread mayonnaise on buns. Using tongs, place shredded beef on hoagie buns; top with tomatoes and basil.
FREEZE OPTION: Freeze the cooled meat mixture in freezer containers. To use, partially thaw in refrigerator overnight. Heat through in a saucepan, stirring occasionally and adding a little broth if necessary.
1 SANDWICH: 549 cal., 26g fat (7g sat. fat), 79mg chol., 669mg sod., 46g carb. (14g sugars, 2g fiber), 31g pro.

BRITTANY ALLYN
Mesa, AZ

CHIPOTLE CHILI SLOPPY JOES

Kids and teens love this zesty take on that all-time classic loose-meat sandwich. The leftovers, if there are any, freeze well, too.
—Brittany Allyn, Mesa, AZ

Prep: 15 min. • **Cook:** 20 min.
Makes: 6 servings

- **1 lb. lean ground beef (90% lean)**
- **1 cup finely chopped sweet onion**
- **½ cup finely chopped green pepper**
- **1 jalapeno pepper, seeded and finely chopped, optional**
- **½ cup chili sauce**
- **½ cup water**
- **1 to 2 chipotle peppers in adobo sauce, finely chopped**
- **1 Tbsp. packed brown sugar**
- **1 tsp. yellow mustard**
- **6 kaiser rolls or hamburger buns, split**
- **2 Tbsp. butter, softened**
- **Pickle slices, optional**

1. Preheat broiler. In a large skillet, cook beef, onion, green pepper and, if desired, jalapeno over medium heat until beef is no longer pink, breaking up the beef into crumbles, for 5-7 minutes; drain.
2. Stir in chili sauce, water, chipotle peppers, brown sugar and mustard; bring to a boil. Simmer, uncovered, until slightly thickened, 8-10 minutes, stirring occasionally.
3. Lightly spread cut sides of rolls with butter; arrange on a baking sheet, buttered side up. Broil 3-4 in. from heat until lightly toasted, about 30 seconds. Fill with beef mixture and, if desired, pickles.

FREEZE OPTION: Freeze the cooled meat mixture in freezer containers. To use, partially thaw in refrigerator overnight. Heat through in a saucepan, stirring occasionally and adding a little water if necessary. Prepare sandwiches as directed.

NOTE: Wear disposable gloves when cutting hot peppers; the oils can burn skin. Avoid touching your face.

1 SANDWICH: 313 cal., 12g fat (5g sat. fat), 57mg chol., 615mg sod., 32g carb. (11g sugars, 2g fiber), 19g pro. **DIABETIC EXCHANGES:** 2 starch, 2 lean meat, 1 fat.

SO EASY GAZPACHO

My daughter received this recipe from a friend a few years ago. I tried it and loved it, so now it makes an appearance on my menus, too. This cold soup certainly is the talk of the party!
—Lorna Sirtoli, Cortland, NY

Prep: 10 min. + chilling • **Makes:** 5 servings

- **2 cups tomato juice**
- **4 medium tomatoes, peeled and finely chopped**
- **½ cup chopped, seeded and peeled cucumber**
- **⅓ cup finely chopped onion**
- **¼ cup olive oil**
- **¼ cup cider vinegar**
- **1 tsp. sugar**
- **1 garlic clove, minced**
- **¼ tsp. salt**
- **¼ tsp. pepper**

In a large bowl, combine all ingredients. Cover and refrigerate until chilled, at least 4 hours.

1 CUP: 146 cal., 11g fat (2g sat. fat), 0 chol., 387mg sod., 11g carb. (8g sugars, 2g fiber), 2g pro.

SESAME CHICKEN VEGGIE WRAPS

I'm always on the lookout for fast, nutritious recipes that will appeal to my kids. They love edamame, so these wraps are a smart choice for those on-the-go days.
—Elisabeth Larsen, Pleasant Grove, UT

Takes: 30 min. • **Makes:** 8 servings

- **1 cup frozen shelled edamame**

DRESSING

- **2 Tbsp. orange juice**
- **2 Tbsp. olive oil**
- **1 tsp. sesame oil**
- **½ tsp. ground ginger**
- **¼ tsp. salt**
- **⅛ tsp. pepper**

WRAPS

- **2 cups fresh baby spinach**
- **1 cup thinly sliced cucumber**
- **1 cup fresh sugar snap peas, chopped**
- **½ cup shredded carrots**
- **½ cup thinly sliced sweet red pepper**
- **1 cup chopped cooked chicken breast**
- **8 whole wheat tortillas (8 in.), room temperature**

1. Cook edamame according to the package directions. Drain; rinse with cold water and drain well. Whisk together orange juice, oils and seasonings for dressing.
2. In a large bowl, combine the remaining vegetables, chicken and edamame; toss with dressing. Place about ½ cup mixture on each tortilla. Fold bottom and sides of tortilla over filling and roll up.
1 WRAP: 214 cal., 7g fat (1g sat. fat), 13mg chol., 229mg sod., 28g carb. (2g sugars, 5g fiber), 12g pro. **DIABETIC EXCHANGES:** 2 starch, 1 lean meat, 1 fat.

WINNING CREAM OF CAULIFLOWER SOUP

Generally, my husband isn't a soup fan—but his spoon is poised and ready for this version. I adapted the rich and creamy concoction from one I tasted at a local restaurant. It's since become a popular item in our house.
—Carol Reaves, San Antonio, TX

Prep: 30 min. • **Cook:** 40 min.
Makes: 8 servings (about 2 qt.)

- **2 medium onions, chopped**
- **2 medium carrots, grated**
- **2 celery ribs, sliced**
- **2 garlic cloves, minced**
- **¼ cup plus 6 Tbsp. butter, divided**
- **1 medium head cauliflower, chopped**
- **5 cups chicken broth**
- **¼ cup minced fresh parsley**
- **1 tsp. salt**
- **1 tsp. coarsely ground pepper**
- **½ tsp. dried basil**
- **½ tsp. dried tarragon**
- **6 Tbsp. all-purpose flour**
- **1 cup whole milk**
- **½ cup heavy whipping cream**
- **¼ cup sour cream**
- **Fresh tarragon, optional**

1. In a soup kettle or Dutch oven, saute the onions, carrots, celery and garlic in ¼ cup butter until tender. Add cauliflower, broth, parsley, salt and pepper, basil and tarragon. Cover and simmer until the vegetables are tender, 30 minutes.
2. Meanwhile, in a saucepan, melt remaining butter. Stir in flour until smooth. Gradually stir in the milk and whipping cream. Bring to a boil; cook and stir until thickened, 2 minutes. Add to cauliflower mixture. Cook until thickened, stirring frequently, 10 minutes. Remove from the heat; stir in sour cream. Garnish soup with tarragon if desired.
1 CUP: 286 cal., 23g fat (14g sat. fat), 68mg chol., 1083mg sod., 17g carb. (8g sugars, 4g fiber), 6g pro.

PASTA FAGIOLI SOUP

My husband enjoys my version of this dish so much, he stopped ordering it at restaurants. He'd rather savor it when we have it at home. It's so easy to make, and yet it's hearty enough to be a full dinner.
—Brenda Thomas, Springfield, MO

Takes: 30 min. • **Makes:** 5 servings

- **½ lb. Italian turkey sausage links, casings removed, crumbled**
- **1 small onion, chopped**
- **1½ tsp. canola oil**
- **1 garlic clove, minced**
- **2 cups water**
- **1 can (15½ oz.) great northern beans, rinsed and drained**
- **1 can (14½ oz.) diced tomatoes, undrained**
- **1 can (14½ oz.) reduced-sodium chicken broth**
- **¾ cup uncooked elbow macaroni**
- **¼ tsp. pepper**
- **1 cup fresh spinach leaves, cut as desired**
- **5 tsp. shredded Parmesan cheese**

1. In a large saucepan, cook sausage over medium heat until no longer pink; drain, remove from pan and set aside. In the same pan, saute the onion in oil until tender. Add garlic; saute 1 minute longer.

2. Add the water, beans, tomatoes, broth, macaroni and pepper; bring to a boil. Cook, uncovered, until the macaroni is tender, for 8-10 minutes.

3. Reduce heat to low; stir in sausage and spinach. Cook until the spinach is wilted, 2-3 minutes. Garnish with cheese.

1⅓ CUPS: 228 cal., 7g fat (1g sat. fat), 29mg chol., 841mg sod., 27g carb. (4g sugars, 6g fiber), 16g pro.

READER REVIEW

"I love this pasta fagioli soup! I made it twice and still dream about it after it's long gone..."

VENOMOUS354, TASTEOFHOME.COM

BBQ CHICKEN SANDWICHES

These great sandwiches are a cinch to make. For a spicier taste, eliminate the ketchup and increase the amount of salsa to 1 cup.
—*Leticia Lewis, Kennewick, WA*

Prep: 20 min. • **Cook:** 15 min.
Makes: 6 servings

- ½ **cup chopped onion**
- ½ **cup diced celery**
- 1 **garlic clove, minced**
- 1 **Tbsp. butter**
- ½ **cup salsa**
- ½ **cup ketchup**
- 2 **Tbsp. brown sugar**
- 2 **Tbsp. cider vinegar**
- 1 **Tbsp. Worcestershire sauce**
- ½ **tsp. chili powder**
- ¼ **tsp. salt**
- ⅛ **tsp. pepper**
- 2 **cups shredded cooked chicken**
- 6 **hamburger buns, split and toasted**

1. In a large saucepan, saute the onion, celery and garlic in butter until tender. Stir in salsa, ketchup, brown sugar, vinegar, Worcestershire sauce, chili powder, salt and pepper.
2. Stir in chicken. Bring to a boil. Reduce heat; cover and simmer for 15 minutes. Serve about ⅓ cup chicken mixture on each bun.
FREEZE OPTION: Freeze the cooled meat mixture in freezer containers. To use, partially thaw in refrigerator overnight. Heat through in a saucepan, stirring occasionally and adding a little water if necessary. Serve in buns.
1 SANDWICH: 284 cal., 8g fat (3g sat. fat), 47mg chol., 770mg sod., 35g carb. (12g sugars, 3g fiber), 18g pro. **DIABETIC EXCHANGES:** 2 starch, 2 lean meat.

QUICK CALZONES

We came up with a winning way to use up leftover pasta sauce—hearty calzones that taste like they're made from scratch. Frozen bread dough makes them a snap to assemble, and with the Parmesan and Italian seasoning, they taste just like pizza!
—Taste of Home *Test Kitchen*

Takes: 30 min. • **Makes:** 4 servings

- 1 **loaf (1 lb.) frozen bread dough, thawed**
- 1 **cup pasta sauce with meat**
- ¼ **cup shredded part-skim mozzarella cheese**
- 1 **to 2 Tbsp. 2% milk**
- ½ **tsp. Italian seasoning**
- 1 **Tbsp. grated Parmesan cheese**

1. Preheat oven to 350°. On a lightly floured surface, divide dough into four portions. Roll each into a 6-in. circle. Spread ¼ cup sauce over half of each circle to within ½ in. of edge; top with 1 Tbsp. mozzarella cheese. Fold the dough over filling; pinch edges to seal. Place on a greased baking sheet.
2. Brush milk over tops; sprinkle with Italian seasoning and Parmesan cheese. Bake until golden brown, 20-25 minutes.
1 CALZONE: 430 cal., 12g fat (3g sat. fat), 26mg chol., 1037mg sod., 63g carb. (6g sugars, 4g fiber), 21g pro.

SPAGHETTI & MEATBALL SOUP

A couple of nights each week our family ends up eating in shifts because everyone is going every which way, all at the same time. Having a hearty soup simmering in the slow cooker is an easy way to give us all a warm meal.
—Susan Stetzel, Gainesville, NY

Prep: 45 min. • **Cook:** 6¼ hours
Makes: 8 servings (3¼ qt.)

- **1 cup soft bread crumbs**
- **¾ cup 2% milk**
- **2 large eggs, lightly beaten**
- **½ cup freshly grated Parmesan cheese**
- **¾ tsp. salt**
- **½ tsp. garlic powder**
- **½ tsp. pepper**
- **2 lbs. bulk Italian sausage, mild**

SOUP

- **4 cups beef stock**
- **1 jar (24 oz.) marinara sauce**
- **3 cups water**
- **1 tsp. dried basil**
- **Parmesan rind, optional**
- **8 oz. angel hair pasta, broken into 1½-in. pieces**
- **Additional freshly grated Parmesan cheese, optional**

1. Preheat oven to 400°. In a large bowl, mix bread crumbs and milk. Let stand 5 minutes; drain. Stir in eggs, cheese and seasonings. Add sausage; mix lightly but thoroughly. Shape into 1-in. balls. Place meatballs on a greased rack in a 15x10x1-in. baking pan. Bake until cooked through, 12-15 minutes.
2. Transfer meatballs to a 6-qt. slow cooker. Add stock, marinara sauce, water, basil and, if desired, Parmesan rind. Cook, covered, on low 6-8 hours to allow flavors to blend.
3. Discard Parmesan rind. Stir in pasta; cook, covered, on high until pasta is tender, 15-20 minutes longer. If desired, serve soup with additional cheese.
NOTE: To make soft bread crumbs, tear bread into pieces and place in a food processor or blender. Cover and pulse until crumbs form. One slice of bread yields ½-¾ cup crumbs.
1½ CUPS: 394 cal., 26g fat (9g sat. fat), 95mg chol., 1452mg sod., 23g carb. (9g sugars, 2g fiber), 17g pro.

BACON & SWISS CHICKEN SANDWICHES

I created this sandwich based on one that my daughter ordered at a restaurant. She likes to dip her sandwich in the extra honey-mustard sauce. It's delicious.
—Marilyn Moberg, Papillion, NE

Takes: 25 min. • **Makes:** 4 servings

- **¼ cup reduced-fat mayonnaise**
- **1 Tbsp. Dijon mustard**
- **1 Tbsp. honey**
- **4 boneless skinless chicken breast halves (4 oz. each)**
- **½ tsp. Montreal steak seasoning**
- **4 slices Swiss cheese**
- **4 whole wheat hamburger buns, split**
- **2 bacon strips, cooked and crumbled**
- **Lettuce leaves and tomato slices, optional**

1. In a small bowl, mix mayonnaise, mustard and honey. Set honey-mustard aside. Pound chicken breast halves with a meat mallet to ½-in. thickness. Sprinkle with steak seasoning. Grill chicken, covered, over medium heat or broil 4 in. from heat until a thermometer reads 165°, 4-6 minutes on each side. Top meat with cheese during the last 1 minute of cooking.
2. Grill buns over medium heat, cut side down, until toasted, 30-60 seconds. Serve chicken on buns with bacon, mayonnaise mixture and, if desired, lettuce and tomato.
1 SANDWICH: 410 cal., 17g fat (6g sat. fat), 91mg chol., 667mg sod., 29g carb. (9g sugars, 3g fiber), 34g pro. **DIABETIC EXCHANGES:** 4 lean meat, 2 starch, 2 fat.

SUSAN STETZEL
Gainesville, NY

WILD RICE SOUP

As the oldest of eight girls growing up on the farm, I began cooking at an early age. This soup—which I tried for the first time at my sister's house—brings me compliments no matter where I serve it.
—Elienore Myhre, Balaton, MN

Prep: 30 min. • **Cook:** 1 hour
Makes: 8 servings (about 2 qt.)

- **⅓ cup uncooked wild rice**
- **1 Tbsp. canola oil**
- **1 qt. water**
- **1 medium onion, chopped**
- **1 celery rib, finely chopped**
- **1 medium carrot, finely chopped**
- **½ cup butter**
- **½ cup all-purpose flour**
- **3 cups chicken broth**
- **2 cups half-and-half cream**
- **½ tsp. dried rosemary, crushed**
- **1 tsp. salt**

1. In a medium saucepan, combine the rice, oil and water; bring to a boil. Reduce heat; cover and simmer for 30 minutes.
2. Meanwhile, in a Dutch oven, cook onion, celery and carrot in butter until vegetables are almost tender. Stir in flour until blended; cook and stir for 2 minutes. Slowly stir in broth and undrained rice. Bring to a boil; cook and stir until slightly thickened, 2 minutes. Reduce the heat; stir in cream, rosemary and salt. Simmer, uncovered, until the rice is tender, for about 20 minutes.
1 CUP: 270 cal., 19g fat (11g sat. fat), 61mg chol., 797mg sod., 17g carb. (4g sugars, 1g fiber), 5g pro.

PRESSURE-COOKER CUBAN PULLED PORK SANDWICHES

I lived in Florida for a while and loved the Cuban pulled pork sandwiches that are popular there. So I decided to put my pressure cooker to good use by making some myself.
—Lacie Griffin, Austin, TX

Prep: 20 min. • **Cook:** 25 min. + releasing
Makes: 16 servings

- **1 boneless pork shoulder butt roast (4 to 5 lbs.)**
- **2 tsp. salt**
- **2 tsp. pepper**
- **1 Tbsp. olive oil**
- **1 cup orange juice**
- **½ cup lime juice**
- **12 garlic cloves, minced**
- **2 Tbsp. spiced rum, optional**
- **2 Tbsp. ground coriander**
- **2 tsp. white pepper**
- **1 tsp. cayenne pepper**

SANDWICHES

- **2 loaves (1 lb. each) French bread**
- **Yellow mustard, optional**
- **16 dill pickle slices**
- **1½ lbs. thinly sliced deli ham**
- **1½ lbs. Swiss cheese, sliced**

1. Cut pork into 2-in.-thick pieces; season with salt and pepper. Select saute setting on a 6-qt. electric pressure cooker; adjust for high heat. Add oil; working in batches, brown pork on all sides. Remove from cooker.
2. Add the orange and lime juices, stirring to scrape browned bits from bottom of cooker. Add garlic, rum if desired, coriander, white pepper and cayenne pepper. Return pork and any collected juices to cooker. Lock the lid in place; make sure vent is closed. Select manual setting; adjust pressure to high and set time for 25 minutes.
3. When finished cooking, naturally release pressure for 10 minutes, then quick-release any remaining pressure according to the manufacturer's instructions. Remove roast; when cool enough to handle, shred with two forks. Remove 1 cup cooking liquid from cooker; add to pork and toss together.
4. Cut each loaf of bread in half lengthwise. If desired, spread mustard over cut sides of bread. Layer bottom halves of bread with pickles, pork, ham and cheese. Replace tops. Cut each loaf into eight slices.
1 SANDWICH: 573 cal., 28g fat (12g sat. fat), 126mg chol., 1240mg sod., 35g carb. (5g sugars, 2g fiber), 45g pro.

CHICKEN SALAD CROISSANTS

This tempting chicken salad gets its special taste from Swiss cheese and pickle relish. It's my brother's favorite—he insists that I make it whenever he visits.
—Laura Koziarski, Battle Creek, MI

Takes: 15 min. • **Makes:** 6 servings

- **⅔ cup mayonnaise**
- **½ cup dill pickle relish**
- **1 Tbsp. minced fresh parsley**
- **1 tsp. lemon juice**
- **½ tsp. seasoned salt**
- **⅛ tsp. pepper**
- **2 cups cubed cooked chicken**
- **1 cup cubed Swiss cheese**
- **6 croissants, split**
- **Lettuce leaves**

Mix first six ingredients; stir in chicken and cheese. Serve on croissants lined with lettuce.

1 SANDWICH: 607 cal., 41g fat (14g sat. fat), 109mg chol., 1001mg sod., 34g carb. (13g sugars, 2g fiber), 25g pro.

SAUSAGE & CHICKEN GUMBO

This recipe for the classic southern comfort food was the first thing I ever cooked for my girlfriend. It was simple to make, but it tasted gourmet. Lucky for me, it was love at first bite.
—Kael Harvey, Brooklyn, NY

Prep: 35 min. • **Cook:** 6 hours
Makes: 6 servings

- **¼ cup all-purpose flour**
- **¼ cup canola oil**
- **4 cups chicken broth, divided**
- **1 pkg. (14 oz.) smoked sausage, cut into ½-in. slices**
- **1 cup frozen sliced okra, thawed**
- **1 small green pepper, chopped**
- **1 medium onion, chopped**
- **1 celery rib, chopped**
- **3 garlic cloves, minced**
- **½ tsp. pepper**
- **¼ tsp. salt**
- **¼ tsp. cayenne pepper**
- **2 cups coarsely shredded cooked chicken**
- **Hot cooked rice**

1. In a heavy saucepan, mix flour and oil until smooth; cook and stir mixture over medium heat until light brown, 4 minutes. Reduce the heat to medium-low; cook and stir until dark reddish brown, about 15 minutes (do not burn). Gradually stir in 3 cups broth; transfer to a 4- or 5-qt. slow cooker.

2. Stir in the sausage, vegetables, garlic and seasonings. Cook, covered, on low until the flavors are blended, 6-8 hours. Stir in chicken and remaining broth; heat through. Serve gumbo with rice.

1 CUP: 427 cal., 31g fat (9g sat. fat), 89mg chol., 1548mg sod., 11g carb. (4g sugars, 1g fiber), 25g pro.

DID YOU KNOW?

Gumbo is a hearty, stew-like soup usually served with rice. It starts with a dark roux of flour and oil or butter. It may contain shellfish, chicken, sausage, ham, tomatoes, onions, garlic, sweet peppers and celery. In addition to the roux, okra is used as a thickening agent.

CAESAR CHICKEN WRAPS

When we have chicken for dinner, I cook extra so I can make these full-flavored roll-ups the next day. Featuring Caesar salad dressing, cream cheese, red pepper, black olives and a hint of garlic, the wraps are perfect alongside fruit or corn on the cob.
—*Christi Martin, Elko, NV*

Takes: 30 min. • **Makes:** 5 servings

- **½ cup creamy Caesar salad dressing**
- **½ cup grated Parmesan cheese, divided**
- **1 tsp. lemon juice**
- **1 garlic clove, minced**
- **¼ tsp. pepper**
- **1 pkg. (8 oz.) cream cheese, softened**
- **3 cups shredded romaine**
- **½ cup diced sweet red pepper**
- **1 can (2¼ oz.) sliced ripe olives, drained**
- **5 flour tortillas (10 in.)**
- **1¾ cups cubed cooked chicken**

1. In a small bowl, combine the salad dressing, ¼ cup Parmesan cheese, lemon juice, garlic and pepper. In a small bowl, beat the cream cheese until smooth. Add half of the salad dressing mixture and mix well; set aside.
2. In a large bowl, combine the romaine, red pepper and olives. Add the remaining salad dressing mixture; toss to coat. Spread about ¼ cup cream cheese mixture over each tortilla. Top with the romaine mixture and chicken; sprinkle with remaining Parmesan cheese. Roll up; cut in half.
1 SERVING: 614 cal., 36g fat (15g sat. fat), 108mg chol., 1065mg sod., 36g carb. (2g sugars, 7g fiber), 29g pro.

SHRIMP PO'BOYS WITH PINEAPPLE SLAW

This twist on the traditional po'boy sandwich adds flavor and veggies while reducing fat and calories. For a smoked flavor, grill the shrimp. For a lower-carb option, just serve the po'boy open-faced on a baguette half.
—*Melissa Pelkey Hass, Waleska, GA*

Takes: 30 min. • **Makes:** 6 servings

- **⅓ cup egg substitute**
- **½ cup panko (Japanese) bread crumbs**
- **2 Tbsp. reduced-sodium Creole seasoning**
- **1 lb. uncooked shrimp (16-20 per lb.), peeled and deveined**
- **2 cups broccoli coleslaw mix**
- **1 cup unsweetened pineapple tidbits, drained, 3 Tbsp. liquid reserved**
- **2 green onions, chopped**
- **½ cup reduced-fat mayonnaise**
- **6 hoagie buns, split and toasted**
- **4 Tbsp. reduced-fat tartar sauce**
- **3 medium tomatoes, sliced**

1. Preheat oven to 400°. Pour egg substitute into a shallow bowl. In a separate shallow bowl, mix bread crumbs and Creole seasoning. Dip shrimp in egg substitute, then in crumb mixture, patting to help coating adhere. Bake in a greased 15x10x1-in. pan until shrimp turn pink, 7-9 minutes. Keep warm.
2. Meanwhile, combine the broccoli slaw, pineapple and green onions. In a small bowl, whisk together the mayonnaise and reserved pineapple liquid until smooth. Add to broccoli mixture; toss to coat.
3. To serve, spread hoagie buns with tartar sauce. Divide tomato slices and shrimp among buns. Top with pineapple broccoli slaw.
1 SANDWICH: 420 cal., 13g fat (2g sat. fat), 99mg chol., 1430mg sod., 54g carb. (15g sugars, 3g fiber), 23g pro.

SATISFYING TOMATO SOUP

I was craving tomato soup one day. Instead of reaching for a can, I decided to make my own. My sister Joan likes it chunky, so she doesn't puree the mixture. Pair it with a classic grilled cheese sandwich or, if you want to wow them, cut the sandwich into cubes for croutons.
—Marian Brown, Mississauga, ON

Takes: 30 min. • **Makes:** 4 servings

- **2 tsp. canola oil**
- **¼ cup finely chopped onion**
- **¼ cup finely chopped celery**
- **2 cans (14½ oz. each) diced tomatoes, undrained**
- **1½ cups water**
- **2 tsp. brown sugar**
- **½ tsp. salt**
- **½ tsp. dried basil**
- **¼ tsp. dried oregano**
- **¼ tsp. coarsely ground pepper**
- **Minced fresh basil, optional**

1. In a large saucepan, heat oil over medium-high heat. Add onion and celery; cook and stir until tender, 2-4 minutes. Add remaining ingredients. Bring to a boil. Reduce heat; simmer, uncovered, for 10 minutes to allow flavors to blend.

2. Puree soup using an immersion blender. Or cool soup slightly and puree in batches in a blender; return to pan and heat through. If desired, top with fresh minced basil.

FREEZE OPTION: Freeze the cooled soup in freezer containers. To use, partially thaw in refrigerator overnight. Heat through in a saucepan, stirring occasionally and adding a little water if necessary.

GRILLED CHEESE CROUTONS: For croutons that won't immediately absorb all the soup, make a grilled cheese sandwich that is crispy and a little drier than normal. Start by buttering one side of two slices of hearty, day-old bread. Place one slice in a skillet over medium-low heat; top with your favorite cheese slices. Top with the second slice, butter side up, and cook until dark golden brown, 4-5 minutes. Flip and cook another 4-5 minutes. Remove and cut into cubes.

1¼ CUPS: 76 cal., 2g fat (0 sat. fat), 0 chol., 627mg sod., 13g carb. (9g sugars, 4g fiber), 2g pro.

BACON & CHEESE SANDWICHES

This mean melt—with bacon, Dijon mustard and two kinds of cheese—is the perfect marriage of a delicious melty filling and crispy, buttery bread.
—Sharon Delaney-Chronis, South Milwaukee, WI

Takes: 25 min. • **Makes:** 4 servings

- **¼ cup mayonnaise**
- **2 tsp. Dijon mustard**
- **8 slices sourdough bread**
- **8 slices Swiss cheese (¾ oz. each)**
- **8 slices cheddar cheese (¾ oz. each)**
- **8 slices tomato**
- **4 slices sweet onion**
- **8 cooked bacon strips**
- **2 Tbsp. butter, softened**

1. In a small bowl, mix the mayonnaise and mustard; spread over four bread slices. Layer with the cheeses, tomato, onion and bacon. Top with remaining bread. Butter outsides of the sandwiches.

2. On a griddle, toast the sandwiches over medium heat until golden brown and cheese is melted, 2-3 minutes on each side.

1 SANDWICH: 743 cal., 51g fat (22g sat. fat), 124 chol., 627mg sod., 36g carb. (9g sugars, 1g fiber), 37g pro.

CASHEW TURKEY SALAD SANDWICHES

One bite and you'll be hooked on this slightly sweet sandwich. It's protein-packed so you can feel good while you munch!
—Mary Wilhelm, Sparta, WI

Takes: 15 min. • **Makes:** 4 servings

- **¼ cup reduced-fat mayonnaise**
- **2 Tbsp. reduced-fat plain yogurt**
- **1 green onion, chopped**
- **¼ tsp. salt**
- **¼ tsp. pepper**
- **1½ cups cubed cooked turkey breast**
- **¼ cup thinly sliced celery**
- **2 Tbsp. chopped dried apricots**
- **2 Tbsp. chopped unsalted cashews**
- **8 slices pumpernickel bread**
- **4 lettuce leaves**

1. In a bowl, mix the first five ingredients. Stir in turkey, celery, apricots and cashews.
2. Line half of the bread slices with lettuce. Top with turkey mixture and remaining bread.
1 SANDWICH: 298 cal., 9g fat (2g sat. fat), 51mg chol., 664mg sod., 32g carb. (4g sugars, 4g fiber), 22g pro. **DIABETIC EXCHANGES:** 2 starch, 2 lean meat, 1½ fat.

PUMPKIN SOUP WITH SOURDOUGH SAGE CROUTONS

I'm a big fan of cream-style soups, and this one is a favorite in our house. The recipe is inspired by traditional fall flavors—pumpkin, nutmeg and sage. For a tasty variation, use butternut squash in place of the pumpkin.
—Jenn Tidwell, Fair Oaks, CA

Prep: 35 min. • **Cook:** 30 min.
Makes: 10 servings (2½ qt. soup)

- **1 large onion, chopped**
- **2 medium carrots, thinly sliced**
- **3 Tbsp. olive oil**
- **9 cups cubed fresh pumpkin**
- **3 cans (14½ oz. each) chicken broth**
- **2 Tbsp. minced fresh sage**
- **1½ tsp. garlic powder**
- **½ tsp. salt**
- **½ tsp. pepper**
- **⅛ tsp. ground nutmeg**

SWEET CREAM
- **3 oz. cream cheese, softened**
- **¼ cup 2% milk**
- **2 Tbsp. confectioners' sugar**

CROUTONS
- **3 slices sourdough bread, cubed**
- **2 Tbsp. olive oil**
- **2 Tbsp. butter, melted**
- **2 Tbsp. minced fresh sage**

1. In a Dutch oven, saute onion and carrots in oil for 5 minutes. Add the pumpkin; cook 5-6 minutes longer. Stir in the broth, sage, garlic powder, salt, pepper and nutmeg; bring to a boil. Reduce heat; cover and simmer until the pumpkin is tender, 15-20 minutes.
2. Cool slightly. In a blender, process soup in batches until smooth. Return all to pan and heat through.
3. For sweet cream, combine ingredients until smooth. For croutons, place bread in a small bowl; drizzle with oil and butter. Sprinkle with the sage and toss to coat. Transfer to a small skillet; cook and stir over medium heat until lightly toasted, 4-6 minutes.
4. Garnish individual servings with sweet cream and croutons.
1 CUP SOUP WITH 3 TBSP. CROUTONS AND 2 TSP SWEET CREAM: 199 cal., 13g fat (4g sat. fat), 18mg chol., 778mg sod., 19g carb. (7g sugars, 1g fiber), 4g pro.

HEARTY VEGETABLE SOUP

A friend gave me the brilliant idea to use V8 tomato juice in soup because it provides more flavor. Packed with veggies of all kinds, this soup just feels good to eat.

—Janice Steinmetz, Somers, CT

Prep: 25 min. • **Cook:** 1 hour 20 min.
Makes: 16 servings (4 qt.)

- **1 Tbsp. olive oil**
- **8 medium carrots, sliced**
- **2 large onions, chopped**
- **4 celery ribs, chopped**
- **1 large green pepper, seeded and chopped**
- **1 garlic clove, minced**
- **2 cups chopped cabbage**
- **2 cups frozen cut green beans (about 8 oz.)**
- **2 cups frozen peas (about 8 oz.)**
- **1 cup frozen corn (about 5 oz.)**
- **1 can (15 oz.) garbanzo beans or chickpeas, rinsed and drained**
- **1 bay leaf**
- **2 tsp. chicken bouillon granules**
- **1½ tsp. dried parsley flakes**
- **1 tsp. salt**
- **1 tsp. dried marjoram**
- **1 tsp. dried thyme**
- **½ tsp. dried basil**
- **¼ tsp. pepper**
- **4 cups water**
- **1 can (28 oz.) diced tomatoes, undrained**
- **2 cups V8 juice**

1. In a stockpot, heat oil over medium-high heat; saute carrots, onions, celery and green pepper until crisp-tender. Add garlic; cook and stir 1 minute. Stir in the remaining ingredients; bring to a boil.

2. Reduce the heat; simmer, covered, until the vegetables are tender, 1 to 1½ hours. Remove the bay leaf.

1 CUP: 105 cal., 2g fat (0 sat. fat), 0 chol., 488mg sod., 20g carb. (9g sugars, 5g fiber), 4g pro. **DIABETIC EXCHANGES:** 1 starch.

WHITE BEAN & CHICKEN ENCHILADA SOUP

I made this soup to please my daughters' craving for creaminess, my husband's for spice and mine for white beans. Garnish as you like with jalapenos, sour cream and green onions.
—Darcy Gonzalez, Palmdale, CA

Prep: 15 min. • **Cook:** 20 min.
Makes: 8 servings (3 qt.)

- **4 cans (15½ oz. each) great northern beans, rinsed and drained**
- **3 boneless skinless chicken breasts (6 oz. each), cubed**
- **½ medium onion, chopped**
- **1 garlic clove, minced**
- **2 cups frozen corn, thawed**
- **1 can (10¾ oz.) condensed cream of chicken soup, undiluted**
- **1 carton (32 oz.) reduced-sodium chicken broth**
- **1 Tbsp. ground cumin**
- **2 seeded and chopped jalapeno peppers, divided**
- **1 tsp. pepper**
- **2 green onions, chopped**
- **Sour cream, shredded cheddar cheese and tortilla chips**
- **Fresh cilantro leaves, optional**

1. In a large stockpot, combine first eight ingredients. Add 1 chopped jalapeno and ground pepper. Bring to a boil. Reduce heat; simmer, covered, until chicken is no longer pink and the soup is heated through, about 15-20 minutes.
2. Serve with remaining chopped jalapeno; top with green onions, sour cream, cheese and tortilla chips. If desired, garnish with cilantro leaves.
1½ CUPS: 301 cal., 5g fat (1g sat. fat), 41mg chol., 1121mg sod., 37g carb. (1g sugars, 12g fiber), 25g pro.

READER REVIEW

"Great soup recipe. It was a warm bowl of comfort on a winter day."

GRAMMY DEBBIE, TASTEOFHOME.COM

GRILLED VEGGIE SANDWICHES WITH CILANTRO PESTO

While vacationing in Sedona, Arizona, I fell in love with this pesto-kissed sandwich. Home again, I developed a version that tastes just like the original.
—Carolyn Phenicie, Titusville, PA

Prep: 20 min. • **Grill:** 20 min. + standing
Makes: 4 servings

- **⅔ cup packed fresh cilantro sprigs**
- **¼ cup packed fresh parsley sprigs**
- **2 Tbsp. grated Parmesan cheese**
- **2 garlic cloves, peeled**
- **2 Tbsp. water**
- **1 Tbsp. pine nuts**
- **1 Tbsp. olive oil**

SANDWICHES

- **2 large sweet red peppers**
- **4 slices eggplant (½ in. thick)**
- **Cooking spray**
- **½ tsp. salt**
- **¼ tsp. pepper**
- **½ cup shredded part-skim mozzarella cheese**
- **4 kaiser rolls, split**

1. For pesto, place cilantro, parsley, Parmesan cheese and garlic in a small food processor; pulse until chopped. Add water and pine nuts; process until blended. Continue processing; slowly add oil.
2. Grill peppers, covered, over medium heat until skins are blistered and blackened, turning occasionally, 10-15 minutes. Immediately place peppers in a large bowl; let stand, covered, for 20 minutes. Peel off and discard charred skin. Cut peppers in half; remove stems and seeds.
3. Lightly spritz both sides of eggplant slices with the cooking spray; sprinkle with salt and pepper. Grill, covered, over medium heat until tender, for 3-5 minutes on each side. Top with the peppers; sprinkle with mozzarella cheese. Grill, covered, until cheese is melted, about 2-3 minutes; remove from grill.
4. Spread roll bottoms with pesto. Top with eggplant stacks and roll tops.
1 SANDWICH: 310 cal., 12g fat (3g sat. fat), 11mg chol., 755mg sod., 40g carb. (6g sugars, 4g fiber), 12g pro. **DIABETIC EXCHANGES:** 2 starch, 1 lean meat, 1 vegetable, 1 fat.

BISTRO TURKEY SANDWICH

As a turkey lover who can't get enough during the holidays, I was inspired to come up with this restaurant-worthy sandwich. Soft, rich cheese like Brie takes it up an extra notch.
—Grace Voltolina, Westport, CT

Takes: 30 min. • **Makes:** 4 servings

- **2 Tbsp. butter, divided**
- **1 large Granny Smith or Honeycrisp apple, cut into ¼-in. slices**
- **½ tsp. sugar**
- **¼ tsp. ground cinnamon**
- **½ medium sweet onion, sliced**
- **¼ cup whole-berry or jellied cranberry sauce**
- **4 ciabatta rolls, split**
- **1 lb. cooked turkey, sliced**
- **8 slices Camembert or Brie cheese (about 8 oz.)**
- **3 cups arugula (about 2 oz.)**

1. Preheat broiler. In a skillet, heat 1 Tbsp. butter over medium heat; saute apple with sugar and cinnamon until crisp-tender, 3-4 minutes. Remove from pan.
2. In same pan, melt the remaining butter over medium heat; saute onion until lightly browned, 3-4 minutes. Remove from heat; stir in sauteed apple.
3. Spread cranberry sauce onto bottom of rolls; layer with turkey, apple mixture and cheese. Place on a baking sheet alongside roll tops, cut side up.
4. Broil 3-4 in. from heat until cheese begins to melt and roll tops are golden brown, 45-60 seconds. Add arugula; close sandwiches.
1 SANDWICH: 797 cal., 28g fat (14g sat. fat), 171mg chol., 1196mg sod., 87g carb. (16g sugars, 6g fiber), 55g pro.

BRATS WITH SAUERKRAUT

I've made many variations of this excellent main dish. The bratwurst can be plain, smoked or cheese-flavored, served whole or cut in slices, with a bun or without. At a party or potluck, it draws a crowd.
—Darlene Dixon, Hanover, MN

Prep: 10 min. • **Cook:** 6 hours
Makes: 8 servings

- **8 uncooked bratwurst links**
- **1 can (14 oz.) sauerkraut, rinsed and well drained**
- **2 medium apples, peeled and finely chopped**
- **3 bacon strips, cooked and crumbled**
- **¼ cup packed brown sugar**
- **¼ cup finely chopped onion**
- **1 tsp. ground mustard**
- **8 brat buns, split**

1. Place bratwurst in a 5-qt. slow cooker. In a large bowl, combine the sauerkraut, apples, bacon, brown sugar, onion and mustard; spoon over bratwurst.
2. Cover and cook on low until a thermometer inserted in the sausage reads 160°, 6-8 hours.
3. Place brats in buns; using a slotted spoon, top with sauerkraut mixture.
1 SANDWICH: 534 cal., 28g fat (11g sat. fat), 53mg chol., 1188mg sod., 51g carb. (18g sugars, 4g fiber), 21g pro.

SAUSAGE BEAN SOUP

You're moments away from a flavor-packed soup that will keep you toasty warm on even the chilliest night. It's the kind of recipe we Minnesotans can't get enough of.
—Marlene Muckenhirn, Delano, MN

Takes: 25 min. • **Makes:** 6 servings

- **¾ lb. bulk Italian sausage**
- **½ cup chopped onion**
- **1 garlic clove, minced**
- **1 can (16 oz.) butter beans, rinsed and drained**
- **1 can (15 oz.) black beans, rinsed and drained**
- **1 can (14½ oz.) diced tomatoes, undrained**
- **1 Tbsp. minced fresh basil or 1 tsp. dried basil**
- **1 can (14½ oz.) reduced-sodium beef broth**
- **2 Tbsp. shredded Parmesan cheese**

1. In a large saucepan, cook and crumble sausage with onion and garlic over medium heat until no longer pink, 5-7 minutes; drain.
2. Stir in beans, tomatoes, basil and broth; bring to a boil. Reduce heat; simmer, covered, 10 minutes. Serve with cheese.

1 CUP: 268 cal., 13g fat (4g sat. fat), 33mg chol., 908mg sod., 27g carb. (4g sugars, 7g fiber), 15g pro.

HEALTH TIP: To cut about 130mg sodium per serving, use no-salt-added diced tomatoes and skip the Parmesan cheese. Use no-salt-added beans to save almost 300mg more.

SLOW-COOKER LASAGNA SOUP

Try this soup if you're looking for a fun and healthy twist on traditional lasagna.
—Sharon Gerst, North Liberty, IA

Prep: 35 min. • **Cook:** 5 hours + standing
Makes: 8 servings (2½ qt.)

- **1½ lbs. bulk Italian sausage**
- **1 large onion, chopped**
- **2 medium carrots, chopped**
- **2 cups sliced fresh mushrooms**
- **3 garlic cloves, minced**
- **1 carton (32 oz.) chicken broth**
- **2 cans (14½ oz. each) Italian stewed tomatoes**
- **1 can (15 oz.) tomato sauce**
- **6 lasagna noodles, broken into 1-in. pieces**
- **2 cups coarsely chopped fresh spinach**
- **1 cup cubed or shredded part-skim mozzarella cheese**
- **½ cup shredded Parmesan cheese**
- **Thinly sliced fresh basil, optional**

1. In a large skillet, cook the sausage over medium-high heat until no longer pink, breaking into crumbles, 8-10 minutes; drain. Transfer to a 5- or 6-qt. slow cooker.
2. Add onion and carrots to same skillet; cook and stir until softened, 2-4 minutes. Stir in mushrooms and garlic; cook and stir until the mushrooms are softened, 2-4 minutes. Transfer to slow cooker. Stir in the broth, tomatoes and tomato sauce. Cook, covered, on low until vegetables are tender, 4-6 hours.
3. Skim fat from soup. Add lasagna; cook until tender, 1 hour longer. Stir in spinach. Remove insert; let stand 10 minutes. Divide mozzarella cheese among serving bowls; ladle soup over cheese. Sprinkle with Parmesan cheese and, if desired, basil.

1⅓ CUPS: 420 cal., 24g fat (9g sat. fat), 63mg chol., 1731mg sod., 30g carb. (8g sugars, 4g fiber), 21g pro.

Side Dishes, Salads & More

A memorable menu isn't complete without on-the-side sensations that complement the main course. Start here for the freshest salads, sides and condiments to round out the meal.

ROBIN HAAS
Jamaica Plain, MA

SPINACH SALAD WITH TORTELLINI & ROASTED ONIONS

Spinach and tortellini go so well together, and this salad makes an easy meal with leftover cooked chicken. What really makes it special are the roasted onions that add oomph to bottled salad dressing.
—Robin Haas, Jamaica Plain, MA

Prep: 20 min. • **Bake:** 20 min.
Makes: 6 servings

- **2 cups chopped sweet onion (about 1 large)**
- **1 Tbsp. canola oil**
- **1 pkg. (9 oz.) refrigerated cheese tortellini**
- **½ to ⅔ cup Italian salad dressing**
- **1 Tbsp. red wine vinegar**
- **10 oz. fresh baby spinach (about 12 cups)**
- **2 cups cubed cooked chicken breast (about 10 oz.)**
- **1 can (12 oz.) marinated quartered artichoke hearts, drained**
- **1 can (2¼ oz.) sliced ripe olives, drained**
- **½ cup julienned roasted sweet red peppers**
- **½ cup shaved Parmesan cheese**

1. Preheat oven to 425°. Toss onion with oil; spread into a foil-lined 15x10x1-in. baking pan. Roast until softened and lightly browned, 20-25 minutes, stirring occasionally.
2. Cook tortellini according to the package directions. Drain and rinse gently with cold water; drain well.
3. Place ½ cup salad dressing, vinegar and roasted onion in a blender. Cover; process until blended, thinning with additional dressing if desired.
4. To serve, place spinach, chicken, artichoke hearts, olives, peppers and tortellini in a large bowl; toss with onion mixture. Top with the Parmesan cheese.
2 CUPS: 448 cal., 22g fat (6g sat. fat), 59mg chol., 887mg sod., 33g carb. (9g sugars, 3g fiber), 24g pro.

THAI CHICKEN COLESLAW

My love of Thai peanut sauce inspired this tasty salad creation that always has me going back for seconds. It also make a delicious side when prepared without chicken.
—Jodi Ollerman, West Richland, WA

Prep: 20 min. + chilling • **Makes:** 4 servings

- **¼ cup lime juice**
- **¼ cup reduced-sodium soy sauce**
- **¼ cup creamy peanut butter**
- **2 Tbsp. honey**
- **1 Tbsp. Sriracha chili sauce**
- **1 garlic clove, minced**
- **1 tsp. minced fresh gingerroot or ¼ tsp. ground ginger**
- **1 tsp. sesame oil**

SALAD

- **1 pkg. (14 oz.) coleslaw mix**
- **1½ cups shredded rotisserie chicken, chilled**
- **4 green onions, chopped**
- **¼ cup chopped fresh cilantro**
- **Chopped honey-roasted peanuts, optional**

1. For dressing, whisk first eight ingredients until blended.
2. Place first four salad ingredients in a large bowl; toss with dressing. Refrigerate, covered, for 1 hour. If desired, sprinkle each serving with peanuts.
1 CUP: 286 cal., 13g fat (3g sat. fat), 47mg chol., 835mg sod., 23g carb. (15g sugars, 4g fiber), 21g pro.

CHIVE & ONION HASH BROWN POTATOES

A friend once told me about a cheesy, buttery potato dish her mother used to make. Here's my re-creation—and my friend actually liked it better than her mom's version.
—Barb Templin, Norwood, MN

Prep: 15 min. • **Bake:** 45 min. + standing
Makes: 12 servings (¾ cup each)

- **1½ cups half-and-half cream**
- **1 container (8 oz.) spreadable chive and onion cream cheese**
- **2 Tbsp. dried minced onion**
- **1 tsp. salt**
- **½ tsp. pepper**
- **2 pkg. (20 oz. each) refrigerated shredded hash brown potatoes**
- **2 cups shredded Swiss cheese**
- **3 Tbsp. minced fresh chives, divided**
- **2 Tbsp. butter, cubed**

1. Preheat oven to 375°. In a Dutch oven, combine the first five ingredients; cook and stir over medium heat until blended. Stir in the potatoes.
2. In a greased 13x9-in. or 3-qt. baking dish, layer a third of the hash brown mixture and ⅔ cup Swiss cheese; sprinkle with 1 Tbsp. chives. Repeat layers. Top with remaining hash brown mixture and cheese; dot with butter.
3. Bake, covered, for 35 minutes. Bake, uncovered, 10-20 minutes longer or until edges begin to brown and potatoes are heated through. Let stand 10 minutes before serving. Sprinkle with remaining chives.
¾ CUP: 285 cal., 17g fat (11g sat. fat), 57mg chol., 423mg sod., 23g carb. (3g sugars, 1g fiber), 9g pro.

BLACK-EYED PEA SALAD

My husband and I love southern food—so much so, we took a cooking class while visiting Savannah, Georgia. People go nuts for this black-eyed pea salad at picnics and potlucks.
—Danielle Lee, Sewickley, PA

Prep: 25 min. + chilling • **Makes:** 10 servings

- **2 cans (15½ oz. each) black-eyed peas, rinsed and drained**
- **2 cups grape tomatoes, halved**
- **1 each small green, yellow and red peppers, finely chopped**
- **1 small red onion, chopped**
- **1 celery rib, chopped**
- **2 Tbsp. minced fresh basil**

DRESSING

- **¼ cup red wine vinegar or balsamic vinegar**
- **1 Tbsp. stone-ground mustard**
- **1 tsp. minced fresh oregano or ¼ tsp. dried oregano**
- **¾ tsp. salt**
- **½ tsp. freshly ground pepper**
- **¼ cup olive oil**

1. In a large bowl, combine peas, tomatoes, peppers, onion, celery and basil.
2. For dressing, in a small bowl, whisk vinegar, mustard, oregano, salt and pepper. Gradually whisk in oil until blended. Drizzle over salad; toss to coat. Refrigerate, covered, at least 3 hours before serving.

¾ CUP: 130 cal., 6g fat (1g sat. fat), 0 chol., 319mg sod., 15g carb. (3g sugars, 3g fiber), 5g pro. **DIABETIC EXCHANGES:** 1 starch, 1 fat.

YOGURT GRAPE SALAD

The cool colors and tangy flavors of vanilla yogurt and cream cheese are brightened with the sweetness and crunch of cheery red grapes in this refreshing salad.
—Geraldine Saucier, Albuquerque, NM

Takes: 10 min. • **Makes:** 8 servings

- **1 cup (8 oz.) vanilla yogurt**
- **2 oz. cream cheese, softened**
- **1 Tbsp. honey**
- **½ tsp. ground cinnamon**
- **½ tsp. minced fresh mint**
- **6 cups seedless red grapes**

Process first five ingredients in a food processor until smooth. Place grapes and yogurt mixture in a bowl; toss to coat. Refrigerate until serving.

¾ CUP: 149 cal., 3g fat (2g sat. fat), 9mg chol., 58mg sod., 30g carb. (27g sugars, 1g fiber), 2g pro.

REFRIGERATOR GARDEN PICKLES

Canning isn't necessary for these pickles; they'll keep in the fridge for up to a month.
—Linda Chapman, Meriden, IA

Prep: 20 min. • **Cook:** 15 min. + chilling
Makes: 7 pints

- **6 cups sugar**
- **6 cups white vinegar**
- **¼ cup celery seed**
- **¼ cup mustard seed**
- **2 Tbsp. canning salt**
- **10 medium carrots, halved lengthwise and cut into 2-in. pieces**
- **3 medium cucumbers, sliced**
- **3 medium sweet red peppers, cut into 1-in. pieces**
- **2 large onions, halved and sliced**
- **1 bunch green onions, cut into 2-in. pieces**

1. In a Dutch oven, combine the first five ingredients; bring to a boil, stirring to dissolve sugar. Meanwhile, place the remaining ingredients in a large bowl.
2. Pour hot liquid over vegetables; cool. Transfer to jars, if desired; cover tightly. Refrigerate for 6-8 hours before serving. Store in the refrigerator for up to 1 month.

¼ CUP: 55 cal., 0 fat (0 sat. fat), 0 chol., 28mg sod., 13g carb. (11g sugars, 1g fiber), 1g pro.

JAMBALAYA RICE SALAD

My cold rice salad has a little hint of spice for a classic jambalaya-style kick. Shrimp, tomatoes, ham and peppers give it bright color and a delightful texture.
—Karen Rahn, Hixon, TN

Prep: 20 min. • **Cook:** 15 min. + chilling
Makes: 8 servings

- **1⅓ cups uncooked long grain rice**
- **2 Tbsp. olive oil**
- **2 cups cubed fully cooked ham**
- **⅓ cup chopped onion**
- **2 garlic cloves, minced**
- **1 tsp. dried oregano**
- **1 tsp. dried thyme**
- **½ to 1 tsp. salt**
- **¼ to ½ tsp. cayenne pepper**
- **¼ tsp. pepper**
- **⅓ cup red wine vinegar**
- **1½ lbs. peeled and deveined cooked shrimp (31-40 per lb.)**
- **2 celery ribs, thinly sliced**
- **1 small green pepper, julienned**
- **1 small sweet red pepper, julienned**
- **1 pint cherry tomatoes, halved**
- **2 green onions, sliced**

1. Prepare rice according to the package directions; cool. In a large skillet, heat oil over medium heat. Add ham and onion; cook and stir until onion is tender, about 5 minutes. Add next six ingredients; cook and stir 2 minutes. Remove from heat; stir in vinegar.
2. Combine rice, ham mixture, shrimp, celery and peppers. Refrigerate, covered, at least 2 hours. Add tomatoes; toss to combine. Sprinkle with onions.
1¼ CUPS: 309 cal., 7g fat (1g sat. fat), 150mg chol., 709mg sod., 32g carb. (2g sugars, 2g fiber), 28g pro. **DIABETIC EXCHANGES:** 4 lean meat, 2 starch, 1 vegetable, 1 fat.

PENNSYLVANIA DUTCH COLESLAW

My mother used to make this salad on holidays. With the abundance of cabbage grown here in the Northwest, the recipe is perfect for us.
—Deb Darr, Falls City, OR

Prep: 15 min. + chilling • **Makes:** 16 servings

- **1 medium head green cabbage, shredded (about 8 cups)**
- **1 cup shredded red cabbage**
- **4 to 5 carrots, shredded**
- **1 cup mayonnaise**
- **2 Tbsp. cider vinegar**
- **½ cup sugar**
- **1 tsp. salt**
- **¼ tsp. pepper**

In a large bowl, combine cabbage and carrots; set aside. In a small bowl, combine all the remaining ingredients; pour over cabbage mixture. Toss well and refrigerate overnight.
¾ CUP: 146 cal., 11g fat (2g sat. fat), 5mg chol., 239mg sod., 11g carb. (9g sugars, 2g fiber), 1g pro.

READER REVIEW

"This coleslaw is a wonderful side dish for family and friends. Everyone loved it!"

2124ARIZONA, TASTEOFHOME.COM

TEXAS GARLIC MASHED POTATOES

These creamy potatoes get their flavor burst from garlic and caramelized onions. Their savory goodness makes any meal better.
—Richard Markle, Midlothian, TX

Prep: 20 min. • **Cook:** 30 min.
Makes: 6 servings

- **1 whole garlic bulb**
- **1 tsp. plus 1 Tbsp. olive oil, divided**
- **1 medium white onion, chopped**
- **4 medium potatoes, peeled and quartered**
- **¼ cup butter, softened**
- **¼ cup sour cream**
- **¼ cup grated Parmesan cheese**
- **¼ cup 2% milk**
- **½ tsp. salt**
- **¼ tsp. pepper**

1. Preheat oven to 425°. Remove papery outer skin from garlic bulb, but do not peel or separate cloves. Cut top off of garlic bulb, exposing individual cloves. Brush cut cloves with 1 tsp. oil. Wrap in foil. Bake until cloves are soft, 30-35 minutes.
2. Meanwhile, in a large skillet over low heat, heat remaining oil. Add the chopped onion; cook until golden brown, 15-20 minutes, stirring occasionally. Transfer to a food processor. Process until blended; set aside.
3. Place potatoes in a large saucepan; add water to cover. Bring to a boil. Reduce heat; cook, uncovered, until tender, 15-20 minutes. Drain; return to pan. Squeeze softened garlic onto potatoes; add the butter, sour cream, cheese, milk, salt, pepper and onion. Beat until mashed.
FREEZE OPTION: Place cooled mashed potato mixture in a freezer container and freeze. To use, partially thaw in refrigerator overnight. Microwave, covered, on high, stirring twice and adding a little milk if necessary, until heated through.
⅔ CUP: 236 cal., 14g fat (7g sat. fat), 31mg chol., 313mg sod., 25g carb. (4g sugars, 2g fiber), 4g pro.

SPECIAL SQUASH CASSEROLE

Squash has traditionally been a food our family passes up, but this luscious casserole is an exception to the rule. You won't find it among our Thanksgiving leftovers—it's one of the first dishes to go back to the kitchen empty.
—Kathleen Cox, Wyoming, MI

Prep: 50 min. • **Bake:** 1 hour
Makes: 10 servings

- **3 lbs. butternut squash, peeled, seeded and cubed**
- **¾ cup 2% milk**
- **6 Tbsp. butter, melted**
- **3 large eggs, lightly beaten**
- **½ tsp. vanilla extract**
- **¾ cup sugar**
- **3 Tbsp. all-purpose flour**
- **½ tsp. ground cinnamon**
- **⅛ tsp. ground cloves**
- **⅛ tsp. ground nutmeg**

TOPPING

- **½ cup crushed vanilla wafers (about 15 wafers)**
- **¼ cup packed brown sugar**
- **2 Tbsp. butter, melted**

1. Place squash in a large saucepan or Dutch oven; cover with water. Bring to a boil; cover and cook until tender, 25-30 minutes. Drain and place in a large bowl; beat just until smooth.
2. Beat in the milk, butter, eggs and vanilla. Combine the dry ingredients; gradually add to squash mixture and mix well.
3. Transfer to a greased 2-qt. baking dish. Cover and bake at 350° for 45 minutes. Meanwhile, in a small bowl, combine topping ingredients until crumbly.
4. Sprinkle topping over squash. Bake, uncovered, for 12-15 minutes longer or until heated through.
¾ CUP: 279 cal., 12g fat (7g sat. fat), 91mg chol., 146mg sod., 41g carb. (26g sugars, 4g fiber), 4g pro.

HOMEMADE CANNED SPAGHETTI SAUCE

This DIY spaghetti sauce is a tomato grower's dream come true! Use up your garden bounty and enjoy it later in the year.
—Tonya Branham, Mount Olive, AL

Prep: 1½ hours + simmering
Process: 40 min. • **Makes:** 9 qt.

- **25 lbs. tomatoes (about 80 medium)**
- **4 large green peppers, seeded**
- **4 large onions, cut into wedges**
- **2 cans (12 oz. each) tomato paste**
- **¼ cup canola oil**
- **⅔ cup sugar**
- **¼ cup salt**
- **8 garlic cloves, minced**
- **4 tsp. dried oregano**
- **2 tsp. dried parsley flakes**
- **2 tsp. dried basil**
- **2 tsp. crushed red pepper flakes**
- **2 tsp. Worcestershire sauce**
- **2 bay leaves**
- **1 cup plus 2 Tbsp. bottled lemon juice**

1. In a Dutch oven, bring 2 qt. water to a boil. Using a slotted spoon, place tomatoes, one at a time, in boiling water for 30-60 seconds. Remove each tomato and immediately plunge into ice water. Peel and quarter tomatoes; place in a stockpot.
2. Pulse the green peppers and onions in batches in a food processor until finely chopped; transfer to stockpot. Stir in next 11 ingredients. Add water to cover; bring to a boil. Reduce heat; simmer, uncovered, 4-5 hours, stirring occasionally.
3. Discard bay leaves. Add 2 Tbsp. lemon juice to each of nine hot 1-qt. jars. Ladle hot mixture into jars, leaving ½-in. headspace. Remove air bubbles and adjust headspace, if necessary, by adding hot mixture. Wipe rims. Center lids on jars; screw on bands until fingertip tight.
4. Place jars into canner with simmering water, ensuring the jars are completely covered with water. Bring to a boil; process for 40 minutes. Remove jars and cool.
NOTE: The processing time listed is for altitudes of 1,000 feet or less. For altitudes up to 3,000 feet, add 5 minutes; 6,000 feet, add 10 minutes; 8,000 feet, add 15 minutes; 10,000 feet, add 20 minutes.
¾ CUP: 118 cal., 5g fat (0 sat. fat), 0 chol., 614mg sod., 17g carb. (11g sugars, 4g fiber), 3g pro. **DIABETIC EXCHANGES:** 1 starch, 1 fat.

CHEESY ZUCCHINI SAUTE

Although I no longer have a garden of my own, friends and neighbors keep me amply supplied with squash. As a thank-you, I tell them how to make this refreshing zucchini saute. It's quick, easy and tasty!

—Doris Biggs, Felton, DE

Takes: 20 min. • **Makes:** 6 servings

- ½ **cup chopped onion**
- ¼ **cup butter, cubed**
- 3 **cups coarsely shredded zucchini**
- 2 **tsp. minced fresh basil or ½ tsp. dried basil**
- ½ **tsp. salt**
- ⅛ **tsp. garlic powder**
- 1 **cup shredded cheddar cheese**
- 1 **cup diced fresh tomato**
- 2 **Tbsp. sliced ripe olives**

1. In a large skillet, saute onion in butter until crisp-tender. Stir in the zucchini, basil, salt and garlic powder. Cook and stir for 4-5 minutes or until zucchini is crisp-tender. Sprinkle with the cheese, tomato and olives.

2. Cover and cook for 4-5 minutes or until cheese is melted. Serve immediately.

1 CUP: 157 cal., 13g fat (9g sat. fat), 40mg chol., 416mg sod., 5g carb. (3g sugars, 1g fiber), 5g pro.

TOMATO FETA SALAD

One summer I combined my love for onions with a bumper crop of tomatoes and a homemade balsamic dressing. The result was this salad that receives thumbs-up approval whenever it's served.

—Robert Golus, Greer, SC

Takes: 20 min. • **Makes:** 4 servings

- 2 **Tbsp. balsamic vinegar**
- 1½ **tsp. minced fresh basil or ½ tsp. dried basil**
- ½ **tsp. salt**
- ½ **cup coarsely chopped sweet onion**
- 1 **lb. grape or cherry tomatoes, halved**
- 2 **Tbsp. olive oil**
- ¼ **cup crumbled feta cheese**

In a large bowl, combine the vinegar, basil and salt. Add onion; toss to coat. Let stand 5 minutes. Add tomatoes, oil and feta cheese; toss to coat. Serve with a slotted spoon.

¾ CUP: 121 cal., 9g fat (2g sat. fat), 8mg chol., 412mg sod., 9g carb. (3g sugars, 2g fiber), 3g pro.

THREE-GREEN SALAD

Looking for the perfect salad to accompany a favorite lasagna or pasta dish? Give this one a try. It's loaded with veggies, and the bold flavor and crunch can't be beat.
—Gina Squires, Salem, OR

Prep: 15 min. + chilling
Makes: 12 servings (about ¾ cup dressing)

- 4 **cups torn iceberg lettuce**
- 4 **cups torn leaf lettuce**
- 4 **cups torn fresh spinach**
- 1 **medium cucumber, sliced**
- 2 **carrots, sliced**
- 2 **celery ribs, sliced**
- 6 **fresh broccoli florets, sliced**
- 3 **fresh cauliflowerets, sliced**
- 6 **radishes, sliced**
- 4 **green onions, sliced**
- 5 **fresh mushrooms, sliced**

ITALIAN DRESSING

- ⅓ **cup olive oil**
- ¼ **cup plus 2 Tbsp. red wine vinegar**
- 2 **Tbsp. grated Parmesan cheese**
- 1 **tsp. sugar**
- 1 **to 2 garlic cloves, minced**
- ¼ **tsp. dried oregano**
- ¼ **tsp. dried basil**
- **Pinch salt and pepper**

1. In a large salad bowl, toss the greens and vegetables. Cover and chill. In a blender, combine all dressing ingredients; cover and process until blended. Pour into a jar with tight-fitting lid; chill for at least 30 minutes.
2. Shake dressing before serving; pour desired amount over salad and toss to coat.

1 CUP SALAD WITH 1 TBSP. DRESSING: 136 cal., 12g fat (2g sat. fat), 1mg chol., 51mg sod., 5g carb. (2g sugars, 2g fiber), 2g pro.

TEST KITCHEN TIP

Here's an easy tip that makes it easy to remove the core from a head of iceberg lettuce. Hold the head with both hands and firmly hit the head, core side down, against a countertop. Then twist the core and it should come right out. To clean the lettuce, run water into the area where the core was removed. Invert the lettuce and allow the water to drain out before using.

YELLOW SQUASH & ZUCCHINI GRATIN

This gratin is the perfect way to use up an abundance of summer squash. Easy to prepare, it takes just 10 minutes in the oven and serves up bubbly and delicious.
—Jonathan Lawler, Greenfield, IN

Prep: 25 min. • **Bake:** 10 min.
Makes: 6 servings

- 2 **Tbsp. butter**
- 2 **medium zucchini, cut into ¼-in. slices**
- 2 **medium yellow summer squash, cut into ¼-in. slices**
- 2 **shallots, minced**
- ½ **tsp. sea salt**
- ¼ **tsp. coarsely ground pepper**
- 4 **garlic cloves, minced**
- ½ **cup heavy whipping cream**
- 1 **cup panko (Japanese) bread crumbs, divided**
- ½ **cup grated Parmesan cheese, divided**

1. Preheat oven to 450°. In a large skillet, melt butter over medium heat; add zucchini, yellow squash and shallots. Sprinkle with salt and pepper. Cook, stirring occasionally, until zucchini and squash are crisp-tender, 4-6 minutes. Add garlic; cook 1 minute more.
2. Add the cream; cook until thickened, 3-5 minutes. Remove from heat; stir in ½ cup bread crumbs and ¼ cup cheese. Spoon mixture into a greased 11x7-in. or 2-qt. baking dish. Sprinkle with the remaining bread crumbs and cheese. Bake until golden brown, 8-10 minutes.

1 CUP: 203 cal., 14g fat (8g sat. fat), 39mg chol., 357mg sod., 15g carb. (4g sugars, 2g fiber), 6g pro.

MILD TOMATO SALSA

I got this salsa recipe from my sister, and my children and I have been making batches of it ever since. We pair pint jars with packages of tortilla chips for zesty Christmas gifts. When the kids give this present to their teachers, they can truthfully say they helped make it.
—Pamela Lundstrum, Bird Island, MN

Prep: 40 min. + simmering • **Process:** 20 min.
Makes: 10 pints

- **10½ lbs. tomatoes (about 35 medium), peeled and quartered**
- **4 medium green peppers, chopped**
- **3 large onions, chopped**
- **2 cans (12 oz. each) tomato paste**
- **1¾ cups white vinegar**
- **½ cup sugar**
- **1 medium sweet red pepper, chopped**
- **1 celery rib, chopped**
- **15 garlic cloves, minced**
- **4 to 5 jalapeno peppers, seeded and chopped**
- **¼ cup canning salt**
- **¼ to ½ tsp. hot pepper sauce**

1. In a large stockpot, cook the tomatoes, uncovered, over medium heat 20 minutes. Drain, reserving 2 cups liquid. Return tomatoes to the pot.
2. Stir in green peppers, onions, tomato paste, vinegar, sugar, red pepper, celery, garlic, jalapenos, canning salt, hot pepper sauce and reserved tomato liquid. Bring to a boil. Reduce heat; simmer, uncovered, 1 hour, stirring frequently.
3. Ladle hot mixture into 10 hot 1-pint jars, leaving ½-in. headspace. Remove air bubbles and adjust headspace, if necessary, by adding hot mixture. Wipe rims. Center lids on jars; screw on bands until fingertip tight.
4. Place jars into canner with simmering water, ensuring that they are completely covered with water. Bring water to a boil; process jars for 20 minutes. Remove jars and cool.
NOTE: Wear disposable gloves when cutting hot peppers; the oils can burn skin. Avoid touching your face.
2 TBSP.: 14 cal., 0 fat (0 sat. fat), 0 chol., 182mg sod., 3g carb. (2g sugars, 1g fiber), 0 pro.

SWEET POTATO PANZANELLA

This is my favorite fall lunch dish. It is filled with flavor and texture but isn't too high in calories.
—Mary Leverette, Columbia, SC

Takes: 30 min. • **Makes:** 8 servings

- **2 cups cubed peeled sweet potatoes**
- **4 cups cubed French bread**
- **4 Tbsp. olive oil, divided**
- **⅛ tsp. salt**
- **⅛ tsp. pepper**
- **4 cups fresh baby spinach**
- **½ small red onion, thinly sliced**
- **¼ cup minced fresh basil**
- **¼ cup minced fresh cilantro**
- **⅓ cup red wine vinegar**

1. Preheat oven to 450°. Place sweet potatoes and water to cover in a large saucepan; bring to a boil. Reduce heat; cook, covered, just until tender, 8-12 minutes. Drain; cool slightly.
2. Meanwhile, toss bread cubes with 2 Tbsp. oil, salt and pepper. Spread evenly in an ungreased 15x10x1-in. pan. Bake until golden brown, about 5 minutes. Transfer to a large bowl; cool slightly.
3. Add spinach, onion, herbs and sweet potatoes to toasted bread. In a small bowl, whisk together vinegar and remaining oil. Drizzle over salad; toss gently to combine.
¾ CUP: 142 cal., 7g fat (1g sat. fat), 0 chol., 150mg sod., 17g carb. (3g sugars, 2g fiber), 2g pro. **DIABETIC EXCHANGES:** 1 starch, 1½ fat.

MARY LEVERETTE
Columbia, SC

TWO-BERRY FLUFF SALAD

This fluffy salad is a welcome treat on warm Texas afternoons. There's a blueberry orchard near our home, so we often pick up berries to use in this recipe and others. When fresh berries aren't in season, you can substitute frozen berries with equally good results.
—Karen Wenzel, Conroe, TX

Takes: 15 min.
Makes: 12 servings (¾ cup each)

- **1 pkg. (8 oz.) cream cheese, softened**
- **1½ cups confectioners' sugar**
- **2 cups heavy whipping cream**
- **8 cups fresh strawberries (about 2 lbs.), sliced**
- **2 cups fresh blueberries**
- **Additional fresh strawberries and blueberries, optional**

1. In a large bowl, beat the cream cheese and confectioners' sugar until smooth. Slowly add cream, beating until thick and fluffy.
2. Fold in 8 cups strawberries and 2 cups blueberries. If desired, top with additional strawberries and blueberries.

¾ CUP: 305 cal., 21g fat (13g sat. fat), 64mg chol., 72mg sod., 28g carb. (24g sugars, 3g fiber), 3g pro.

ACORN SQUASH WITH CRANBERRY STUFFING

If you have squash or cranberry lovers at the table, here's your new go-to recipe. It's colorful, the blend of flavors is delicious and it's a fitting addition to a Thanksgiving menu.
—Dorothy Pritchett, Wills Point, TX

Prep: 10 min. • **Bake:** 55 min.
Makes: 4 servings

- **2 medium acorn squash**
- **¼ cup chopped celery**
- **2 Tbsp. chopped onion**
- **2 Tbsp. butter**
- **1 medium tart apple, peeled and diced**
- **½ tsp. salt**
- **½ tsp. lemon juice**
- **⅛ tsp. pepper**
- **1 cup fresh or frozen cranberries**
- **½ cup sugar**
- **2 Tbsp. water**

1. Cut squash in half; discard seeds. Cut a thin slice from the bottom of squash halves so they sit flat. Place squash hollow side down in an ungreased 13x9-in. baking dish; add ½ in. water. Cover and bake at 375° for 45 minutes.
2. Meanwhile, in a small skillet, saute celery and onion in butter until tender. Add the apple, salt, lemon juice and pepper. Cook, uncovered, over medium-low heat until apple is tender, stirring occasionally. Stir in the cranberries, sugar and water. Cook and stir until berries pop and liquid is syrupy.
3. Turn squash halves over; fill with cranberry mixture. Cover and bake 10-15 minutes longer or until squash is tender.

1 SERVING: 270 cal., 6g fat (4g sat. fat), 15mg chol., 367mg sod., 57g carb. (36g sugars, 5g fiber), 2g pro.

SLOW-COOKER LOADED MASHED POTATOES

Every holiday season, my mother could be counted on to deliver her famous cream cheese mashed potatoes. I keep the tradition going, but I boost the cheese factor.
—Ann Nolte, Riverview, FL

Prep: 25 min. + chilling • **Cook:** 3 hours
Makes: 10 servings

- **3 lbs. cubed peeled potatoes (about 9 medium)**
- **1 pkg. (8 oz.) cream cheese, softened**
- **1 cup sour cream**
- **½ cup butter, cubed**
- **¼ cup 2% milk**
- **½ lb. bacon strips, cooked and crumbled**
- **1½ cups shredded cheddar cheese**
- **1½ cups shredded pepper jack cheese**
- **4 green onions, thinly sliced**
- **½ tsp. onion powder**
- **½ tsp. garlic powder**
- **Salt and pepper to taste**

1. Place potatoes in a Dutch oven, adding water to cover. Bring to a boil; reduce heat and simmer, uncovered, until tender, 10-15 minutes. Drain; return to pan. Mash with cream cheese, sour cream, butter and milk. Stir in bacon, cheeses, onions and seasonings. Cover; refrigerate overnight.
2. Transfer to a greased 3- or 4-qt. slow cooker. Cook, covered, on low 3-3½ hours.
¾ CUP: 505 cal., 36g fat (20g sat. fat), 109mg chol., 530mg sod., 31g carb. (3g sugars, 3g fiber), 16g pro.

VEGGIE-FILLED MACARONI & CHEESE

This creamy mac and cheese definitely doesn't come from a box. A bounty of vegetables add crunch and color. You can also use frozen mixed veggies if you don't have fresh on hand.
—Marsha Morril, Harrisburg, OR

Prep: 30 min. • **Bake:** 15 min.
Makes: 12 servings

- **1½ cups uncooked elbow macaroni**
- **3 cups fresh broccoli florets**
- **2 cups fresh cauliflowerets**
- **3 large carrots, halved lengthwise and thinly sliced**
- **2 celery ribs, sliced**
- **1 Tbsp. butter**
- **1 medium onion, chopped**
- **¼ cup all-purpose flour**
- **1 cup 2% milk**
- **1 cup chicken broth**
- **3 cups shredded sharp cheddar cheese**
- **1 Tbsp. Dijon mustard**
- **¼ tsp. salt**
- **⅛ tsp. pepper**
- **¼ tsp. paprika**

1. Preheat oven to 350°. In a 6-qt. stockpot, cook macaroni according to the package directions, adding broccoli, cauliflower, carrots and celery during the last 6 minutes of cooking. Drain; transfer to a greased 13x9-in. baking dish.
2. Meanwhile, in a large saucepan, heat butter over medium-high heat; saute onion until tender. Stir in flour until blended. Gradually stir in milk and broth; bring to a boil. Cook and stir until thickened, about 2 minutes; stir in cheese, mustard, salt and pepper.
3. Add to macaroni mixture, stirring to coat; sprinkle with paprika. Bake, uncovered, until heated through, 15-20 minutes.
1 CUP: 200 cal., 11g fat (6g sat. fat), 33mg chol., 391mg sod., 15g carb. (3g sugars, 2g fiber), 10g pro.

READER REVIEW

"This is a great meal for kids. My 4-year-old gobbled it up and said, "More, please!"

PEISPUDS, TASTEOFHOME.COM

TZATZIKI POTATO SALAD

My son has an egg allergy, so this potato salad is perfect for him. For extra color, add radishes, apple and garlic dill pickles.
—Cindy Romberg, Mississauga, ON

Prep: 25 min. + chilling
Makes: 12 servings (¾ cup each)

- **3 lbs. small red potatoes, halved**
- **1 carton (12 oz.) refrigerated tzatziki sauce**
- **2 celery ribs, thinly sliced**
- **½ cup plain Greek yogurt**
- **2 green onions, chopped**
- **2 Tbsp. snipped fresh dill**
- **2 Tbsp. minced fresh parsley**
- **½ tsp. salt**
- **¼ tsp. celery salt**
- **¼ tsp. pepper**
- **1 Tbsp. minced fresh mint, optional**

1. Place potatoes in a Dutch oven; add water to cover. Bring to a boil. Reduce heat; cook, uncovered, until tender, 10-15 minutes. Drain and place in a large bowl. Refrigerate, covered, until chilled.

2. In a small bowl, mix tzatziki sauce, celery, yogurt, green onions, dill, parsley, salt, celery salt, pepper and, if desired, mint. Spoon over potatoes; toss to coat.

¾ CUP: 128 cal., 3g fat (2g sat. fat), 7mg chol., 190mg sod., 21g carb. (3g sugars, 2g fiber), 4g pro. **DIABETIC EXCHANGES:** 1½ starch, ½ fat.

QUICK & EASY HONEY MUSTARD

This fast, easy mustard with rice vinegar and honey has more flavor than any other honey mustard dressing I have ever tried.
—Sharon Rehm, New Blaine, AR

Takes: 5 min. • **Makes:** 1 cup

- **½ cup stone-ground mustard**
- **¼ cup honey**
- **¼ cup rice vinegar**

In a bowl, whisk all ingredients. Refrigerate until serving.

1 TBSP.: 28 cal., 1g fat (0 sat. fat), 0 chol., 154mg sod., 6g carb. (5g sugars, 0 fiber), 0 pro.

SLOW-COOKED BROCCOLI

This crumb-topped side dish is quick to assemble and full of flavor. Since it simmers in a slow cooker, it frees up my oven for other things. This is a tremendous help when I'm preparing several items for a big meal at home.
—Connie Slocum, Antioch, TN

Prep: 10 min. • **Cook:** 2¾ hours
Makes: 10 servings

- **6 cups frozen chopped broccoli, partially thawed**
- **1 can (10¾ oz.) condensed cream of celery soup, undiluted**
- **1½ cups shredded sharp cheddar cheese, divided**
- **¼ cup chopped onion**
- **½ tsp. Worcestershire sauce**
- **¼ tsp. pepper**
- **1 cup crushed butter-flavored crackers (about 25)**
- **2 Tbsp. butter**

1. In a large bowl, combine the broccoli, soup, 1 cup cheese, onion, Worcestershire sauce and pepper. Pour into a greased 3-qt. slow cooker. Sprinkle crackers on top; dot with butter.

2. Cover and cook on high for 2½-3 hours. Sprinkle with remaining cheese. Cook until the cheese is melted, 10 minutes longer.

½ CUP: 159 cal., 11g fat (6g sat. fat), 25mg chol., 431mg sod., 11g carb. (2g sugars, 1g fiber), 6g pro.

BACON-GRUYERE SMASHED POTATOES

Gruyere cheese, bacon, sweet onions and herbs take smashed potatoes to a whole new level of amazing. This loaded side dish is so rich and satisfying, it could almost be eaten on its own.

—Lisa Speer, Palm Beach, FL

Prep: 20 min. • **Cook:** 1 hour
Makes: 16 servings (¾ cup each)

- **½ cup butter, divided**
- **3 large sweet onions, halved and thinly sliced**
- **1½ tsp. salt, divided**
- **¾ tsp. pepper, divided**
- **3 tsp. minced fresh thyme or 1 tsp. dried thyme**
- **3½ lbs. medium red potatoes, halved**
- **1 cup 2% milk**
- **10 slices bacon strips, cooked and crumbled**
- **1 cup shredded Gruyere or white cheddar cheese**
- **Chopped fresh parsley, optional**

1. In a large skillet, heat ¼ cup butter over medium-high heat. Add onions, ¼ tsp. salt and ⅛ tsp. pepper; cook and stir 8-10 minutes or until softened. Reduce heat to medium-low; cook 40-50 minutes or until deep golden brown, stirring occasionally and stirring in thyme during last 5 minutes.

2. Place potatoes in a 6-qt stockpot; add water to cover. Bring to a boil. Reduce heat; cook, uncovered, 20-25 minutes or until tender. Drain; return to pan. Add milk and remaining butter, salt and pepper. Coarsely mash the potatoes with a masher, leaving small chunks. Stir in bacon and onions; sprinkle with cheese. Let stand, covered, until cheese melts. If desired, sprinkle with parsley.

¾ CUP: 205 cal., 11g fat (6g sat. fat), 29mg chol., 427mg sod., 21g carb. (5g sugars, 2g fiber), 7g pro.

BUTTERNUT SQUASH APPLE BAKE

Even those who aren't fans of squash enjoy this side dish. Sweet slices of butternut squash are topped with apples covered in a cinnamon-sugar glaze for a quick and easy dinner accompaniment.

—Ellie Klopping, Toledo, OH

Prep: 15 min. • **Bake:** 45 min.
Makes: 8 servings

- **1 butternut squash (2 lbs.), peeled and cut into ½-in. slices**
- **3 medium tart apples, peeled and thinly sliced**
- **⅓ cup packed brown sugar**
- **1½ tsp. all-purpose flour**
- **¼ tsp. ground cinnamon**
- **2 Tbsp. butter, melted**

1. Preheat oven to 350°. Layer squash and apples in a 13x9-in. baking dish coated with cooking spray. Mix brown sugar, flour and cinnamon; sprinkle over top. Drizzle with melted butter.

2. Bake, covered, until squash and apples are tender, 45-55 minutes.

1 SERVING: 120 cal., 3g fat (2g sat. fat), 8mg chol., 36mg sod., 25g carb. (15g sugars, 4g fiber), 1g pro. **DIABETIC EXCHANGES:** 1 starch, ½ fruit, ½ fat.

BACON-CORN STUFFED PEPPERS

Filled with corn, salsa, green onions, mozzarella cheese and bacon, these grilled pepper halves are sure to liven up your next cookout. They have a wonderful taste and give a fun twist to the usual corn on the cob.
—Mitzi Sentiff, Annapolis, MD

Prep: 20 min. • **Grill:** 25 min.
Makes: 4 servings

- **2 cups frozen corn, thawed**
- **⅓ cup salsa**
- **6 green onions, chopped**
- **1 medium green pepper, halved and seeded**
- **1 medium sweet red pepper, halved and seeded**
- **¼ cup shredded part-skim mozzarella cheese**
- **2 bacon strips, cooked and crumbled**
- **Additional salsa, optional**

1. In a large bowl, combine the corn, salsa and onions. Spoon into pepper halves. Place each stuffed pepper half on a piece of heavy-duty foil (about 18x12 in.). Fold foil around peppers and seal tightly.
2. Grill, covered, over medium heat until peppers are crisp-tender, 25-30 minutes. Carefully open packets to allow steam to escape. Sprinkle with cheese and bacon. Return to the grill until cheese is melted, 3-5 minutes. Serve with extra salsa if desired.
1 STUFFED PEPPER HALF: 130 cal., 4g fat (1g sat. fat), 9mg chol., 207mg sod., 21g carb. (5g sugars, 3g fiber), 6g pro. **DIABETIC EXCHANGES:** 1 starch, 1 vegetable, ½ fat.

READER REVIEW

"My family loved this recipe! Grandma, sister, Dad, brother, Mom, hubby! I am making it again for Christmas dinner; it will look so pretty with green and red peppers!"

HEATHERBRESSLAW, TASTEOFHOME.COM

TWICE-BAKED SWEET POTATOES WITH BACON

These sweet spuds always take my guests by surprise because of their smoky, creamy flavor and the pretty presentation. You'll get major kudos when you place these on your table.
—Cynthia Boberskyj, Rochester, NY

Prep: 20 min. • **Bake:** 1¼ hours
Makes: 6 servings

- **6 medium sweet potatoes (about 12 oz. each)**
- **¼ cup butter, softened**
- **½ tsp. salt**
- **⅛ tsp. pepper**
- **2 cups shredded cheddar cheese**
- **6 bacon strips, cooked and crumbled**

1. Preheat oven to 375°. Scrub sweet potatoes; pierce several times with a fork. Place in a foil-lined 15x10x1-in. baking pan; bake until tender, 1-1¼ hours. Cool slightly.
2. Cut a thin slice off the top of each potato; discard slice. Scoop out pulp, leaving thin shells. In a large bowl, mash pulp with butter, salt and pepper; stir in cheese and bacon. Spoon into potato shells.
3. Return to pan. Bake until heated through, 15-20 minutes.

1 STUFFED POTATO: 611 cal., 24g fat (13g sat. fat), 66mg chol., 683mg sod., 84g carb. (34g sugars, 10g fiber), 17g pro.

TEST KITCHEN TIP
When purchasing sweet potatoes, select those that are firm with no cracks or bruises. If stored in a cool, dark, well-ventilated place, they'll remain fresh for about two weeks. If the temperature is above 60°, they'll sprout sooner or become woody. Once cooked, sweet potatoes can be stored for up to a week in the refrigerator.

CHEESY SLOW-COOKED CORN

Even those who usually don't reach for corn will ask for seconds once they try this side dish. Folks love the flavor, and I love how easy it is to make with ingredients I have on hand.
—Mary Ann Truitt, Wichita, KS

Prep: 5 min. • **Cook:** 3 hours
Makes: 12 servings

- **9½ cups (48 oz.) frozen corn**
- **11 oz. cream cheese, softened**
- **¼ cup butter, cubed**
- **3 Tbsp. water**
- **3 Tbsp. milk**
- **2 Tbsp. sugar**
- **6 slices process American cheese, cut into small pieces**

In a 4- or 5-qt. slow cooker, combine all ingredients. Cook, covered, on low, until heated through and the cheese is melted, 3-4 hours, stirring once.

1 CUP: 265 cal., 16g fat (9g sat. fat), 39mg chol., 227mg sod., 27g carb. (6g sugars, 2g fiber), 7g pro.

POPPY SEED DRESSING

The best way to dress up seasonal fruit is with this sweet and tangy topping.
—Patricia Staudt, Marble Rock, IA

Takes: 5 min.
Makes: 12 servings (2 Tbsp. each)

- **1 cup canola oil**
- **⅓ cup white vinegar**
- **¾ cup sugar**
- **1½ tsp. onion salt**
- **1 tsp. ground mustard**
- **1 Tbsp. poppy seeds**
- **Fresh fruit or salad greens of choice**

Place first five ingredients in a blender; cover and process until sugar is dissolved. Stir in poppy seeds. Refrigerate, covered, until serving. Serve with fruit or salad greens.

2 TBSP. DRESSING: 219 cal., 19g fat (1g sat. fat), 0 chol., 225mg sod., 13g carb. (13g sugars, 0 fiber), 0 pro.

SIMPLE AU GRATIN POTATOES

These cheesy potatoes are always welcome at our dinner table, and they're so simple to make. They make a perfect complement to ham but also go well with pork, chicken and other mains.
—Cris O'Brien, Virginia Beach, VA

Prep: 20 min. • **Bake:** 1½ hours
Makes: 8 servings

- **3 Tbsp. butter**
- **3 Tbsp. all-purpose flour**
- **1½ tsp. salt**
- **⅛ tsp. pepper**
- **2 cups 2% milk**
- **1 cup shredded cheddar cheese**
- **5 cups thinly sliced peeled potatoes (about 6 medium)**
- **½ cup chopped onion**
- **Additional pepper, optional**

1. Preheat oven to 350°. In a large saucepan, melt butter over low heat. Stir in flour, salt and pepper until smooth. Gradually add milk. Bring to a boil; cook and stir 2 minutes or until thickened. Remove from heat; stir in cheese until melted. Add potatoes and onion.
2. Transfer to a greased 2-qt. baking dish. Cover and bake 1 hour. Uncover; bake until the potatoes are tender, 30-40 minutes. If desired, top with additional pepper.
¾ CUP: 224 cal., 10g fat (7g sat. fat), 35mg chol., 605mg sod., 26g carb. (4g sugars, 2g fiber), 7g pro.

WHITE ALE POTATO SALAD

Take this one outside! My grown-up recipe uses beer instead of mayo, so you don't need to worry about keeping it cool. It's a really popular recipe on my blog, *girllikestoeat.com*.
—Jenny MacBeth, Pittsburgh, PA

Prep: 15 min. • **Cook:** 20 min. + chilling
Makes: 12 servings (¾ cup each)

- **2 lbs. fingerling or small red potatoes, cut into 1-in. pieces**

DRESSING

- **½ cup white ale**
- **3 Tbsp. olive oil**
- **2 Tbsp. balsamic vinegar**
- **2 Tbsp. Dijon mustard**
- **1 pkg. Italian salad dressing mix**

SALAD

- **4 cups fresh arugula (about 2½ oz.) or chopped fresh kale**
- **1½ cups grape tomatoes**
- **6 green onions, chopped**
- **10 bacon strips, cooked and crumbled**
- **1 cup crumbled Gorgonzola or feta cheese**
- **¼ cup minced fresh chives**

1. Place potatoes in a large saucepan; add water to cover. Bring to a boil. Reduce heat; cook, uncovered, 12-15 minutes or until tender. Drain; transfer to a large bowl.
2. In a small bowl, whisk dressing ingredients until blended. Pour over warm potatoes and toss to coat. Cool slightly. Refrigerate salad, covered, until cold, about 1 hour.
3. To serve, add arugula, tomatoes, green onions and bacon to potatoes; toss gently to combine. Sprinkle with cheese and chives. Serve immediately.
¾ CUP: 185 cal., 9g fat (3g sat. fat), 15mg chol., 536mg sod., 19g carb. (4g sugars, 2g fiber), 7g pro.

WENDY'S APPLE POMEGRANATE SALAD

My grandparents grew pomegranates, pecans and walnuts and would send us some each year. Some of my best memories are the days I used to spend with my grandmother in the kitchen, learning how to cook with her. Whenever I make this, it's like having lunch with her again.
—Wendy Ball, Battle Creek, MI

Takes: 20 min. • **Makes:** 8 servings

- **1 bunch romaine, torn (about 8 cups)**
- **½ cup pomegranate seeds**
- **½ cup chopped pecans or walnuts, toasted**
- **½ cup shredded Parmesan cheese**
- **1 large Granny Smith apple, chopped**
- **1 Tbsp. lemon juice**
- **¼ cup olive oil**
- **¼ cup white wine vinegar**
- **2 Tbsp. sugar**
- **¼ tsp. salt**

1. In a large bowl, combine the romaine, pomegranate seeds, pecans and cheese. Toss apple with lemon juice and add to salad.
2. In a small bowl, whisk remaining ingredients until blended. Drizzle over salad; toss to coat. Serve immediately.
NOTE: To toast nuts, bake in a shallow pan in a 350° oven for 5-10 minutes or cook in a skillet over low heat until lightly browned, stirring occasionally.
1 CUP: 165 cal., 13g fat (2g sat. fat), 4mg chol., 163mg sod., 10g carb. (8g sugars, 2g fiber), 3g pro. **DIABETIC EXCHANGES:** 2½ fat, 1 vegetable.

CHERRY JAM

We live in Door County, an area known for its wonderful tart cherries. This beautiful sweet jam makes lovely gifts.
—Karen Haen, Sturgeon Bay, WI

Prep: 35 min. • **Process:** 5 min.
Makes: 6 half-pints

- **2½ lbs. fresh tart cherries, pitted**
- **1 pkg. (1¾ oz.) powdered fruit pectin**
- **½ tsp. butter**
- **4¾ cups sugar**

1. In a food processor, cover and process cherries in batches until finely chopped. Transfer to a Dutch oven; stir in pectin and butter. Bring to a full rolling boil over high heat, stirring constantly. Stir in sugar; return to a full rolling boil. Boil and stir 1 minute.
2. Remove from heat; skim off foam. Ladle hot mixture into six hot sterilized half-pint jars, leaving ¼-in. headspace. Remove air bubbles and adjust headspace, if necessary, by adding hot mixture. Wipe rims. Center lids on jars; screw on bands until fingertip tight.
3. Place jars into canner with simmering water, ensuring the jars are completely covered with water. Bring to a boil; process for 5 minutes. Remove jars and cool.
NOTE: The processing time listed is for altitudes of 1,000 feet or less. Add 1 minute to the processing time for each 1,000 feet of additional altitude.
2 TBSP.: 89 cal., 0 fat (0 sat. fat), 0 chol., 1mg sod., 23g carb. (22g sugars, 0 fiber), 0 pro.

Hearty Main Dishes

Not sure what to serve for dinner? Let our most-requested entrees help. From beef and chicken to pork and fish—and even a few meat-free options—these recipes have you covered!

ASPARAGUS HAM DINNER

I've been making this light meal for my family for years now, and it's always well-received. With asparagus, tomato, pasta and chunks of ham, this skillet dish is a tempting blend of flavors and textures.

—Rhonda Zavodny, David City, NE

Takes: 25 min. • **Makes:** 6 servings

- **2 cups uncooked corkscrew or spiral pasta**
- **¾ lb. fresh asparagus, cut into 1-in. pieces**
- **1 medium sweet yellow pepper, julienned**
- **1 Tbsp. olive oil**
- **6 medium tomatoes, diced**
- **6 oz. boneless fully cooked ham, cubed**
- **¼ cup minced fresh parsley**
- **½ tsp. salt**
- **½ tsp. dried oregano**
- **½ tsp. dried basil**
- **⅛ to ¼ tsp. cayenne pepper**
- **¼ cup shredded Parmesan cheese**

Cook pasta according to package directions. Meanwhile, in a large cast-iron or other heavy skillet, saute asparagus and yellow pepper in oil until crisp-tender. Add tomatoes and ham; heat through. Drain pasta; add to vegetable mixture. Stir in the parsley and seasonings. Sprinkle with cheese.

1⅓ CUPS: 204 cal., 5g fat (1g sat. fat), 17mg chol., 561mg sod., 29g carb. (5g sugars, 3g fiber), 12g pro. **DIABETIC EXCHANGES:** 1½ starch, 1 lean meat, 1 vegetable, ½ fat.

READER REVIEW

"Yum! Great way to use up leftover ham and add in a lot of vegetables. This was particularly good with whole-wheat pasta."

CURLYLIS85, TASTEOFHOME.COM

EASY CORNED BEEF & CABBAGE

I first tried this simple way to cook traditional corned beef and cabbage for St. Patrick's Day a few years ago. Now it's a regular in my menu planning. It's terrific with Dijon mustard and a wedge of soda or rye bread.
—*Karen Waters, Laurel, MD*

Prep: 15 min. • **Cook:** 8 hours
Makes: 8 servings

- **1 medium onion, cut into wedges**
- **4 large red potatoes, quartered**
- **1 lb. baby carrots**
- **3 cups water**
- **3 garlic cloves, minced**
- **1 bay leaf**
- **2 Tbsp. sugar**
- **2 Tbsp. cider vinegar**
- **½ tsp. pepper**
- **1 corned beef brisket with spice packet (2½ to 3 lbs.), cut in half**
- **1 small head cabbage, cut into wedges**

1. Place the onion, potatoes and carrots in a 6- to 7-qt. slow cooker. Combine the water, garlic, bay leaf, sugar, vinegar, pepper and the spice packet contents; pour over vegetables. Top with brisket and cabbage.
2. Cover and cook on low until the meat and vegetables are tender, 8-9 hours. Discard bay leaf before serving.
1 SERVING: 414 cal., 19g fat (6g sat. fat), 97mg chol., 1191mg sod., 38g carb. (11g sugars, 6g fiber), 23g pro.

BLACK BEAN & RICE ENCHILADAS

I love Mexican food, and I'm always looking for ways to make it more healthy. I reinvented one of my favorite restaurant dishes so it suits my taste and lifestyle.
—*Christie Ladd, Mechanicsburg, PA*

Prep: 40 min. • **Bake:** 30 min.
Makes: 8 servings

- **1 Tbsp. olive oil**
- **1 green pepper, chopped**
- **1 medium onion, chopped**
- **3 garlic cloves, minced**
- **1 can (15 oz.) black beans, rinsed and drained**
- **1 can (14½ oz.) diced tomatoes and green chilies**
- **¼ cup picante sauce**
- **1 Tbsp. chili powder**
- **1 tsp. ground cumin**
- **¼ tsp. crushed red pepper flakes**
- **2 cups cooked brown rice**
- **8 flour tortillas (6 in.), warmed**
- **1 cup salsa**
- **1 cup shredded reduced-fat cheddar cheese**
- **3 Tbsp. chopped fresh cilantro leaves**

1. Preheat oven to 350°. In a large nonstick skillet, heat oil over medium heat. Add green pepper, onion and garlic; saute until tender. Add the next six ingredients; bring to a boil. Reduce heat; simmer, uncovered, until heated through. Add rice; cook 5 minutes longer.
2. Spoon a rounded ½ cup of rice mixture down center of each tortilla. Fold sides over filling and roll up. Place seam side down in a 13x9-in. baking dish coated with cooking spray. Spoon remaining rice mixture along sides of dish. Top tortillas with salsa. Bake, covered, for 25 minutes. Uncover; sprinkle with cheese. Bake until the cheese is melted, 2-3 minutes longer. Sprinkle with cilantro before serving.
1 ENCHILADA: 279 cal., 8g fat (2g sat. fat), 10mg chol., 807mg sod., 39g carb. (4g sugars, 5g fiber), 11g pro. **DIABETIC EXCHANGES:** 2½ starch, 1 lean meat, 1 vegetable.

STUFFED PEPPERS FOR FOUR

Truly a meal in one, this quick supper has it all: veggies, meat, pasta and sauce—everything packed into tender bell peppers. Bonus: they look pretty on your table.
—Taste of Home *Test Kitchen*

Takes: 30 min. • **Makes:** 4 servings

- ½ **cup uncooked orzo pasta**
- 4 **medium sweet peppers (any color)**
- ¼ **cup water**
- 1 **lb. ground beef**
- ½ **cup chopped onion**
- 2 **cups pasta sauce**
- 1 **cup frozen broccoli-cauliflower blend, thawed and chopped**
- ½ **cup grated Parmesan cheese, divided**

1. Cook orzo according to package directions; drain. Cut and discard tops from the peppers; remove seeds. Place peppers in a 3-qt. round microwave-safe dish. Add water; microwave, covered, on high until peppers are crisp-tender, 7-9 minutes.
2. In a large skillet, cook and crumble beef with onion over medium heat until no longer pink, 5-7 minutes; drain. Stir in pasta sauce, vegetables, ¼ cup cheese and orzo. Spoon into peppers. Sprinkle with remaining cheese.
3. Microwave, uncovered, on high until heated through, 1-2 minutes.
1 STUFFED PEPPER: 448 cal., 18g fat (7g sat. fat), 79mg chol., 734mg sod., 41g carb. (15g sugars, 6g fiber), 30g pro.

BASIL PORK CHOPS

These tender glazed chops get a kick of flavor from basil, chili powder and a little brown sugar. Serve with your favorite roasted veggies and you've got a comforting meal for a busy night.
—Lisa Gilliland, Fort Collins, CO

Takes: 25 min. • **Makes:** 4 servings

- ¼ **cup packed brown sugar**
- 1½ **tsp. dried basil**
- ½ **tsp. salt**
- ½ **tsp. chili powder**
- 2 **Tbsp. canola oil, divided**
- 4 **boneless pork loin chops (½ in. thick and 4 oz. each)**

1. Mix first four ingredients; gradually stir in 1 Tbsp. oil (mixture will be crumbly). Rub over both sides of pork chops.
2. In a large skillet, heat remaining oil over medium heat; cook the pork chops until a thermometer reads 145°, 4-6 minutes per side. Let stand 5 minutes before serving.
1 PORK CHOP: 152 cal., 8g fat (1g sat. fat), 14mg chol., 312mg sod., 14g carb. (13g sugars, 0 fiber), 6g pro.

EASY GLAZED SALMON

It only takes four ingredients and less than a half hour to make this delightful main dish.
—Tara Ernspiker, Falling Waters, WV

Takes: 25 min. • **Makes:** 4 servings

- ⅓ **cup packed brown sugar**
- ¼ **cup unsweetened pineapple juice**
- 2 **Tbsp. soy sauce**
- 4 **salmon fillets (6 oz. each)**

1. Line a 15x10x1-in. baking pan with foil; grease the foil. Set aside. In a small bowl, combine the brown sugar, pineapple juice and soy sauce. Place salmon skin side down on prepared pan. Spoon sauce mixture over fish.
2. Bake, uncovered, at 350° for 20-25 minutes or until fish flakes easily with a fork, basting frequently with pan juices.
1 FILLET: 394 cal., 18g fat (4g sat. fat), 100mg chol., 568mg sod., 20g carb. (19g sugars, 0 fiber), 35g pro..

BROILED COD

This is the easiest and tastiest fish you're likely to serve. Even finicky eaters who think they don't like fish love the beautiful, flaky results.
—Kim Russell, North Wales, PA

Takes: 30 min. • **Makes:** 2 servings

- **¼ cup fat-free Italian salad dressing**
- **½ tsp. sugar**
- **⅛ tsp. salt**
- **⅛ tsp. garlic powder**
- **⅛ tsp. curry powder**
- **⅛ tsp. paprika**
- **⅛ tsp. pepper**
- **2 cod fillets (6 oz. each)**
- **2 tsp. butter**

1. Preheat broiler. In a shallow bowl, mix first seven ingredients; add cod, turning to coat. Let stand 10-15 minutes.

2. Place fillets on a greased rack of a broiler pan; discard remaining marinade. Broil 3-4 in. from heat until fish just begins to flake easily with a fork, 10-12 minutes. Top with butter.

1 FILLET: 168 cal., 5g fat (3g sat. fat), 75mg chol., 365mg sod., 2g carb. (2g sugars, 0 fiber), 27g pro. **DIABETIC EXCHANGES:** 4 lean meat, 1 fat.

MOIST & TENDER TURKEY BREAST

We were on vacation the first time I cooked a turkey in a slow cooker. It simmered while we were out having fun, and we came back to a spectacularly juicy bird. Now it's a part of the dinner rotation at home, too. You won't want to wait for Thanksgiving to try it.
—Heidi Vawdrey, Riverton, UT

Prep: 10 min. • **Cook:** 4 hours
Makes: 12 servings

- **1 bone-in turkey breast (6 to 7 lbs.)**
- **4 fresh rosemary sprigs**
- **4 garlic cloves, peeled**
- **½ cup water**
- **1 Tbsp. brown sugar**
- **½ tsp. coarsely ground pepper**
- **¼ tsp. salt**

Place the turkey breast, rosemary, garlic and water in a 6-qt. slow cooker. Mix brown sugar, pepper and salt; sprinkle over turkey. Cook, covered, on low or until turkey is tender and a thermometer inserted in turkey reads at least 170°, 4-6 hours.

5 OZ. COOKED TURKEY: 318 cal., 12g fat (3g sat. fat), 122mg chol., 154mg sod., 2g carb. (1g sugars, 0 fiber), 47g pro.

VEGETARIAN LINGUINE

Looking for a filling alternative to meat and potatoes? Try this colorful pasta dish. My oldest son came up with the skillet recipe to take advantage of fresh mushrooms, zucchini, basil and other vegetables plus some creamy provolone cheese.
—Jane Bone, Cape Coral, FL

Takes: 30 min. • **Makes:** 6 servings

- 6 **oz. uncooked linguine**
- 2 **Tbsp. butter**
- 1 **Tbsp. olive oil**
- 2 **medium zucchini, thinly sliced**
- ½ **lb. fresh mushrooms, sliced**
- 1 **large tomato, chopped**
- 2 **green onions, chopped**
- 1 **garlic clove, minced**
- ½ **tsp. salt**
- ¼ **tsp. pepper**
- 1 **cup shredded provolone cheese**
- 3 **Tbsp. shredded Parmesan cheese**
- 2 **tsp. minced fresh basil**

Cook the linguine according to the package directions. Meanwhile, in a large skillet, heat butter and oil over medium heat. Add zucchini and mushrooms; saute 3-5 minutes. Add the tomato, onions, garlic and seasonings. Reduce heat; simmer, covered, about 3 minutes. Drain linguine; add to vegetable mixture. Sprinkle with cheeses and basil. Toss to coat.

1½ CUPS: 260 cal., 13g fat (7g sat. fat), 25mg chol., 444mg sod., 26g carb. (3g sugars, 2g fiber), 12g pro. **DIABETIC EXCHANGES:** 1½ starch, 1½ fat, 1 medium-fat meat, 1 vegetable.

ALMOND CHICKEN & STRAWBERRY-BALSAMIC SAUCE

Crispy chicken with a sweet-tart sauce is served alongside wilted spinach for a meal that's both easy and elegant. I created the recipe years ago for a contest, and it won the grand prize!
—Virginia Anthony, Jacksonville, FL

Prep: 20 min. • **Cook:** 20 min.
Makes: 4 servings

- ½ **cup panko (Japanese) bread crumbs**
- ⅓ **cup unblanched almonds, coarsely ground**
- ½ **tsp. salt**
- ¼ **tsp. pepper**
- 4 **boneless skinless chicken breast halves (4 oz. each)**
- 3 **tsp. canola oil, divided**
- ¼ **cup chopped shallots**
- ⅓ **cup reduced-sodium chicken broth**
- ⅓ **cup strawberry preserves**
- 3 **Tbsp. balsamic vinegar**
- 1 **Tbsp. minced fresh rosemary or 1 tsp. dried rosemary, crushed**
- 1 **pkg. (9 oz.) fresh baby spinach**

1. In a shallow dish, combine bread crumbs, almonds, salt and pepper. Add the chicken, one piece at a time, turning to coat.
2. In a large nonstick skillet, cook the chicken in 2 tsp. oil over medium heat until the juices run clear, 4-5 minutes on each side. Remove and keep chicken warm.
3. In the same pan, cook shallots in remaining oil until tender. Stir in the broth, preserves, vinegar and rosemary. Bring to a boil. Reduce the heat; simmer until thickened, 5-6 minutes.
4. Meanwhile, in a large saucepan, bring ½ in. of water to a boil. Add spinach; cover and boil until wilted, 3-5 minutes. Drain; serve with chicken and sauce.

1 SERVING: 349 cal., 13g fat (2g sat. fat), 63mg chol., 476mg sod., 31g carb. (19g sugars, 3g fiber), 29g pro.

ARTICHOKE CHICKEN

Rosemary, mushrooms and artichokes come together to give chicken a wonderful, savory flavor. I've served this dish to a large group by doubling the recipe. It's a hit with everyone—especially my family!

—Ruth Stenson, Santa Ana, CA

Prep: 15 min. • **Bake:** 50 min.
Makes: 8 servings

- **8 boneless skinless chicken breast halves (4 oz. each)**
- **2 Tbsp. butter**
- **2 jars (6 oz. each) marinated quartered artichoke hearts, drained**
- **1 jar (4½ oz.) whole mushrooms, drained**
- **½ cup chopped onion**
- **⅓ cup all-purpose flour**
- **1½ tsp. dried rosemary, crushed**
- **¾ tsp. salt**
- **¼ tsp. pepper**
- **2 cups chicken broth or 1 cup broth and 1 cup dry white wine**
- **Hot cooked noodles**
- **Minced fresh parsley**

1. In a large skillet, brown chicken in butter. Remove chicken to an ungreased 13x9-in. baking dish. Arrange the artichokes and mushrooms on top of chicken; set aside.

2. Saute onion in pan juices until crisp-tender. Combine the flour, rosemary, salt and pepper. Stir into pan until blended. Add chicken broth. Bring to a boil; cook and stir until thickened and bubbly, 2 minutes. Remove from the heat and spoon over chicken.

3. Bake chicken uncovered at 350° until a thermometer reads 170°, about 40 minutes. Serve with pasta and sprinkle with parsley.

FREEZE OPTION: Cool unbaked casserole; cover and freeze. To use, partially thaw in refrigerator overnight. Remove from the refrigerator 30 minutes before baking. Preheat oven to 350°. Bake casserole as directed, increasing time as necessary to heat through and for a thermometer inserted in center to read 170°.

1 SERVING: 232 cal., 9g fat (3g sat. fat), 81mg chol., 752mg sod., 7g carb. (1g sugars, 1g fiber), 28g pro.

PORK SHEPHERD'S PIE

Of all the shepherd's pie recipes I've tried throughout the years, this one is definitely my favorite. I enjoy cooking for my family, who all agree this savory pie is a keeper.
—Mary Arthurs, Etobicoke, ON

Prep: 30 min. • **Bake:** 45 min.
Makes: 6 servings

PORK LAYER
- **1 lb. ground pork**
- **1 small onion, chopped**
- **2 garlic cloves, minced**
- **1 cup cooked rice**
- **½ cup pork gravy or ¼ cup chicken broth**
- **½ tsp. salt**
- **½ tsp. dried thyme**

CABBAGE LAYER
- **1 medium carrot, diced**
- **1 small onion, chopped**
- **2 Tbsp. butter or margarine**
- **6 cups chopped cabbage**
- **1 cup chicken broth**
- **½ tsp. salt**
- **¼ tsp. pepper**

POTATO LAYER
- **2 cups mashed potatoes**
- **¼ cup shredded cheddar cheese**

In a skillet over medium heat, brown pork until no longer pink. Add onion and garlic. Cook until vegetables are tender; drain. Stir in rice, gravy, salt and thyme. Spoon into a greased 11x7-in. baking dish. In the same skillet, saute carrot and onion in butter over medium heat for 5 minutes. Stir in the cabbage; cook for 1 minute. Add broth, salt and pepper; cover and cook for 10 minutes. Spoon over pork layer. Spoon or pipe mashed potatoes on top; sprinkle with cheese. Bake, uncovered, at 350° for 45 minutes or until browned.

1 CUP: 365 cal., 19g fat (8g sat. fat), 66mg chol., 1045mg sod., 28g carb. (5g sugars, 4g fiber), 19g pro.

ROAST BEEF & GRAVY

This is the easiest way to make roast beef and gravy. On busy days, I put the roast in the slow cooker and forget about it. Serve with mashed potatoes to soak up that gravy and a fruit salad.
—Abby Metzger, Larchwood, IA

Prep: 15 min. • **Cook:** 8 hours
Makes: 10 servings

- **1 boneless beef chuck roast (3 lbs.)**
- **2 cans (10¾ oz. each) condensed cream of mushroom soup, undiluted**
- **⅓ cup sherry or beef broth**
- **1 envelope onion soup mix**

1. Cut chuck roast in half; place in a 3-qt. slow cooker. In a large bowl, combine the remaining ingredients; pour over roast.
2. Cover and cook on low for 8-10 hours or until meat is tender.

FREEZE OPTION: Place sliced pot roast in freezer containers; top with cooking juices. Cool and freeze. To use, partially thaw in refrigerator overnight. Heat through in a covered saucepan, gently stirring and adding a little water if necessary.

1 SERVING: 267 cal., 14g fat (6g sat. fat), 90mg chol., 517mg sod., 4g carb. (0 sugars, 0 fiber), 27g pro.

READER REVIEW

"Delicious! Roast was very tender and the gravy was wonderful over mashed potatoes. I love mushrooms and added a can to mine."
GUNSLINGER, TASTEOFHOME.COM

BEST-EVER FRIED CHICKEN

Family reunions and neighborly gatherings will be out of this world when you serve this crispy, juicy and perfectly seasoned fried chicken. I grew up on a farm, and every year when it was time to bale hay, my dad hired farmhands to help. The crew looked forward to coming because they knew they would be treated to Mom's delicious fried chicken.
—Lola Clifton, Vinton, VA

Prep: 15 min. • **Cook:** 20 min.
Makes: 4 servings

- **1¾ cups all-purpose flour**
- **1 Tbsp. dried thyme**
- **1 Tbsp. paprika**
- **2 tsp. salt**
- **2 tsp. garlic powder**
- **1 tsp. pepper**
- **1 large egg**
- **⅓ cup whole milk**
- **2 Tbsp. lemon juice**
- **1 broiler/fryer chicken (3 to 4 lbs.), cut up**
- **Oil for deep-fat frying**

1. In a shallow bowl, mix first six ingredients. In a separate shallow bowl, whisk egg, milk and lemon juice until blended. Dip chicken in flour mixture to coat all sides; shake off excess. Dip in egg mixture, then again in flour mixture.
2. In an electric skillet or deep fryer, heat oil to 375°. Fry chicken, a few pieces at a time, until golden brown and the chicken juices run clear, for 6-10 minutes on each side. Drain the chicken on paper towels.
1 SERVING: 811 cal., 57g fat (9g sat. fat), 176mg chol., 725mg sod., 26g carb. (2g sugars, 2g fiber), 47g pro.

TORTELLINI CARBONARA

Bacon, cream and Parmesan cheese combine for a creamy sauce that's heavenly poured over pasta. This recipe is great for company.
—Cathy Croyle, Davidsville, PA

Takes: 20 min. • **Makes:** 4 servings

- **1 pkg. (9 oz.) refrigerated cheese tortellini**
- **8 bacon strips, chopped**
- **1 cup heavy whipping cream**
- **½ cup grated Parmesan cheese**
- **½ cup chopped fresh parsley**

1. Cook tortellini according to the package directions; drain.
2. Meanwhile, in a large skillet, cook bacon over medium heat until crisp, stirring occasionally. Remove with a slotted spoon; drain on paper towels. Pour off drippings.
3. In the same pan, combine cream, cheese, parsley and bacon; heat through over medium heat. Stir in tortellini. Serve immediately.
1 CUP: 527 cal., 36g fat (20g sat. fat), 121mg chol., 728mg sod., 33g carb. (3g sugars, 2g fiber), 19g pro.

TEST KITCHEN TIP
Traditional carbonara often has eggs in the sauce. If you'd like to add a little extra protein, halve the cream in this recipe and temper two whisked eggs into the sauce. To temper eggs, remove the pan from the heat before gradually adding a small amount of the hot cream mixture to two whisked eggs— then add it all back to the pan. Tempering keeps the eggs from getting hot too quickly, which can result in scrambled eggs!

KILNER

SPINACH & ARTICHOKE PIZZA

My from-scratch pizza has a whole wheat crust flavored with beer. Top it with spinach, artichoke hearts, tomatoes and fresh basil.
—Raymonde Bourgeois, Swastika, ON

Prep: 25 min. • **Bake:** 20 min. • **Makes:** 6 slices

- **1½ to 1¾ cups white whole wheat flour**
- **1½ tsp. baking powder**
- **¼ tsp. salt**
- **¼ tsp. each dried basil, oregano and parsley flakes**
- **¾ cup beer or nonalcoholic beer**

TOPPINGS

- **1½ tsp. olive oil**
- **1 garlic clove, minced**
- **2 cups shredded Italian cheese blend**
- **2 cups fresh baby spinach**
- **1 can (14 oz.) water-packed quartered artichoke hearts, drained and coarsely chopped**
- **2 medium tomatoes, seeded and coarsely chopped**
- **2 Tbsp. thinly sliced fresh basil**

1. Preheat oven to 425°. In a large bowl, whisk 1½ cups flour, baking powder, salt and dried herbs until blended. Add beer, stirring just until moistened.
2. Turn dough onto a well-floured surface; knead gently 6-8 times, adding additional flour if needed. Press dough to fit a greased 12-in. pizza pan. Pinch the edge to form a rim. Bake until edge is lightly browned, 8 minutes.
3. Mix oil and garlic; spread over the crust. Sprinkle with ½ cup of cheese; layer with spinach, artichoke hearts and tomatoes. Sprinkle with remaining cheese. Bake until crust is golden and cheese is melted, about 8-10 minutes. Sprinkle with fresh basil.
1 SLICE: 290 cal., 10g fat (6g sat. fat), 27mg chol., 654mg sod., 32g carb. (1g sugars, 5g fiber), 14g pro. **DIABETIC EXCHANGES:** 2 starch, 1 medium-fat meat, 1 vegetable.

FAVORITE HAMBURGER STEW

A woman at our church gave me this recipe when I needed a way to use up our bounty of home-canned tomatoes. My husband loves it, and it's easy to warm up for a carefree dinner in the winter months.
—Marcia Clay, Truman, MN

Prep: 20 min. • **Cook:** 65 min. • **Makes:** 4 qt.

- **2 lbs. ground beef**
- **2 medium onions, chopped**
- **4 cans (14½ oz. each) stewed tomatoes, undrained**
- **8 medium carrots, thinly sliced**
- **4 celery ribs, thinly sliced**
- **2 medium potatoes, peeled and cubed**
- **2 cups water**
- **½ cup uncooked long grain rice**
- **3 tsp. salt**
- **1 tsp. pepper**

1. In a Dutch oven, cook beef and onions over medium heat until the meat is no longer pink; drain. Add the tomatoes, carrots, celery, potatoes, water, rice, salt and pepper; bring to a boil. Reduce heat; cover and simmer mixture until vegetables and rice are tender, 30 minutes.
2. Uncover; simmer until thickened to desired consistency, 20-30 minutes longer.
FREEZE OPTION: Freeze the cooled stew in freezer containers. To use, partially thaw the stew in refrigerator overnight. Heat through in a saucepan, stirring occasionally and adding a little water if necessary.
1 CUP: 165 cal., 6g fat (2g sat. fat), 30mg chol., 584mg sod., 16g carb. (5g sugars, 2g fiber), 12g pro.

SAGE CHICKEN CORDON BLEU

I love to surprise my family with creative meals during the week. I usually double this recipe so we can enjoy leftovers the next day.
—Martha Stine, Johnstown, PA

Prep: 20 min. • **Bake:** 40 min.
Makes: 6 servings

- **6 boneless skinless chicken breast halves (4 oz. each)**
- **½ to ¾ tsp. rubbed sage**
- **6 slices thinly sliced deli ham**
- **6 slices part-skim mozzarella cheese, halved**
- **1 medium tomato, seeded and chopped**
- **⅓ cup dry bread crumbs**
- **2 Tbsp. grated Parmesan cheese**
- **2 Tbsp. minced fresh parsley**
- **4 Tbsp. butter, divided**

1. Preheat oven to 350°. Pound the chicken breasts with a meat mallet to ⅛-in. thickness; sprinkle with sage. Place the ham, mozzarella cheese and tomato down the center of each; roll up chicken from a long side, tucking in the ends. Secure with toothpicks.
2. In a shallow bowl, toss bread crumbs with Parmesan cheese and parsley. In a shallow microwave-safe dish, microwave 3 Tbsp. butter until melted. Dip the chicken in butter, then roll in crumb mixture. Place in a greased 11x7-in. baking dish, seam side down. Melt the remaining butter; drizzle over top.
3. Bake, uncovered, until a thermometer inserted in chicken reads 165°, 40-45 minutes. Discard toothpicks before serving.
1 SERVING: 328 cal., 17g fat (9g sat. fat), 112mg chol., 575mg sod., 8g carb. (2g sugars, 1g fiber), 35g pro.

EASY BEEF STROGANOFF

Here's a lighter take on my mother-in-law's amazing beef stroganoff. We call it "special noodles" in our house.
—Jennifer Riordan, St. Louis, MO

Takes: 30 min. • **Makes:** 6 servings

- **4½ cups uncooked yolk-free noodles**
- **1 lb. lean ground beef (90% lean)**
- **½ lb. sliced fresh mushrooms**
- **1 large onion, halved and sliced**
- **3 garlic cloves, minced**
- **1 Tbsp. reduced-fat butter**
- **2 Tbsp. all-purpose flour**
- **1 can (14½ oz.) reduced-sodium beef broth**
- **2 Tbsp. tomato paste**
- **1 cup reduced-fat sour cream**
- **¼ tsp. salt**
- **¼ tsp. pepper**
- **Chopped fresh parsley, optional**

1. Cook noodles according to the package directions. Meanwhile, in a large saucepan, cook the beef, mushrooms and onion over medium heat until meat is no longer pink. Add the garlic; cook 1 minute longer. Drain. Remove and keep warm.
2. In the same pan, melt butter. Stir in flour until smooth; gradually add the broth and tomato paste. Bring to a boil; cook and stir until thickened, 2 minutes.
3. Carefully return beef mixture to the pan. Add the sour cream, salt and pepper; cook and stir until heated through (do not boil). Drain noodles; serve with beef mixture. If desired, top with chopped parsley.
NOTE: This recipe was tested with Land O'Lakes light stick butter.
1 SERVING: 326 cal., 7g fat (3g sat. fat), 48mg chol., 342mg sod., 39g carb. (8g sugars, 3g fiber), 24g pro. **DIABETIC EXCHANGES:** 2 starch, 2 lean meat, 1 vegetable.

5i

APPLE-DIJON PORK ROAST

This favorite dish takes minutes to assemble and is incredibly delicious. I serve it with rice or noodles, then spoon the tangy sauce as gravy over everything.

—Cindy Steffen, Cedarburg, WI

Prep: 15 min. • **Cook:** 4 hours
Makes: 8 servings

- **1 boneless pork loin roast (2 to 3 lbs.)**
- **1 can (14½ oz.) chicken broth**
- **1 cup unsweetened apple juice**
- **½ cup Dijon mustard**
- **6 Tbsp. cornstarch**
- **6 Tbsp. cold water**
- **Coarsely ground pepper, optional**

1. Place roast in a 5-qt. slow cooker. In a small bowl, combine the broth, apple juice and mustard; pour over roast. Cover and cook on low until tender, 4-5 hours. Remove roast and keep warm.

2. For gravy, strain cooking juices and skim fat. Pour juices into a small saucepan. Combine cornstarch and water until smooth; gradually stir into juices. Bring to a boil; cook and stir until thickened, 2 minutes. Serve with pork. If desired, top with coarsely ground pepper.

4 OZ. COOKED PORK: 197 cal., 7g fat (2g sat. fat), 56mg chol., 413mg sod., 11g carb. (3g sugars, 0 fiber), 23g pro.

HOMEMADE MANICOTTI

These tender manicotti are much easier to stuff than the purchased variety. People are always amazed when I tell them I make my own noodles. My son fixed this recipe for friends, and they were extremely impressed with his cooking skills.

—Richard Bunt, Painted Post, NY

Prep: 70 min. • **Bake:** 40 min.
Makes: 6 servings

CREPE NOODLES

- **1½ cups all-purpose flour**
- **1 cup milk**
- **3 large eggs**
- **½ tsp. salt**

FILLING

- **1½ lbs. ricotta cheese**
- **¼ cup grated Romano cheese**
- **1 large egg**
- **1 Tbsp. minced fresh parsley or 1 tsp. dried parsley flakes**
- **1 jar (26 oz.) meatless spaghetti sauce**
- **Grated Romano cheese, optional**

1. Place flour in a bowl; whisk in milk, eggs and salt until smooth. Heat a lightly greased 8-in. skillet; pour about 2 Tbsp. batter into center of skillet. Spread into a 5-in. circle. Cook over medium heat until set; do not brown or turn. Repeat with the remaining batter, making 18 crepes. Stack the crepes between waxed paper; set aside.

2. For filling, combine the cheeses, egg and parsley. Spoon 3-4 Tbsp. down the center of each crepe; roll up. Pour half of the spaghetti sauce into an ungreased 13x9-in. baking dish. Place rolled crepes, seam side down, over sauce; pour remaining sauce over top.

3. Cover and bake at 350° for 20 minutes. Uncover and bake until heated through, 20 minutes longer. If desired sprinkle with Romano cheese.

3 MANICOTTI: 480 cal., 22g fat (11g sat. fat), 201mg chol., 1128mg sod., 44g carb. (17g sugars, 3g fiber), 27g pro.

EGG ROLL NOODLE BOWL

We dearly love Asian egg rolls, but they can be challenging to make. Simplify everything with this deconstructed egg roll in a bowl made on the stovetop.
—Courtney Stultz, Weir, KS

Takes: 30 min. • **Makes:** 4 servings

- 1 **Tbsp. sesame oil**
- ½ **lb. ground pork**
- 1 **Tbsp. soy sauce**
- 1 **garlic clove, minced**
- 1 **tsp. ground ginger**
- ½ **tsp. salt**
- ¼ **tsp. ground turmeric**
- ¼ **tsp. pepper**
- 6 **cups shredded cabbage (about 1 small head)**
- 2 **large carrots, shredded (about 2 cups)**
- 4 **oz. rice noodles**
- 3 **green onions, thinly sliced**
- **Additional soy sauce, optional**

1. In a large skillet, heat oil over medium-high heat; cook and crumble pork until browned, 4-6 minutes. Stir in the soy sauce, garlic and seasonings. Add cabbage and carrots; cook, stirring occasionally, until the vegetables are tender, 4-6 minutes longer.
2. Cook rice noodles according to package directions; drain and immediately add to pork mixture, tossing to combine. Sprinkle with green onions. If desired, serve with additional soy sauce.
1½ CUPS: 302 cal., 12g fat (4g sat. fat), 38mg chol., 652mg sod., 33g carb. (2g sugars, 4g fiber), 14g pro. **DIABETIC EXCHANGES:** 2 medium-fat meat, 2 vegetable, 1½ starch, ½ fat.

TEST KITCHEN TIP
Egg Roll Noodle Bowl can easily be adapted to a meatless dish. Omit the ground pork and add mushrooms for extra heartiness and scrambled eggs or tofu for protein.

COURTNEY STULTZ
Weir, KS

CAN-CAN CHICKEN

Here's a tasty take on the popular beer-can chicken. Once the bird is on the grill, the work's basically done. And cleanup is a cinch—a must for a guy like me.
—Steve Bath, Lincoln, NE

Prep: 30 min. + chilling
Grill: 1¼ hours • **Makes:** 6 servings

- 1 **Tbsp. kosher salt**
- 1 **tsp. sugar**
- 1 **tsp. onion powder**
- 1 **tsp. garlic powder**
- 1 **tsp. cayenne pepper**
- 1 **tsp. paprika**
- 1 **tsp. ground mustard**
- 1 **broiler/fryer chicken (3½ to 4 lbs.)**
- 1 **can (12 oz.) beer**

1. In a bowl, mix the first seven ingredients. Using your fingers, carefully loosen the skin from chicken; rub seasoning mixture under and over skin. Tuck wings under the chicken. Refrigerate, covered, 1 hour.
2. Completely cover all sides of an 8- or 9-in. baking pan with foil. Place a beer-can chicken rack securely in pan. Remove half of the beer from can. Using a can opener, make additional large holes in top of can; place can in rack.
3. Stand chicken vertically on rack; place on grill rack. Grill, covered, over indirect medium heat until a thermometer inserted in thickest part of thigh reads 170°-175°, 1¼-1½ hours.
4. Carefully remove pan from the grill; tent chicken with foil. Let chicken stand 15 minutes before carving.
1 SERVING: 377 cal., 20g fat (5g sat. fat), 122mg chol., 1067mg sod., 4g carb. (3g sugars, 0 fiber), 39g pro.

FANTASTIC FISH TACOS

Searching for a lighter alternative to traditional fried fish tacos, I came up with this crispy, crunchy entree with easy toppings.
—Jennifer Palmer, Rancho Cucamonga, CA

Takes: 30 min. • **Makes:** 4 servings

- **½ cup fat-free mayonnaise**
- **1 Tbsp. lime juice**
- **2 tsp. fat-free milk**
- **1 large egg**
- **1 tsp. water**
- **⅓ cup dry bread crumbs**
- **2 Tbsp. salt-free lemon-pepper seasoning**
- **1 lb. mahi mahi or cod fillets, cut into 1-in. strips**
- **4 corn tortillas (6 in.), warmed**

TOPPINGS

- **1 cup coleslaw mix**
- **2 medium tomatoes, chopped**
- **1 cup shredded reduced-fat Mexican cheese blend**
- **1 Tbsp. minced fresh cilantro**

1. For sauce, in a small bowl, mix mayonnaise, lime juice and milk; refrigerate until serving.
2. In a shallow bowl, whisk together egg and water. In another bowl, toss bread crumbs with lemon pepper. Dip fish in egg mixture, then in the crumb mixture, patting to help coating adhere.
3. Place a large nonstick skillet over medium-high heat. Add fish; cook until golden brown and the fish just begins to flake easily with a fork, 2-4 minutes per side. Serve in tortillas with toppings and sauce.
1 TACO: 321 cal., 10g fat (5g sat. fat), 148mg chol., 632mg sod., 29g carb. (5g sugars, 4g fiber), 34g pro. **DIABETIC EXCHANGES:** 4 lean meat, 2 starch.

CLASSIC CHICKEN POTPIE

Our neighbors are always after me to make a yummy potpie. That's all the encouragement I need, since we love the dish, too!
—Ada-May Smith, Citrus Springs, FL

Prep: 20 min. • **Bake:** 20 min. + standing
Makes: 8 servings

- **3 cups frozen mixed vegetables (about 16 oz.), thawed**
- **2¼ cups cubed cooked chicken**
- **1 cup frozen pearl onions, thawed**
- **1 jar (4½ oz.) sliced mushrooms, drained**
- **¼ cup butter**
- **¼ cup all-purpose flour**
- **¾ tsp. dried thyme**
- **1 can (14½ oz.) chicken broth**
- **2 tsp. chicken bouillon granules**
- **Pastry for single-crust pie (9 in.)**

1. Preheat oven to 450°. In a greased deep 2½-qt. baking dish, combine the vegetables, chicken, onions and mushrooms.
2. In a small saucepan, melt the butter over medium heat. Stir in flour and thyme until blended; gradually whisk in broth and bouillon. Bring to a boil, stirring constantly; cook and stir until thickened, about 2 minutes. Pour over vegetable mixture.
3. Roll pastry dough to fit top of dish; place over filling. Trim and flute edge. Cut slits in the crust.
4. Bake until golden brown and filling is heated through, 18-20 minutes. Let stand 5 minutes before serving.
1 SERVING: 363 cal., 21g fat (12g sat. fat), 82mg chol., 757mg sod., 28g carb. (4g sugars, 4g fiber), 16g pro.
PASTRY FOR SINGLE-CRUST PIE (9 IN.): Combine 1¼ cups all-purpose flour and ¼ tsp. salt; cut in ½ cup cold butter until crumbly. Gradually add 3-5 Tbsp. ice water, tossing with a fork until the dough holds together when pressed. Wrap in plastic wrap and refrigerate dough 1 hour.

ORANGE-GLAZED PORK LOIN

This is one of the best pork recipes I've ever tried. My family looks forward to this roast for dinner, and guests always want the recipe. The flavorful rub and the glaze sparked with orange juice are also outstanding on pork chops.
—Lynnette Miete, Alna, ME

Prep: 10 min. • **Bake:** 1 hour 20 min. + standing
Makes: 16 servings

- **1 tsp. salt**
- **1 garlic clove, minced**
- **2 to 3 fresh thyme sprigs or ¼ tsp. dried thyme**
- **¼ tsp. ground ginger**
- **¼ tsp. pepper**
- **1 boneless pork loin roast (5 lbs.)**

GLAZE

- **1 cup orange juice**
- **¼ cup packed brown sugar**
- **1 Tbsp. Dijon mustard**
- **⅓ cup cold water**
- **1 Tbsp. cornstarch**

1. Preheat oven to 350°. Combine first five ingredients; rub over roast. Place fat-side up on a rack in a shallow roasting pan. Bake, uncovered, for 1 hour.
2. Meanwhile, in a saucepan over medium heat, combine orange juice, brown sugar and mustard. In a small bowl, mix the water and cornstarch until smooth. Add to orange juice mixture. Bring to a boil; cook and stir for 2 minutes. Reserve 1 cup glaze for serving; brush half of remaining glaze over roast.
3. Bake until a thermometer reads 145°, 20-40 minutes longer, brushing occasionally with remaining glaze. Let stand 10 minutes before slicing. Reheat reserved glaze; serve with the roast.

4 OZ. COOKED PORK WITH 1 TBSP. GLAZE: 199 cal., 7g fat (2g sat. fat), 71mg chol., 212mg sod., 6g carb. (5g sugars, 0 fiber), 28g pro.
DIABETIC EXCHANGES: 4 lean meat, ½ starch.

LE CREUSET

SKILLET MAC & CHEESE

This skillet version of the great comfort food is so simple and so full of melty, cheesy goodness, it almost seems too good to be true. Serve it plain or dress it up with arugula and cherry tomatoes for extra flavor and color.
—Ann Bowers, Rockport, TX

Takes: 25 min. • **Makes:** 4 servings

- **2 cups uncooked elbow macaroni (about 8 oz.)**
- **2 Tbsp. butter**
- **2 Tbsp. all-purpose flour**
- **1½ cups half-and-half cream**
- **¾ lb. process cheese (Velveeta), cubed**
- **Optional toppings: fresh arugula, halved cherry tomatoes and coarsely ground pepper**

1. Cook macaroni according to the package directions; drain.
2. Meanwhile, in a large cast-iron or other heavy skillet, melt butter over medium heat. Stir in flour until smooth; gradually whisk in cream. Bring to a boil, stirring constantly. Cook and stir until thickened, about 2 minutes. Reduce heat; stir in cheese until melted.
3. Add macaroni; cook and stir until heated through. Top as desired.
1½ CUPS: 600 cal., 37g fat (23g sat. fat), 144mg chol., 1185mg sod., 40g carb. (9g sugars, 1g fiber), 23g pro.

READER REVIEW

"I have tried many mac and cheese recipes, and this is the best and creamiest so far. I used regular milk instead of half and half, a ½ lb. Velveeta and ½ tsp. each of garlic and onion powders. I topped it with fresh parsley and crumbled bacon. It's my new go-to mac and cheese recipe!"

NICOLE, TASTEOFHOME.COM

BEEF FILETS WITH PORTOBELLO SAUCE

These tasty steaks seem special but they are fast enough for everyday dinners. We enjoy the mushroom-topped fillets with crusty French bread, mixed salad and a light lemon dessert.
—Christel Stein, Tampa, FL

Takes: 20 min. • **Makes:** 2 servings

- **2 beef tenderloin steaks (4 oz. each)**
- **1¾ cups sliced baby portobello mushrooms (about 4 oz.)**
- **½ cup dry red wine or reduced-sodium beef broth**
- **1 tsp. all-purpose flour**
- **½ cup reduced-sodium beef broth**
- **1 tsp. ketchup**
- **1 tsp. steak sauce**
- **1 tsp. Worcestershire sauce**
- **½ tsp. ground mustard**
- **¼ tsp. pepper**
- **⅛ tsp. salt**
- **1 Tbsp. minced fresh chives, optional**

1. Place a large skillet coated with cooking spray over medium-high heat; brown steaks on both sides. Remove from pan.
2. Add mushrooms and wine to pan; bring to a boil over medium heat, stirring to loosen browned bits from pan. Cook until liquid is reduced by half, 2-3 minutes. Mix flour and broth until smooth; stir into pan. Stir in all remaining ingredients except chives; bring to a boil.
3. Return steaks to pan; cook, uncovered, until meat reaches desired doneness (for medium-rare, a thermometer should read 135°; medium, 140°), 1-2 minutes per side. If desired, sprinkle with chives.
1 SERVING: 247 cal., 7g fat (3g sat. fat), 51mg chol., 369mg sod., 7g carb. (3g sugars, 1g fiber), 27g pro. **DIABETIC EXCHANGES:** 3 lean meat, 1 vegetable.

SLOW-ROASTED CHICKEN WITH VEGETABLES

Even a beginner cook could make this and it would turn out perfectly—the recipe couldn't be easier. A few minutes of prep and you will come home to a delicious dinner.
—Anita Bell, Hermitage, TN

Prep: 15 min. • **Cook:** 6 hours + standing
Makes: 6 servings

- **2 medium carrots, peeled, halved lengthwise and cut into 3-in. pieces**
- **2 celery ribs, halved lengthwise and cut into 3-in. pieces**
- **8 small red potatoes, quartered**
- **¾ tsp. salt, divided**
- **⅛ tsp. pepper**
- **1 medium lemon, halved**
- **2 garlic cloves, minced**
- **1 broiler/fryer chicken (3 to 4 lbs.)**
- **1 Tbsp. dried rosemary, crushed**
- **1 Tbsp. lemon juice**
- **1 Tbsp. olive oil**
- **2½ tsp. paprika**

1. Place carrots, celery and potatoes in a 6-qt. slow cooker; sprinkle with ¼ tsp. salt and pepper. Place the lemon halves and garlic in chicken cavity. Tuck wings under chicken; tie drumsticks together. Place chicken over the vegetables in slow cooker, breast side up. Mix together rosemary, lemon juice, oil, paprika and remaining salt in small bowl; rub mixture over the chicken.
2. Cook, covered, on low until a thermometer inserted in the thigh reads at least 170° and the vegetables are tender, about 6-8 hours.
3. Remove chicken from slow cooker; tent with foil. Let stand 15 minutes before carving. Serve with vegetables.

3 OZ. COOKED CHICKEN WITH ⅔ CUP VEGETABLES: 329 cal., 17g fat (4g sat. fat), 88mg chol., 400mg sod., 14g carb. (2g sugars, 3g fiber), 29g pro.

SMOTHERED BURRITOS

My brother-in-law teased that I knew how to make only five things using ground beef. I proved him wrong with a new invention—these amazing burritos.
—Kim Kenyon, Greenwood, MO

Takes: 30 min. • **Makes:** 4 servings

- **1 can (10 oz.) green enchilada sauce**
- **¾ cup salsa verde**
- **1 lb. ground beef**
- **4 flour tortillas (10 in.)**
- **1½ cups shredded cheddar cheese, divided**

1. Preheat oven to 375°. In a small bowl, mix enchilada sauce and salsa verde.
2. In a large skillet, cook beef over medium heat 8-10 minutes or until no longer pink, breaking into crumbles; drain. Stir in ½ cup sauce mixture.
3. Spoon ⅔ cup beef mixture across center of each tortilla; top each with 3 Tbsp. cheese. Fold bottom and sides of tortilla over filling and roll up.
4. Place burritos in a greased 11x7-in. baking dish. Pour remaining sauce mixture over top; sprinkle with remaining ¾ cup cheese. Bake, uncovered, 10-15 minutes or until the cheese is melted.

1 BURRITO: 624 cal., 33g fat (15g sat. fat), 115mg chol., 1470mg sod., 44g carb. (6g sugars, 2g fiber), 36g pro.

ANITA BELL
Hermitage, TN

FREEZE OPTION: Cool the two unbaked casseroles; cover and freeze. To use, partially thaw in the refrigerator overnight. Remove from refrigerator 30 minutes before baking. Preheat oven to 350°. Cover casserole with foil; bake 50 minutes. Uncover; bake until heated through and a thermometer inserted in center reads 165°, 15-20 minutes longer.

2 STUFFED SHELLS: 397 cal., 23g fat (14g sat. fat), 94mg chol., 1097mg sod., 24g carb. (5g sugars, 2g fiber), 24g pro.

CHEESE-STUFFED SHELLS

When I was living in California, I tasted this rich, cheesy pasta dish at a neighborhood Italian restaurant. I got the recipe, made a few little changes to it, and now I think it's even better!
—Lori Mecca, Grants Pass, OR

Prep: 35 min. • **Bake:** 50 min.
Makes: 12 servings (2 casseroles)

- **1 lb. bulk Italian sausage**
- **1 large onion, chopped**
- **1 pkg. (10 oz.) frozen chopped spinach, thawed and squeezed dry**
- **1 pkg. (8 oz.) cream cheese, cubed**
- **1 large egg, lightly beaten**
- **2 cups shredded part-skim mozzarella cheese, divided**
- **2 cups shredded cheddar cheese**
- **1 cup 4% cottage cheese**
- **1 cup grated Parmesan cheese**
- **¼ tsp. salt**
- **¼ tsp. pepper**
- **⅛ tsp. ground cinnamon, optional**
- **24 jumbo pasta shells, cooked and drained**

SAUCE

- **1 can (29 oz.) tomato sauce**
- **1 Tbsp. dried minced onion**
- **1½ tsp. dried basil**
- **1½ tsp. dried parsley flakes**
- **2 garlic cloves, minced**
- **1 tsp. sugar**
- **1 tsp. dried oregano**
- **½ tsp. salt**
- **¼ tsp. pepper**

1. In a large skillet, cook sausage and onion over medium heat until meat is no longer pink; drain. Transfer to a large bowl. Stir in the spinach, cream cheese and egg. Add 1 cup mozzarella cheese, cheddar cheese, cottage cheese, Parmesan cheese, salt, pepper and cinnamon if desired.
2. Stuff pasta shells with sausage mixture. Arrange in two shallow 2-qt. or 11x7-in. baking dishes coated with cooking spray. Combine the sauce ingredients; spoon over shells.
3. Cover and bake at 350° for 45 minutes. Uncover; sprinkle with remaining mozzarella. Bake 5-10 minutes longer or until bubbly and cheese is melted. Let stand for 5 minutes before serving.

5i

ROASTED CHICKEN

You can't go wrong with tender roasted chicken. Here a simple blend of seasonings makes this a snap to prepare, and it smells heavenly as it roasts.
—Marian Platt, Sequim, WA

Prep: 10 min. • **Bake:** 1¼ hours + standing
Makes: 12 servings

- **¾ tsp. onion salt**
- **¾ tsp. celery salt**
- **¾ tsp. seasoned salt**
- **½ tsp. pepper**
- **2 broiler/fryer chickens (3 to 4 lbs. each)**

1. Preheat oven to 400°. Mix seasonings.
2. Place chickens on a rack in a roasting pan, breasts side up. Rub seasonings over outside and inside of chickens. Tuck under wings; tie together drumsticks. Roast chickens until a thermometer inserted in thickest part of thigh reads 170°-175°, 1¼-1½ hours. (Cover loosely with foil if chickens brown too quickly.)
3. Remove from oven; tent with foil. Let stand 15 minutes before carving.

1 SERVING: 293 cal., 17g fat (5g sat. fat), 104mg chol., 370mg sod., 0 carb. (0 sugars, 0 fiber), 33g pro.

READER REVIEW
"Very easy and tasty! I poured a little olive oil over the chicken and then topped it with the seasoning. Delicious and moist!"
DARRR, TASTEOFHOME.COM

Casserole Entrees

Hearty and heartwarming, a casserole is the ultimate comfort food. For a family dinner or a potluck supper, these savory dishes are perfect one-dish wonders.

CHICKEN ZUCCHINI CASSEROLE

A co-worker shared this recipe with me—it was originally her grandmother's. When I make it, I use precooked chicken from the grocery store and fresh zucchini my neighbor gives me from his garden.

—Bev Dutro, Dayton, OH

Prep: 20 min. • **Bake:** 45 min.
Makes: 6 servings

- **1 pkg. (6 oz.) stuffing mix**
- **¾ cup butter, melted**
- **3 cups diced zucchini**
- **2 cups cubed cooked chicken breast**
- **1 can (10¾ oz.) condensed cream of chicken soup, undiluted**
- **1 medium carrot, shredded**
- **½ cup chopped onion**
- **½ cup sour cream**

1. Preheat oven to 350°. Combine stuffing mix and butter. Set aside ½ cup for topping. Add the zucchini, chicken, soup, carrot, onion and sour cream to the remaining stuffing mixture.

2. Transfer to a greased 11x7-in. baking dish. Sprinkle with the reserved stuffing mixture. Bake, uncovered, for 40-45 minutes or until golden brown and bubbly.

1 CUP: 481 cal., 31g fat (18g sat. fat), 115mg chol., 1174mg sod., 27g carb. (6g sugars, 2g fiber), 21g pro.

READER REVIEW

"This recipe is amazing! We chopped up a jalapeno and cut the butter just a little. It's a must-try recipe!"

BARBARA, TASTEOFHOME.COM

CHEESY PIZZA CASSEROLE

I first made this recipe after discovering it in the reader's exchange of our local electric cooperative's magazine. Serve it whenever you've got a crowd to please!
—Judy Chandler, Franklin, KY

Prep: 25 min. • **Bake:** 25 min.
Makes: 10 servings

- **1 lb. ground beef**
- **1 pkg. (3½ oz.) sliced pepperoni**
- **1 medium onion, chopped**
- **1 medium green pepper, chopped**
- **1 jar (4½ oz.) sliced mushrooms, drained**
- **7 oz. vermicelli, cooked and drained**
- **⅓ cup butter, melted**
- **1 can (15 oz.) tomato sauce, divided**
- **1 cup shredded Swiss cheese**
- **4 cups shredded part-skim mozzarella cheese**
- **½ tsp. dried oregano**
- **½ tsp. dried basil**

1. Preheat oven to 350°. In a large skillet, cook the beef, pepperoni, onion and green pepper over medium heat until the meat is no longer pink; drain. Stir in mushrooms; set aside.
2. Combine vermicelli and butter in a greased 13x9-in. baking dish; toss to coat. Pour 1 cup tomato sauce over the pasta; top with half the meat mixture. Combine the Swiss and mozzarella cheeses; sprinkle half over top. Sprinkle with oregano and basil. Layer with the remaining meat and cheese mixtures. Pour the remaining tomato sauce over top.
3. Bake, uncovered, for 25-30 minutes or until bubbly.
1 SERVING: 422 cal., 25g fat (14g sat. fat), 83mg chol., 764mg sod., 21g carb. (4g sugars, 2g fiber), 28g pro.

CRUNCHY ALMOND TURKEY CASSEROLE

One of my cousins gave me the recipe for this comforting casserole. The almonds and water chestnuts give it a fun crunch.
—Jill Black, Troy, ON

Prep: 15 min. • **Bake:** 35 min.
Makes: 8 servings

- **2 cans (10¾ oz. each) condensed cream of mushroom soup, undiluted**
- **½ cup mayonnaise**
- **½ cup sour cream**
- **2 Tbsp. chopped onion**
- **2 Tbsp. lemon juice**
- **1 tsp. salt**
- **½ tsp. white pepper**
- **5 cups cubed cooked turkey**
- **3 cups cooked rice**
- **4 celery ribs, chopped**
- **1 can (8 oz.) sliced water chestnuts, drained**
- **1 cup sliced almonds**

TOPPING

- **1½ cups crushed Ritz crackers (about 40 crackers)**
- **⅓ cup butter, melted**
- **¼ cup sliced almonds**

1. Preheat oven to 350°. In a large bowl, combine the soup, mayonnaise, sour cream, onion, lemon juice, salt and pepper. Stir in the turkey, rice, celery, water chestnuts and almonds.
2. Transfer to a greased 13x9-in. baking dish. Bake, uncovered, for 25 minutes. Combine the topping ingredients; sprinkle over the turkey mixture. Return to oven; bake until bubbly and golden brown, another 10-15 minutes.
1 CUP: 678 cal., 41g fat (12g sat. fat), 105mg chol., 1211mg sod., 43g carb. (5g sugars, 4g fiber), 34g pro.

SALSA VERDE CHICKEN CASSEROLE

This is a rich and surprisingly tasty rendition of all the Tex-Mex dishes we love packed into one fantastic casserole. Best of all, it's ready in hardly any time!
—Janet McCormick, Proctorville, OH

Takes: 30 min. • **Makes:** 6 servings

- 2 **cups shredded rotisserie chicken**
- 1 **cup sour cream**
- 1½ **cups salsa verde, divided**
- 8 **corn tortillas (6 in.)**
- 2 **cups chopped tomatoes**
- ¼ **cup minced fresh cilantro**
- 2 **cups shredded Monterey Jack cheese**
- **Optional toppings: avocado slices, thinly sliced green onions or fresh cilantro leaves**

1. Preheat oven to 400°. Combine chicken, sour cream and ¾ cup salsa in a bowl. Spread ¼ cup of the remaining salsa on the bottom of a greased 8-in. square baking dish.
2. Layer with half the tortillas and chicken mixture; sprinkle with half the tomatoes, minced cilantro and half the cheese. Repeat layers with the remaining tortillas, chicken mixture, tomatoes and cheese.
3. Bake, uncovered, for 20-25 minutes or until bubbly. Serve with the remaining salsa and, if desired, optional toppings.
1 SERVING: 400 cal., 23g fat (13g sat. fat), 102mg chol., 637mg sod., 22g carb. (5g sugars, 3g fiber), 26g pro.

ANGEL HAIR SHRIMP BAKE

Shrimp and pasta blend beautifully with the herbs, salsa and three kinds of cheese in this hearty layered casserole. Whatever the occasion, bake up a dish of succulent shrimp goodness to share.
—Susan Davidson, Elm Grove, WI

Prep: 25 min. • **Bake:** 25 min.
Makes: 8 servings

- 1 **pkg. (9 oz.) refrigerated angel hair pasta**
- 1½ **lbs. uncooked medium shrimp, peeled and deveined**
- ¾ **cup crumbled feta cheese**
- ½ **cup shredded Swiss cheese**
- 1 **jar (16 oz.) chunky salsa**
- ½ **cup shredded Monterey Jack cheese**
- ¾ **cup minced fresh parsley**
- 1 **tsp. dried basil**
- 1 **tsp. dried oregano**
- 2 **large eggs**
- 1 **cup half-and-half cream**
- 1 **cup plain yogurt**
- **Chopped fresh parsley, optional**

1. Preheat oven to 350°. In a greased 13x9-in. baking dish, layer half the pasta, shrimp, feta cheese, Swiss cheese and salsa. Repeat layers. Sprinkle with Monterey Jack cheese, parsley, basil and oregano.
2. In a small bowl, whisk the eggs, cream and yogurt; pour over casserole. Bake, uncovered, until a thermometer reads 160°, 25-30 minutes. Let stand 5 minutes before serving. If desired, top with parsley.
1 CUP: 220 cal., 8g fat (5g sat. fat), 144mg chol., 452mg sod., 15g carb. (4g sugars, 2g fiber), 17g pro. **DIABETIC EXCHANGES:** 2½ lean meat, 1½ starch.

HOT BROWN TURKEY CASSEROLE

If you've ever tried the famous Hot Brown sandwich at The Brown Hotel in Louisville, Kentucky, you'll love this homemade version. It can be assembled ahead and refrigerated; just up the baking time if cooking it from cold.
—Diane Halferty, Corpus Christi, TX

Prep: 40 min. • **Bake:** 20 min.
Makes: 12 servings

- **¼ cup butter**
- **¼ cup all-purpose flour**
- **4 cups 2% milk**
- **1 large egg**
- **⅔ cup grated Parmesan cheese, divided**
- **¼ tsp. salt**
- **¼ tsp. pepper**
- **12 slices bread, toasted and divided**
- **2 lbs. thinly sliced cooked turkey or chicken**
- **¼ tsp. paprika**
- **6 bacon strips, cooked and crumbled**
- **1 cup tomatoes, chopped and seeded**
- **1 tsp. minced fresh parsley**

1. Preheat oven to 350°. In a large saucepan, melt butter over medium heat. Stir in flour until smooth; gradually whisk in milk. Bring to a boil, stirring constantly; cook until slightly thickened, 6-8 minutes. Remove from heat.
2. In a small bowl, lightly beat egg. Gradually whisk in ½ cup of the sauce. Slowly return all to the pan, whisking constantly. Add ½ cup Parmesan cheese, salt and pepper. Cook and stir until thickened. (Do not allow to boil.)
3. In a greased 13x9-in. baking dish, layer six toast slices and sliced turkey; pour the sauce over top. Sprinkle with paprika, bacon and the remaining Parmesan cheese.
4. Bake until heated through, 20-25 minutes. Top with tomatoes and parsley. Cut remaining toast slices in half diagonally;serve on the side.
1 SERVING: 316 cal., 13g fat (6g sat. fat), 117mg chol., 472mg sod., 19g carb. (6g sugars, 1g fiber), 30g pro.

MOTHER'S HAM CASSEROLE

This casserole, one of my mother's favorite dishes, always brings back fond memories of her whenever I prepare it. It's a terrific use of leftover ham from a holiday dinner.
—Linda Childers, Murfreesboro, TN

Prep: 35 min. • **Bake:** 25 min.
Makes: 6 servings

- **2 cups cubed peeled potatoes**
- **1 large carrot, sliced**
- **2 celery ribs, chopped**
- **3 cups water**
- **2 cups cubed fully cooked ham**
- **2 Tbsp. chopped green pepper**
- **2 tsp. finely chopped onion**
- **7 Tbsp. butter, divided**
- **3 Tbsp. all-purpose flour**
- **1½ cups 2% milk**
- **¾ tsp. salt**
- **⅛ tsp. pepper**
- **1 cup shredded cheddar cheese**
- **½ cup soft bread crumbs**

1. Preheat oven to 375°. In a saucepan, bring the potatoes, carrot, celery and water to a boil. Reduce heat; cover and cook about 15 minutes or until tender. Drain.
2. In a large skillet, saute the ham, green pepper and onion in 3 Tbsp. butter until tender. Add to the potato mixture. Transfer to a greased 1½-qt. baking dish.
3. In a large saucepan, melt the remaining butter; stir in flour until smooth. Gradually add the milk, salt and pepper. Bring to a boil; cook and stir for 2 minutes or until thickened. Reduce heat; add cheese and stir until melted.
4. Pour over ham mixture. Sprinkle with bread crumbs. Bake, uncovered, for 25-30 minutes or until heated through.
1 CUP: 374 cal., 25g fat (15g sat. fat), 89mg chol., 1208mg sod., 22g carb. (5g sugars, 2g fiber), 17g pro.

PINEAPPLE HAM CASSEROLE

Living in Hawaii, I wanted to share a recipe that features pineapple. It's our most important fruit crop, and it really shines in this dish.

—Marsha Fleming, Kula, HI

Prep: 15 min. • **Bake:** 30 min.
Makes: 4 servings

- **2 cups uncooked wide egg noodles**
- **½ cup chopped celery**
- **2 Tbsp. butter, divided**
- **1 pkg. cream cheese, cubed**
- **¾ cup whole milk**
- **2 cups cubed fully cooked ham**
- **2 cans (8 oz. each) crushed pineapple, drained**
- **2 tsp. Worcestershire sauce**
- **½ tsp. salt**
- **Dash pepper**
- **¼ cup dry bread crumbs**

1. Preheat oven to 350°. Cook egg noodles according to the package directions; drain. In a large skillet, saute celery in 1 Tbsp. butter until tender. Stir in cream cheese and milk; cook and stir until cheese is melted. Add the noodles, ham, pineapple, Worcestershire sauce, salt and pepper.
2. Transfer to an ungreased 1½-qt. baking dish. Melt remaining butter; toss with bread crumbs. Sprinkle over top. Bake, uncovered, 30-35 minutes or until heated through.
1 SERVING: 527 cal., 34g fat (19g sat. fat), 139mg chol., 1541mg sod., 34g carb. (11g sugars, 1g fiber), 22g pro.

COMFORTING TUNA CASSEROLE

My mother gave me the recipe for this classic casserole many years ago. Sometimes I use sliced stuffed olives instead of pimientos.

—Dorothy Coleman, Hobe Sound, FL

Prep: 15 min. • **Bake:** 20 min.
Makes: 2 servings

- **1¾ cups uncooked wide egg noodles**
- **6 tsp. reduced-fat butter, divided**
- **4 tsp. all-purpose flour**
- **¼ tsp. salt**
- **Dash pepper**
- **¾ cup 2% milk**
- **3 oz. reduced-fat cream cheese**
- **1 pouch (2½ oz.) albacore white tuna in water**
- **2 Tbsp. diced pimientos**
- **2 tsp. minced chives**
- **2 slices Muenster cheese (¾ oz. each)**
- **2 Tbsp. soft bread crumbs**

1. Preheat oven to 350°. Cook the noodles according to package directions. Meanwhile, in a small saucepan over medium heat, melt 5 tsp. butter. Stir in the flour, salt and pepper until blended; gradually add the milk. Bring to a boil over medium heat; cook and stir for 1-2 minutes or until thickened. Reduce heat to medium-low; add the cream cheese, tuna, pimientos and chives. Cook and stir until the cheese is melted.
2. Drain the noodles. Spread ¼ cup tuna mixture into a 3-cup baking dish coated with cooking spray. Layer with half the noodles, ½ cup tuna mixture and one slice cheese. Repeat layers.
3. Microwave the remaining butter on high, stirring every 30 seconds; stir in the bread crumbs. Sprinkle over top of casserole. Bake, uncovered, until bubbly, 20-25 minutes.
1½ CUPS: 493 cal., 26g fat (15g sat. fat), 118mg chol., 941mg sod., 37g carb. (7g sugars, 2g fiber), 28g pro.

ZUCCHINI LASAGNA

I plant zucchini in our garden every year, and we always seem to have more than we can use. This recipe is a particularly delicious way to use our abundant crop.

—Charlotte McDaniel, Williamsville, IL

Prep: 20 min. • **Bake:** 40 min. + standing
Makes: 6 servings

- **1 lb. lean ground beef (90% lean)**
- **¼ cup chopped onion**
- **½ tsp. dried oregano**
- **½ tsp. dried basil**
- **¼ tsp. salt**
- **¼ tsp. pepper**
- **1 can (15 oz.) tomato sauce**
- **1 large egg, lightly beaten**
- **1 cup 2% cottage cheese**
- **4 medium zucchini (about 1¾ lbs.)**
- **3 Tbsp. all-purpose flour**
- **1 cup shredded part-skim mozzarella cheese**
- **Additional shredded mozzarella cheese, optional**

1. Preheat oven to 375°. In large skillet, cook and crumble the beef with the onion over medium-high heat until the meat is no longer pink, 5-7 minutes. Stir in the seasonings and tomato sauce. Bring to boil; simmer, uncovered, for 5 minutes. In a bowl, mix the egg and cottage cheese.

2. Trim the ends of zucchini; cut lengthwise into ¼-in.-thick slices. Layer half the slices in a 13x9-in. baking dish coated with cooking spray; dust with half the flour. Top with the cottage cheese mixture and half the meat sauce. Add the remaining zucchini; dust with remaining flour. Spread with remaining meat sauce; sprinkle with 1 cup mozzarella cheese.

3. Bake, uncovered, until heated through, about 40 minutes. If desired, sprinkle with additional cheese. Let stand 10 minutes before serving.

1 SERVING: 273 cal., 13g fat (5g sat. fat), 92mg chol., 725mg sod., 14g carb. (6g sugars, 3g fiber), 27g pro. **DIABETIC EXCHANGES:** 3 lean meat, 1 starch, 1 fat.

SHRIMP & CRAB CASSEROLE

A medley of seafood and other flavors combine in this rich, satisfying dish. Make it a day in advance for company—or any night you crave an easy, elegant meal.
—Jan Bartley, Evergreen, NC

Prep: 25 min. • **Bake:** 40 min.
Makes: 8 servings

- **2 pkg. (8.8 oz. each) ready-to-serve long grain and wild rice**
- **¼ cup butter, cubed**
- **2 celery ribs, chopped**
- **1 medium onion, chopped**
- **3 Tbsp. all-purpose flour**
- **1½ cups half-and-half cream**
- **1 tsp. seafood seasoning**
- **¾ tsp. salt**
- **½ tsp. hot pepper sauce**
- **¼ tsp. pepper**
- **1½ lbs. uncooked shrimp (31-40 per lb.), peeled and deveined**
- **2 cans (6 oz. each) lump crabmeat, drained**
- **1 cup shredded Colby-Monterey Jack cheese**

1. Preheat oven to 350°. Spread rice into a greased 13x9-in. baking dish. In a large skillet, heat butter over medium-high heat. Add celery and onion; cook and stir until tender, 6-8 minutes. Stir in the flour until blended; gradually whisk in cream. Bring to a boil, stirring constantly; cook and stir 1-2 minutes or until thickened.

2. Stir in seafood seasoning, salt, pepper sauce and pepper. Fold in shrimp and crab. Spoon over rice. Sprinkle with cheese. Bake, covered until shrimp turn pink, 40-45 minutes. Let stand 5 minutes.

NOTE: To make ahead, prepare as directed, cooling sauce slightly before adding shrimp and crab. Cover and refrigerate overnight. Remove from the refrigerator 30 minutes before baking. Bake as directed.

1 SERVING: 376 cal., 17g fat (10g sat. fat), 195mg chol., 1127mg sod., 24g carb. (3g sugars, 1g fiber), 29g pro.

CHEESY CHILE CASSEROLE

A short list of ingredients packs full flavor in this easy-to-assemble casserole. Serve it as the star of your next meal.
—Phyllis Bidwell, Las Vegas, NV

Prep: 10 min. • **Bake:** 40 min.
Makes: 8 servings

- **2 cups shredded Monterey Jack cheese**
- **2 cups shredded cheddar cheese**
- **1 can (7 oz.) whole green chiles, rinsed and seeded**
- **2 large eggs**
- **2 Tbsp. all-purpose flour**
- **1 can (12 oz.) evaporated milk**
- **1 can (8 oz.) tomato sauce or 1 cup fresh salsa, drained, divided**

1. In a large bowl, combine cheeses. In a greased 2-qt. baking dish, layer cheese and chiles. Whisk the eggs, flour and milk; pour over cheese mixture.

2. Bake at 350° for 30 minutes. Top with half the tomato sauce or salsa; bake another 10 minutes or until heated through. Let stand for 5 minutes before serving. Serve with the remaining sauce.

1 PIECE: 304 cal., 21g fat (14g sat. fat), 125mg chol., 538mg sod., 9g carb. (5g sugars, 0 fiber), 18g pro.

EGGPLANT ROLLATINI

While these eggplant roll-ups may take some time to prepare, the final results taste like a fine dining restaurant. Your family will request this dish time and again.
—Nancy Sousley, Lafayette, IN

Prep: 1 hour • **Bake:** 30 min.
Makes: 5 servings

- 1 **large eggplant**
- 1 **Tbsp. salt**

SAUCE
- 1 **small onion, chopped**
- ¼ **cup olive oil**
- 2 **garlic cloves, minced**
- 1 **can (15 oz.) tomato sauce**
- 1 **can (14½ oz.) diced tomatoes**
- ½ **cup chicken broth**
- ¼ **cup tomato paste**
- 2 **Tbsp. minced fresh parsley**
- 2 **tsp. sugar**
- ½ **tsp. salt**
- ½ **tsp. dried basil**
- ¼ **tsp. pepper**
- ⅛ **tsp. crushed red pepper flakes**

FILLING
- 1 **carton (15 oz.) ricotta cheese**
- 1 **cup shredded part-skim mozzarella cheese**
- ½ **cup grated Parmesan cheese**
- ¼ **cup minced fresh parsley**
- 1 **large egg, lightly beaten**
- ⅛ **tsp. pepper**

COATING
- 3 **large eggs, lightly beaten**
- 1 **cup seasoned bread crumbs**
- 1 **cup grated Parmesan cheese, divided**
- 2 **garlic cloves, minced**
- 2 **Tbsp. minced fresh parsley**
- **Dash each salt and pepper**
- **Oil for frying**

1. Peel and slice eggplant lengthwise into fifteen ⅛-in.-thick slices. Place in a colander over a plate; sprinkle with salt and toss. Let stand for 30 minutes.
2. Meanwhile, for sauce, in a large saucepan, saute onion in oil. Add garlic; cook 1 minute longer. Stir in the remaining ingredients. Bring to a boil. Reduce heat; simmer, uncovered, 20-25 minutes or until flavors are blended, stirring occasionally. Rinse and drain eggplant.
3. In a large bowl, combine filling ingredients; set aside.
4. For the coating, place the eggs in a shallow bowl. In another shallow bowl, combine the bread crumbs, ½ cup Parmesan cheese, garlic, parsley, salt and pepper. Dip eggplant slices in the beaten eggs, then in the bread crumb mixture.
5. In an electric skillet, heat ½ in. oil to 375°. Fry the eggplant in batches for 2-3 minutes on each side or until golden brown. Drain on paper towels.
6. Preheat oven to 375°. Spoon 1 cup sauce into an ungreased 13x9-in. baking dish. Spread 2 rounded Tbsp. filling over each eggplant slice. Carefully roll up each slice and place it seam side down in baking dish. Spoon the remaining sauce over the roll-ups. Sprinkle with the remaining Parmesan cheese. Cover and bake for 30-35 minutes or until bubbly.
3 EACH: 726 cal., 48g fat (15g sat. fat), 181mg chol., 3182mg sod., 44g carb. (19g sugars, 7g fiber), 35g pro.

LEMON CHICKEN & RICE

On our busy ranch, we often need meals we can put on the table in a hurry. This all-in-one chicken dish—with its delicate lemon flavor—fits the bill, and it's inexpensive to boot.
—Kat Thompson, Prineville, OR

Takes: 30 min. • **Makes:** 4 servings

- 2 **Tbsp. butter**
- 1 **lb. boneless skinless chicken breasts, cut into strips**
- 1 **medium onion, chopped**
- 1 **large carrot, thinly sliced**
- 2 **garlic cloves, minced**
- 1 **Tbsp. cornstarch**
- 1 **can (14½ oz.) chicken broth**
- 2 **Tbsp. lemon juice**
- ¼ **tsp. salt**
- 1 **cup frozen peas**
- 1½ **cups uncooked instant rice**

1. In a large cast-iron or other heavy skillet, heat butter over medium-high heat; saute chicken, onion, carrot and garlic until the chicken is no longer pink, 5-7 minutes.
2. In a small bowl, mix cornstarch, broth, lemon juice and salt until smooth. Gradually add to the skillet; bring to a boil. Cook and stir until thickened, 1-2 minutes.
3. Stir in the peas; return to a boil. Stir in the rice. Remove from heat; let stand, covered, 5 minutes.
1 SERVING: 370 cal., 9g fat (4g sat. fat), 80mg chol., 746mg sod., 41g carb. (4g sugars, 3g fiber), 29g pro. **DIABETIC EXCHANGES:** 3 starch, 3 lean meat, 1½ fat.

EASY CHEESY LOADED GRITS

A tasty bowl of grits inspired me to develop my own version made with sausage, green chiles and cheeses. It just might be better than the original!

—Joan Hallford, North Richland Hills, TX

Prep: 35 min. • **Bake:** 50 min. + standing
Makes: 8 servings

- **1 lb. mild or spicy bulk pork sausage**
- **1 small onion, chopped**
- **4 cups water**
- **½ tsp. salt**
- **1 cup quick-cooking grits**
- **3 cans (4 oz. each) chopped green chiles**
- **1½ cups shredded sharp cheddar cheese, divided**
- **1½ cups shredded Monterey Jack cheese, divided**
- **2 Tbsp. butter**
- **¼ tsp. hot pepper sauce**
- **2 large eggs, lightly beaten**
- **¼ tsp. paprika**
- **Chopped fresh cilantro**

1. Preheat oven to 325°. In a large skillet, cook the sausage and onion over medium heat 6-8 minutes or until sausage is no longer pink, breaking up sausage into crumbles; drain.
2. In a large saucepan, bring water and salt to a boil. Slowly stir in the grits. Reduce heat to medium-low; cook, covered, about 5 minutes or until thickened, stirring occasionally. Remove from heat.
3. Add green chiles, ¾ cup cheddar cheese, ¾ cup Monterey Jack cheese, butter and pepper sauce; stir until cheese is melted. Stir in eggs, then the sausage mixture.
4. Transfer to a greased 13x9-in. baking dish. Top with the remaining cheeses; sprinkle with paprika. Bake, uncovered, until golden brown and set, 50-60 minutes. Let stand 10 minutes before serving. Sprinkle with cilantro.
1 CUP: 399 cal., 28g fat (15g sat. fat), 116mg chol., 839mg sod., 19g carb. (2g sugars, 2g fiber), 18g pro.

FLORENTINE SPAGHETTI BAKE

This enticing sausage dish appeals to most every appetite, from basic meat-and-potatoes fans to gourmets. My daughter, a Montana wheat rancher's wife, serves it often to satisfy her hardworking family.

—Lorraine Martin, Lincoln, CA

Prep: 30 min. • **Bake:** 1 hour + standing
Makes: 9 servings

- **8 oz. uncooked spaghetti**
- **1 lb. bulk Italian sausage**
- **1 large onion, chopped**
- **1 garlic clove, minced**
- **1 jar (24 oz.) pasta sauce**
- **1 can (4 oz.) mushroom stems and pieces, drained**
- **1 large egg, lightly beaten**
- **2 cups 4% cottage cheese**
- **1 pkg. (10 oz.) frozen chopped spinach, thawed and squeezed dry**
- **¼ cup grated Parmesan cheese**
- **½ tsp. seasoned salt**
- **¼ tsp. pepper**
- **2 cups shredded part-skim mozzarella cheese**

1. Preheat oven to 375°. Cook pasta according to package directions. Meanwhile, in a large skillet over medium heat, cook sausage and onion, crumbling meat, until the sausage is no longer pink. Add garlic; cook 1 minute longer. Drain. Stir in the pasta sauce and mushrooms. Bring to a boil. Reduce heat; cover and cook until heated through, about 15 minutes.
2. Drain the pasta. Combine the egg with the next five ingredients. Spread 1 cup sausage mixture in a greased 13x9-in. baking dish. Top with spaghetti and remaining sausage mixture. Layer with egg mixture and mozzarella cheese.
3. Cover and bake 45 minutes. Uncover; bake until lightly browned and heated through, about 15 minutes longer. Let stand 15 minutes before cutting.
1 PIECE: 449 cal., 23g fat (9g sat. fat), 83mg chol., 1218mg sod., 35g carb. (10g sugars, 4g fiber), 25g pro.

CHICKEN ENCHILADA BAKE

Good thing the recipe makes a lot, because your family won't want to stop eating this cheesy southwestern casserole. The green enchilada sauce brightens it right up.
—Melanie Burns, Pueblo West, CO

Prep: 20 min. • **Bake:** 50 min. + standing
Makes: 10 servings

- **4½ cups shredded rotisserie chicken**
- **1 can (28 oz.) green enchilada sauce**
- **1¼ cups sour cream**
- **9 corn tortillas (6 in.), cut into 1½-in. pieces**
- **4 cups shredded Monterey Jack cheese**

1. Preheat oven to 375°. In a greased 13x9-in. baking dish, layer half of each of the following: chicken, enchilada sauce, sour cream, tortillas and cheese. Repeat layers.
2. Bake, covered, for 40 minutes. Uncover; bake until bubbly, about 10 minutes longer. Let stand 15 minutes before serving.
FREEZE OPTION: Cover and freeze unbaked casserole. To use, partially thaw in refrigerator overnight. Remove from refrigerator about 30 minutes before baking. Bake at 375° as directed, increasing time as necessary to heat through and until a thermometer inserted in the center reads 165°.
1 CUP: 469 cal., 29g fat (14g sat. fat), 113mg chol., 1077mg sod., 16g carb. (3g sugars, 1g fiber), 34g pro.

CORNBREAD TACO BAKE

Cornbread and beef bake together in one casserole dish, making this dish so convenient. It's packed with tempting seasonings, and the cheese and onions make an attractive topping.
—Vicki Good, Oscoda, MI

Prep: 20 min. • **Bake:** 25 min.
Makes: 6 servings

- **1½ lbs. ground beef**
- **1 can (15¼ oz.) whole kernel corn, drained**
- **1 can (8 oz.) tomato sauce**
- **½ cup water**
- **½ cup chopped green pepper**
- **1 envelope taco seasoning**
- **1 pkg. (8½ oz.) cornbread/muffin mix**
- **1 can (2.8 oz.) french-fried onions, divided**
- **⅓ cup shredded cheddar cheese**

1. Preheat oven to 400°. In a large skillet, cook beef over medium heat until no longer pink; drain. Stir in the corn, tomato sauce, water, green pepper and taco seasoning. Spoon into a greased 2-qt. baking dish.
2. Prepare cornbread mix according to the package directions for cornbread. Stir in half the onions. Spread over the beef mixture. Bake, uncovered, for 20 minutes.
3. Sprinkle with cheese and the remaining onions. Bake 3-5 minutes longer or until the cheese is melted and a toothpick inserted into the cornbread layer comes out clean.
1 SERVING: (1 piece) equals 575 cal., 27 g fat (10 g sat. fat), 91 mg chol., 1,443 mg sod., 50 g carb., 2 g fiber, 29 g pro.

TEST KITCHEN TIP
Make your own taco seasoning at home by combining ¼ cup flour, ¼ cup chili powder, 3 Tbsp. dried minced onion, 1 Tbsp. garlic powder, 2½ tsp. salt, 2 tsp. dried oregano, 2 tsp. ground cumin, 1½ tsp. cayenne pepper and 1 tsp. ground coriander. You can adjust the mix to your personal preference by using more or less of each spice—and also control the amount of salt!

NEW ENGLAND LAMB BAKE

This hearty dish is perfect for warming up on a chilly winter evening. When you smell it baking, you'll be glad you stayed home.
—Frank Grady, Fort Kent, ME

Prep: 25 min. • **Bake:** 1½ hours
Makes: 8 servings

- **1 Tbsp. canola oil**
- **2 lbs. boneless leg of lamb, cut into 1-in. cubes**
- **1 large onion, chopped**
- **¼ cup all-purpose flour**
- **3 cups chicken broth**
- **2 large leeks (white portion only), cut into ½-in. slices**
- **2 large carrots, sliced**
- **2 Tbsp. minced fresh parsley, divided**
- **½ tsp. dried rosemary, crushed**
- **½ tsp. salt**
- **¼ tsp. pepper**
- **¼ tsp. dried thyme**
- **3 large potatoes, peeled and sliced**
- **3 Tbsp. butter, melted and divided**

1. Preheat oven to 375°. In a Dutch oven, heat oil over medium heat. Add lamb and onion; cook and stir until meat is no longer pink. Stir in flour until blended. Gradually add broth. Bring to a boil; cook until thickened, 1-2 minutes, stirring to loosen browned bits from the pan. Add leeks, carrots, 1 Tbsp. parsley, rosemary, salt, pepper and thyme.
2. Spoon into a greased 13x9-in. or 3-qt. baking dish. Cover with potato slices; brush with 2 Tbsp. melted butter. Bake 1 hour; brush potatoes with the remaining butter. Return to oven; bake until meat is tender and potatoes are golden, 30 minutes to 1 hour more. Cool briefly; sprinkle with remaining parsley.
FREEZE OPTION: Remove baking dish from oven; cool completely. Before adding the remaining parsley, cover dish and freeze. Freeze the parsley separately. To use, partially thaw lamb in refrigerator overnight. Remove from refrigerator 30 minutes before baking; thaw remaining parsley. Preheat oven to 350°. Reheat, covered, until a thermometer reads 165°, about 1 hour. Sprinkle with the remaining parsley.
1 SERVING: 356 cal., 13g fat (5g sat. fat), 82mg chol., 631mg sod., 34g carb. (4g sugars, 4g fiber), 25g pro. **DIABETIC EXCHANGES:** 3 starch, 3 lean meat, 1½ fat.

CHIPOTLE TURKEY CHILAQUILES

As a frugal mom, I try to use leftovers in ways that provide good nutrition. This recipe does just that. Best of all, it lets my children enjoy the flavors of their Mexican heritage.
—Aimee Day, Ferndale, WA

Prep: 30 min. • **Bake:** 25 min.
Makes: 8 servings

- **15 corn tortillas (6 in.), torn into 1½-in. pieces**
- **3 cups shredded cooked turkey or chicken**
- **1 large onion, chopped**
- **4 garlic cloves, minced**
- **⅓ cup lime juice**
- **2 chipotle peppers in adobo sauce**
- **2 cans (15 oz. each) black beans, rinsed and drained**
- **3 cups crumbled queso fresco or shredded part-skim mozzarella cheese**
- **3 cups turkey or chicken broth**
- **Chopped fresh cilantro**
- **Hot cooked rice, optional**
- **Sour cream, optional**

1. Preheat oven to 400°. In batches, arrange the corn tortilla pieces in a single layer on an ungreased baking sheet and bake 6-8 minutes or until crisp.
2. In a large bowl, toss turkey with onion and garlic. Place the lime juice and peppers in a blender; cover and process until blended.
3. Arrange half the tortilla pieces in a greased 13x9-in. baking dish. Layer with the turkey mixture, beans, 1½ cups cheese and chipotle mixture. Top with remaining tortilla pieces and cheese. Pour broth over top.
4. Bake, uncovered, for 25-30 minutes or until the cheese is melted. Sprinkle with cilantro. If desired, serve with rice and sour cream.
1½ CUPS: 364 cal., 8g fat (3g sat. fat), 56mg chol., 766mg sod., 44g carb. (3g sugars, 7g fiber), 29g pro.

CORN DOG CASSEROLE

Reminiscent of traditional corn dogs, this fun main dish really hits the spot. It tastes especially good right from the oven.
—Marcy Suzanne Olipane, Belleville, IL

Prep: 25 min. • **Bake:** 30 min.
Makes: 10 servings

- 2 **cups thinly sliced celery**
- 2 **Tbsp. butter**
- 1½ **cups sliced green onions**
- 1½ **lbs. hot dogs**
- 2 **large eggs**
- 1½ **cups 2% milk**
- 2 **tsp. rubbed sage**
- ¼ **tsp. pepper**
- 2 **pkg. (8½ oz. each) cornbread/muffin mix**
- 2 **cups shredded sharp cheddar cheese, divided**

1. Preheat oven to 400°. In a small skillet, saute celery in butter for 5 minutes. Add onions; saute 5 minutes longer or until the vegetables are tender. Place in a large bowl; set aside.
2. Cut hot dogs into ½-in. slices. In the same skillet, saute hot dogs for 5 minutes or until lightly browned; add to vegetables.
3. In a large bowl, whisk eggs, milk, sage and pepper. Set aside 1 cup of the hot dog mixture; add the rest to the egg mixture. Stir in the cornbread mixes. Add 1½ cups cheese. Spread into a shallow 3-qt. baking dish. Top with the reserved hot dog mixture and the remaining cheese.
4. Bake, uncovered, for 30 minutes or until golden brown.
1 CUP: 578 cal., 38g fat (16g sat. fat), 108mg chol., 1307mg sod., 40g carb. (13g sugars, 2g fiber), 19g pro.

FRITO PIE

Frito pie is legendary in the Southwest for being spicy, salty and cheesy-fabulous. Here's my easy take on this crunchy classic.
—Jan Moon, Alamogordo, NM

Takes: 30 min. • **Makes:** 6 servings

- 1 **lb. ground beef**
- 1 **medium onion, chopped**
- 2 **cans (15 oz. each) Ranch Style beans (pinto beans in seasoned tomato sauce)**
- 1 **pkg. (9¾ oz.) Fritos corn chips**
- 2 **cans (10 oz. each) enchilada sauce**
- 2 **cups shredded cheddar cheese**
- **Thinly sliced green onions, optional**

1. Preheat oven to 350°. In a large skillet, cook beef and onion over medium heat 6-8 minutes or until beef is no longer pink and onion is tender, breaking up beef into crumbles; drain. Stir in beans; heat through.
2. Reserve 1 cup corn chips for topping. Place the remaining corn chips in a greased 13x9-in. baking dish. Layer with the meat mixture, enchilada sauce and cheese; top with the reserved chips.
3. Bake, uncovered, for 15-20 minutes or until the cheese is melted. If desired, sprinkle with green onions.
1 SERVING: 731 cal., 41g fat (14g sat. fat), 84mg chol., 1733mg sod., 54g carb. (6g sugars, 8g fiber), 34g pro.

SPAGHETTI SQUASH MEATBALL CASSEROLE

One of our favorite comfort food dinners is spaghetti and meatballs. We're crazy about this lightened-up, healthier version—and the same flavors with more nutritious ingredients!
—Courtney Stultz, Weir, KS

Prep: 35 min. • **Bake:** 30 min.
Makes: 6 servings

- **1 medium spaghetti squash (about 4 lbs.)**
- **½ tsp. salt, divided**
- **½ tsp. fennel seed**
- **¼ tsp. ground coriander**
- **¼ tsp. dried basil**
- **¼ tsp. dried oregano**
- **1 lb. lean ground beef (90% lean)**
- **2 tsp. olive oil**
- **1 medium onion, chopped**
- **1 garlic clove, minced**
- **2 cups chopped collard greens**
- **1 cup chopped fresh spinach**
- **1 cup reduced-fat ricotta cheese**
- **2 plum tomatoes, chopped**
- **1 cup pasta sauce**
- **1 cup shredded part-skim mozzarella cheese**

1. Cut spaghetti squash lengthwise in half; discard seeds. Place the squash halves on a microwave-safe plate, cut side down. Microwave, uncovered, on high until tender, 15-20 minutes. Cool slightly.
2. Preheat oven to 350°. Mix ¼ tsp. salt with the remaining seasonings; add to beef, mixing lightly but thoroughly. Shape into 1½-in. balls. In a large skillet, brown the meatballs over medium heat; remove from pan.
3. In same pan, heat oil over medium heat; saute onion until tender, 3-4 minutes. Add garlic; cook and stir 1 minute. Stir in the collard greens, spinach, ricotta cheese and remaining salt; remove from heat.
4. Using a fork, separate the strands of the spaghetti squash; stir into the greens mixture. Transfer to a greased 13x9-in. baking dish. Top with tomatoes, meatballs, sauce and cheese. Bake, uncovered, until the meatballs are cooked through, 30-35 minutes.
1 SERVING: 362 cal., 16g fat (6g sat. fat), 69mg chol., 618mg sod., 32g carb. (7g sugars, 7g fiber), 26g pro. **DIABETIC EXCHANGES:** 3 lean meat, 2 starch, 1 fat.

5i

CHEESEBURGER & FRIES CASSEROLE

Kids love this casserole because it combines two of their favorite fast foods. I like the fact that I can whip it up with just a few ingredients and almost no prep time.
—Karen Owen, Rising Sun, IN

Prep: 10 min. • **Bake:** 50 min.
Makes: 8 servings

- **2 lbs. lean ground beef (90% lean)**
- **1 can (10¾ oz.) condensed golden mushroom soup, undiluted**
- **1 can (10¾ oz.) condensed cheddar cheese soup, undiluted**
- **1 pkg. (20 oz.) frozen crinkle-cut french fries**

1. Preheat oven to 350°. In a large skillet, cook beef over medium heat until no longer pink; drain. Stir in soups. Pour into a greased 13x9-in. baking dish.
2. Arrange the french fries on top. Bake, uncovered, for 50-55 minutes or until the fries are golden brown.
1½ CUPS: 352 cal., 17g fat (5g sat. fat), 62mg chol., 668mg sod., 25g carb. (1g sugars, 2g fiber), 25g pro.

CREAMY TURKEY CASSEROLE

This satisfying supper puts Thanksgiving leftovers to terrific use. I sometimes make turkey just so I'll have ingredients for the casserole!

—Mary Jo O'Brien, Hastings, MN

Prep: 15 min. • **Bake:** 40 min.
Makes: 12 servings

- **1 can (10¾ oz.) condensed cream of celery soup, undiluted**
- **1 can (10¾ oz.) condensed cream of mushroom soup, undiluted**
- **1 can (10¾ oz.) condensed cream of onion soup, undiluted**
- **5 oz. process cheese (Velveeta), cubed**
- **⅓ cup mayonnaise**
- **3½ to 4 cups shredded cooked turkey**
- **1 pkg. (16 oz.) frozen broccoli florets or cuts, thawed**
- **1½ cups cooked white rice**
- **1½ cups cooked wild rice**
- **1 can (8 oz.) sliced water chestnuts, drained**
- **1 jar (4 oz.) sliced mushrooms, drained**
- **1½ to 2 cups salad croutons**

1. Preheat oven to 350°. Combine undiluted soups, cheese and mayonnaise. Stir in the turkey, broccoli, rice, water chestnuts and mushrooms.

2. Transfer to a greased 13x9-in. baking dish. Bake, uncovered, for 30 minutes; stir. Sprinkle with salad croutons. Bake until bubbly, for 8-12 minutes longer.

¾ CUP: 311 cal., 14g fat (4g sat. fat), 52mg chol., 846mg sod., 25g carb. (3g sugars, 3g fiber), 20g pro.

READER REVIEW

"This is so yummy! I have made it several times, with great reviews each time. My mom has even asked for the recipe. It makes a lot, but freezes well. Perfect for a cold winter night."

KAREN421, TASTEOFHOME.COM

BAKED CHOPS & COTTAGE FRIES

Convenience items such as frozen vegetables and a jar of cheese sauce make it a snap to assemble this delectable pork chop supper. It's a simple one-dish meal.
—Gregg Voss, Emerson, NE

Prep: 20 min. • **Bake:** 55 min.
Makes: 6 servings

- **6 bone-in pork loin chops (1 in. thick and 7 oz. each)**
- **1 Tbsp. olive oil**
- **½ tsp. seasoned salt**
- **1 jar (8 oz.) process cheese sauce**
- **½ cup 2% milk**
- **4 cups frozen cottage (waffle) fries**
- **1 can (2.8 oz.) french-fried onions, divided**
- **4 cups frozen broccoli florets**

1. In a large skillet, brown pork chops in oil; sprinkle with seasoned salt. In a small bowl, combine cheese sauce and milk until blended.
2. Spread into a greased 13x9-in. baking dish. Top with cottage fries and half the onions. Layer with broccoli and pork chops.
3. Cover and bake at 350° for 45 minutes. Sprinkle with remaining onions. Bake until a thermometer reads 160°, 10 minutes longer.
1 SERVING: 533 cal., 28g fat (11g sat. fat), 116mg chol., 1208mg sod., 28g carb. (6g sugars, 3g fiber), 38g pro.

READER REVIEW

"This turned out really well—the flavors were good. I couldn't find cottage fries, so I used natural-cut potato fries instead. I'll definitely make it again."

COOKIESNOB, TASTEOFHOME.COM

SPICY CHICKEN & BACON MAC

I've been working to perfect a creamy, spicy mac and cheese for years. After adding smoky bacon, chicken, jalapenos and spicy cheese, this is the ultimate! I use rotisserie chicken and precooked bacon when I'm pressed for time.
—Sarah Gilbert, Aloha, OR

Takes: 30 min. • **Makes:** 6 servings

- **1½ cups uncooked cavatappi pasta or elbow macaroni**
- **3 Tbsp. butter**
- **3 Tbsp. all-purpose flour**
- **1½ cups heavy whipping cream**
- **½ cup 2% milk**
- **1 tsp. Cajun seasoning**
- **¼ tsp. salt**
- **¼ tsp. pepper**
- **2 cups shredded pepper jack cheese**
- **2 cups shredded cooked chicken**
- **6 bacon strips, cooked and crumbled**
- **1 jalapeno pepper, seeded and chopped**
- **1 cup crushed kettle-cooked potato chips or panko (Japanese) bread crumbs**

1. Cook the pasta according to package directions for al dente; drain. Preheat broiler.
2. In a 10-in. ovenproof skillet, heat butter over medium heat. Stir in the flour until blended; cook and stir until lightly browned, 1-2 minutes (do not burn). Gradually whisk in cream, milk, Cajun seasoning, salt and pepper. Bring to a boil, stirring constantly. Reduce heat; cook and stir until thickened, about 5 minutes. Stir in cheese until melted. Add the pasta, chicken, bacon and jalapeno; cook and stir until heated through. Sprinkle chips over top.
3. Broil 3-4 in. from heat until the chips are browned, about 30 seconds.
1 CUP: 673 cal., 50g fat (28g sat. fat), 175mg chol., 705mg sod., 26g carb. (3g sugars, 1g fiber), 32g pro.

GREEN BEAN CHICKEN CASSEROLE

My husband, who proclaims he's strictly a meat-and-potatoes man, asked for seconds the first time I threw together this homey all-in-one meal. My daughter and several guests raved about it, too.
—DeLissa Mingee, Warr Acres, OK

Prep: 15 min. • **Bake:** 25 min.
Makes: 2 casseroles (4 servings each)

- **1 pkg. (6 oz.) long grain and wild rice mix**
- **4 cups cubed cooked chicken**
- **1¾ cups frozen french-style green beans**
- **1 can (10¾ oz.) condensed cream of mushroom soup, undiluted**
- **1 can (10¾ oz.) condensed cream of broccoli soup, undiluted**
- **1 can (4 oz.) mushroom stems and pieces, drained**
- **⅔ cup chopped onion**
- **⅔ cup chopped green pepper**
- **1 envelope onion soup mix**
- **¾ cup shredded Colby cheese**
- **1⅓ cup french-fried onions**

Preheat oven to 350°. Prepare wild rice according to package directions. Stir in the chicken, beans, soups, mushrooms, onion, green pepper and soup mix. Spoon into two greased 1½-qt. baking dishes. Sprinkle with cheese. Cover and bake for 25-30 minutes or until heated through. Uncover and sprinkle each with half the French-fried onions; bake 5 minutes longer or until onions are golden.
FREEZE OPTION: Cover and freeze unbaked casseroles for up to 3 months. Completely thaw in the refrigerator. Remove from the refrigerator 30 minutes before baking. Cover and bake at 350° for 60-65 minutes or until heated through. Uncover and sprinkle with French-fried onions; bake 5 minutes longer.
1 CUP: 400 cal., 17g fat (6g sat. fat), 76mg chol., 1319mg sod., 34g carb. (4g sugars, 3g fiber), 27g pro.

CHICKEN TORTILLA BAKE

My mother often made this heartwarming casserole when I was growing up. Chicken, cheese and zippy green chiles are a classic combination.
—Jerri Moror, Rio Rancho, NM

Prep: 20 min. • **Bake:** 30 min.
Makes: 8 servings

- **3 cups shredded cooked chicken**
- **2 cans (4 oz. each) chopped green chiles**
- **1 cup chicken broth**
- **1 can (10¾ oz.) condensed cream of mushroom soup, undiluted**
- **1 can (10¾ oz.) condensed cream of chicken soup, undiluted**
- **1 small onion, finely chopped**
- **12 corn tortillas, warmed**
- **2 cups shredded cheddar cheese**

1. Preheat oven to 350°. In a large bowl, combine chicken, chiles, broth, soups and onion; set aside. Layer half the tortillas in a greased 13x9-in. baking dish, cutting to fit pan if desired. Top with half the chicken mixture and half the cheese. Repeat layers.
2. Bake, uncovered, for 30 minutes or until heated through.
FREEZE OPTION: Cover and freeze unbaked casserole. To use, partially thaw in refrigerator overnight. Remove from refrigerator about 30 minutes before baking. Preheat oven to 350°. Bake casserole as directed, increasing time as necessary to heat through and for a thermometer inserted in center to read 165°.
1 SERVING: 359 cal., 17g fat (8g sat. fat), 81mg chol., 1007mg sod., 26g carb. (2g sugars, 3g fiber), 25g pro.

FREEZE OPTION: Sprinkle cheese over cooled unbaked casserole. Cover and freeze. To use, partially thaw in refrigerator overnight. Remove from refrigerator 30 minutes before baking. Bake casserole as directed, increasing time as necessary to heat through and for a thermometer inserted in center to read 165°. If desired, serve with jalapeno slices.

1 SERVING: 390 cal., 15g fat (6g sat. fat), 81mg chol., 814mg sod., 29g carb. (3g sugars, 6g fiber), 32g pro.

PORK & GREEN CHILE CASSEROLE

Because I have two jobs—working at a local hospital and also part time for some area doctors—I'm always on the lookout for good quick recipes to fix for my family. Some of my co-workers and I often exchange recipes. This casserole was brought to a picnic at my house and has a delightful kick.

—Dianne Esposite, New Middletown, OH

Prep: 20 min. • **Bake:** 30 min.
Makes: 6 servings

- **1½ lbs. boneless pork, cut into ½-in. cubes**
- **1 Tbsp. canola oil**
- **1 can (15 oz.) black beans, rinsed and drained**
- **1 can (10¾ oz.) condensed cream of chicken soup, undiluted**
- **1 can (14½ oz.) diced tomatoes, undrained**
- **2 cans (4 oz. each) chopped green chiles**
- **1 cup quick-cooking brown rice**
- **¼ cup water**
- **2 to 3 Tbsp. salsa**
- **1 tsp. ground cumin**
- **½ cup shredded cheddar cheese**
- **Sliced jalapeno pepper, optional**

1. Preheat oven to 350°. In a large skillet, brown pork in oil; drain. Stir in the beans, soup, tomatoes, chiles, rice, water, salsa and cumin.

2. Pour into an ungreased 2-qt. baking dish. Bake, uncovered, 30 minutes or until bubbly. Sprinkle with cheese; let stand 5 minutes before serving. Top with jalapeno if desired.

TOMATO, SAUSAGE & CHEDDAR BREAD PUDDING

If you love bread pudding, this savory dish is the perfect way to have it as your entire meal, not just dessert!

—Holly Jones, Kennesaw, GA

Prep: 30 min. • **Bake:** 45 min.
Makes: 12 servings

- **3 cups shredded sharp cheddar cheese**
- **1 can (28 oz.) diced tomatoes, drained**
- **1 lb. bulk Italian sausage, cooked and crumbled**
- **4 green onions, thinly sliced**
- **¼ cup minced fresh basil or 1 Tbsp. dried basil**
- **¼ cup packed brown sugar**
- **1 tsp. dried oregano**
- **1 tsp. garlic powder**
- **3 cups cubed French bread**
- **6 large eggs**
- **1½ cups heavy whipping cream**
- **½ tsp. salt**
- **½ tsp. pepper**
- **½ cup grated Parmesan cheese**

1. Preheat oven to 350°. In a large bowl, combine the first eight ingredients. Stir in the bread. Transfer to a greased 13x9-in. baking dish.

2. In the same bowl, whisk eggs, cream, salt and pepper; pour over the bread mixture. Sprinkle with Parmesan cheese. Bake for 45-50 minutes or until a knife inserted in the center comes out clean.

1 SERVING: 430 cal., 32g fat (18g sat. fat), 206mg chol., 822mg sod., 16g carb. (8g sugars, 2g fiber), 19g pro.

Slow-Cooker Dinners

All hail the almighty slow cooker! Turn to these handy set-it-and-forget-it recipes that slowly simmer in the miracle of a machine that does (almost) all the work for you!

CHICKEN SOFT TACOS

My family loves these tacos. The chicken cooks in the slow-cooker, so it's convenient to throw together before I leave for work. At the end of the day, all I have to do is roll up the filling in tortillas with the remaining ingredients and dinner's ready in minutes. The chicken also makes a great topping for salad.
—Cheryl Newendorp, Pella, IA

Prep: 30 min. • **Cook:** 5 hours
Makes: 5 servings

- **1 broiler/fryer chicken (3½ lbs.), cut up and skin removed**
- **1 can (8 oz.) tomato sauce**
- **1 can (4 oz.) chopped green chiles**
- **⅓ cup chopped onion**
- **2 Tbsp. chili powder**
- **2 Tbsp. Worcestershire sauce**
- **¼ tsp. garlic powder**
- **10 flour tortillas (8 in.), warmed**
- **1¼ cups shredded cheddar cheese**
- **1¼ cups salsa**
- **1¼ cups shredded lettuce**
- **1 large tomato, chopped**
- **¾ cup sour cream, optional**

1. Place the chicken in a 4-qt. slow cooker. In a small bowl, combine the tomato sauce, chiles, onion, chili powder, Worcestershire sauce and garlic powder; pour over chicken. Cover and cook on low for 5-6 hours or until chicken is tender and juices run clear.
2. Remove the chicken. Shred meat with two forks and return to the slow cooker; heat through. Spoon ½ cup chicken mixture down the center of each tortilla. Top with cheese, salsa, lettuce, tomato and sour cream if desired; roll up.
2 TACOS: 749 cal., 29g fat (13g sat. fat), 157mg chol., 1454mg sod., 64g carb. (6g sugars, 5g fiber), 52g pro.

SLOW-COOKED TURKEY SANDWICHES

These sandwiches have been such a hit at office potlucks that I keep copies of the recipe in my desk to hand out.
—Diane Twait Nelsen, Ringsted, IA

Prep: 15 min. • **Cook:** 3 hours
Makes: 18 servings

- **6 cups cubed cooked turkey**
- **2 cups cubed process cheese (Velveeta)**
- **1 can (10¾ oz.) condensed cream of chicken soup, undiluted**
- **1 can (10¾ oz.) condensed cream of mushroom soup, undiluted**
- **½ cup finely chopped onion**
- **½ cup chopped celery**
- **18 wheat sandwich buns, split**

In a 4-qt. slow cooker, combine the first six ingredients. Cover and cook on low until vegetables are tender and cheese is melted, 3-4 hours. Stir mixture; spoon ½ cup onto each bun.

1 SANDWICH: 263 cal., 9g fat (3g sat. fat), 62mg chol., 680mg sod., 26g carb. (5g sugars, 4g fiber), 20g pro.

HUNGARIAN GOULASH

Here is an heirloom recipe that is very close to my heart. My grandmother made this for my mother when she was a child, and Mom made it for us to enjoy. Paprika and caraway add wonderful flavor and sour cream gives it a creamy richness.
—Marcia Doyle, Pompano, FL

Prep: 20 min. • **Cook:** 7 hours
Makes: 12 servings

- **3 medium onions, chopped**
- **2 medium carrots, chopped**
- **2 medium green peppers, chopped**
- **3 lbs. beef stew meat**
- **¾ tsp. salt, divided**
- **¾ tsp. pepper, divided**
- **2 Tbsp. olive oil**
- **1½ cups reduced-sodium beef broth**
- **¼ cup all-purpose flour**
- **3 Tbsp. paprika**
- **2 Tbsp. tomato paste**
- **1 tsp. caraway seeds**
- **1 garlic clove, minced**
- **Dash sugar**
- **12 cups uncooked whole wheat egg noodles**
- **1 cup reduced-fat sour cream**

1. Place onions, carrots and green peppers in a 5-qt. slow cooker. Sprinkle meat with ½ tsp. salt and ½ tsp. pepper. In a large skillet, brown meat in oil in batches. Transfer to slow cooker.
2. Add broth to skillet, stirring to loosen browned bits from pan. Combine the flour, paprika, tomato paste, caraway seeds, garlic, sugar and remaining salt and pepper; stir into the skillet. Bring to a boil; cook and stir for 2 minutes or until thickened. Pour over meat. Cover and cook on low for 7-9 hours or until meat is tender.
3. Cook noodles according to the package directions. Stir sour cream into slow cooker. Drain noodles; serve with goulash.

⅔ CUP GOULASH WITH 1 CUP NOODLES: 388 cal., 13g fat (4g sat. fat), 78mg chol., 285mg sod., 41g carb. (5g sugars, 7g fiber), 31g pro. **DIABETIC EXCHANGES:** 3 lean meat, 2 starch, 1 vegetable, 1 fat.

CREAMY BRATWURST STEW

I adapted a baked stew recipe from the newspaper to create a simple slow-cooked version. Rich, hearty and creamy, it is the best comfort food for cold winter nights.
—Susan Holmes, Germantown, WI

Prep: 20 min. • **Cook:** 6½ hours
Makes: 8 servings

- **1¾ lbs. potatoes (about 4 medium), peeled and cubed**
- **2 medium carrots, chopped**
- **2 celery ribs, chopped**
- **1 medium onion, chopped**
- **1 medium green pepper, chopped**
- **2 lbs. uncooked bratwurst links**
- **½ cup chicken broth**
- **1 tsp. salt**
- **1 tsp. dried basil**
- **½ tsp. pepper**
- **2 cups half-and-half cream**
- **1 Tbsp. cornstarch**
- **3 Tbsp. cold water**

1. Place first five ingredients in a 5-qt. slow cooker; toss to combine. Top with bratwurst. Mix broth and seasonings; pour over top.
2. Cook, covered, on low until sausage is cooked through and vegetables are tender, 6-7 hours. Remove sausages from slow cooker; cut into 1-in. slices. Add to potato mixture; stir in cream.
3. Mix cornstarch and water until smooth; stir into stew. Cook, covered, on high until thickened, about 30 minutes.

1 CUP: 544 cal., 39g fat (15g sat. fat), 114mg chol., 1367mg sod., 25g carb. (5g sugars, 2g fiber), 19g pro.

BLACK BEAN CHICKEN NACHOS

One of my favorite local restaurants, Zeppelins, has the best chicken nachos. Their dish inspired me to create my own homemade version but with the added convenience of using the slow cooker. I always use fresh cilantro because it's economical and makes the dish pop with flavor.
—Natalie Hess, Pennsville, NJ

Prep: 10 min. • **Cook:** 4 hours
Makes: 8 servings

- **1½ lbs. boneless skinless chicken breast**
- **2 jars (16 oz. each) black bean and corn salsa**
- **1 each medium green pepper and sweet red pepper, chopped**
- **Tortilla chips**
- **2 cups shredded Mexican cheese blend**
- **Fresh cilantro leaves**
- **Optional toppings: minced fresh cilantro, pickled jalapeno slices and sour cream**

1. Place chicken, salsa and peppers in a 3- or 4-qt. slow cooker. Cook, covered, on low until meat is tender, 4-5 hours.
2. Remove chicken; shred with two forks. Return to slow cooker. Using a slotted spoon, serve chicken over chips; sprinkle with cheese and cilantro. Add toppings of choice.

½ CUP CHICKEN MIXTURE: 280 cal., 11g fat (5g sat. fat), 72mg chol., 708mg sod., 20g carb. (5g sugars, 8g fiber), 27g pro.

TEST KITCHEN TIP
With its slightly sharp flavor, cilantro—also known as Chinese parsley—gives a distinctive taste to Mexican, Latin American and Asian dishes. (The spice coriander comes from the seed of the cilantro plant.) Like all other fresh herbs, cilantro should be used as soon as possible.

TARRAGON CHICKEN

I made this one night when I had friends coming over for dinner. Everyone loved the fresh taste from the vegetables and tarragon. Even my picky husband liked it. Serve it with crusty French bread to soak up the delicious sauce.
—Shanelle Lee, Ephrata, PA

Prep: 30 min. • **Cook:** 6 hours
Makes: 6 servings

- **1 lb. fresh baby carrots**
- **½ lb. medium fresh mushrooms, halved**
- **1 small onion, chopped**
- **6 bone-in chicken thighs (about 2¼ lbs.), skin removed**
- **1 cup chicken broth**
- **1 tsp. dried tarragon**
- **½ tsp. salt**
- **¼ tsp. pepper**
- **2 Tbsp. cornstarch**
- **½ cup heavy whipping cream**

1. In a 5-qt. slow cooker, combine carrots, mushrooms and onion. Top with chicken. In a small bowl, combine broth, tarragon, salt and pepper; pour over chicken. Cook, covered, on low until chicken is tender, 6-8 hours. Remove chicken; when cool enough to handle, shred with two forks. Transfer the chicken and vegetables to a serving platter; keep warm.
2. Pour juices into a small saucepan. Skim fat. In a small bowl, mix cornstarch with ½ cup cooking juices until smooth. Whisk into pan. Bring to a boil; cook and stir 1-2 minutes or until thickened. Add cream; heat through. Serve with chicken and vegetables.

1 CHICKEN THIGH WITH ⅓ CUP SAUCE: 309 cal., 17g fat (7g sat. fat), 110mg chol., 497mg sod., 12g carb. (5g sugars, 2g fiber), 26g pro.

BUTTERMILK-MUSHROOM PORK CHOPS

I went through several variations before creating these pork chops that my family considers perfect! I wanted something rich and delicious and still relatively good for you. Consider this meal for Sunday dinner—you can toss the ingredients in the slow cooker in the morning and let it cook while you attend church or do other activites.
—Kristin Stone, Little Elm, TX

Prep: 25 min. • **Cook:** 3½ hours
Makes: 6 servings

- ¼ **cup all-purpose flour**
- 1 **tsp. salt, divided**
- ½ **tsp. pepper**
- 6 **boneless pork loin chops (6 to 8 oz. each)**
- 2 **Tbsp. canola oil**
- 1 **Tbsp. butter**
- 1 **lb. medium fresh mushrooms, quartered**
- ½ **cup white wine or chicken broth**
- 1 **Tbsp. minced fresh basil**
- 1 **can (10¾ oz.) condensed cream of mushroom soup, undiluted**
- 1 **cup buttermilk**
- **Hot cooked egg noodles**
- **Additional basil**

1. In a shallow bowl, mix flour, ½ tsp. salt and pepper. Add pork chops, one at a time, and toss to coat; shake off excess.
2. In a large skillet, heat oil over medium-high heat; brown pork chops in batches. Transfer meat and drippings to a 4-qt. slow cooker.
3. In same skillet, heat butter over medium heat. Add mushrooms; cook and stir until tender, 6-8 minutes. Add wine, stirring to loosen browned bits from the pan. Pour the mushroom mixture over pork chops; sprinkle with basil.
4. Cook, covered, on low until meat is tender, 3-4 hours. Whisk together soup, buttermilk and remaining salt; pour over pork chops. Cook, covered, 30 minutes longer. Stir before serving. Serve with noodles; sprinkle with additional basil.
NOTE: Warmed buttermilk will appear curdled.
1 CHOP WITH ¾ CUP SAUCE: 376 cal., 19g fat (6g sat. fat), 91mg chol., 836mg sod., 11g carb. (2g sugars, 1g fiber), 37g pro.

5i

SLOW-COOKED HAM

Entertaining doesn't get much easier than serving this tasty five-ingredient ham from the slow cooker. Bonus: The leftovers are delicious in casseroles!
—Heather Spring, Sheppard Air Force Base, TX

Prep: 5 min. • **Cook:** 6 hours
Makes: 20 servings

- ½ **cup packed brown sugar**
- 1 **tsp. ground mustard**
- 1 **tsp. prepared horseradish**
- 2 **Tbsp. plus ¼ cup cola, divided**
- 1 **fully cooked boneless ham (5 to 6 lbs.), cut in half**

In a small bowl, combine the brown sugar, mustard, horseradish and 2 Tbsp. cola. Rub over ham. Transfer to a 5-qt. slow cooker; add remaining cola to slow cooker. Cover and cook on low for 6-8 hours or until a thermometer reads 140°.
3 OZ. COOKED HAM: 143 cal., 4g fat (1g sat. fat), 58mg chol., 1180mg sod., 6g carb. (6g sugars, 0 fiber), 21g pro.

READER REVIEW
"Absolutely fantastic! My family asks for this often and my kids point out when ham is on sale in the grocery store! I usually freeze the leftovers and use them in all my casserole/egg bake recipes."
DANA03, TASTEOFHOME.COM

SLOW-COOKED SWEET & SOUR PORK

Even though I've been making this sweet and sour pork for over 20 years, my family still enjoys it to this day. That's how you know a recipe is a keeper!
—Martha Nickerson, Hancock, ME

Prep: 20 min. • **Cook:** 6½ hours
Makes: 6 servings

- **2 Tbsp. plus 1½ tsp. paprika**
- **1½ lbs. boneless pork loin roast, cut into 1-in. strips**
- **1 Tbsp. canola oil**
- **1 can (20 oz.) unsweetened pineapple chunks**
- **1 medium onion, chopped**
- **1 medium green pepper, chopped**
- **¼ cup cider vinegar**
- **3 Tbsp. brown sugar**
- **3 Tbsp. reduced-sodium soy sauce**
- **1 Tbsp. Worcestershire sauce**
- **½ tsp. salt**
- **2 Tbsp. cornstarch**
- **¼ cup cold water**
- **Thinly sliced green onions, optional**
- **Hot cooked rice, optional**

1. Place paprika in a shallow bowl. Add pork, a few pieces at a time, and turn to coat. In a nonstick skillet, brown pork in oil in batches over medium-high heat. Transfer to a 3-qt. slow cooker.
2. Drain pineapple, reserving juice; refrigerate the pineapple. Add the pineapple juice, onion, green pepper, vinegar, brown sugar, soy sauce, Worcestershire sauce and salt to slow cooker. Cover and cook on low for 6-8 hours or until meat is tender.
3. Combine the cornstarch and water until smooth; stir into pork mixture. Add pineapple. Cover and cook 30 minutes longer or until sauce is thickened. If desired, sprinkle with green onions and serve over rice.
1 CUP: 312 cal., 10g fat (3g sat. fat), 73mg chol., 592mg sod., 28g carb. (21g sugars, 2g fiber), 278g pro. **DIABETIC EXCHANGES:** 3 lean meat, 1 fruit, ½ starch, ½ fat.

SLOW-COOKED TURKEY SLOPPY JOES

These tangy sandwiches go over well at gatherings large and small. I frequently take them to potlucks, and I'm always asked what my secret ingredient is.
—Marylou LaRue, Freeland, MI

Prep: 15 min. • **Cook:** 4 hours
Makes: 8 servings

- **1 lb. lean ground turkey**
- **1 small onion, chopped**
- **½ cup chopped celery**
- **¼ cup chopped green pepper**
- **1 can (10¾ oz.) reduced-sodium condensed tomato soup, undiluted**
- **½ cup ketchup**
- **2 Tbsp. prepared mustard**
- **1 Tbsp. brown sugar**
- **¼ tsp. pepper**
- **8 hamburger buns, split**

1. In a large skillet coated with cooking spray, cook the turkey, onion, celery and green pepper over medium heat until meat is no longer pink; drain. Stir in the soup, ketchup, mustard, brown sugar and pepper.
2. Transfer to a 3-qt. slow cooker. Cover and cook on low for 4 hours. Serve on buns.
1 SANDWICH: 247 cal., 7g fat (2g sat. fat), 45mg chol., 553mg sod., 32g carb. (0 sugars, 2g fiber), 14g pro. **DIABETIC EXCHANGES:** 2 starch, 1½ lean meat.

LOUISIANA RED BEANS & RICE

Smoked turkey sausage and red pepper flakes add zip to this slow-cooked version of the New Orleans classic. For extra heat, add a splash of red pepper sauce.

—Julia Bushree, Menifee, CA

Prep: 20 min. • **Cook:** 3 hours
Makes: 8 servings

- **4 cans (16 oz. each) kidney beans, rinsed and drained**
- **1 can (14½ oz.) diced tomatoes, undrained**
- **1 pkg. (14 oz.) smoked turkey sausage, sliced**
- **3 celery ribs, chopped**
- **1 large onion, chopped**
- **1 cup chicken broth**
- **1 medium green pepper, chopped**
- **1 small sweet red pepper, chopped**
- **6 garlic cloves, minced**
- **1 bay leaf**
- **½ tsp. crushed red pepper flakes**
- **2 green onions, chopped**
- **Hot cooked rice**

1. In a 4- or 5-qt. slow cooker, combine the first 11 ingredients. Cook, covered, on low until vegetables are tender, 3-4 hours.

2. Stir before serving. Remove bay leaf. Serve with green onions and rice.

FREEZE OPTION: Discard bay leaf and freeze cooled bean mixture in freezer containers. To use, partially thaw in refrigerator overnight. Heat through in a saucepan; stir occasionally, adding a little broth or water if necessary. Serve as directed.

1 CUP: 291 cal., 3g fat (1g sat. fat), 32mg chol., 1070mg sod., 44g carb. (8g sugars, 13g fiber), 24g pro.

SLOW-COOKER BEEF STROGANOFF

No more standing and stirring at the stove. This creamy Stroganoff preps in a skillet, then cooks all day while you're away.

—Sarah Vasques, Milford, NH

Prep: 20 min. • **Cook:** 4 hours
Makes: 7 servings

- **2 lbs. beef top sirloin steak, cut into thin strips**
- **3 Tbsp. olive oil**
- **1 cup water**
- **1 envelope (1½ oz.) beef Stroganoff seasoning for the slow cooker**
- **1 lb. sliced baby portobello mushrooms**
- **1 small onion, chopped**
- **3 Tbsp. butter**
- **¼ cup port wine or beef broth**
- **2 tsp. ground mustard**
- **1 tsp. sugar**
- **1½ cups sour cream**
- **Hot cooked egg noodles**
- **Minced fresh parsley, optional**

1. In a large skillet, brown meat in oil. Add water and seasoning mix, stirring to loosen browned bits from pan. Transfer meat and drippings to a 3-qt. slow cooker.

2. In the same skillet, saute the mushrooms and onion in butter until tender. Combine the wine, mustard and sugar; stir into the mushroom mixture. Add to slow cooker; stir to combine.

3. Cover and cook on low for 3-4 hours or until meat is tender. Stir in sour cream. Serve with noodles. Sprinkle with parsley if desired.

1 CUP: 418 cal., 25g fat (12g sat. fat), 100mg chol., 812mg sod., 10g carb. (4g sugars, 1g fiber), 32g pro.

SARAH VASQUES
Milford, NH

SLOW-COOKED MEATBALL STEW

I came up with this meal as another way to use frozen meatballs. It's quick to put together in the morning and ready when my husband gets home in the evening.

—Iris Schultz, Miamisburg, OH

Prep: 20 min. • **Cook:** 9 hours
Makes: 6 servings

- **3 medium potatoes, peeled and cut into ½-in. cubes**
- **1 lb. fresh baby carrots, quartered**
- **1 large onion, chopped**
- **3 celery ribs, sliced**
- **1 pkg. (12 oz.) frozen fully cooked home-style meatballs**
- **1 can (10¾ oz.) condensed tomato soup, undiluted**
- **1 can (10½ oz.) beef gravy**
- **1 cup water**
- **1 envelope onion soup mix**
- **2 tsp. beef bouillon granules**

1. Place the potatoes, carrots, onion, celery and meatballs in a 5-qt. slow cooker. Combine the remaining ingredients; pour over meatball mixture.

2. Cover and cook on low for 9-10 hours or until vegetables are crisp-tender.

1 CUP: 291 cal., 8g fat (3g sat. fat), 51mg chol., 1400mg sod., 41g carb. (12g sugars, 4g fiber), 14g pro.

BEEF BURGUNDY WITH NOODLES

Here's a classic recipe that's more than just stew served over noodles. To keep things easy I trim the meat and cut up the vegetables the night before I plan to serve. The next day, I toss all the ingredients into the slow cooker. Shortly before dinnertime, I cook the noodles and bake some cheesy garlic toast to complete the meal.
—Mary Jo Miller, Mansfield, OH

Prep: 10 min. • **Cook:** 5 hours
Makes: 6 servings

- **1½ lbs. beef stew meat, cut into 1-in. cubes**
- **½ lb. whole fresh mushrooms, halved**
- **4 medium carrots, chopped**
- **1 can (10¾ oz.) condensed golden mushroom soup, undiluted**
- **1 large onion, cut into thin wedges**
- **½ cup Burgundy wine or beef broth**
- **¼ cup quick-cooking tapioca**
- **½ tsp. salt**
- **¼ tsp. dried thyme**
- **¼ tsp. pepper**
- **Hot cooked egg noodles**

1. In a 5-qt. slow cooker, combine the first 10 ingredients.
2. Cover and cook on low for 5-6 hours or until meat is tender. Serve with noodles.
1 CUP: 273 cal., 9g fat (3g sat. fat), 73mg chol., 642mg sod., 19g carb. (5g sugars, 3g fiber), 24g pro.

DID YOU KNOW?
The secret to making this classic dish outstanding is to use both good-quality meat and red wine. Select a drinkable wine and not one labeled for cooking.

BAYOU GULF SHRIMP GUMBO

This recipe skips the traditional hard-to-find spices and still delivers the true seafood flavor beloved in the Louisiana bayou and beyond.
—Wolfgang Hanau, West Palm Beach, FL

Prep: 35 min. • **Cook:** 5 hours
Makes: 6 servings

- **½ lb. bacon strips, chopped**
- **3 celery ribs, chopped**
- **1 medium onion, chopped**
- **1 medium green pepper, chopped**
- **2 garlic cloves, minced**
- **2 bottles (8 oz. each) clam juice**
- **1 can (14½ oz.) diced tomatoes, undrained**
- **2 Tbsp. Worcestershire sauce**
- **1 tsp. dried marjoram**
- **2 lbs. uncooked large shrimp, peeled and deveined**
- **2½ cups frozen sliced okra, thawed**
- **Hot cooked brown rice, optional**

1. In a large skillet, cook bacon over medium heat until crisp. Remove to paper towels with a slotted spoon; drain, reserving 2 Tbsp. drippings. Saute the celery, onion, green pepper and garlic in drippings until tender.
2. Transfer to a 4-qt. slow cooker. Stir in the bacon, clam juice, tomatoes, Worcestershire sauce and marjoram. Cover and cook on low for 4 hours.
3. Stir in shrimp and okra. Cover and cook 1 hour longer or until shrimp turn pink and okra is heated through. Serve with rice if desired.
1½ CUPS: 285 cal., 12g fat (4g sat. fat), 204mg chol., 1074mg sod., 13g carb. (6g sugars, 3g fiber), 32g pro.

HONEY PULLED PORK SUBS

Honey and ground ginger are the flavor boosters behind my no-stress sandwiches. A bottle of your favorite barbecue sauce quickly ties it all together.
—Denise Davis, Porter, ME

Prep: 15 min. • **Cook:** 5 hours
Makes: 16 servings

- **1 small onion, finely chopped**
- **1 boneless pork shoulder butt roast (2½ lbs.)**
- **1 bottle (18 oz.) barbecue sauce**
- **½ cup water**
- **¼ cup honey**
- **6 garlic cloves, minced**
- **1 tsp. seasoned salt**
- **1 tsp. ground ginger**
- **8 submarine buns, split**

1. Place onion and roast in a 5-qt. slow cooker. In a small bowl, combine the barbecue sauce, water, honey, garlic, seasoned salt and ginger; pour over meat. Cover and cook on high for 5-6 hours or until meat is tender.
2. Remove meat; cool slightly. Shred meat with two forks and return to the slow cooker; heat through. Serve on buns. Cut sandwiches in half.

FREEZE OPTION: Place individual portions of cooled meat mixture in freezer containers. To use, partially thaw in refrigerator overnight. Microwave, covered, on high in a microwave-safe dish until heated through, gently stirring and adding a little water if necessary. Serve on a bun.
½ SANDWICH: 417 cal., 13g fat (4g sat. fat), 81mg chol., 867mg sod., 44g carb. (12g sugars, 2g fiber), 29g pro.

SLOW-COOKER BBQ CHICKEN

Of all the recipes I make in my slow cooker, this one is my favorite. If you like your barbecue sweet with a little kick of spice, this will be your new go-to as well.
—Yvonne McKim, Vancouver, WA

Prep: 15 min. • **Cook:** 5 hours
Makes: 12 servings

- **6 chicken leg quarters, skin removed**
- **¾ cup ketchup**
- **½ cup orange juice**
- **¼ cup packed brown sugar**
- **¼ cup red wine vinegar**
- **¼ cup olive oil**
- **4 tsp. minced fresh parsley**
- **2 tsp. Worcestershire sauce**
- **1 tsp. garlic salt**
- **½ tsp. pepper**
- **2 Tbsp. plus 2 tsp. cornstarch**
- **¼ cup water**

1. Using a sharp knife, cut through the joint of each leg quarter to separate into two pieces. Place chicken in a 4-qt. slow cooker.
2. In a small bowl, mix the ketchup, orange juice, brown sugar, vinegar, olive oil, parsley, Worcestershire sauce, garlic salt and pepper; pour over chicken. Cook, covered, on low until meat is tender, 5-6 hours.
3. Remove chicken to a serving platter; keep warm. Skim the fat from cooking juices; pour into a measuring cup to measure 2 cups. Transfer to a small saucepan; bring to a boil. In a small bowl, mix cornstarch and water until smooth; stir into cooking juices. Return to a boil, stirring constantly; cook and stir until thickened, 1-2 minutes. Serve with chicken.
1 SERVING: 179 cal., 9g fat (2g sat. fat), 45mg chol., 392mg sod., 12g carb. (9g sugars, 0 fiber), 13g pro. **DIABETIC EXCHANGES:** 2 lean meat, 1 starch, 1 fat.

SLOW-COOKER TATER TOT CASSEROLE

What's not to love about classic Tater Tot casserole—especially when it's made in the slow cooker? I guarantee you will want to add this family-pleasing potluck favorite to your regular rotation.
—Nick Iverson, Denver, CO

Prep: 25 min. • **Cook:** 6 hours + standing
Makes: 12 servings

- **2 lbs. ground beef**
- **1 large onion, chopped**
- **1 lb. sliced fresh mushrooms**
- **3 garlic cloves, minced**
- **2 cans (10¾ oz. each) condensed cream of mushroom soup, undiluted**
- **½ tsp. salt**
- **½ tsp. pepper**
- **1 lb. frozen cut green beans**
- **1 bag (32 oz.) frozen Tater Tots**
- **1 cup shredded cheddar cheese**

1. In a large skillet cook beef over medium-high heat until no longer pink, breaking into crumbles, 5-6 minutes; drain and transfer to a 5-qt. slow cooker. Add onions and mushrooms to skillet; cook over medium-high heat until vegetables are tender, 8-10 minutes. Add garlic; cook 1 minute more. Stir in condensed soup, salt and pepper. Place meat mixture in slow cooker; add green beans and stir to combine. Top with Tater Tots and cheese.
2. Cook, covered, on low 6-8 hours. Let stand, uncovered, 15 minutes before serving.
1 SERVING: 383 cal., 22g fat (7g sat. fat), 58mg chol., 941mg sod., 27g carb. (3g sugars, 4g fiber), 20g pro.

TEST KITCHEN TIP
For more color, use frozen mixed vegetables in place of green beans in this family-friendly dish.

GREEN CHILE RIBS

I like my food with a spicy kick; my wife does not. These ribs with green chiles suit her taste. For more heat, add cayenne or jalapenos.
—Guy Newton, Nederland, CO

Prep: 20 min. • **Cook:** 5 hours
Makes: 8 servings

- **4 lbs. pork baby back ribs**
- **2 Tbsp. ground cumin, divided**
- **2 Tbsp. olive oil**
- **1 small onion, finely chopped**
- **1 jar (16 oz.) salsa verde**
- **3 cans (4 oz. each) chopped green chiles**
- **2 cups beef broth**
- **¼ cup minced fresh cilantro**
- **1 Tbsp. all-purpose flour**
- **3 garlic cloves, minced**
- **¼ tsp. cayenne pepper**
- **Additional minced fresh cilantro**

1. Cut ribs into serving-size pieces; rub with 1 Tbsp. cumin. In a large skillet, heat oil over medium-high heat. Brown ribs in batches. Place ribs in a 6-qt. slow cooker.

2. Add onion to same pan; cook and stir 2-3 minutes or until onion is tender. Add the salsa verde, green chiles, broth, ¼ cup cilantro, flour, garlic, cayenne and remaining cumin to slow cooker. Cook, covered, on low 5-6 hours or until meat is tender. Sprinkle with additional cilantro.

1 SERVING: 349 cal., 25g fat (8g sat. fat), 81mg chol., 797mg sod., 8g carb. (2g sugars, 1g fiber), 24g pro.

PORK TACOS WITH MANGO SALSA

I'e made quite a few tacos in my day, and these are my all-time favorite. Nothing beats the tender filling made in a slow cooker. Make the mango salsa from scratch if you have time. It's worth it!
—Amber Massey, Argyle, TX

Prep: 25 min. • **Cook:** 6 hours
Makes: 12 servings

- **2 Tbsp. lime juice**
- **2 Tbsp. white vinegar**
- **3 Tbsp. chili powder**
- **2 tsp. ground cumin**
- **1½ tsp. salt**
- **½ tsp. pepper**
- **3 cups cubed fresh pineapple**
- **1 small red onion, coarsely chopped**
- **2 chipotle peppers in adobo sauce**
- **1 bottle (12 oz.) dark Mexican beer**
- **3 lbs. pork tenderloin, cut into 1-in. cubes**
- **¼ cup chopped fresh cilantro**
- **1 jar (16 oz.) mango salsa**
- **24 corn tortillas (6 in.), warmed**

OPTIONAL TOPPINGS
- **Cubed fresh pineapple**
- **Cubed avocado**
- **Queso fresco**

1. Puree first nine ingredients in a blender; stir in beer. In a 5- or 6-qt. slow cooker, combine pork and pineapple mixture. Cook, covered, on low until pork is very tender, 6-8 hours. Stir to break up pork.

2. Stir cilantro into salsa. Using a slotted spoon, serve pork mixture in tortillas; add salsa and toppings as desired.

FREEZE OPTION: Freeze cooled meat mixture and cooking juices in freezer containers. To use, partially thaw taco filling in refrigerator overnight. Heat through in a saucepan, stirring occasionally.

2 TACOS: 282 cal., 6g fat (2g sat. fat), 64mg chol., 678mg sod., 31g carb. (5g sugars, 5g fiber), 26g pro. **DIABETIC EXCHANGES:** 3 lean meat, 2 starch.

CAJUN-STYLE BEANS & SAUSAGE

Beans and rice make the perfect meal because they're well-balanced, an excellent source of protein, and easy to prepare. The sausage adds full flavor to the recipe, and traditional pork sausage lovers won't even notice that chicken sausage is used in this dish.
—Robin Haas, Cranston, RI

Prep: 25 min. • **Cook:** 6 hours
Makes: 8 servings

- **1 pkg. (12 oz.) fully cooked spicy chicken sausage links, halved lengthwise and cut into ½-in. slices**
- **2 cans (16 oz. each) red beans, rinsed and drained**
- **2 cans (14½ oz. each) diced tomatoes, undrained**
- **3 medium carrots, chopped**
- **1 large onion, chopped**
- **1 large green pepper, chopped**
- **½ cup chopped roasted sweet red peppers**
- **3 garlic cloves, minced**
- **1 tsp. Cajun seasoning**
- **1 tsp. dried oregano**
- **½ tsp. dried thyme**
- **½ tsp. pepper**
- **5⅓ cups cooked brown rice**

1. In a large skillet coated with cooking spray, brown sausage. Transfer to a 5-qt. slow cooker. Stir in beans, tomatoes, vegetables, garlic and seasonings.
2. Cook, covered, on low 6-8 hours or until vegetables are tender. Serve with rice.
1 CUP SAUSAGE AND BEAN MIXTURE WITH ⅔ CUP RICE: 355 cal., 5g fat (1g sat. fat), 33mg chol., 759mg sod., 58g carb. (7g sugars, 11g fiber), 18g pro.

EASY & ELEGANT HAM

I love to serve my large family this moist, tender ham. It can be readied quickly in the morning, frees up my oven, tastes outstanding, and will feed a big crowd. Pineapple, cherries and an orange glaze make it a real showstopper.
—Denise DiPace, Medford, NJ

Prep: 5 min. • **Cook:** 6 hours
Makes: 20 servings

- **2 cans (20 oz. each) sliced pineapple**
- **1 fully cooked boneless ham (about 6 lbs.), cut in half**
- **1 jar (6 oz.) maraschino cherries, well drained**
- **1 jar (12 oz.) orange marmalade**

1. Drain pineapple, reserving juice; set juice aside. Place half the pineapple in an ungreased 6-qt. slow cooker. Top with the ham pieces. Add the cherries, remaining pineapple and reserved pineapple juice. Spoon marmalade over ham. Cover and cook on low until heated through, 6-7 hours.
2. Remove to a warm serving platter. Serve pineapple and cherries with sliced ham.
5 OZ.: 212 cal., 5g fat (2g sat. fat), 69mg chol., 1424mg sod., 18g carb. (18g sugars, 0 fiber), 25g pro.

AUTUMN PUMPKIN CHILI

We have this chili often because everyone loves it, even the most finicky grandchildren. The pumpkin adds wonderful creamy texture. It's a keeper in my book!
—Kimberly Nagy, Port Hadlock, WA

Prep: 20 min. • **Cook:** 7 hours
Makes: 4 servings

- 1 **medium onion, chopped**
- 1 **small green pepper, chopped**
- 1 **small sweet yellow pepper, chopped**
- 1 **Tbsp. canola oil**
- 1 **garlic clove, minced**
- 1 **lb. ground turkey**
- 1 **can (15 oz.) solid-pack pumpkin**
- 1 **can (14½ oz.) diced tomatoes, undrained**
- 4½ **tsp. chili powder**
- ¼ **tsp. pepper**
- ¼ **tsp. salt**
- **Optional toppings: shredded cheddar cheese, sour cream and sliced green onions**

1. Saute the onion and green and yellow peppers in oil in a large skillet until tender. Add garlic; cook 1 minute longer. Crumble turkey into skillet. Cook over medium heat until meat is no longer pink.
2. Transfer to a 3-qt. slow cooker. Stir in the pumpkin, tomatoes, chili powder, pepper and salt. Cover and cook on low for 7-9 hours. Serve with toppings of your choice.
1¼ CUPS: 281 cal., 13g fat (3g sat. fat), 75mg chol., 468mg sod., 20g carb. (9g sugars, 7g fiber), 25g pro. **DIABETIC EXCHANGES:** 3 lean meat, 1 starch, 1 vegetable, 1 fat.

BEEF & RICE STUFFED CABBAGE ROLLS

This recipe is special to me because it's an easy one-pot meal that tastes like you spent the whole day in the kitchen. My family loves it.
—Lynn Bowen, Geraldine, AL

Prep: 20 min. • **Cook:** 6 hours
Makes: 6 servings

- 12 **cabbage leaves**
- 1 **cup cooked brown rice**
- ¼ **cup finely chopped onion**
- 1 **large egg, lightly beaten**
- ¼ **cup fat-free milk**
- ½ **tsp. salt**
- ¼ **tsp. pepper**
- 1 **lb. lean ground beef (90% lean)**

SAUCE

- 1 **can (8 oz.) tomato sauce**
- 1 **Tbsp. brown sugar**
- 1 **Tbsp. lemon juice**
- 1 **tsp. Worcestershire sauce**

1. In batches, cook cabbage in boiling water 3-5 minutes or until crisp-tender. Drain; cool slightly. Trim the thick vein from the bottom of each cabbage leaf, making a V-shaped cut.
2. In a large bowl, combine rice, onion, egg, milk, salt and pepper. Add beef; mix lightly but thoroughly. Place about ¼ cup beef mixture on each cabbage leaf. Pull together cut edges of leaf to overlap; fold over filling. Fold in sides and roll up.
3. Place six rolls in a 4- or 5-qt. slow cooker, seam side down. In a bowl, mix sauce ingredients; pour half of the sauce over cabbage rolls. Top with remaining rolls and sauce. Cook, covered, on low 6-8 hours or until a thermometer inserted in beef reads 160° and cabbage is tender.
2 CABBAGE ROLLS: 204 cal., 7g fat (3g sat. fat), 83mg chol., 446mg sod., 16g carb. (5g sugars, 2g fiber), 18g pro. **DIABETIC EXCHANGES:** 2 lean meat, 1 starch.

ASIAN BBQ PORK BUNS

Here's a quick way to get a delicious and comforting dinner on the table. Sometimes I add a little reduced-sodium soy sauce to the barbecue sauce. If your family loves Asian food like mine does, they will fall for these pork buns.
—*Teresa Ralston, New Albany, OH*

Prep: 25 min. • **Cook:** 6 hours
Makes: 8 servings

- **1 boneless pork shoulder butt roast (3 lbs.)**
- **1¾ tsp. salt, divided**
- **1¼ tsp. coarsely ground pepper, divided**
- **1 Tbsp. canola oil**
- **½ cup water**
- **1 bottle (12 oz.) regular chili sauce (such as Heinz)**
- **½ cup hoisin sauce**
- **3 Tbsp. rice vinegar**
- **1 Tbsp. minced fresh gingerroot**
- **4 cups coleslaw mix**
- **¼ cup Asian toasted sesame salad dressing**
- **8 split sesame seed hamburger buns, toasted**

1. Sprinkle pork roast with 1½ tsp. salt and 1 tsp. pepper. In a large skillet, heat oil over medium-high heat. Add pork; brown on all sides. Transfer pork and drippings to a greased 4-qt. slow cooker. Add water; cook, covered, on low until pork is tender, 5-6 hours. Remove pork; discard cooking juices.

2. When pork is cool enough to handle, shred meat with two forks. Return to slow cooker. Stir together chili sauce, hoisin sauce, vinegar and ginger. Pour over pork; toss to coat. Cook until heated through, about 1 hour.

3. Meanwhile, toss the coleslaw mix with the dressing and remaining salt and pepper. Serve the shredded pork topped with coleslaw on toasted buns.

1 SANDWICH: 533 cal., 24g fat (8g sat. fat), 102mg chol., 1,862mg sod., 45g carb. (20g sugars, 2g fiber), 35g pro.

TERESA RALSTON
New Albany, OH

SLOW-COOKED PORK TACOS

This wonderful taco filling also is great wrapped in Bibb lettuce leaves instead of tortillas. Use any leftovers to make burritos the next day.
—Kathleen Wolf, Naperville, IL

Prep: 20 min. • **Cook:** 4 hours
Makes: 10 servings

- **2 lbs. boneless pork sirloin chops, cut into 2-in. pieces**
- **1½ cups salsa verde**
- **1 medium sweet red pepper, chopped**
- **1 medium onion, chopped**
- **¼ cup chopped dried apricots**
- **2 Tbsp. lime juice**
- **2 garlic cloves, minced**
- **1 tsp. ground cumin**
- **½ tsp. salt**
- **¼ tsp. white pepper**
- **Dash hot pepper sauce**
- **10 flour tortillas (8 in.), warmed**
- **Optional toppings: chopped tomatoes, cubed avocado, reduced-fat sour cream, shredded reduced-fat cheddar cheese and sliced green onions**

1. In a 3-qt. slow cooker, combine all the ingredients except tortillas and toppings. Cook, covered, on high until meat is tender, 4-5 hours.
2. Shred pork with two forks. Serve in tortillas; top as desired.
1 TACO: 310 cal., 9g fat (3g sat. fat), 55mg chol., 596mg sod., 34g carb. (4g sugars, 2g fiber), 23g pro. **DIABETIC EXCHANGES:** 3 lean meat, 2 starch.

READER REVIEW

"Delicious recipe! Not too spicy and the apricots gave it a sweet flavor that was fantastic. This is going onto our menu rotation."

RAINDROP74, TASTEOFHOME.COM

CHICKEN STEW WITH GNOCCHI

My chicken stew fills the house with an amazing aroma as it gently bubbles in the slow cooker. One whiff and my family heads to the kitchen to see if it's ready.
—Marge Drake, Juniata, NE

Prep: 25 min. • **Cook:** 6½ hours
Makes: 8 servings (3 qt.)

- **3 medium parsnips, peeled and cut into ½-in. pieces**
- **2 large carrots, cut into ½-in. slices**
- **2 celery ribs, chopped**
- **1 large sweet potato, peeled and cut into 1-in. cubes**
- **4 green onions, chopped**
- **3 lbs. bone-in chicken thighs, skin removed**
- **½ tsp. dried sage leaves**
- **¼ tsp. salt**
- **¼ tsp. pepper**
- **4 cups chicken broth**
- **1 cup water**
- **3 Tbsp. cornstarch**
- **¼ cup cold water**
- **1 pkg. (16 oz.) potato gnocchi**
- **Hot pepper sauce and thinly sliced green onions, optional**

1. Place the parsnips, carrots, celery, sweet potato and onions in a 5-qt. slow cooker. Top with chicken; sprinkle with the sage, salt and pepper. Add broth and water. Cover and cook on low for 6-8 hours or until chicken is tender.
2. Remove chicken; when cool enough to handle, remove meat from bones and discard bones. Cut meat into bite-size pieces and return to the slow cooker.
3. Mix the cornstarch and cold water until smooth; stir into stew. Add gnocchi. Cover and cook on high for 30 minutes or until thickened. If desired, season with hot pepper sauce, and sprinkle with sliced green onion.
1½ CUPS: 405 cal., 11g fat (3g sat. fat), 92mg chol., 922mg sod., 46g carb. (10g sugars, 5g fiber), 29g pro.

GROUND BEEF SPINACH ALFREDO LASAGNA

With ground beef, spinach, two types of sauce and three kinds of cheese, this lasagna goes beyond the expected. When serving, be sure to scoop all the way down to the bottom of the slow cooker so you get a good sampling of all the layers.
—Deborah Bruno, Mira Loma, CA

Prep: 20 min. • **Cook:** 4 hours
Makes: 8 servings

- 1 **lb. ground beef**
- 1 **medium onion, chopped**
- 2 **garlic cloves, minced**
- 1 **jar (24 oz.) spaghetti sauce**
- 1 **carton (15 oz.) ricotta cheese**
- ½ **cup grated Parmesan cheese**
- 2 **Tbsp. minced fresh parsley**
- ½ **tsp. pepper**
- 1 **pkg. (8 oz.) no-cook lasagna noodles**
- 8 **cups shredded part-skim mozzarella cheese**
- 1 **pkg. (10 oz.) frozen chopped spinach, thawed and squeezed dry**
- 1 **jar (15 oz.) Alfredo sauce**

1. In a large skillet, cook beef, onion and garlic over medium heat 6-8 minutes or until the beef is no longer pink, breaking up beef into crumbles; drain. Stir in spaghetti sauce.
2. In a small bowl, mix the ricotta cheese, Parmesan cheese, parsley and pepper. Spread 1 cup meat mixture onto the bottom of an ungreased 5- or 6-qt. slow cooker. Arrange four noodles over sauce, breaking noodles to fit if necessary; layer with half of the ricotta mixture, 2 cups mozzarella cheese and 1 cup meat mixture.
3. Top with four noodles, spinach, Alfredo sauce and 2 cups of the mozzarella cheese. Continue layering with four noodles, the remaining ricotta mixture, 2 cups mozzarella cheese and 1 cup meat mixture. Add any remaining noodles; top with remaining meat mixture and mozzarella cheese.
4. Cook, covered, on low 4-5 hours or until noodles are tender.

1 PIECE: 757 cal., 40g fat (23g sat. fat), 143mg chol., 1362mg sod., 43g carb. (13g sugars, 4g fiber), 55g pro.

MELT-IN-YOUR-MOUTH SAUSAGES

My family loves this recipe. It's such a good all-around dish, either for sandwiches like these or served over hot cooked spaghetti.
—Ilean Schultheiss, Cohocton, NY

Prep: 10 min. • **Cook:** 4 hours
Makes: 8 servings

- **8 Italian sausage links (2 lbs.)**
- **1 jar (26 oz.) meatless spaghetti sauce**
- **½ cup water**
- **1 can (6 oz.) tomato paste**
- **1 large green pepper, thinly sliced**
- **1 large onion, thinly sliced**
- **1 Tbsp. grated Parmesan cheese**
- **1 tsp. dried parsley flakes**
- **8 brat buns, split**
- **Additional Parmesan cheese, optional**

1. Place sausages in a large skillet; cover with water. Bring to a boil. Reduce heat; cover and simmer for 10 minutes or until a thermometer reads 160°; drain well.
2. Meanwhile, in a 3-qt. slow cooker, combine the spaghetti sauce, water, tomato paste, green pepper, onion, cheese and parsley. Add sausages. Cover and cook on low until vegetables are tender, 4-5 hours. Serve in buns. Sprinkle sandwiches with additional cheese if desired.

1 SANDWICH: 557 cal., 29g fat (9g sat. fat), 62mg chol., 1510mg sod., 51g carb. (14g sugars, 4g fiber), 24g pro.

SLOW-COOKED SUNDAY CHICKEN

Here's a hearty dish for two that satisfies the biggest appetites. It's loaded with homey, old-fashioned flavor.
—Ruthann Martin, Louisville, OH

Prep: 15 min. • **Cook:** 6 hours
Makes: 2 servings

- **2 small carrots, cut into 2-in. pieces**
- **½ medium onion, chopped**
- **½ celery rib, cut into 2-in. pieces**
- **1 cup cut fresh green beans (2-in. pieces)**
- **2 small red potatoes, halved**
- **2 bone-in chicken breast halves (7 oz. each), skin removed**
- **2 bacon strips, cooked and crumbled**
- **¾ cup hot water**
- **1 tsp. chicken bouillon granules**
- **¼ tsp. salt**
- **¼ tsp. dried thyme**
- **¼ tsp. dried basil**
- **Pinch pepper**

1. In a 3-qt. slow cooker, layer the first seven ingredients in the order listed. Combine the water, bouillon, salt, thyme, basil and pepper; pour over the top. Do not stir.
2. Cover and cook on low until vegetables are tender and a thermometer inserted in chicken reads 170°, 6-8 hours. Remove chicken and vegetables. Thicken cooking juices for gravy if desired.

1 SERVING: 304 cal., 7g fat (2g sat. fat), 94mg chol., 927mg sod., 21g carb. (8g sugars, 5g fiber), 37g pro.

TEST KITCHEN TIP

The Department of Agriculture recommends that you don't wash or rinse chicken before cooking. If you do, bacteria can spread to kitchen surfaces and utensils and contaminate other foods.

Breads, Rolls & Muffins

Is there anything better than smelling freshly baked bread? Sure there is—eating it! These homemade delights run the gamut from breakfast to dinner, with lots of delicious stops on the way.

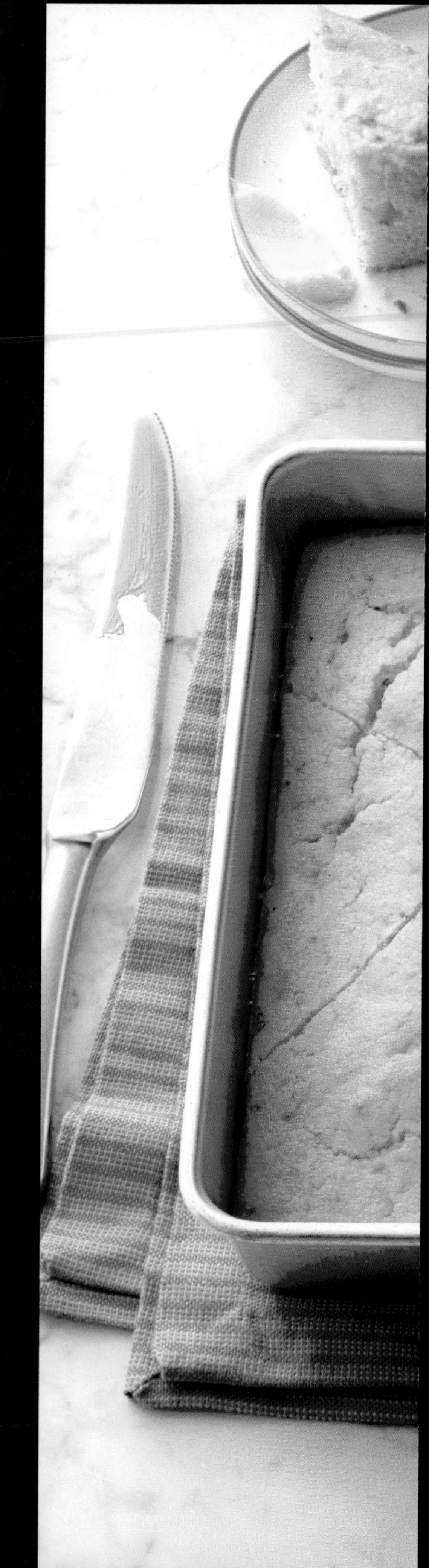

APPALACHIAN CORNBREAD

On this westernmost Appalachian ridge, we get abundant rain and sunshine, which means a super sweet corn crop. With staggered plantings, there is enough to eat from mid-July through August, plus plenty to freeze for the long winter. This cornbread is just one way we use the bounty!
—Anne Wiehler, Farmington, PA

Prep: 15 min. • **Bake:** 20 min.
Makes: 9 servings

- 2 **Tbsp. chopped onion**
- 4 **Tbsp. canola oil, divided**
- 1 **cup all-purpose flour**
- 1 **cup cornmeal**
- 2 **Tbsp. sugar**
- 4 **tsp. baking powder**
- ½ **tsp. salt**
- 2 **large eggs, room temperature**
- 1 **cup whole milk**
- ½ **cup fresh or frozen corn, thawed**
- ⅓ **cup shredded cheddar cheese**
- ¼ **cup salsa**
- 2 **Tbsp. minced chives**

1. Preheat oven to 425°. Grease a 9-in. square baking pan; set aside. In a small saucepan, saute onion in 1 Tbsp. oil until tender.
2. In a large bowl, combine flour, cornmeal, sugar, baking powder and salt. In another bowl, whisk eggs, milk and the remaining oil. Stir in the corn, cheese, salsa, chives and reserved onion. Stir into the dry ingredients just until combined.
3. Transfer to prepared baking pan. Bake 20-25 minutes or until a toothpick inserted in the center comes out clean and top is lightly browned. Cut into squares; serve warm.
1 PIECE: 229 cal., 10g fat (3g sat. fat), 55mg chol., 395mg sod., 29g carb. (5g sugars, 2g fiber), 6g pro.

WONDERFUL ENGLISH MUFFINS

When I was growing up on a farm, my mom always seemed to be making homemade bread...nothing tasted so good! Now I like to make these simple yet delicious muffins for my own family.
—Linda Rasmussen, Twin Falls, ID

Prep: 30 min. + rising • **Cook:** 25 min.
Makes: 12 muffins

- **1 cup whole milk**
- **¼ cup butter, cubed**
- **2 Tbsp. sugar**
- **1 tsp. salt**
- **2 pkg. (¼ oz. each) active dry yeast**
- **1 cup warm water (110° to 115°)**
- **2 cups all-purpose flour**
- **3 to 3½ cups whole wheat flour**
- **1 Tbsp. sesame seeds**
- **1 Tbsp. poppy seeds**
- **Cornmeal**

1. Scald milk in a saucepan; add butter, sugar and salt. Stir until the butter melts; cool to lukewarm. In a small bowl, dissolve yeast in warm water; add to the milk mixture. Stir in all-purpose flour and 1 cup whole wheat flour until smooth. Add sesame seeds, poppy seeds and enough of the remaining whole wheat flour to make a soft dough.
2. Turn dough onto a floured surface; knead until smooth and elastic, about 8-10 minutes. Place in a greased bowl, turning once to grease top. Cover with a towel and let rise until doubled, about 1 hour.
3. Punch dough down. Roll to ⅓-in. thickness on a cornmeal-covered surface. Cut into circles with a 3½-in. or 4-in. cutter; cover and let rise until nearly doubled, about 30 minutes.
4. Place muffins, cornmeal side down, in a greased skillet; cook over medium-low heat for 12-14 minutes or until bottoms are browned. Turn and cook about 12-14 minutes or until browned. Cool on wire racks; split and toast to serve.
1 MUFFIN: 240 cal., 6g fat (3g sat. fat), 13mg chol., 248mg sod., 41g carb. (4g sugars, 4g fiber), 7g pro.

GARLIC BREAD

As an accompaniment, this bread could not be tastier or simpler to make. Minced fresh garlic is key to these flavor-packed crusty slices, which our family would snap up warm from the oven.
—Grace Yaskovic, Lake Hiawatha, NJ

Takes: 20 min. • **Makes:** 8 servings

- **½ cup butter, melted**
- **3 to 4 garlic cloves, minced**
- **1 loaf (1 lb.) French bread, halved lengthwise**
- **2 Tbsp. minced fresh parsley**

1. In a small bowl, combine butter and garlic. Brush over cut sides of bread; sprinkle with parsley. Place, cut side up, on a baking sheet.
2. Bake at 350° for 8 minutes. Broil 4-6 in. from the heat for 2 minutes or until golden brown. Cut into 2-in. slices. Serve warm.
1 PIECE: 258 cal., 13g fat (7g sat. fat), 31mg chol., 462mg sod., 30g carb. (1g sugars, 2g fiber), 5g pro.

MUENSTER BREAD

The recipe makes a beautiful, round loaf. With a layer of gooey cheese peeking out of every slice, it's definitely worth the effort.
—Melanie Mero, Ida, MI

Prep: 20 min. + rising • **Bake:** 40 min. + cooling
Makes: 1 loaf (16 slices)

- **2 pkg. (¼ oz. each) active dry yeast**
- **1 cup warm whole milk (110° to 115°)**
- **½ cup butter, softened**
- **2 Tbsp. sugar**
- **1 tsp. salt**
- **3¼ to 3¾ cups all-purpose flour**
- **1 large egg plus 1 large egg yolk**
- **4 cups shredded Muenster cheese**
- **1 large egg white, beaten**

1. In a large bowl, dissolve yeast in milk. Add the butter, sugar, salt and 2 cups flour; beat until smooth. Stir in enough of the remaining flour to form a soft dough.
2. Turn dough onto a floured surface; knead until smooth and elastic, 6-8 minutes. Place in a greased bowl, turning once to grease top. Cover with a towel and let rise in a warm place until doubled, about 1 hour.
3. In a large bowl, beat egg and yolk; stir in cheese. Punch down dough; roll into a 16-in. circle. Place in a greased 10-in. cast-iron skillet or 9-in. round baking pan, letting the dough drape over the edges. Spoon the cheese mixture into center of dough. Gather dough up over the filling in 1½-in. pleats. Gently squeeze pleats together at top and twist to make a topknot. Allow to rise 10-15 minutes. Preheat oven to 375°.
4. Brush the loaf with egg white. Bake for 40-45 minutes. Cool on a wire rack about 20 minutes. Serve warm.
1 SLICE: 273 cal., 16g fat (9g sat. fat), 71mg chol., 399mg sod., 22g carb. (3g sugars, 1g fiber), 11g pro.

SWIRLED PUMPKIN YEAST BREAD

I call this my hostess-gift bread, but it's fantastic for any occasion at all. Swirls of cinnamon sugar make every slice irresistible.
—Shirley Runkle, St. Paris, OH

Prep: 45 min. + rising • **Bake:** 50 min. + cooling
Makes: 2 loaves (16 slices each)

- **3 cups whole wheat flour**
- **2 cups quick-cooking oats**
- **⅔ cup packed brown sugar**
- **2 pkg. (¼ oz. each) active dry yeast**
- **2½ tsp. pumpkin pie spice**
- **1½ tsp. salt**
- **1 tsp. sugar**
- **4½ to 5 cups all-purpose flour**
- **1½ cups warm water (120° to 130°)**
- **1 cup canned pumpkin**
- **⅓ cup canola oil**
- **⅓ cup unsweetened applesauce**
- **2 large eggs**
- **½ cup raisins**

FILLING

- **½ cup packed brown sugar**
- **1 tsp. ground cinnamon**
- **¼ cup butter, softened**

1. In a large bowl, mix first seven ingredients and 2 cups of the all-purpose flour. In a small saucepan, heat the water, pumpkin, oil and applesauce to 120°-130°. Add to the dry ingredients; beat on medium speed for 2 minutes. Add eggs; beat on high 2 minutes. Stir in raisins and enough of the remaining all-purpose flour to form a firm dough.
2. Turn dough onto a floured surface; knead until smooth and elastic, 6-8 minutes. Place in a greased bowl, turning once to grease the top. Cover with plastic wrap; let rise in a warm place until doubled, about 1 hour.
3. Mix brown sugar and cinnamon. Punch down the dough. Turn onto a lightly floured surface; divide in half. Roll each half into an 18x9-in. rectangle. Spread each with 2 Tbsp. butter to within ½ in. of edges and sprinkle with ¼ cup of the brown sugar mixture. Roll each up jelly-roll style, starting with a short side; pinch seam to seal. Place in greased 9x5-in. loaf pans, seam side down. Cover with towels; let rise in a warm place until doubled, about 30 minutes. Preheat oven to 350°.
4. Bake until golden brown, 50-60 minutes. Cool 10 minutes before removing from pans to wire racks to cool.
1 SLICE: 202 cal., 5g fat (1g sat. fat), 15mg chol., 130mg sod., 36g carb. (10g sugars, 3g fiber), 5g pro.

TEST KITCHEN TIP

Most bread recipes that call for whole wheat flour also call for water—water brings out the flour's wheat flavor and makes for a crisper crust. Use milk instead of water for bread with a softer interior and crust. It does not matter whether the whole wheat flour you use is store-bought or freshly ground.

LEMON POUND CAKE MUFFINS

I make these lemony muffins for all kinds of occasions. My family is always asking for them. They have a rich cakelike taste and a sweet, tangy flavor. They're so unbelievably good!
—Lola Baxter, Winnebago, MN

Prep: 15 min. • **Bake:** 20 min. • **Makes:** 1 dozen

- ½ **cup butter, softened**
- 1 **cup sugar**
- 2 **large egg, room temperatures**
- ½ **cup sour cream**
- 1 **tsp. vanilla extract**
- ½ **tsp. lemon extract**
- 1¾ **cups all-purpose flour**
- ½ **tsp. salt**
- ¼ **tsp. baking soda**

GLAZE

- 2 **cups confectioners' sugar**
- 3 **Tbsp. lemon juice**

1. Preheat oven to 400°. In a large bowl, cream butter and sugar until light and fluffy. Add the eggs, one at a time, beating well after each addition. Beat in the sour cream and extracts. Combine the flour, salt and baking soda; add to the creamed mixture just until moistened.

2. Fill 12 greased or paper-lined muffin cups three-fourths full. Bake until a toothpick inserted in the center comes out clean, 18-20 minutes. Cool in pan for 5 minutes before removing from pan to a wire rack.

3. Combine glaze ingredients; drizzle over muffins. Serve warm.

1 MUFIN: 311 cal., 10g fat (6g sat. fat), 63mg chol., 218mg sod., 51g carb. (36g sugars, 1g fiber), 3g pro.

ALOHA QUICK BREAD

The addition of coconut, orange zest, pineapple and nuts gives a new twist to banana bread. I sometimes serve slices of it for dessert.
—Lanita Anderson, Chesapeake, VA

Prep: 15 min. • **Bake:** 80 min. + cooling
Makes: 1 loaf

- ½ **cup butter, softened**
- 1 **cup sugar**
- 2 **large eggs, room temperature**
- 1 **cup mashed ripe bananas (about 2 medium)**
- ¼ **cup whole milk**
- 1 **Tbsp. grated orange zest**
- 1 **tsp. vanilla extract**
- ½ **tsp. almond extract**
- 2 **cups all-purpose flour**
- 1 **tsp. baking soda**
- ½ **tsp. salt**
- 1 **cup sweetened shredded coconut**
- ½ **cup chopped nuts**
- ½ **cup crushed pineapple, drained**

1. Preheat oven to 350°. In a bowl, cream butter and sugar. Add eggs, one at a time, beating well after each addition. Beat in banana, milk, orange zest and extracts.

2. Combine flour, baking soda and salt; add to the creamed mixture just until moistened. Fold in coconut, nuts and pineapple. Transfer to a greased 9x5-in. loaf pan.

3. Bake for 1 hour and 20 minutes or until a toothpick inserted in the center comes out clean. Cool for 10 minutes before removing from pan to a wire rack.

1 SLICE: 239 cal., 11g fat (6g sat. fat), 42mg chol., 236mg sod., 33g carb. (18g sugars, 1g fiber), 4g pro.

SWIRL CINNAMON BREAD

If you like cinnamon, you'll love this quick bread! It's crusty on top, soft and moist inside. Prettily wrapped loaves make great holiday gifts, too!
—Taste of Home *Test Kitchen*

Prep: 25 min. • **Bake:** 45 min. + cooling
Makes: 1 loaf (12 slices)

- **2 cups all-purpose flour**
- **¾ cup sugar**
- **½ tsp. baking soda**
- **½ tsp. plus 1½ tsp. ground cinnamon, divided**
- **¼ tsp. salt**
- **1 large egg, room temperature**
- **1 cup reduced-fat plain yogurt**
- **¼ cup canola oil**
- **1 tsp. vanilla extract**
- **¼ cup packed brown sugar**

1. Preheat oven to 350°. In a large bowl, combine flour, sugar, baking soda, ½ tsp. cinnamon and salt. In a small bowl, whisk egg, yogurt, oil and vanilla. Stir into the dry ingredients just until moistened. In a small bowl, combine the brown sugar and the remaining cinnamon.
2. Coat an 8x4-in. loaf pan with cooking spray. Spoon a third of the batter into the pan; top with a third of the brown sugar mixture. Repeat the layers twice more. Cut through the batter with a knife to swirl the brown sugar mixture.
3. Bake for 45-55 minutes or until a toothpick inserted in the center comes out clean. Cool for 10 minutes before removing from pan to a wire rack.
1 SLICE: 203 cal., 6g fat (1g sat. fat), 19mg chol., 124mg sod., 35g carb. (19g sugars, 1g fiber), 4g pro.

PUMPKIN OAT MUFFINS

It isn't considered Thanksgiving or Christmas in our house until these are on the table! Enjoy the flavors of pumpkin pie in muffin form any time of the year.
—*Carol Hale, Sarver, PA*

Takes: 30 min. • **Makes:** 1 dozen

- **1 cup all-purpose flour**
- **½ cup packed brown sugar**
- **2 tsp. baking powder**
- **1 tsp. pumpkin pie spice**
- **½ tsp. salt**
- **¼ tsp. baking soda**
- **1 large egg, room temperature, lightly beaten**
- **¾ cup canned pumpkin**
- **¼ cup whole milk**
- **¼ cup canola oil**
- **1 cup old-fashioned oats**
- **½ cup raisins**

TOPPING

- **⅓ cup packed brown sugar**
- **1 Tbsp. all-purpose flour**
- **¾ tsp. pumpkin pie spice**
- **1 Tbsp. cold butter**

1. Preheat oven to 375°. In a large bowl, combine first six ingredients. Combine egg, pumpkin, milk and oil; add to dry ingredients just until moistened. Stir in oats and raisins.
2. Fill 12 greased or paper-lined muffin cups two-thirds full. In a small bowl, combine the brown sugar, flour and pie spice; cut in butter until crumbly. Sprinkle 1 rounded teaspoonful over each muffin. Bake 15-20 minutes or until a toothpick comes out clean.
3. Cool for 5 minutes before removing from pan to a wire rack. Serve warm.
1 MUFFIN: 204 cal., 7g fat (2g sat. fat), 21mg chol., 214mg sod., 34g carb. (19g sugars, 2g fiber), 3g pro.

READER REVIEW

"These muffins were excellent! Quick to mix up, moist inside and crunchy on top. I substituted dried cranberries for the raisins. This recipe is a keeper!"

COOKIE65, TASTEOFHOME.COM

SWISS CHEESE BREAD

This bread will receive rave reviews, whether you serve it as an appetizer or alongside a meal. For real convenience, make it ahead of time and freeze it!

—Karla Boice, Mahtomedi, MN

Takes: 30 min. • **Makes:** 24 servings

- **1 loaf (18-20 in.) French bread**
- **8 oz. (2 sticks) butter, softened**
- **2 cups shredded Swiss cheese**
- **¾ tsp. celery seed**
- **¾ tsp. garlic powder**
- **3 Tbsp. dehydrated parsley flakes**

1. Preheat oven to 425°. Cut bread in half. Make diagonal cuts, 1 in. apart, deep into the bread but not through bottom. Combine all remaining ingredients. Spread half the butter mixture between bread slices. Spread the remaining mixture over top and sides.

2. Place the bread on double thickness of foil; cover loosely with more foil. Bake for 20-30 minutes. For last 5 minutes, remove foil covering bread to allow it to brown.

1 PIECE: 154 cal., 11g fat (6g sat. fat), 29mg chol., 217mg sod., 10g carb. (1g sugars, 1g fiber), 4g pro.

SAUSAGE CHEESE MUFFINS

These small savory muffins are fun to serve as appetizers or at brunch. With just five ingredients, the tasty bites are easy to whip up to take to the office, a friend's house or any gathering.

—Willa Paget, Nashville, TN

Prep: 25 min. • **Bake:** 15 min. • **Makes:** 4 dozen

- **1 lb. bulk spicy pork sausage**
- **1 can (10¾ oz.) condensed cheddar cheese soup, undiluted**
- **½ cup whole milk**
- **2 to 3 tsp. rubbed sage**
- **3 cups biscuit/baking mix**

In a skillet over medium heat, cook sausage until no longer pink; drain. Combine soup, milk, sage and sausage. Stir in the biscuit mix just until moistened. Fill greased miniature muffin cups two-thirds full. Bake at 400° for 15-20 minutes or until muffins test done.

2 MINI MUFFINS: 112 cal., 7g fat (2g sat. fat), 9mg chol., 366mg sod., 11g carb. (1g sugars, 0 fiber), 3g pro.

YUMMY APRICOT PECAN BREAD

This delectable bread—always perfect with coffee or as a gift—is really quick and easy to prepare.
—*Joan Hallford, North Richland Hills, TX*

Prep: 20 min. • **Bake:** 40 min.
Makes: 2 loaves (12 slices each)

- **2½ cups all-purpose flour**
- **¾ cup sugar**
- **2 tsp. baking soda**
- **1 tsp. ground cinnamon**
- **¼ tsp. salt**
- **¼ tsp. ground nutmeg**
- **1 cup 2% milk**
- **2 large eggs, room temperature**
- **⅓ cup butter, melted**
- **2 cups shredded cheddar cheese**
- **1 cup finely chopped dried apricots**
- **¾ cup finely chopped pecans**

TOPPING
- **3 Tbsp. packed brown sugar**
- **1 Tbsp. butter**
- **½ tsp. ground cinnamon**

1. Preheat oven to 350°. Grease two 8x4-in. loaf pans; set aside. In a large bowl, combine the first six ingredients. In a small bowl, beat the milk, eggs and butter; stir into the dry ingredients just until moistened. Fold in the cheese, apricots and pecans. Spoon into the prepared loaf pans. Combine the topping ingredients; sprinkle over batter.
2. Bake for 40-45 minutes or until a toothpick comes out clean. Cool for 10 minutes before removing from pans to wire racks.
FREEZE OPTION: Securely wrap and freeze individual cooled loaves. To use, thaw at room temperature
1 SLICE: 189 cal., 9g fat (4g sat. fat), 36mg chol., 223mg sod., 23g carb. (11g sugars, 1g fiber), 5g pro.

JOAN HALLFORD
North Richland Hills, TX

5i

POTATO PAN ROLLS

My family loves these rolls and requests them often. Because the recipes calls for quick-rise yeast, a pan never takes long to make.
—*Connie Storckman, Evanston, WY*

Prep: 15 min. + rising • **Bake:** 20 min.
Makes: 16 rolls

- **4½ to 5 cups all-purpose flour**
- **3 Tbsp. sugar**
- **2 pkg. (¼ oz. each) quick-rise yeast**
- **1½ tsp. salt**
- **1¼ cups water**
- **3 Tbsp. butter**
- **½ cup mashed potatoes (without added milk and butter)**
- **Additional all-purpose flour**

1. In a large bowl, combine 2 cups flour, the sugar, yeast and salt. In a small saucepan, heat water and butter to 120°-130°. Add to the dry ingredients; beat until smooth. Stir in mashed potatoes and enough of the remaining flour to form a soft dough.
2. Turn dough onto a floured surface; knead until smooth and elastic, about 6-8 minutes. Cover and let rest for 10 minutes. Divide into 16 pieces. Shape each piece into a ball. Place in two greased 8- or 9-in. cast-iron skillets or round baking pans. Cover and let rise in a warm place until doubled, about 30 minutes.
3. Preheat oven to 400°. Sprinkle tops of rolls with additional flour. Bake until golden brown, 18-22 minutes. Remove from pans to wire racks to cool.
1 ROLL: 163 cal., 3g fat (1g sat. fat), 6mg chol., 239mg sod., 30g carb. (3g sugars, 1g fiber), 4g pro.

PISTACHIO QUICK BREAD

I love making batches of these special loaves to give away for the holidays. They also freeze well so there's always one ready for company.
—Judy Fischer, Green Bay, WI

Prep: 20 min. • **Bake:** 35 min. + cooling
Makes: 2 loaves (12 slices each)

- **1 pkg. white cake mix (regular size)**
- **1 pkg. (3.4 oz.) instant pistachio pudding mix**
- **4 large eggs, room temperature**
- **1 cup sour cream**
- **¼ cup water**
- **¼ cup canola oil**
- **⅓ cup sugar**
- **¾ tsp. ground cinnamon**

1. Preheat oven to 350°. In a large bowl, combine the cake and pudding mixes. Add the eggs, sour cream, water and oil; beat until blended (batter will be thick).
2. Combine sugar and cinnamon. Spoon half of the batter into two greased 8x4-in. loaf pans; sprinkle each with 2 Tbsp. cinnamon sugar. Spread with the remaining batter; sprinkle with the remaining cinnamon sugar.
3. Bake for 35-40 minutes or until a toothpick inserted in the center comes out clean. Cool in pans for 10 minutes before removing to wire racks.

1 SLICE: 169 cal., 7g fat (2g sat. fat), 42mg chol., 218mg sod., 24g carb. (16g sugars, 0 fiber), 2g pro.

DID YOU KNOW?

If you want to use egg substitute or egg whites instead of eggs, leave at least 1 whole egg in the mix, as the yolk adds flavor, tenderness and protein, and helps to blend liquids, like oil and water, that are hard to combine. For the rest, substitute 2 egg whites or ¼ cup fat-free egg substitute for each whole egg. Packaged cake mixes usually include ingredients that help with tenderness, texture, etc., so using only egg whites often works fine.

STICKY BUNS

It's impossible to eat just one of these soft, gooey sticky buns—they are full of old-fashioned goodness.
—Dorothy Showalter, Broadway, VA

Prep: 30 min. + rising • **Bake:** 20 min. + cooling
Makes: 1 dozen

- **2 tsp. active dry yeast**
- **1¼ cups warm water (110° to 115°)**
- **3 Tbsp. butter, softened**
- **3 Tbsp. sugar**
- **2 Tbsp. nonfat dry milk powder**
- **1 tsp. salt**
- **3¼ to 3¾ cups bread flour**

SAUCE

- **½ cup packed brown sugar**
- **¼ cup butter, cubed**
- **¼ cup corn syrup**
- **½ cup chopped pecans**

FILLING

- **⅓ cup butter, softened**
- **1 Tbsp. sugar**
- **1 tsp. ground cinnamon**

1. Dissolve yeast in warm water. Add the butter, sugar, milk powder and salt, then beat in 2 cups of flour on low for 3 minutes. Stir in enough of the remaining flour to form a soft dough.
2. Turn dough onto a floured surface; knead until smooth and elastic, 6-8 minutes. Place in a greased bowl, turning once to grease top. Cover dough and let rise in a warm place until doubled, about 1 hour.
3. Meanwhile, in a small saucepan, make sauce by combining brown sugar, butter and corn syrup; cook over medium heat until the sugar is dissolved. Stir in pecans. Pour into a greased 13x9-in. baking dish.
4. Punch down dough. Turn onto a floured surface; roll into a 16x10-in. rectangle. Make the filling by combining butter, sugar and cinnamon; spread to within ¾ in. of edges. Roll up jelly-roll style, starting with a long side; pinch seam to seal. Cut into 12 slices; place slices cut side down over sauce. Cover with a kitchen towel; let rise in a warm place until doubled, about 45 minutes.
5. Preheat oven to 375°. Bake until golden brown, 20-25 minutes. Cool 3 minutes before inverting onto a serving platter.

1 BUN: 314 cal., 15g fat (8g sat. fat), 32mg chol., 334mg sod., 42g carb. (17g sugars, 1g fiber), 5g pro.

TROPICAL MUFFINS

I entered these muffins at our county fair and won the grand champion award for baked goods. They're so moist and flavorful, they don't need butter. If you don't like the flavor of rum, omit the extract or substitute vanilla or coconut extract.

—Sylvia Osborn, Clay Center, KS

Prep: 20 min. • **Bake:** 25 min.
Makes: about 1 dozen

- **¼ cup butter, softened**
- **½ cup sugar**
- **1 large egg, room temperature**
- **1 cup sour cream**
- **1½ tsp. rum extract**
- **1½ cups all-purpose flour**
- **1 tsp. baking powder**
- **½ tsp. baking soda**
- **½ tsp. salt**
- **1 can (8 oz.) crushed pineapple, drained**
- **½ cup sweetened shredded coconut**
- **⅓ cup chopped pecans**

1. In a large bowl, cream the butter and sugar until light and fluffy. Beat in the egg, sour cream and extract. Combine the flour, baking powder, baking soda and salt; stir into the creamed mixture just until moistened. Fold in the pineapple, coconut and pecans.

2. Fill 12 greased or paper-lined muffin cups two-thirds full. Bake at 375° for 22-25 minutes or until a toothpick comes out clean. Cool for 5 minutes before removing from pan to a wire rack.

FREEZE OPTION: Freeze cooled muffins in an airtight container. To use, thaw at room temperature or, if desired, microwave each muffin on high for 20-30 seconds or until heated through.

1 MUFFIN: 225 cal., 11g fat (6g sat. fat), 41mg chol., 249mg sod., 26g carb. (13g sugars, 1g fiber), 3g pro.

ZUCCHINI NUT BREAD

Lighter and fluffier than most zucchini breads, this recipe is an ideal way to put that vegetable to good use!

—Kevin Bruckerhoff, Columbia, MO

Prep: 15 min. • **Bake:** 55 min. + cooling
Makes: 2 loaves (12 slices each)

- **2 cups sugar**
- **1 cup canola oil**
- **3 large eggs, room temperature**
- **2 tsp. vanilla extract**
- **3 cups all-purpose flour**
- **1 tsp. salt**
- **1 tsp. baking soda**
- **1 tsp. grated lemon zest**
- **1 tsp. ground cinnamon**
- **¼ tsp. baking powder**
- **2 cups shredded zucchini (about 2 medium)**
- **½ cup chopped walnuts or pecans**

1. Preheat oven to 350°. Grease two 8x4-in. loaf pans. In a large bowl, beat sugar, oil, eggs and vanilla until well blended. In another bowl, whisk the flour, salt, baking soda, lemon zest, cinnamon and baking powder; gradually beat into the sugar mixture, mixing just until moistened. Stir in zucchini and walnuts.

2. Transfer batter to the prepared pans. Bake for 55-65 minutes or until a toothpick inserted in center comes out clean. Cool 10 minutes before removing from the pans to wire racks to cool.

1 SLICE: 229 cal., 11g fat (1g sat. fat), 26mg chol., 165mg sod., 29g carb. (17g sugars, 1g fiber), 3g pro.

SPICED APPLE CORNBREAD

There's nothing better than a big piece of cornbread to go with a supper of fried chicken, chops or baked ham. I've sweetened the pot with a little apple and spice for a most tender and moist cornbread.

—Kelly Williams, Forked River, NJ

Prep: 15 min. • **Bake:** 40 min.
Makes: 12 servings

- 2 **cups all-purpose flour**
- 2 **cups yellow cornmeal**
- 1 **Tbsp. baking powder**
- 1 **tsp. salt**
- ½ **tsp. ground cinnamon**
- ½ **tsp. pumpkin pie spice**
- ½ **cup butter, softened**
- 1½ **cups sugar**
- ½ **tsp. vanilla extract**
- 4 **large eggs, room temperature**
- 2 **cups water**
- 1 **cup shredded peeled apple**

1. Preheat oven to 400°. Whisk together the first six ingredients. In a large bowl, beat butter and sugar until blended. Add vanilla and eggs, one at a time, beating well after each. Stir in the flour mixture alternately with water, adding water slowly (mixture may appear slightly curdled). Stir in apple.

2. Transfer to a greased 10-in. cast-iron skillet (pan will be very full). Bake on a lower oven rack until a toothpick inserted in the center comes out clean, 40-50 minutes. Serve warm.

1 SLICE: 371 cal., 10g fat (5g sat. fat), 82mg chol., 404mg sod., 64g carb. (27g sugars, 2g fiber), 6g pro.

PUMPKIN SPICE BREAD

One bite and you'll agree this bread tastes just like pumpkin pie without the crust!

—Delora Lucas, Belle, WV

Prep: 10 min. • **Bake:** 1 hour + cooling
Makes: 2 loaves

- 3 **cups sugar**
- 1 **cup vegetable oil**
- 4 **large eggs, room temperature, lightly beaten**
- 1 **can (15 oz.) solid-pack pumpkin**
- 3½ **cups all-purpose flour**
- 1 **tsp. baking soda**
- 1 **tsp. salt**
- 1 **tsp. ground cinnamon**
- 1 **tsp. ground nutmeg**
- ½ **tsp. baking powder**
- ½ **tsp. ground cloves**
- ½ **tsp. ground allspice**
- ½ **cup water**

1. Preheat oven to 350°. Grease two 9x5-in. loaf pans; set aside. In a large bowl, combine sugar, oil and eggs. Add the pumpkin and mix well. Combine the flour, baking soda, salt, cinnamon, nutmeg, baking powder, cloves and allspice; add to the pumpkin mixture alternately with water, beating well after each addition.

2. Pour batter into prepared pans. Bake for 60-65 minutes or until a toothpick inserted in the center comes out clean. Cool in pans for 10 minutes before removing to a wire rack to cool completely.

1 SLICE: 197 cal., 8g fat (1g sat. fat), 27mg chol., 128mg sod., 30g carb. (19g sugars, 1g fiber), 2g pro.

TRADITIONAL CHOCOLATE CHIP MUFFINS

Muffins are one of my favorite things to bake, and these are the best. I always keep some in the freezer for breakfast on the run—I can zap one in the microwave before I head out the door.

—Kelly Kirby, Mill Bay, NS

Prep: 15 min. • **Bake:** 25 min. • **Makes:** 1 dozen

- ½ **cup butter, softened**
- 1 **cup sugar**
- 2 **large eggs, room temperature**
- 1 **cup plain yogurt**
- 1 **tsp. vanilla extract**
- 2 **cups all-purpose flour**
- 1 **tsp. baking soda**
- ½ **tsp. baking powder**
- ½ **tsp. salt**
- ¾ **cup semisweet chocolate chips**

TOPPING

- ¼ **cup semisweet chocolate chips**
- 2 **Tbsp. brown sugar**
- 2 **Tbsp. chopped walnuts, optional**
- 1 **tsp. ground cinnamon**

1. Preheat oven to 350°. In a large bowl, cream butter and sugar until light and fluffy. Add the eggs, one at a time, beating well after each addition. Beat in yogurt and vanilla. Combine the flour, baking soda, baking powder and salt; add to the creamed mixture just until moistened. Fold in the chocolate chips. Fill 12 paper-lined muffin cups two-thirds full.

2. Combine the topping ingredients; sprinkle over batter. Bake for 25-30 minutes or until a toothpick inserted in the center comes out clean. Cool for 5 minutes before removing from pan to wire rack. Serve warm.

1 MUFFIN: 308 cal., 13g fat (8g sat. fat), 58mg chol., 319mg sod., 45g carb. (28g sugars, 1g fiber), 5g pro.

TEST KITCHEN TIP
When you want fresh muffins in the morning, do some of the prep work the night before, combining the dry ingredients in an airtight container and measuring any other ingredients that will hold. The next morning, quickly stir up the batter and pop the muffins in the oven.

5i

QUICK & EASY BREAD BOWLS

Impress friends and family by serving cream soups or dips in bread bowls. It's one of the most popular recipes on my blog, *yammiesnoshery.com.*

—Rachel Preus, Marshall, MI

Prep: 35 min. + rising • **Bake:** 20 min+ cooling
Makes: 6 servings

- 2 **Tbsp. active dry yeast**
- 3 **cups warm water (110° to 115°)**
- 2 **Tbsp. sugar**
- 2 **tsp. salt**
- 6½ **to 7½ cups bread flour**
- **Cornmeal and sesame seeds, optional**

1. In a small bowl, dissolve yeast in warm water. In a large bowl, combine sugar, salt, yeast mixture and 3 cups flour; beat on medium speed 3 minutes. Stir in enough of the remaining flour to form a soft dough (dough will be sticky).

2. Turn dough onto a floured surface; knead until smooth and elastic, 6-8 minutes. Place in a greased bowl, turning once to grease the top. Cover with a kitchen towel and let rise in a warm place until doubled, about 30 minutes.

3. Preheat oven to 500°. Punch dough down. Divide and shape into six balls. Place balls 3 in. apart on two baking sheets that have been generously sprinkled with cornmeal or greased. Cover with a kitchen towel; let rise in a warm place until doubled, about 15 minutes. Spray loaves with water; if desired, generously sprinkle with sesame seeds. Using a sharp knife, score surface with shallow cuts in an X pattern. Bake 2 minutes. Reduce oven setting to 425°. Bake until golden brown and internal temperature reaches 190-200°. Remove from pans to wire racks to cool.

4. Cut a thin slice off the top of bread. Hollow out the bottom portion of loaf, leaving a ¼-in. shell (discard removed bread or save for another use, such as croutons).

1 BREAD BOWL: 283 cal., 1g fat (0 sat. fat), 0 chol., 396mg sod., 57g carb. (2g sugars, 2g fiber), 10g pro.

ALMOND STREUSEL ROLLS

Try my prize-winning pastry! These rolls are so popular that they often don't even cool completely before the pan is empty.
—Perlene Hoekema, Lynden, WA

Prep: 40 min. + rising • **Bake:** 35 min. + cooling
Makes: 1 dozen

- **2 pkg. (¼ oz. each) active dry yeast**
- **¾ cup warm water (110° to 115°)**
- **¾ cup warm whole milk (110° to 115°)**
- **¼ cup butter, softened**
- **½ cup sugar**
- **2 large eggs**
- **1 tsp. salt**
- **5¼ to 5½ cups all-purpose flour**

FILLING

- **½ cup almond paste**
- **¼ cup butter, softened**
- **½ cup packed brown sugar**
- **¼ tsp. almond extract**

TOPPING

- **3 Tbsp. sugar**
- **1 Tbsp. all-purpose flour**
- **1 Tbsp. butter**

ICING

- **1½ cups confectioners' sugar**
- **¼ tsp. almond extract**
- **1 to 2 Tbsp. whole milk**

1. In a large bowl, dissolve the yeast in warm water. Add the milk, butter, sugar, eggs, salt and 2 cups flour. Beat until smooth. Stir in enough remaining flour to form a soft dough.
2. Turn dough onto a floured surface; knead until smooth and elastic, about 6-8 minutes. Place in a greased bowl, turning once to grease the top. Cover and let rise in a warm place until doubled, about 1 hour.
3. Punch dough down; roll out to a 15x10-in. rectangle. In a large bowl, beat the filling ingredients until smooth. Spread over dough.
4. Roll up jelly-roll style, starting with a short side; seal seams. Cut into 12 slices. Place in a greased 13x9-in. baking pan or 12-in. ovenproof skillet. Cover and let rise in a warm place until doubled, about 30 minutes.
5. Combine topping ingredients; sprinkle over rolls. Bake at 350° for 35-40 minutes or until golden brown. Cool on a wire rack.
6. In a small bowl, combine confectioners' sugar, extract and enough milk to achieve drizzling consistency; drizzle over rolls.
1 ROLL: 482 cal., 13g fat (6g sat. fat), 61mg chol., 308mg sod., 83g carb. (37g sugars, 2g fiber), 8g pro.

PERLENE HOEKEMA
Lynden, WA

ELVIS BANANA BREAD

As a toddler, my son loved bananas, and we always had them in the house. When we didn't eat them all before they were too ripe, we experimented beyond basic banana bread. That's how we came up with Elvis bread!
—Elizabeth Somppi, Greenfield, WI

Prep: 30 min. • **Bake:** 45 min. + cooling
Makes: 3 mini loaves (6 slices each)

- **2 cups all-purpose flour**
- **1 cup sugar**
- **1 tsp. baking powder**
- **1 tsp. baking soda**
- **1 tsp. salt**
- **1 tsp. pumpkin pie spice**
- **4 medium ripe bananas, mashed**
- **2 large eggs, room temperature**
- **½ cup creamy peanut butter**
- **¼ cup unsweetened applesauce**
- **¼ cup canola oil**
- **2 tsp. vanilla extract**
- **⅔ cup semisweet chocolate chips**

1. Preheat oven to 350°. In a large bowl, whisk the first six ingredients. In another bowl, whisk the bananas, eggs, peanut butter, applesauce, oil and vanilla until blended. Add to the flour mixture; stir just until moistened. Fold in chocolate chips.
2. Transfer to three 5¾x3x2-in. pans coated with cooking spray. Bake 45-50 minutes or until a toothpick inserted in center comes out clean. Cool in pans 10 minutes before removing to a wire rack to cool.
FREEZE OPTION: Securely wrap cooled loaves; freeze. Thaw at room temperature or, if desired, microwave each loaf on high for 60-75 seconds or until heated through.
1 SLICE: 227 cal., 9g fat (2g sat. fat), 24mg chol., 266mg sod., 34g carb. (19g sugars, 2g fiber), 4g pro.

ZUCCHINI-CHOCOLATE CHIP MUFFINS

Whenever I make these muffins, I freeze several. As I'm leaving for work, I take one out of the freezer to enjoy at the office with a cup of coffee.

—Janet Pierce DeCori, Rockton, IL

Prep: 20 min. • **Bake:** 20 min.
Makes: 1 dozen

- **1½ cups all-purpose flour**
- **¾ cup sugar**
- **1 tsp. baking soda**
- **1 tsp. ground cinnamon**
- **½ tsp. salt**
- **1 large egg, room temperature, lightly beaten**
- **½ cup canola oil**
- **¼ cup whole milk**
- **1 Tbsp. lemon juice**
- **1 tsp. vanilla extract**
- **1 cup shredded zucchini**
- **¼ cup miniature semisweet chocolate chips**
- **¼ cup chopped walnuts**

1. Preheat oven to 350°. In a bowl, combine the flour, sugar, baking soda, cinnamon and salt. Beat the egg, oil, milk, lemon juice and vanilla; stir into the dry ingredients just until moistened. Fold in zucchini, chocolate chips and walnuts. Fill 12 greased or paper-lined muffin cups two-thirds full.
2. Bake for 20-25 minutes or until a toothpick comes out clean.

FREEZE OPTION: Freeze cooled muffins in an airtight container. To use, thaw at room temperature or, if desired, microwave each muffin on high for 20-30 seconds or until heated through.

1 MUFFIN: 234 cal., 13g fat (2g sat. fat), 16mg chol., 213mg sod., 28g carb. (15g sugars, 1g fiber), 3g pro.

SOUR CREAM CUT-OUT BISCUITS

After trying countless ways to make biscuits and never being completely satisfied, I decided to incorporate sour cream. Success! Split them while warm, spread on some butter and enjoy.

—Lorraine Caland, Shuniah, ON

Takes: 30 min. • **Makes:** 10 biscuits

- **2 cups all-purpose flour**
- **2 Tbsp. sugar**
- **3 tsp. baking powder**
- **½ tsp. salt**
- **½ tsp. baking soda**
- **1 cup sour cream**
- **1 Tbsp. butter, melted**

1. Preheat oven to 425°. In a large bowl, whisk flour, sugar, baking powder, salt and baking soda. Stir in sour cream just until moistened.
2. Turn onto a lightly floured surface; knead gently 8-10 times. Pat or roll dough to ½-in. thickness; cut with a floured 2¼-in. biscuit cutter. Place 1 in. apart on an ungreased baking sheet. Bake until golden brown, 10-12 minutes. Brush biscuits with butter; serve warm.

1 BISCUIT: 159 cal., 6g fat (4g sat. fat), 9mg chol., 343mg sod., 22g carb. (3g sugars, 1g fiber), 3g pro.

ALMOND TEA BREAD

My aunt brought her tea bread recipe with her from Scotland, and a fresh-baked loaf has become a family tradition during the holidays. Each slice is loaded with red cherries.
—Kathleen Showers, Briggsdale, CO

Prep: 15 min. • **Bake:** 1¼ hours + cooling
Makes: 2 loaves (16 slices each)

- **1 can (8 oz.) almond paste**
- **¼ cup butter, softened**
- **1 cup sugar**
- **3 large eggs, room temperature**
- **1½ cups fresh pitted cherries or blueberries**
- **3 cups all-purpose flour, divided**
- **4 tsp. baking powder**
- **½ tsp. salt**
- **¾ cup whole milk**

1. Preheat oven to 350°. Grease and flour two 8x4-in. loaf pans; set aside. In a large bowl, combine almond paste and butter; beat until well blended. Gradually add sugar, beating until light and fluffy. Add the eggs, one at a time, beating well after each addition. In a small bowl, gently toss the cherries with 1 Tbsp. flour. Set aside.
2. Combine baking powder, salt and remaining flour; add to the creamed mixture alternately with milk, beating well after each addition.
3. Spoon a sixth of the batter into each of the prepared loaf pans; sprinkle layers with half of the fruit. Cover with another layer of batter and sprinkle with the remaining fruit. Top with the remaining batter; smooth with spatula.
4. Bake for 1¼ hours or until a toothpick inserted in the center comes out clean. Cool for 10 minutes before removing from pans to wire racks to cool completely.
1 SLICE: 130 cal., 4g fat (1g sat. fat), 25mg chol., 111mg sod., 21g carb. (10g sugars, 1g fiber), 3g pro.

5i

FRENCH LOAVES

My kids love to help me make this delicious bread recipe. It's quite easy, and they enjoy the fact that they can be eating fresh bread in less than two hours!
—Denise Boutin, Grand Isle, VT

Prep: 30 min. + rising • **Bake:** 15 min.
Makes: 2 loaves (12 slices each)

- **2 Tbsp. active dry yeast**
- **2 cups warm water (110° to 115°)**
- **2 tsp. salt**
- **1 tsp. sugar**
- **4½ to 5 cups bread flour**
- **1 tsp. cornmeal**

1. In a large bowl, dissolve the yeast in warm water. Add salt, sugar and 2 cups of flour. Beat until smooth. Stir in enough of the remaining flour to form a soft dough.
2. Turn dough onto a floured surface; knead until smooth and elastic, about 6-8 minutes. Place in a greased bowl, turning once to grease the top. Cover and let rise in a warm place until doubled, about 1 hour.
3. Punch dough down. Turn onto a lightly floured surface; divide in half. Shape into 12-in.-long loaves.
4. Place seam side down on a greased baking sheet. Cover and let rise until doubled, about 30 minutes.
5. Preheat oven to 450°. Sprinkle loaves with cornmeal. With a sharp knife, make four shallow slashes across the top of each loaf. Bake 15-20 minutes or until golden brown. Cool on a wire rack.
1 SLICE: 79 cal., 0 fat (0 sat. fat), 0 chol., 197mg sod., 17g carb. (0 sugars, 1g fiber), 3g pro. **DIABETIC EXCHANGES:** 1 starch.

READER REVIEW

"My first time making bread from scratch and it came out perfect! Great tasting bread that we used to make delicious garlic bread. Easy and foolproof enough for a first-timer. I'd recommend this to anyone!"

HEATHERBETHER80, TASTEOFHOME.COM

S'MORES MONKEY BREAD MUFFINS

When it comes to mini versions of anything, I'm sold! These muffins are ooey-gooey individual monkey breads made with frozen dinner rolls, graham cracker crumbs, chocolate chips, and mini marshmallows. They couldn't be easier to make, and kids just love them.
—Tina Butler, Royse City, TX

Prep: 35 min. • **Bake:** 15 min. • **Makes:** 1 dozen

- **15 frozen bread dough dinner rolls, thawed but still cold**
- **1⅓ cups graham cracker crumbs**
- **½ cup sugar**
- **6 Tbsp. butter, cubed**
- **1 cup miniature semisweet chocolate chips, divided**
- **¾ cup miniature marshmallows**

ICING

- **1 cup confectioners' sugar**
- **½ tsp. butter, softened**
- **1 to 2 Tbsp. 2% milk**

1. Preheat oven to 375°. Line 12 muffin cups with foil liners.
2. Using a sharp knife, cut each dinner roll into four pieces. In a shallow bowl, mix cracker crumbs and sugar. In a large microwave-safe bowl, microwave butter until melted. Dip three pieces of dough in the butter, then roll in the crumb mixture to coat; place in a prepared muffin cup. Repeat until all the muffin cups are filled. Sprinkle tops with ¾ cup chocolate chips and marshmallows.
3. Toss the remaining dough pieces with the remaining butter, rewarming the butter if necessary. Place two additional dough pieces into each cup; sprinkle with the remaining chocolate chips.
4. Bake until golden brown, 15-20 minutes. Cool 5 minutes before removing from pan to a wire rack. Mix the icing ingredients; spoon over tops. Serve warm.
1 MUFFIN: 351 cal., 13g fat (6g sat. fat), 16mg chol., 337mg sod., 57g carb. (29g sugars, 3g fiber), 6g pro.

SOFT SESAME BREADSTICKS

Go for homemade goodness with soft and chewy breadsticks. For variety, skip the sesame seeds and sprinkle with a little garlic salt and Parmesan cheese.
—*Nancy Johnson, Connersville, IN*

Takes: 30 min. • **Makes:** 1 dozen

- **1¼ cups all-purpose flour**
- **2 tsp. sugar**
- **1½ tsp. baking powder**
- **½ tsp. salt**
- **⅔ cup whole milk**
- **3 Tbsp. butter, melted**
- **2 tsp. sesame seeds**

1. Preheat oven to 450°. In a small bowl, combine flour, sugar, baking powder and salt. Gradually add milk and stir to form a soft dough. Turn onto a floured surface and knead gently 3-4 times. Roll into a 10x5x½-in. rectangle; cut into 12 breadsticks.
2. Place butter in a 13x9-in. baking pan. Place breadsticks in butter and turn to coat. Sprinkle with sesame seeds. Bake until golden brown, 14-18 minutes. Serve warm.
3 BREADSTICKS: 257 cal., 11g fat (6g sat. fat), 29mg chol., 553mg sod., 34g carb. (5g sugars, 1g fiber), 6g pro.

HANDY SAUSAGE BISCUITS

These are similar to old-fashioned biscuits made from scratch, but they're even better thanks to the tasty sausage throughout. It's almost impossible to stop eating them. I like to serve these biscuits with an egg dish or soup.
—*Nancy Parker, Seguin, TX*

Prep: 25 min. • **Bake:** 10 min.
Makes: 2 dozen

- **¾ lb. bulk pork sausage**
- **2⅔ cups all-purpose flour**
- **2 Tbsp. sugar**
- **1½ tsp. baking powder**
- **½ tsp. baking soda**
- **½ tsp. salt**
- **½ cup shortening**
- **1 pkg. (¼ oz.) active dry yeast**
- **¼ cup warm water (110° to 115°)**
- **1 cup buttermilk**
- **Melted butter**

1. Preheat oven to 450°. In a skillet, cook sausage over medium heat until no longer pink; drain well and set aside. In a bowl, combine flour, sugar, baking powder, baking soda and salt; cut in shortening until crumbly. Stir in the sausage.
2. In another bowl, dissolve yeast in water; let stand for 5 minutes. Add buttermilk. Stir into the dry ingredients just until moistened.
3. On a lightly floured surface, gently knead dough 6-8 times. Roll out to ½-in. thickness; cut with a 2 in. biscuit cutter. Place on lightly greased baking sheets.
4. Brush tops with butter. Bake 10-12 minutes or until golden brown. Serve warm.
1 BISCUIT: 131 cal., 7g fat (2g sat. fat), 8mg chol., 211mg sod., 12g carb. (2g sugars, 0 fiber), 3g pro.

PRETTY PUMPKIN CINNAMON BUNS

I make sticky buns and cinnamon rolls quite often because my husband loves them. One day, I had some fresh pumpkin on hand and decided to try pumpkin cinnamon buns. We loved the results!
—Glenda Joseph, Chambersburg, PA

Prep: 45 min. + rising • **Bake:** 25 min.
Makes: 2 dozen

- 2 **Tbsp. active dry yeast**
- ½ **cup warm water (110° to 115°)**
- 4 **large eggs**
- 1 **cup shortening**
- 1 **cup canned pumpkin**
- 1 **cup warm whole milk (110° to 115°)**
- ½ **cup sugar**
- ½ **cup packed brown sugar**
- ⅓ **cup instant vanilla pudding mix**
- ⅓ **cup instant butterscotch pudding mix**
- 1 **tsp. salt**
- 8 **to 9 cups all-purpose flour**

FILLING
- ¼ **cup butter, melted**
- 1 **cup packed brown sugar**
- 2 **tsp. ground cinnamon**

ICING
- 3 **Tbsp. water**
- 2 **Tbsp. butter, softened**
- 1 **tsp. ground cinnamon**
- 2 **cups confectioners' sugar**
- 1½ **tsp. vanilla extract**

1. In a large bowl, dissolve the yeast in warm water. Add the eggs, shortening, pumpkin, milk, sugars, pudding mixes, salt and 6 cups of flour. Beat until smooth. Stir in enough of the remaining flour to form a soft dough (dough will be sticky).
2. Turn dough onto a floured surface; knead until smooth and elastic, 6-8 minutes. Place in a greased bowl, turning once to grease top. Cover and let rise in a warm place until doubled, about 1 hour.
3. Punch dough down; divide in half. Roll each portion into a 12x8-in. rectangle; brush with butter. Combine brown sugar and cinnamon; sprinkle over dough to within ½ in. of edges.
4. Roll up jelly-roll style, starting with a long side; pinch seams to seal. Cut each roll into 12 slices. Place slices cut side down in two greased 13x9-in. baking pans. Cover and let rise until doubled, about 30 minutes.
5. Bake at 350° for 22-28 minutes or until golden brown. In a small bowl, combine the water, butter and cinnamon. Add the confectioners' sugar and vanilla; beat until smooth. Spread over buns. Serve warm.
1 BUN: 399 cal., 13g fat (4g sat. fat), 40mg chol., 188mg sod., 65g carb. (31g sugars, 2g fiber), 6g pro.

WINNING CRANBERRY MUFFINS

Our town is the hub of the area's large cranberry bogs, which are beautiful year-round. The fresh cranberries make the perfect addition to these tasty treats! These muffins are my husband's favorite, and my friends like them, too.
—Dorothy Bateman, Carver, MA

Takes: 30 min.
Makes: 12 standard or 6 jumbo muffins

- 1 **cup fresh cranberries, quartered**
- 8 **Tbsp. sugar, divided**
- 1¾ **cups all-purpose flour**
- 2½ **tsp. baking powder**
- ¼ **tsp. salt**
- 1 **large egg, room temperature**
- ¾ **cup whole milk**
- ⅓ **cup vegetable oil**
- 1 **tsp. grated lemon zest, optional**
- **Cinnamon sugar**

1. Preheat oven to 400° Sprinkle quartered cranberries with 2 Tbsp. of sugar; set aside. Sift the remaining 6 Tbsp. sugar, flour, baking powder and salt into large bowl.
2. In another bowl, beat the egg, milk and oil. Make a hole in the center of the dry ingredients; pour in the liquid ingredients. Stir just until moistened. Add berries and, if desired, lemon zest. Fill 12 greased standard or 6 greased jumbo muffin cups. Sprinkle with cinnamon sugar.
3. Bake for 18 minutes for standard muffins or for 22 minutes for jumbo muffins.
1 STANDARD MUFFIN: 171 cal., 7g fat (1g sat. fat), 20mg chol., 146mg sod., 24g carb. (10g sugars, 1g fiber), 3g pro.

Cakes, Pies & Desserts

Indulge your craving for something special with this fabulous collection of goodies—just the thing to end a meal on a sweet note or for a perfect treat any time!

BLUEBERRY LATTICE BARS

Since our area hosts an annual blueberry festival, my daughters and I are always looking for exciting, new berry recipes to enter in the cooking contest. These lovely yummy bars won a blue ribbon one year.
—Debbie Ayers, Baileyville, ME

Prep: 25 min. + chilling
Bake: 30 min. + cooling • **Makes:** 2 dozen

- **1⅓ cups butter, softened**
- **⅔ cup sugar**
- **¼ tsp. salt**
- **1 large egg, room temperature**
- **½ tsp. vanilla extract**
- **3¾ cups all-purpose flour**

FILLING

- **3 cups fresh or frozen blueberries**
- **1 cup sugar**
- **3 Tbsp. cornstarch**

1. Cream butter, sugar and salt until light and fluffy; beat in egg and vanilla. Gradually beat in flour. Divide dough in half; shape each half into a 1-in.-thick rectangle. Wrap and refrigerate 2 hours or overnight.
2. Preheat oven to 375°. Place blueberries, sugar and cornstarch in a small saucepan. Bring to a boil over medium heat, stirring frequently; cook and stir until thickened, about 2 minutes. Cool slightly.
3. Roll each portion of the dough between two sheets of plastic wrap into a 14x10-in. rectangle. Place rectangles on separate baking sheets; freeze until firm, 5-10 minutes. Place one rectangle in a greased 13x9-in. baking pan, pressing onto bottom and about ½ in. up the sides. Add the filling.
4. Cut the remaining rectangle into ½-in. strips; freeze 5-10 minutes to firm. Arrange strips over the filling in crisscross fashion. If desired, press edges with a fork to seal the strips. Bake until the top crust is golden brown, 30-35 minutes. Cool on a wire rack. Cut into bars.
1 BAR: 233 cal., 11g fat (7g sat. fat), 35mg chol., 109mg sod., 32g carb. (16g sugars, 1g fiber), 3g pro.

WINNING APRICOT BARS

This recipe is down-home baking at its best, and it represents all regions of the country. It's won blue ribbons at county fairs and cookie contests in several states! Easy to make, it's perfect for potluck suppers, bake sales, lunch boxes or just plain snacking.
—Jill Moritz, Irvine, CA

Prep: 15 min. • **Bake:** 30 min. + cooling
Makes: 2 dozen

- **¾ cup butter, softened**
- **1 cup sugar**
- **1 large egg, room temperature**
- **½ tsp. vanilla extract**
- **2 cups all-purpose flour**
- **¼ tsp. baking powder**
- **1⅓ cups sweetened shredded coconut**
- **½ cup chopped walnuts**
- **1 jar (10 to 12 oz.) apricot preserves**

1. Preheat oven to 350°. In a large bowl, cream the butter and sugar until light and fluffy. Beat in egg and vanilla. In a small bowl, whisk the flour and baking powder; gradually add to the creamed mixture, mixing well. Fold in coconut and walnuts.
2. Press two-thirds of dough onto the bottom of a greased 13x9-in. baking pan. Spread with preserves; crumble the remaining dough over preserves. Bake 30-35 minutes or until golden brown. Cool completely in pan on a wire rack. Cut into bars.
1 BAR: 195 cal., 10g fat (6g sat. fat), 23mg chol., 72mg sod., 27g carb. (16g sugars, 1g fiber), 2g pro.

SUGAR CREAM PIE

I absolutely love creamy sugar pie; especially the one that my grandma made for me. Here in Indiana, we serve it either warm or chilled.
—Laura Kipper, Westfield, IN

Prep: 20 min. • **Bake:** 15 min. + chilling
Makes: 8 servings

- **Pastry for single-crust pie (9 in.)**
- **1 cup sugar**
- **¼ cup cornstarch**
- **2 cups 2% milk**
- **½ cup butter, cubed**
- **1 tsp. vanilla extract**
- **¼ tsp. ground cinnamon**

1. Preheat oven to 450°. Roll out dough to fit a 9-in. pie plate. Transfer crust to pie plate. Trim crust to ½ in. beyond rim of plate; flute edge. Line unpricked crust with a double thickness of heavy-duty foil. Fill with pie weights, dried beans or uncooked rice.
2. Bake 8 minutes. Remove foil and weights; bake for 5-7 minutes longer or until light brown. Place on a wire rack to cool. Reduce oven setting to 375°.
3. Meanwhile, in a large saucepan, combine sugar and cornstarch; stir in milk until smooth. Bring to a boil. Reduce heat; cook and stir for 2 minutes or until thickened and bubbly. Remove from heat; stir in butter and vanilla. Transfer to crust; sprinkle with cinnamon. Bake 15-20 minutes or until golden brown. Cool on a wire rack; refrigerate until chilled.
PASTRY FOR A SINGLE-CRUST PIE (9 IN.): Combine 1¼ cups all-purpose flour and ¼ tsp. salt; cut in ½ cup cold butter until crumbly. Gradually add 3-5 Tbsp. ice water, tossing with a fork until the dough holds together when pressed. Wrap and refrigerate 1 hour.
1 PIECE: 418 cal., 24g fat (15g sat. fat), 66mg chol., 275mg sod., 47g carb. (28g sugars, 1g fiber), 4g pro.

TEST KITCHEN TIP
This delicious creamy treat is an egg-free way to enjoy a custardlike texture. If you're baking for the holidays, try adding ⅛ tsp. each of cloves, nutmeg and ginger when mixing in the cinnamon. Your home will smell heavenly!

SPICED DEVIL'S FOOD CAKE

One of my mom's friends gave her this recipe when I was a child and it has been a family favorite ever since. When your chocolate sweet tooth acts up, this really hits the spot!
—Linda Yeamans, Ashland, OR

Prep: 25 min. • **Bake:** 30 min. + cooling
Makes: 12 servings

- 1 **cup butter, softened**
- 1½ **cups sugar**
- 3 **large eggs, room temperature**
- 1 **tsp. vanilla extract**
- 2 **cups all-purpose flour**
- ¼ **cup baking cocoa**
- 1 **tsp. baking powder**
- 1 **tsp. baking soda**
- 1 **tsp. ground cinnamon**
- ½ **to 1 tsp. ground nutmeg**
- ¼ **to ½ tsp. ground cloves**
- 1 **cup buttermilk**

MOCHA ICING

- 3¾ **cups confectioners' sugar**
- ¼ **cup baking cocoa**
- 6 **Tbsp. strong brewed coffee**
- 6 **Tbsp. butter, melted**
- 1 **tsp. vanilla extract**
- **Toasted whole or chopped almonds, optional**

1. Preheat oven to 350°. Grease and flour two 9-in round baking pans; set aside Cream butter and sugar until light and fluffy. Add the eggs, one at a time, beating well after each addition. Add vanilla.
2. Sift together all the dry ingredients; add to the creamed mixture alternately with buttermilk. Pour batter into prepared pans.
3. Bake until a toothpick inserted in center comes out clean, 30-35 minutes. Cool on wire racks for 10 minutes before removing from pans.
4. In a small bowl, combine all icing ingredients except nuts. Spread frosting between layers and over the top and sides of cake. If desired, top with almonds.
1 SLICE: 543 cal., 23g fat (14g sat. fat), 110mg chol., 389mg sod., 82g carb. (61g sugars, 1g fiber), 5g pro.

CRANBERRY PEACH COBBLER

This cobbler is a little nontraditional but it will soon be at the top of your recipe list. Serve it warm with French vanilla ice cream.
—Grace Sandvigen, Rochester, NY

Prep: 15 min. • **Bake:** 45 min.
Makes: 15 servings

- ½ **cup butter, melted**
- 2 **cans (29 oz. each) sliced peaches**
- 1 **pkg. (15.6 oz.) cranberry-orange quick bread mix**
- 1 **large egg, room temperature**
- 2 **Tbsp. grated orange zest, divided**
- ⅓ **cup dried cranberries**
- ⅓ **cup sugar**

1. Preheat oven to 375°. Pour butter into a 13x9-in. baking dish. Drain peaches, reserving 1 cup juice. Pat peaches dry and set aside. In a large bowl, combine the quick bread mix, egg, 1 Tbsp. orange zest and the reserved peach juice.
2. Drop batter by tablespoonfuls over butter, spreading slightly. Arrange peaches over top; sprinkle with cranberries. Combine sugar and remaining orange zest; sprinkle over peaches. Bake until golden brown, 45-50 minutes. Serve warm.
1 SERVING: 271 cal., 10g fat (5g sat. fat), 33mg chol., 193mg sod., 44g carb. (32g sugars, 1g fiber), 1g pro.

SURPRISE CARROT CAKE

A cousin gave me this carrot cake recipe. It's a potluck delight with its unexpected cream cheese center. My husband and our two children love it, too!
—Lisa Bowen, Little Britain, ON

Prep: 25 min. • **Bake:** 55 min. + cooling
Makes: 16 servings

- **3 cups shredded carrots**
- **1¾ cups sugar**
- **1 cup canola oil**
- **3 large eggs, room temperature**
- **2 cups all-purpose flour**
- **2 tsp. baking soda**
- **2 tsp. ground cinnamon**
- **1 tsp. salt**
- **½ cup chopped pecans**

FILLING

- **1 pkg. (8 oz.) cream cheese, softened**
- **¼ cup sugar**
- **1 large egg, room temperature**

FROSTING

- **1 pkg. (8 oz.) cream cheese, softened**
- **¼ cup butter, softened**
- **2 tsp. vanilla extract**
- **4 cups confectioners' sugar**

1. Preheat oven to 350°. Grease and flour a 10-in. tube pan; set aside. In a large bowl, beat the carrots, sugar, oil and eggs until well blended. In a large bowl, combine the flour, baking soda, cinnamon and salt; gradually beat into the carrot mixture until blended. Stir in the pecans. Pour 3 cups of batter into the prepared pan.
2. In a small bowl, beat the cream cheese and sugar until smooth. Beat in egg. Spoon over the batter in the pan. Top with the remaining batter.
3. Bake for 55-60 minutes or until a toothpick inserted in the center comes out clean. Cool for 10 minutes before removing from pan to a wire rack to cool completely.
4. For frosting, in a small bowl, beat the cream cheese, butter and vanilla until fluffy. Gradually add confectioners' sugar until smooth. Frost cake. Store in the refrigerator.
1 SLICE: 570 cal., 30g fat (10g sat. fat), 92mg chol., 442mg sod., 71g carb. (55g sugars, 2g fiber), 6g pro.

SKILLET PINEAPPLE UPSIDE-DOWN CAKE

This old-fashioned recipe is a traditional favorite for a reason. For a change of pace, you can substitute fresh or frozen peach slices for the pineapple.
—Bernardine Melton, Paola, KS

Prep: 20 min. • **Bake:** 30 min. + cooling
Makes: 10 servings

- **½ cup butter**
- **1 cup packed brown sugar**
- **1 can (20 oz.) sliced pineapple**
- **½ cup chopped pecans**
- **3 large eggs, room temperature, separated**
- **1 cup sugar**
- **1 tsp. vanilla extract**
- **1 cup all-purpose flour**
- **1 tsp. baking powder**
- **¼ tsp. salt**
- **Maraschino cherries**

1. Preheat oven to 375°. Melt butter in a 9- or 10-in. ovenproof skillet. Add brown sugar; mix well until sugar is melted. Drain pineapple, reserving ⅓ cup juice. Arrange about eight pineapple slices in a single layer over the sugar (refrigerate remaining slices for another use). Sprinkle pecans over the pineapple; set aside.
2. In a large bowl, beat egg yolks until thick and lemon-colored. Gradually add sugar, beating well. Blend in vanilla and the reserved pineapple juice. Combine the flour, baking powder and salt; gradually add to the batter and mix well.
3. In a small bowl, beat egg whites on high speed until stiff peaks form; fold into batter. Spoon into skillet.
4. Bake until a toothpick inserted in center comes out clean, 30-35 minutes (cover loosely with foil if cake browns too quickly). Let stand 10 minutes before inverting onto a serving plate. Place a cherry in the center of each pineapple slice.
1 SLICE: 380 cal., 15g fat (7g sat. fat), 88mg chol., 224mg sod., 59g carb. (48g sugars, 1g fiber), 4g pro.

S'MORE CHEESECAKE

Inspired by the old-time campfire snack, this luscious dessert is the grown-up way to do s'mores any time of year.
—Robin Andrews, Cary, NC

Prep: 20 min. • **Bake:** 45 min. + chilling
Makes: 12 servings

- **2¼ cups graham cracker crumbs (about 36 squares)**
- **⅓ cup sugar**
- **½ cup butter, melted**

FILLING

- **2 pkg. (8 oz. each) cream cheese, softened**
- **1 can (14 oz.) sweetened condensed milk**
- **2 tsp. vanilla extract**
- **3 large eggs, room temperature, lightly beaten**
- **1 cup miniature semisweet chocolate chips**
- **1 cup miniature marshmallows**

TOPPING

- **1 cup miniature marshmallows**
- **½ cup semisweet chocolate chips**
- **1 Tbsp. shortening**

1. Preheat oven to 325°. In a small bowl, combine cracker crumbs and sugar; stir in butter. Press onto the bottom and 1¾ in. up the sides of a greased 10-in. springform pan; set aside.
2. In a large bowl, beat the cream cheese, milk and vanilla until smooth. Add eggs; beat on low just until combined. Stir in chocolate chips and marshmallows. Pour over crust. Place on a baking sheet.
3. Bake 40-45 minutes or until center is almost set. Sprinkle with the marshmallows. Bake 4-6 minutes longer or until the marshmallows are puffed.
4. Melt chocolate chips and shortening in a heavy saucepan or microwave; stir until smooth. Drizzle over marshmallows.
5. Cool on a wire rack for 10 minutes. Run a knife around edge of pan to loosen; cool 1 hour longer. Refrigerate overnight. Remove sides of pan. Refrigerate leftovers.
1 SLICE: 486 cal., 27g fat (15g sat. fat), 106mg chol., 292mg sod., 57g carb. (44g sugars, 2g fiber), 8g pro.

PEANUT BUTTER CHOCOLATE CUPCAKES

Chocolate and peanut butter are my two favorite flavors, but I didn't have any luck finding a peanut butter-filled chocolate cupcake recipe. I began experimenting with my go-to cupcake recipe—and this is the happy result.
—Julie Small, Unity, NH

Prep: 30 min. • **Bake:** 25 min. + cooling
Makes: 1 dozen

- **3 oz. cream cheese, softened**
- **¼ cup creamy peanut butter**
- **2 Tbsp. sugar**
- **1 Tbsp. 2% milk**

BATTER

- **2 cups sugar**
- **1¾ cups all-purpose flour**
- **½ cup baking cocoa**
- **1½ tsp. baking powder**
- **1 tsp. salt**
- **¼ tsp. baking soda**
- **2 large eggs, room temperature**
- **1 cup water**
- **1 cup 2% milk**
- **½ cup canola oil**
- **2 tsp. vanilla extract**

FROSTING

- **⅓ cup butter, softened**
- **2 cups confectioners' sugar**
- **6 Tbsp. baking cocoa**
- **3 to 4 Tbsp. 2% milk**

1. Preheat oven to 350°. In a small bowl, beat cream cheese, peanut butter, sugar and milk until smooth; set aside.
2. In a large bowl, combine the sugar, flour, cocoa, baking powder, salt and baking soda. In another bowl, whisk the eggs, water, milk, oil and vanilla. Stir into the dry ingredients just until moistened (batter will be thin).
3. Fill 12 paper-lined jumbo muffin cups half full with batter. Drop a scant tablespoonful of peanut butter mixture into center of each; cover with remaining batter.
4. Bake for 25-30 minutes or until a toothpick inserted into cake comes out clean. Cool for 10 minutes; remove from pans to wire racks. Cool completely.
5. In a large bowl, combine the frosting ingredients until smooth; frost cupcakes. Store in the refrigerator.
1 CUPCAKE: 509 cal., 22g fat (7g sat. fat), 60mg chol., 394mg sod., 75g carb. (55g sugars, 2g fiber), 7g pro.

BLACKBERRY APPLE PIE

My mother made this pie so often she could do it with her eyes closed! We picked the berries ourselves, and the apples came from the trees in our orchard. I can still taste the delicious combination of fruits encased in Mother's flaky pie crust.
—Fran Stanfield, Wilmington, OH

Prep: 20 min. • **Bake:** 50 min.
Makes: 8 servings

- **Pastry for a double-crust pie (9 in.)**
- **5 cups thinly sliced peeled tart apples (about 5 medium)**
- **1 pint fresh blackberries, rinsed and drained**
- **1 Tbsp. lemon juice**
- **¾ cup sugar**
- **2 Tbsp. cornstarch**
- **2 Tbsp. butter**
- **1 large egg, room temperature, lightly beaten**
- **1 Tbsp. water or whole milk**

1. Line a 9-in. pie plate with bottom crust; trim to 1 in. beyond edge of plate. Top with a thin layer of apples. In a large bowl, combine blackberries and remaining apples; sprinkle with lemon juice. Combine the sugar and cornstarch. Add to fruit mixture; toss gently to coat. Spoon into pie shell; dot with butter.
2. Roll out remaining dough; make a lattice crust. Trim, seal and flute edges. Beat egg with water; brush over lattice top and pie edges.
3. Bake at 375° for 50 minutes or until filling is bubbly and apples are tender. Cool on a wire rack. Serve warm or at room temperature.
PASTRY FOR DOUBLE-CRUST PIE (9 IN.): Combine 2½ cups all-purpose flour and ½ tsp. salt; cut in 1 cup cold butter until crumbly. Gradually add ⅓-⅔ cup ice water; toss with a fork until dough holds together when pressed. Divide dough in half. Shape each into a disk; wrap and refrigerate 1 hour or overnight.
1 SLICE: 415 cal., 18g fat (8g sat. fat), 44mg chol., 238mg sod., 62g carb. (32g sugars, 2g fiber), 3g pro.

UPSIDE-DOWN APPLE CAKE

Baked in a Bundt pan and drizzled with icing, this breakfast cake is a special treat. I adapted the recipe from one of my grandmother's.
—Shaunda Wenger, Nibley, UT

Prep: 25 min. • **Bake:** 40 min. + cooling
Makes: 14 servings

- **2 large egg whites, room temperature**
- **1 cup sugar**
- **1 cup sour cream**
- **½ cup unsweetened applesauce**
- **1 tsp. vanilla extract**
- **2 cups all-purpose flour**
- **¾ tsp. baking soda**
- **½ tsp. baking powder**
- **½ tsp. salt**

FILLING
- **2½ cups diced peeled tart apples**
- **½ cup chopped walnuts**
- **¼ cup sugar**
- **2 Tbsp. butter, melted**
- **2 tsp. ground cinnamon**

GLAZE
- **1 cup confectioners' sugar**
- **4 tsp. 2% milk**
- **¼ tsp. vanilla extract**

1. Preheat oven to 350°. Grease and flour a 10-in. fluted tube pan; set aside. In a large bowl, beat egg whites, sugar, sour cream, applesauce and vanilla. Combine flour, baking soda, baking powder and salt; gradually add to the sour cream mixture, beating just until combined.
2. In a large bowl, combine filling ingredients. Spoon half the batter into the prepared pan. Top with half the filling. Repeat layers.
3. Bake for 40-45 minutes or until a toothpick inserted in the center comes out clean. Cool for 10 minutes; invert pan and remove cake to a wire rack to cool completely. Combine glaze ingredients; drizzle over cake.
1 SLICE: 269 cal., 8g fat (4g sat. fat), 46mg chol., 195mg sod., 45g carb. (30g sugars, 1g fiber), 4g pro.

YELLOW CUPCAKES

On any given day, someone probably needs a gorgeous homemade cupcake! This buttery, yellow cake base works with any frosting and decorates beautifully.
—Taste of Home *Test Kitchen*

Prep: 20 min. • **Bake:** 15 min. + cooling
Makes: 2 dozen

- **⅔ cup butter, softened**
- **1¾ cups sugar**
- **2 large eggs, room temperature**
- **1½ tsp. vanilla extract**
- **2½ cups all-purpose flour**
- **2½ tsp. baking powder**
- **½ tsp. salt**
- **1¼ cups 2% milk**
- **Frosting of your choice**

1. Preheat oven to 350°. Line 24 muffin cups with paper liners.
2. In a large bowl, cream butter and sugar until light and fluffy. Add eggs, one at a time, beating well after each addition. Beat in vanilla. In another bowl, whisk flour, baking powder and salt; add to creamed mixture alternately with milk, beating well after each addition.
3. Fill the prepared cups three-fourths full. Bake 15-20 minutes or until a toothpick inserted in center comes out clean. Cool in pans 10 minutes before removing to wire racks to cool completely. Spread with frosting.
1 CUPCAKE: 163 cal., 6g fat (4g sat. fat), 32mg chol., 138mg sod., 25g carb. (15g sugars, 0 fiber), 2g pro.

READER REVIEW

"Just what I have been looking for. Moist and delicious married with perfect vanilla favor. I made raspberry frosting and pressed a red raspberry into each cupcake before baking. They made a beautiful presentation and had a 'to die for' taste."
DRESSAGEDIVA, TASTEOFHOME.COM

CHUNKY MONKEY CUPCAKES

Peanut butter is a favorite of ours, and it brings a fun element to these cupcakes. They're good with or without garnishes.
—Holly Jones, Kennesaw, GA

Prep: 30 min. • **Bake:** 20 min. + cooling
Makes: 2 dozen

- **2 cups mashed ripe bananas (about 5 medium)**
- **1½ cups sugar**
- **3 large eggs, room temperature**
- **½ cup unsweetened applesauce**
- **¼ cup canola oil**
- **3 cups all-purpose flour**
- **1 tsp. baking soda**
- **½ tsp. baking powder**
- **½ tsp. salt**
- **1 cup semisweet chocolate chunks**

FROSTING

- **4 oz. reduced-fat cream cheese**
- **¼ cup creamy peanut butter**
- **3 Tbsp. butter, softened**
- **1 to 1¼ cups confectioners' sugar**
- **Chopped salted peanuts, optional**

1. Preheat oven to 350°. Line 24 muffin cups with paper liners. In a large bowl, beat the first five ingredients until well blended. In another bowl, whisk together flour, baking soda, baking powder and salt; gradually beat into banana mixture. Fold in chocolate chunks.
2. Fill prepared cups three-fourths full. Bake until a toothpick inserted in center comes out clean, 20-25 minutes. Cool in pans about 10 minutes before removing to wire racks to cool completely.
3. For frosting, beat cream cheese, peanut butter and butter until smooth. Gradually beat in enough confectioners' sugar to reach desired consistency. Spread over cupcakes. If desired, sprinkle with peanuts. Refrigerate any leftovers.

1 CUPCAKE: 250 cal., 9g fat (4g sat. fat), 30mg chol., 165mg sod., 40g carb. (25g sugars, 2g fiber), 4g pro.

JUMBLEBERRY CRUMBLE

A friend brought this delicious, down-home dessert to church and was kind enough to give out the recipe. Everyone showered her with compliments! It's especially wonderful served warm or with a dollop of whipped cream.
—Mary Ann Dell, Phoenixville, PA

Prep: 10 min. + standing • **Bake:** 45 min.
Makes: 8 servings

- **3 cups halved fresh strawberries**
- **1½ cups fresh raspberries**
- **1½ cups fresh blueberries**
- **⅔ cup sugar**
- **3 Tbsp. quick-cooking tapioca**
- **½ cup all-purpose flour**
- **½ cup quick-cooking oats**
- **½ cup packed brown sugar**
- **1 tsp. ground cinnamon**
- **⅓ cup butter, melted**
- **Vanilla ice cream or sweetened whipped cream, optional**

1. Preheat oven to 350°. In a large bowl, combine the strawberries, raspberries and blueberries. Combine sugar and tapioca; sprinkle over berries and toss gently. Pour into a greased 11x7-in. baking dish; let stand for 15 minutes.
2. In a small bowl, combine flour, oats, brown sugar and cinnamon. Stir in butter; sprinkle over the berry mixture.
3. Bake 45-50 minutes or until filling is bubbly and topping is golden brown. Serve warm and, if desired, with vanilla ice cream or sweetened whipped cream.

1 SERVING: 290 cal., 8g fat (5g sat. fat), 20mg chol., 84mg sod., 54g carb. (36g sugars, 4g fiber), 2g pro.

DID YOU KNOW?
The only difference between quick-cooking and old-fashioned oats is that quick-cooking oats are cut into smaller pieces so they cook faster. You can use either in your recipes, but quick-cooking will deliver a more delicate texture.

ZUCCHINI BROWNIES

A fast-to-fix peanut butter and chocolate frosting tops these moist brownies that are a sweet way to use up your green garden squash. We really love the cakelike texture of these brownies.
—Allyson Wilkins, Amherst, NH

Prep: 20 min. • **Bake:** 35 min. + cooling
Makes: about 1½ dozen

- 1 **cup butter, softened**
- 1½ **cups sugar**
- 2 **large eggs, room temperature**
- ½ **cup plain yogurt**
- 1 **tsp. vanilla extract**
- 2½ **cups all-purpose flour**
- ¼ **cup baking cocoa**
- 1 **tsp. baking soda**
- ½ **tsp. salt**
- 2 **cups shredded zucchini**

FROSTING

- ⅔ **cup semisweet chocolate chips**
- ½ **cup creamy peanut butter**

1. Preheat oven to 350°. Grease a 13x9-in baking pan; set aside. In a large bowl, cream butter and sugar until light and fluffy. Add eggs, one at a time, beating well after each addition. Beat in yogurt and vanilla. Combine flour, cocoa, baking soda and salt; gradually add to creamed mixture. Stir in zucchini.
2. Pour batter into prepared pan. Bake for 35-40 minutes or until a toothpick inserted in the center comes out clean.
3. For frosting, in a small saucepan, combine chocolate chips and peanut butter. Cook and stir over low heat until smooth. Spread over warm brownies. Cool on a wire rack. Cut into bars.
1 BROWNIE: 307 cal., 17g fat (8g sat. fat), 52mg chol., 283mg sod., 37g carb. (21g sugars, 2g fiber), 5g pro.

5i

RHUBARB CHERRY PIE

As a young girl, I dreamed of being able to make pies like my mother. (Her hefty rolling pin was 2 feet long!) I first made this pie for a church gathering many years ago—ever since, everyone looks for it at every potluck!
—Eunice Hurt, Murfreesboro, TN

Prep: 10 min. + standing • **Bake:** 40 min.
Makes: 8 servings

- 3 **cups sliced fresh or frozen rhubarb (½-in. pieces)**
- 1 **can (16 oz.) pitted tart red cherries, drained**
- 1¼ **cups sugar**
- ¼ **cup quick-cooking tapioca**
- 4 **to 5 drops red food coloring, optional**
- **Pastry for double-crust pie (9 in.)**

1. Preheat oven to 400°. In a large bowl, combine the first five ingredients; let stand for 15 minutes. Line a 9-in. pie plate with pastry; add filling. Top with a lattice crust; flute the edges.
2. Bake 40-50 minutes or until the crust is golden and filling is bubbling.
Pastry for double-crust pie (9 in.): Combine 2½ cups all-purpose flour and ½ tsp. salt; cut in 1 cup cold butter until crumbly. Gradually add ⅓-⅔ cup ice water, tossing with a fork until dough holds together when pressed. Divide dough in half. Shape each into a disk; wrap and refrigerate 1 hour or overnight.
1 SLICE: 433 cal., 14g fat (6g sat. fat), 10mg chol., 206mg sod., 75g carb. (44g sugars, 1g fiber), 3g pro.

LAUREN KNOELKE
Des Moines, IA

TEXAS CHOCOLATE CUPCAKES

I never thought about putting caramel icing on chocolate cupcakes. Boy, was I missing out! My mother-in-law shared this recipe with me. It's to die for!
—Cathy Bodkins, Dayton, VA

Prep: 30 min. • **Bake:** 15 min. + cooling
Makes: 2 dozen

- **2 cups all-purpose flour**
- **2 cups sugar**
- **1 tsp. salt**
- **½ tsp. baking soda**
- **¼ cup baking cocoa**
- **1 cup water**
- **1 cup canola oil**
- **½ cup butter, cubed**
- **2 large eggs, room temperature**
- **⅓ cup buttermilk**
- **1 tsp. vanilla extract**

CARAMEL ICING

- **1 cup packed brown sugar**
- **½ cup butter, cubed**
- **¼ cup whole milk**
- **2 to 2¼ cups confectioners' sugar**

1. Preheat oven to 350°. In a large bowl, combine the flour, sugar, salt and baking soda. In a large saucepan over medium heat, bring the cocoa, water, oil and butter to a boil. Gradually add to the dry ingredients and mix well. Combine the eggs, buttermilk and vanilla; gradually add to batter and mix well (the batter will be very thin).
2. Fill paper-lined muffin cups three-fourths full. Bake 15-20 minutes or until a toothpick inserted in the center comes out clean. Cool for 10 minutes before removing from pans to wire racks to cool completely.
3. For icing, in a heavy saucepan, combine brown sugar, butter and milk. Cook and stir over low heat until the sugar is dissolved. Increase heat to medium. Do not stir. Cook for 3-6 minutes or until bubbles form in the center of the mixture and the syrup turns amber. Remove from the heat; transfer to a small bowl. Cool to room temperature. Gradually beat in confectioners' sugar until smooth. Frost cupcakes.
1 CUPCAKE: 335 cal., 17g fat (6g sat. fat), 39mg chol., 216mg sod., 44g carb. (35g sugars, 0 fiber), 2g pro.

CAST-IRON PEACH CROSTATA

While the crostata, an open-faced fruit tart, is an Italian specialty, my version's peach filling is American all the way.
—Lauren Knoelke, Des Moines, IA

Prep: 45 min. + chilling • **Bake:** 45 min.
Makes: 10 servings

- **1½ cups all-purpose flour**
- **2 Tbsp. plus ¾ cup packed brown sugar, divided**
- **1¼ tsp. salt, divided**
- **½ cup cold unsalted butter, cubed**
- **2 Tbsp. shortening**
- **3 to 5 Tbsp. ice water**
- **8 cups sliced peaches (about 7-8 medium)**
- **1 Tbsp. lemon juice**
- **3 Tbsp. cornstarch**
- **½ tsp. ground cinnamon**
- **¼ tsp. ground nutmeg**
- **1 large egg, beaten**
- **2 Tbsp. sliced almonds**
- **1 Tbsp. coarse sugar**
- **⅓ cup water**
- **1 cup fresh raspberries, optional**

1. Mix flour, 2 Tbsp. brown sugar and 1 tsp. salt; cut in the butter and shortening until crumbly. Gradually add ice water, tossing with a fork until the dough holds together when pressed. Shape into a disk; wrap and refrigerate 1 hour or overnight.
2. Combine peaches and lemon juice. Add the remaining brown sugar, cornstarch, spices and the remaining salt; toss gently. Let stand for 30 minutes.
3. Preheat oven to 400°. On a lightly floured surface, roll dough into a 13-in. circle; transfer to a 10-in. cast-iron skillet, letting excess hang over edge. Using a slotted spoon, transfer peaches into the pastry, reserving the liquid. Fold pastry edge over filling, pleating as you go, leaving the center uncovered. Brush folded pastry with beaten egg; sprinkle with almonds and coarse sugar. Bake until the crust is dark golden and the filling is bubbly, 45-55 minutes.
4. In a small saucepan, combine the reserved liquid and the water; bring to a boil. Simmer until thickened, 1-2 minutes; serve warm with pie. If desired, top with fresh raspberries.
1 SLICE: 322 cal., 13g fat (7g sat. fat), 43mg chol., 381mg sod., 49g carb. (30g sugars, 3g fiber), 4g pro.

WHITE TEXAS SHEET CAKE

This cake gets better the longer it sits, so I try to make it a day ahead. My mother-in-law introduced this deliciously rich sheet cake to me. With its creamy frosting and light almond flavor, no one can stop at just one piece!
—Joanie Ward, Brownsburg, IN

Prep: 20 min. • **Bake:** 20 min. + cooling
Makes: 20 servings

- **2 cups all-purpose flour**
- **2 cups sugar**
- **1 tsp. baking powder**
- **1 tsp. salt**
- **¼ tsp. baking soda**
- **1 cup butter, cubed**
- **1 cup water**
- **2 large eggs, room temperature**
- **½ cup sour cream**
- **1 tsp. almond extract**

FROSTING

- **½ cup butter, cubed**
- **¼ cup 2% milk**
- **4½ cups confectioners' sugar**
- **½ tsp. almond extract**
- **1 cup chopped walnuts**

1. Preheat oven to 375°. Grease a 15x10x1-in. baking pan; set aside. In a large bowl, whisk the first five ingredients. In a small saucepan, combine butter and water; bring just to a boil. Stir into the flour mixture. In a small bowl, whisk the eggs, sour cream and almond extract until blended; add to flour mixture, whisking constantly.
2. Transfer batter to the prepared pan. Bake until golden brown and a toothpick inserted in center comes out clean, 18-22 minutes. Cool on a wire rack 20 minutes.
3. For frosting, combine butter and milk in a large saucepan; bring just to a boil. Remove from heat; gradually stir in confectioners' sugar and extract. Stir in walnuts. Spread over warm cake.
1 PIECE: 409 cal., 19g fat (10g sat. fat), 62mg chol., 304mg sod., 58g carb. (45g sugars, 1g fiber), 4g pro.

TEST KITCHEN TIP
This recipe makes a big, beautiful birthday cake with plenty of room for candles. Just add sprinkles! The roasty flavor of toasted nuts pairs well with decadently sweet desserts. Be sure to toast your walnuts before adding them to the frosting.

VANILLA CREAM FRUIT TART

It's well worth the effort to whip up this creamy tart bursting with juicy summer berries. A friend gave me the recipe, and it always receives rave reviews at gatherings.
—Susan Terzakis, Andover, MA

Prep: 25 min. • **Bake:** 25 min. + chilling
Makes: 12 servings

- **¾ cup butter, softened**
- **½ cup confectioners' sugar**
- **1½ cups all-purpose flour**
- **1 pkg. (10 to 12 oz.) white baking chips, melted and cooled**
- **¼ cup heavy whipping cream**
- **1 pkg. (8 oz.) cream cheese, softened**
- **½ cup pineapple juice**
- **¼ cup sugar**
- **1 Tbsp. cornstarch**
- **½ tsp. lemon juice**
- **1½ to 2 cups fresh strawberries, sliced**
- **1 cup fresh blueberries**
- **1 cup fresh raspberries**

1. Preheat oven to 300°. Grease a 12-in. pizza pan; set aside. Cream the butter and confectioners' sugar until light and fluffy. Beat in flour (mixture will be crumbly). Pat onto prepared pan. Bake until lightly browned, 25-28 minutes. Cool.
2. Cream melted chips until smooth. Beat in cream cheese until smooth. Spread over crust. Refrigerate for 30 minutes. Meanwhile, in a small saucepan, combine pineapple juice, granulated sugar, cornstarch and lemon juice. Bring to a boil over medium heat; cook and stir until thickened, about 2 minutes. Cool.
3. Arrange berries over cream cheese layer; brush with the pineapple mixture. Refrigerate 1 hour before serving.
1 PIECE: 433 cal., 28g fat (17g sat. fat), 60mg chol., 174mg sod., 43g carb. (28g sugars, 2g fiber), 5g pro.

BUTTERMILK CAKE WITH CIDER ICING

One of my favorite cakes, this vintage-style beauty has rich, buttery flavor. I like to make it in a classic Bundt shape. Buttermilk gives the cake an irresistibly tender texture, and watching the apple cider icing drizzle down the sides is almost as marvelous as taking your first bite. Almost.

—Gina Nistico, Denver, CO

Prep: 35 min. • **Bake:** 45 min. + cooling
Makes: 16 servings

- **1 cup butter, softened**
- **2⅓ cups granulated sugar**
- **1½ tsp. vanilla extract**
- **3 large eggs, room temperature**
- **3 cups all-purpose flour**
- **1 tsp. baking powder**
- **½ tsp. baking soda**
- **1 cup buttermilk**

ICING

- **1 cup confectioners' sugar**
- **4 oz. cream cheese, softened**
- **¼ cup butter, softened**
- **¼ to ½ cup apple cider or juice**
- **Freshly grated whole nutmeg, optional**

1. Preheat oven to 350°. Grease and flour a 10-in. fluted tube pan; set aside.

2. Cream the butter and sugar until light and fluffy. Beat in the vanilla and the eggs, one at a time, beating well after each addition. In another bowl, whisk together the flour, baking powder and baking soda; add to the creamed mixture alternately with buttermilk (batter will be thick). Transfer batter to the prepared pan.

3. Bake until a toothpick inserted in the center comes out clean, 45-50 minutes. Cool in pan 10 minutes before removing to a wire rack to cool completely.

4. For the icing, beat confectioners' sugar, cream cheese, butter and enough apple cider to reach desired consistency; spread or spoon over cake. If desired, sprinkle with freshly grated nutmeg.

1 SLICE: 403 cal., 18g fat (11g sat. fat), 81mg chol., 249mg sod., 56g carb. (38g sugars, 1g fiber), 5g pro.

SLOW-COOKER MIXED FRUIT & PISTACHIO CAKE

This cake is easy to make on a lazy day and guaranteed delicious for several days, if you can make it last that long. It's a warm, fragrant welcome in the cooler months.
—Nancy Heishman, Las Vegas, NV

Prep: 20 min. • **Cook:** 2½ hours + cooling
Makes: 8 servings

- **1½ cups all-purpose flour**
- **1½ tsp. ground cinnamon**
- **½ tsp. baking soda**
- **½ tsp. baking powder**
- **½ tsp. ground allspice**
- **¼ tsp. salt**
- **1 can (8 oz.) jellied cranberry sauce**
- **⅓ cup packed brown sugar**
- **⅓ cup buttermilk**
- **¼ cup butter, melted**
- **2 tsp. grated orange zest**
- **½ tsp. orange extract**
- **1 large egg, room temperature**
- **1 cup mixed dried fruit bits**
- **1 cup pistachios**
- **Sweetened whipped cream, optional**

1. Whisk together the first six ingredients. In another bowl, combine the next seven ingredients. Add the cranberry mixture to the flour mixture; stir until smooth. Add dried fruit and pistachios.
2. Pour the batter into a greased 1½-qt. baking dish; place in a 6-qt. slow cooker. Lay a 14x12-in. piece of parchment over top of slow cooker under the lid. Cook, covered, on high until a toothpick inserted in the center comes out clean, about 2½ hours. Remove dish from the slow cooker to a wire rack. Cool for 30 minutes before inverting onto a serving platter.
3. Cut cake into wedges with a serrated knife; if desired, serve with sweetened whipped cream.
1 WEDGE: 375 cal., 14g fat (5g sat. fat), 39mg chol., 349mg sod., 57g carb. (30g sugars, 4g fiber), 7g pro.

5i

SHOOFLY CUPCAKES

These moist old-fashioned molasses cupcakes were my grandmother's specialty. To keep them from disappearing too quickly, she used to store them out of sight. But somehow, we always figured out her hiding places!
—Beth Adams, Jacksonville, FL

Prep: 15 min. • **Bake:** 20 min. + cooling
Makes: 2 dozen

- **4 cups all-purpose flour**
- **2 cups packed brown sugar**
- **¼ tsp. salt**
- **1 cup cold butter, cubed**
- **2 tsp. baking soda**
- **2 cups boiling water**
- **1 cup molasses**

1. Preheat oven to 350°. In a large bowl, combine flour, brown sugar and salt. Cut in butter until crumbly. Set aside 1 cup for topping. Add baking soda to the remaining crumb mixture. Stir in water and molasses.
2. Fill 24 paper-lined muffin cups two-thirds full. Sprinkle with reserved topping. Bake 20-25 minutes or until a toothpick inserted in the center comes out clean. Cool for 10 minutes before removing to wire racks.
1 CUPCAKE: 248 cal., 8g fat (5g sat. fat), 20mg chol., 219mg sod., 43g carb. (26g sugars, 1g fiber), 2g pro.

GRANDMA'S RICE PUDDING

You can whip up this classic dessert on short notice if you keep cooked rice on hand. Cooked rice can be frozen in an airtight container for up to three months. Just thaw it in the refrigerator or microwave when you're ready to use it.
—Margaret DeChant, Newberry, MI

Prep: 10 min. • **Bake:** 45 min.
Makes: 4-6 servings

- **1½ cups cooked rice**
- **¼ cup raisins**
- **2 large eggs**
- **1½ cups whole milk**
- **½ cup sugar**
- **½ tsp. ground nutmeg**
- **Additional milk, optional**

1. Preheat oven to 375°. Place rice and raisins in a greased 1-qt. casserole. In a small bowl, whisk the eggs, milk, sugar and nutmeg; pour over the rice.
2. Bake, uncovered, for 45-50 minutes or until a knife inserted in the center comes out clean. Cool. Pour milk over each serving if desired. Refrigerate leftovers.
1 CUP: 197 cal., 4g fat (2g sat. fat), 79mg chol., 52mg sod., 36g carb. (23g sugars, 0 fiber), 5g pro.

STRAWBERRY SHORTCAKE

I grew up helping my mom make soup and pies in our farmhouse kitchen. This sunny strawberry shortcake recipe brings back memories of family summers on the farm.
—Janet Becker, Anacortes, WA

Prep: 25 min. • **Bake:** 20 min. + cooling
Makes: 9 servings

- **⅔ cup sugar**
- **¼ cup shortening**
- **1 large egg, room temperature**
- **1 tsp. vanilla extract**
- **¼ tsp. salt**
- **1½ cups all-purpose flour**
- **2 tsp. baking powder**
- **½ cup whole milk**
- **1 cup heavy whipping cream, whipped**
- **1½ qt. fresh or frozen strawberries, sliced**

1. Preheat oven to 350°. Grease a 9-in. square baking pan; set aside. In a bowl, cream sugar and shortening. Add egg and vanilla; beat well. Combine dry ingredients and add alternately with milk to the creamed mixture. Spread into the prepared pan. Bake for 20-25 minutes. Cool on wire rack.
2. Cut shortcake into nine pieces. Split each piece horizontally and fill with whipped cream and strawberries. Replace top of cake; garnish with a dollop of whipped cream and more berries. Serve immediately.
1 PIECE: 231 cal., 7g fat (2g sat. fat), 22mg chol., 188mg sod., 39g carb. (20g sugars, 2g fiber), 4g pro.

slowly pour the remaining sauce over cake, allowing sauce to absorb into cake. Cool completely in pan on a wire rack. Invert onto a serving plate. Serve with reserved sauce and, if desired, whipped cream and glazed pecans.

NOTE: To remove cakes easily, use solid shortening for greasing plain and fluted tube pans.

1 SLICE: 371 cal., 17g fat (10g sat. fat), 103mg chol., 233mg sod., 44g carb. (35g sugars, 0 fiber), 3g pro.

BERRY-PATCH BROWNIE PIZZA

I just love the combination of fruit, almonds and chocolate that makes this brownie so distinctive. The fruit lightens the chocolate a bit and makes it feel as though you're eating something both decadent and healthy.
—Sue Kauffman, Columbia City, IN

Prep: 20 min. + chilling
Bake: 15 min. + cooling • **Makes:** 12 servings

- **1 pkg. fudge brownie mix (13x9-in. pan size)**
- **⅓ cup chopped unblanched almonds**
- **1 tsp. almond extract**

TOPPING

- **1 pkg. (8 oz.) cream cheese, softened**
- **1 Tbsp. sugar**
- **1 tsp. vanilla extract**
- **½ tsp. grated lemon zest**
- **2 cups whipped topping**
- **Assorted fresh berries**
- **Fresh mint leaves and coarse sugar, optional**

1. Preheat oven to 375°. Prepare brownie batter according to the package directions for fudgelike brownies, adding almonds and almond extract. Spread into a greased 14-in. pizza pan.
2. Bake until a toothpick inserted in the center comes out clean, 15-18 minutes. Cool completely on a wire rack.
3. Beat the first four topping ingredients until smooth; fold in whipped topping. Spread over crust to within ½ in. of edges; refrigerate, loosely covered, 2 hours.
4. To serve, cut into slices; top with berries of choice. If desired, top with mint and sprinkle with coarse sugar.

1 SLICE: 404 cal., 26g fat (8g sat. fat), 51mg chol., 240mg sod., 39g carb. (26g sugars, 2g fiber), 5g pro.

RICH RUM CAKE

We like a touch of rum for the holidays, and this orangey rum cake is decadent alone or with big swoops of whipped cream.
—Nancy Heishman, Las Vegas, NV

Prep: 35 min. • **Bake:** 25 min. + cooling
Makes: 12 servings

- **4 large eggs, room temperature, separated**
- **2½ cups confectioners' sugar**
- **¾ cup orange juice**
- **¼ cup butter, cubed**
- **¾ cup rum**
- **1 cup all-purpose flour**
- **1 tsp. baking powder**
- **½ tsp. ground cinnamon**
- **¼ tsp. salt**
- **¼ tsp. ground nutmeg**
- **½ cup packed brown sugar, divided**
- **1 tsp. vanilla extract**
- **¾ cup butter, melted**
- **Whipped cream and finely chopped glazed pecans, optional**

1. Place egg whites in a large bowl; let stand at room temperature 30 minutes. For sauce, in a saucepan, combine confectioners' sugar, orange juice and cubed butter; cook and stir over medium-low heat until the sugar is dissolved. Remove from heat; stir in rum. Reserve ¾ cup for serving.
2. Preheat oven to 375°. Grease and flour a 10-in. tube pan; set aside. Sift flour, baking powder, cinnamon, salt and nutmeg together twice; set aside.
3. Beat egg whites on medium until soft peaks form. Gradually add ¼ cup of the brown sugar, 1 Tbsp. at a time, beating on high after each addition until the sugar is dissolved. Continue beating until stiff peaks form.
4. In another bowl, beat egg yolks until slightly thickened. Gradually add the remaining brown sugar and the vanilla, beating on high speed until thick. Fold one-quarter of egg white mixture into batter. Alternately fold in flour mixture and remaining whites. Fold in butter.
5. Transfer batter to the prepared pan. Bake on lowest oven rack 25-30 minutes or until the top springs back when lightly touched. Immediately poke holes in cake with a fork;

YUMMY ZUCCHINI CHOCOLATE CAKE

As a confirmed chocoholic, I declare this my all-time favorite treat. I've changed the original recipe over the years, and no one suspects that it's lighter than most chocolate cakes.
—*Carleta Foltz, Sunrise Beach, MO*

Prep: 20 min. • **Bake:** 30 min.
Makes: 18 servings

- **1¾ cups sugar**
- **½ cup canola oil**
- **2 large eggs, room temperature**
- **⅔ cup unsweetened applesauce**
- **1 tsp. vanilla extract**
- **2½ cups all-purpose flour**
- **½ cup baking cocoa**
- **1 tsp. baking soda**
- **½ tsp. salt**
- **½ cup buttermilk**
- **2 cups shredded zucchini**
- **1 cup (6 oz.) miniature semisweet chocolate chips**
- **½ cup chopped pecans, toasted**

1. Preheat oven to 350°. Coat a 13x9-in. baking pan with cooking spray; set aside.
2. Beat sugar and oil on medium speed for 1 minute. Add eggs, applesauce and vanilla; beat 1 minute. In another bowl, whisk flour, cocoa, baking soda and salt; add to the sugar mixture alternately with buttermilk, beating just until blended. Stir in zucchini.
3. Transfer batter to prepared pan. Bake 20 minutes. Sprinkle with chocolate chips and pecans. Bake until a toothpick inserted in center comes out clean, 10-15 minutes. Cool in pan on a wire rack.
NOTE: To toast nuts, bake in a shallow pan in a 350° oven for 5-10 minutes or cook in a skillet over low heat until lightly browned, stirring occasionally.
1 PIECE: 285 cal., 12g fat (3g sat. fat), 21mg chol., 159mg sod., 43g carb. (27g sugars, 2g fiber), 4g pro.

TEST KITCHEN TIP
If your cake sinks in the center after baking, check your oven temperature. An oven that is not hot enough can cause the cake to rise and then sink. Too short of a baking time can cause similar results. Always use a toothpick to check the cake's doneness.

BANANA-SPLIT BROWNIES

How's this for a dish—all the joy of a banana split in the form of delectable brownie bars.
—*Constance Sheckler, Chestertown, MD*

Prep: 45 min. • **Bake:** 40 min. + cooling
Makes: 2 dozen

- **8 oz. unsweetened chocolate, chopped**
- **¾ cup butter, cubed**
- **3 large eggs, room temperature**
- **2 cups sugar**
- **1 tsp. vanilla extract**
- **1 cup plus 2 Tbsp. all-purpose flour**
- **1 cup maraschino cherries, chopped**

TOPPING

- **1 pkg. (8 oz.) cream cheese, softened**
- **½ cup mashed ripe banana (about 1 medium)**
- **⅓ cup strawberry preserves**
- **1 large egg, room temperature, lightly beaten**
- **¼ cup chopped salted peanuts**
- **Sliced bananas and additional chopped maraschino cherries, optional**

1. Preheat oven to 350°. Grease a 13x9-in. baking pan; set aside. In a microwave, melt chocolate and butter; stir until smooth.
2. In a large bowl, beat eggs and sugar on high speed for 10 minutes. Stir in vanilla and chocolate mixture. Gradually stir in flour. Fold in cherries. Spread into prepared pan.
3. For topping, in a small bowl, beat cream cheese until smooth. Beat in mashed banana and preserves. Add egg; beat on low speed just until blended. Spread over the brownie batter; sprinkle with peanuts.
4. Bake for 40-45 minutes or until topping is set and a toothpick inserted in the brownie portion comes out mostly clean. Cool pan completely on a wire rack.
5. Cut into bars. If desired, serve topped with banana slices and additional cherries. Store in an airtight container in the refrigerator.
1 BROWNIE: 262 cal., 16g fat (9g sat. fat), 57mg chol., 101mg sod., 31g carb. (23g sugars, 2g fiber), 4g pro.

COOKIE SWIRL COBBLER

An extra-rich, chocolate chip cookie dough and a crescent roll topping provide a tasty twist on a classic cherry cobbler. Serve it with a scoop of vanilla ice cream.
—Jeanne Holt, Mendota Heights, MN

Prep: 20 min. • **Bake:** 25 min. + cooling
Makes: 12 servings

- **1 cup (about 8 oz.) refrigerated chocolate chip cookie dough, softened**
- **2 Tbsp. brown sugar**
- **⅓ cup white baking chips**
- **¼ cup plus 2 Tbsp. toasted sliced almonds, divided**
- **1 can (21 oz.) cherry pie filling**
- **½ tsp. almond extract, divided**
- **2 cups fresh or frozen unsweetened raspberries**
- **1 tube (8 oz.) refrigerated crescent rolls**
- **¾ cup confectioners' sugar**
- **3 to 4 tsp. 2% milk**
- **Vanilla ice cream, optional**

1. Preheat oven to 350°. Grease a 13x9-in. baking dish. Combine cookie dough, brown sugar, baking chips and ¼ cup almonds. Set aside. In a large saucepan, heat cherry pie filling over medium heat until bubbly. Remove from heat; stir in ¼ tsp. almond extract. Fold in raspberries. Transfer to baking dish.
2. Unroll crescent dough into one long rectangle; press perforations to seal. Drop spoonfuls of cookie dough mixture over top; spread gently to cover. Roll up jelly-roll style, starting with a long side; pinch seam to seal. Cut crosswise into 12 slices; arrange cut side up on cherry mixture.
3. Bake until golden brown, 25-30 minutes. Cool 10 minutes. Combine confectioners' sugar, the remaining almond extract and enough milk to make a medium-thick glaze. Drizzle rolls with glaze; sprinkle with remaining toasted almonds. Serve warm with ice cream, if desired.
NOTE: To toast nuts, bake in a shallow pan in a 350° oven for 5-10 minutes or cook in a skillet over low heat until lightly browned, stirring occasionally.
1 SERVING: 308 cal., 11g fat (4g sat. fat), 2mg chol., 224mg sod., 49g carb. (22g sugars, 2g fiber), 3g pro.

APPLE SNICKERDOODLE DUMP CAKE

With an apple farm just down the road, I'm always looking for creative ways to use those bushels! We love this cozy cake with caramel drizzle and a scoop of vanilla or cinnamon ice cream.
—Rachel Garcia, Honolulu, HI

Prep: 15 min. • **Bake:** 35 min.
Makes: 10 servings

- **6 cups sliced, peeled tart apple (about 8 medium)**
- **⅓ cup packed brown sugar**
- **¼ cup sugar**
- **¼ cup orange juice**
- **1 Tbsp. lemon juice**
- **1 pkg. (17.9 oz.) snickerdoodle cookie mix**
- **½ cup butter, melted**
- **1 cup coarsely chopped pecans or walnuts**

1. Preheat oven to 350°. Toss apples with sugars and fruit juices; spread into a greased 11x7-in. baking dish.
2. Place cookie mix in a bowl; stir in contents of the cinnamon-sugar packet. Sprinkle over apples. Drizzle with butter. Top with pecans.
3. Bake until golden brown and apples are tender, 35-40 minutes. Serve warm.
1 SERVING: 475 cal., 23g fat (7g sat. fat), 24mg chol., 193mg sod., 67g carb. (48g sugars, 3g fiber), 3g pro.

Cookies & Candies

Tasty treats in small bites—these delectable cookies and candies are just what you need for bake sales, holiday sweets trays or an anytime snack.

CHOCOLATE THUMBPRINT COOKIES

My group of friends had a weekly movie night during winters on Martha's Vineyard, and we'd take turns making a chocolate treat to share. These terrific cookies were an instant success. Once they debuted, I had to make them many more times.

—Laura Bryant German, West Warren, MA

Prep: 25 min. + chilling
Bake: 10 min. + cooling
Makes: about 2½ dozen

- ½ **cup butter, softened**
- ⅔ **cup sugar**
- 1 **large egg, room temperature, separated**
- 2 **Tbsp. whole milk**
- 1 **tsp. vanilla extract**
- 1 **cup all-purpose flour**
- ⅓ **cup baking cocoa**
- ¼ **tsp. salt**
- 1 **cup finely chopped walnuts**

FILLING

- ½ **cup confectioners' sugar**
- 1 **Tbsp. butter, softened**
- 2 **tsp. whole milk**
- ¼ **tsp. vanilla extract**
- 24 **milk chocolate kisses**

1. In a large bowl, cream butter and sugar until light and fluffy. Beat in the egg yolk, milk and vanilla. Combine the flour, cocoa and salt; gradually add to creamed mixture and mix well. Cover and refrigerate until easy to handle, about 1 hour.

2. Preheat oven to 350°. In a small bowl, whisk egg white until foamy. Shape dough into 1-in. balls; dip in egg white, then roll in nuts. Place on greased baking sheets. Using a wooden spoon handle, make an indentation in the center of each cookie. Bake until center is set, 10-12 minutes.

3. For filling, combine the confectioners' sugar, butter, milk and vanilla; stir until smooth. Spoon or pipe ¼ tsp. of filling into each warm cookie; gently press a chocolate kiss in the center. Carefully remove from pans to wire racks to cool.

1 COOKIE: 117 cal., 7g fat (3g sat. fat), 16mg chol., 52mg sod., 13g carb. (8g sugars, 1g fiber), 2g pro.

ALMOND SPRITZ COOKIES

You can leave these almond-flavored cookies plain or decorate them with sugar or frosting in a color to suit the season. In our house, it just wouldn't be Christmas without them.
—Tanya Hart, Muncie, IN

Prep: 15 min. • **Bake:** 10 min./batch
Makes: about 7 dozen

- **1 cup butter, softened**
- **½ cup sugar**
- **½ cup packed brown sugar**
- **1 large egg, room temperature**
- **½ tsp. almond extract**
- **½ tsp. vanilla extract**
- **2½ cups all-purpose flour**
- **¼ tsp. baking soda**
- **¼ tsp. salt**
- **Pink and red colored sugar, optional**

1. Preheat oven to 375°. In a large bowl, cream butter and sugars until fluffy. Beat in egg and extracts. Combine the flour, baking soda and salt; gradually add to the creamed mixture and mix well.
2. Using a cookie press fitted with the disk of your choice, press dough 2 in. apart onto ungreased baking sheets. If desired, sprinkle with colored sugar.
3. Bake for 7-9 minutes or until the edges just begin to brown. Cool on wire racks.
2 COOKIES: 87 cal., 5g fat (3g sat. fat), 17mg chol., 68mg sod., 11g carb. (5g sugars, 0 fiber), 1g pro.

5i

OLD-TIME BUTTER CRUNCH CANDY

This candy is the most popular part of the big tray of cookies and sweets I prepare each holiday season. My whole family loves the nutty pieces draped in chocolate.
—Mildred Duffy, Bella Vista, AR

Prep: 15 min. + cooling • **Cook:** 25 min.
Makes: about 2 lbs.

- **1 cup butter**
- **1¼ cup sugar**
- **2 Tbsp. light corn syrup**
- **2 Tbsp. water**
- **2 cups finely chopped toasted almonds**
- **8 milk chocolate candy bars (1.55 oz. each)**

1. Line a 13x9-in. pan with foil; set aside. Using part of the butter, grease the sides of a large heavy saucepan. Add the remaining butter to the saucepan; melt over low heat. Add sugar, corn syrup and water. Cook and stir over medium heat until a candy thermometer reads 300° (hard-crack stage).
2. Remove from the heat and stir in almonds. Quickly pour into the prepared pan, spreading to cover bottom of pan. Cool completely. Carefully invert pan to remove candy in one piece; remove the foil.
3. Melt half the chocolate in a double boiler or microwave-safe bowl; spread over top of candy. Let cool. Turn candy over and repeat with the remaining chocolate; cool. Break into 2-in. pieces. Store in an airtight container.
2 OZ.: 375 cal., 26g fat (12g sat. fat), 35mg chol., 137mg sod., 34g carb. (29g sugars, 3g fiber), 5g pro.

BUTTERFINGER COOKIES

These cookies don't last long—if you want to be sure to get a taste, make a double batch!
—Carol Kitchens, Ridgeland, MS

Prep: 15 min. • **Bake:** 10 min./batch + cooling
Makes: about 4 dozen

- ½ **cup butter, softened**
- ¾ **cup sugar**
- ⅔ **cup packed brown sugar**
- 2 **large egg whites, room temperature**
- 1¼ **cups chunky peanut butter**
- 1½ **tsp. vanilla extract**
- 1 **cup all-purpose flour**
- ½ **tsp. baking soda**
- ¼ **tsp. salt**
- 6 **Butterfinger candy bars (1.9 oz. each), chopped**

1. Preheat oven to 350°. Cream butter and sugars until light and fluffy. Beat in egg whites. Beat in peanut butter and vanilla. In another bowl, combine flour, baking soda and salt; gradually beat into creamed mixture. Stir in candy bars.

2. Shape dough into 1½-in. balls; place 2 in. apart on greased baking sheets. Bake until golden brown, 10-12 minutes. Remove to wire racks to cool.

1 COOKIE: 122 cal., 7g fat (2g sat. fat), 5mg chol., 92mg sod., 15g carb. (10g sugars, 1g fiber), 2g pro.

CHOCOLATE CARAMEL CANDY

This dazzling treat tastes like a Snickers bar but has homemade flavor beyond compare. When I entered it in a recipe contest at our harvest festival, it won five ribbons.
—Jane Meek, Pahrump, NV

Prep: 45 min. + chilling • **Makes:** about 8 dozen

- 2 **tsp. butter**
- 1 **cup milk chocolate chips**
- ¼ **cup butterscotch chips**
- ¼ **cup creamy peanut butter**

FILLING

- ¼ **cup butter**
- 1 **cup sugar**
- ¼ **cup evaporated milk**
- 1½ **cups marshmallow creme**
- ¼ **cup creamy peanut butter**
- 1 **tsp. vanilla extract**
- 1½ **cups chopped salted peanuts**

CARAMEL LAYER

- 1 **pkg. (14 oz.) caramels**
- ¼ **cup heavy whipping cream**

ICING

- 1 **cup milk chocolate chips**
- ¼ **cup butterscotch chips**
- ¼ **cup creamy peanut butter**

1. Line a 13x9-in. pan with foil; grease foil with 2 tsp. of butter and set pan aside.

2. In a small saucepan, combine the milk chocolate chips, butterscotch chips and peanut butter; stir over low heat until melted and smooth. Spread into the prepared pan. Refrigerate until set.

3. For the filling, in a small heavy saucepan, melt butter over medium heat. Add sugar and milk; bring to a gentle boil. Reduce heat to medium-low; cook and stir 5 minutes. Remove from heat; stir in marshmallow creme, peanut butter and vanilla until smooth. Add peanuts. Spread over first layer. Refrigerate until set.

4. For the caramel layer, in a small heavy saucepan, combine caramels and cream; stir over low heat until melted and smooth. Cook and stir 4 minutes. Spread over the filling. Refrigerate until set.

5. For the icing, in another saucepan, combine chips and peanut butter; stir over low heat until melted and smooth. Pour over the caramel layer. Refrigerate for at least 4 hours or overnight.

6. Remove from the refrigerator 20 minutes before cutting. Remove from pan and cut into 1-in. squares. Store in an airtight container.

1 PIECE: 86 cal., 5g fat (2g sat. fat), 4mg chol., 41mg sod., 10g carb. (9g sugars, 0 fiber), 2g pro.

TEST KITCHEN TIP
The foil does more than prevent the candy from sticking—it allows the candy to be lifted out of the pan in one piece so that you can cut it. This keeps the pan from being scratched by the knife and also allows for more even pieces. When lining the pan, make sure the foil extends over the sides of the pan. Once the candy is set, grasp the foil on opposite sides and lift. Place it on a cutting board, remove the foil and cut.

ITALIAN SPRINKLE COOKIES

These cookies take time, effort and equipment, but they are well worth it! My husband and I used to run an Italian-American restaurant, and this recipe goes back generations.
—*Gloria Cracchiolo, Newburgh, NY*

Prep: 25 min. • **Bake:** 15 min./batch + standing
Makes: about 7 dozen

- **6 large eggs, room temperature**
- **5 cups all-purpose flour**
- **2 cups confectioners' sugar**
- **2 Tbsp. plus 1½ tsp. baking powder**
- **1 cup shortening**
- **3 tsp. almond extract**
- **1½ tsp. lemon extract**

GLAZE

- **3¾ cups confectioners' sugar**
- **½ cup warm whole milk**
- **1 tsp. almond extract**
- **1 tsp. vanilla extract**
- **Colored sprinkles**

1. Preheat oven to 350°. Using a heavy-duty mixer, beat eggs on high speed until light and foamy, about 5 minutes; set aside. In a large bowl, combine the flour, confectioners' sugar and baking powder; on low speed, gradually beat in shortening and extracts until the mixture resembles fine crumbs. Gradually add the beaten eggs (dough will be stiff).
2. Roll dough into 1-in. balls. Place 2 in. apart on ungreased baking sheets. Bake for 12-14 minutes (the tops of the cookies will not brown, but bottoms should brown slightly).
3. Meanwhile, in a small bowl, combine the confectioners' sugar, milk and extracts until smooth. As soon as the cookies are removed from the oven, quickly dip two or three at a time into glaze. Remove with a slotted spoon or tongs; place on wire racks to drain. Immediately top with sprinkles. Let cookies dry for 24 hours before storing in airtight containers.
2 COOKIES: 176 cal., 6g fat (1g sat. fat), 31mg chol., 82mg sod., 28g carb. (16g sugars, 0 fiber), 3g pro.

CHERRY CHEESE WINDMILLS

These pretty cookies look fancy, but they are really not much work. They're perfect for any occasion.
—*Helen McGibbon, Downers Grove, IL*

Prep: 25 min. + chilling
Bake: 10 min./batch + cooling
Makes: about 2½ dozen

- **⅓ cup butter, softened**
- **⅓ cup shortening**
- **¾ cup sugar**
- **1 large egg, room temperature**
- **1 Tbsp. milk**
- **1 tsp. vanilla extract**
- **2 cups all-purpose flour**
- **1½ tsp. baking powder**
- **¼ tsp. salt**

FILLING

- **3 oz. cream cheese, softened**
- **¼ cup sugar**
- **¼ tsp. almond extract**
- **½ cup finely chopped maraschino cherries**
- **¼ cup sliced almonds, toasted and chopped**

1. In a large bowl, cream the butter, shortening and sugar until light and fluffy. Beat in the egg, milk and vanilla. Combine the flour, baking powder and salt; gradually add to creamed mixture and mix well. Divide dough in half. Cover and refrigerate for 3 hours or until easy to handle.
2. Preheat oven to 350°. In a small bowl, beat cream cheese, sugar and extract until smooth. Fold in cherries. On a floured surface, roll each portion of dough into a 10-in. square. With a sharp knife or pastry wheel, cut into 2½-in. squares. Place squares 2 in. apart on ungreased baking sheets. Make 1-in. cuts from each corner toward the center of the dough.
3. Drop a teaspoonful of filling in the center of each square; sprinkle with almonds. Fold alternating points to the center to form a windmill; moisten points with water and pinch gently at center to seal. Bake 8-10 minutes or until set. Cool on wire racks.
1 COOKIE: 126 cal., 6g fat (3g sat. fat), 16mg chol., 73mg sod., 15g carb. (8g sugars, 0 fiber), 1g pro.

THUMBPRINT BUTTER COOKIES

These buttery little rounds add beautiful color to a platter of treats. Fill the thumbprint in the center with any fruit preserves you like.
—Taste of Home *Test Kitchen*

Prep: 25 min. • **Bake:** 10 min./batch
Makes: 2½ dozen

- **6 Tbsp. butter, softened**
- **½ cup sugar**
- **1 large egg, room temperature**
- **2 Tbsp. canola oil**
- **1 tsp. vanilla extract**
- **¼ tsp. butter flavoring**
- **1½ cups all-purpose flour**
- **¼ cup cornstarch**
- **1 tsp. baking powder**
- **¼ tsp. salt**
- **3 Tbsp. apricot or other fruit preserves**

1. Preheat oven to 350°. Cream butter and sugar until light and fluffy; beat in egg, oil, vanilla and butter flavoring. In another bowl, whisk together flour, cornstarch, baking powder and salt; gradually beat into the creamed mixture.
2. Shape dough into 1-in. balls; place 2 in. apart on greased baking sheets. Press a deep indentation in the center of each with the end of a wooden spoon handle. Bake until the edges are light brown, 8-10 minutes.
3. Remove from pans to wire racks to cool. Fill with preserves.
1 COOKIE: 75 cal., 3g fat (2g sat. fat), 13mg chol., 52mg sod., 10g carb. (4g sugars, 0 fiber), 1g pro.

CHOCOLATE CARAMEL THUMBPRINTS

Covered in chopped nuts and drizzled with chocolate, these cookies are delicious and pretty, too. Everybody will look forward to munching on them.
—Elizabeth Marino, San Juan Capistrano, CA

Prep: 25 min. + chilling • **Bake:** 10 min./batch
Makes: about 2½ dozen

- **½ cup butter, softened**
- **⅔ cup sugar**
- **1 large egg, room temperature, separated**
- **2 Tbsp. 2% milk**
- **1 tsp. vanilla extract**
- **1 cup all-purpose flour**
- **⅓ cup baking cocoa**
- **¼ tsp. salt**
- **1 cup finely chopped pecans**

FILLING

- **12 to 14 caramels**
- **3 Tbsp. heavy whipping cream**
- **½ cup semisweet chocolate chips**
- **1 tsp. shortening**

1. In a large bowl, cream the butter and sugar until light and fluffy. Beat in egg yolk, milk and vanilla. In another bowl, whisk flour, cocoa and salt; gradually beat into the creamed mixture. Refrigerate, covered, for 1 hour or until easy to handle.
2. Preheat oven to 350°. Shape dough into 1-in. balls. In a shallow bowl, beat egg white. Place pecans in a separate shallow bowl. Dip balls in egg white, then in pecans, patting to help pecans adhere.
3. Place 2 in. apart on greased baking sheets. Press a deep indentation in the center of each with the end of a wooden spoon handle. Bake for 10-12 minutes or until set. Remove from pans to wire racks to cool.
4. In a large heavy saucepan, melt caramels with cream over low heat; stir until smooth. Fill each cookie with about ½ tsp. of the caramel mixture. In a microwave, melt chocolate chips and shortening; stir until smooth. Drizzle over cookies; let stand until set. Store in an airtight container.
1 COOKIE: 128 cal., 8g fat (3g sat. fat), 17mg chol., 55mg sod., 14g carb. (9g sugars, 1g fiber), 2g pro.

CHOCOLATE LEBKUCHEN CHERRY BALLS

Here's my twist on the traditional German holiday lebkuchen—with a surprise inside. Maraschino cherries add a sweet and unexpected punch to the holiday spice of gingersnaps.
—Arlene Erlbach, Morton Grove, IL

Prep: 45 min. + chilling • **Makes:** 5 dozen

- **40 gingersnap cookies**
- **1 pkg. (8 oz.) cream cheese, softened**
- **1½ cups semisweet chocolate chips, divided**
- **1¼ cups sliced almonds, divided**
- **2 Tbsp. chopped candied orange zest**
- **1 tsp. almond extract**
- **60 maraschino cherries, stems removed**

1. Place gingersnaps, cream cheese, ½ cup chocolate chips, ½ cup almonds, orange zest and extract in a food processor; process until combined. Refrigerate until firm enough to form into balls. Pat cherries dry with paper towels. Wrap each cherry with a rounded tablespoonful of cream cheese mixture; shape into a ball. Freeze until firm, about 20 minutes.
2. Chop the remaining sliced almonds; set aside. In a double boiler, melt the remaining chocolate chips; stir until smooth. Dip cherry balls in chocolate; allow excess to drip off. Sprinkle balls with almonds. Place on waxed paper. Refrigerate until set, about 1 hour.
1 BALL: 76 cal., 4g fat (2g sat. fat), 4mg chol., 37mg sod., 10g carb. (7g sugars, 1g fiber), 1g pro.

MOM'S BUTTERMILK COOKIES

I treasure my mother's recipe for these comforting cookie pillows. The tender treats are topped with thick frosting and a sprinkling of chopped walnuts.
—Jane Darling, Simi Valley, CA

Prep: 20 min. • **Bake:** 10 min./batch + cooling
Makes: about 3 dozen

- **½ cup butter, softened**
- **1 cup sugar**
- **1 large egg, room temperature**
- **1 tsp. vanilla extract**
- **2½ cups all-purpose flour**
- **½ tsp. baking soda**
- **½ tsp. salt**
- **½ cup buttermilk**

FROSTING

- **3 Tbsp. butter, softened**
- **3½ cups confectioners' sugar**
- **¼ cup whole milk**
- **1 tsp. vanilla extract**
- **½ cup finely chopped walnuts, optional**

1. Preheat oven to 375°. Cream butter and sugar until light and fluffy. Beat in egg and vanilla. In a separate bowl, whisk flour, baking soda and salt; add to creamed mixture alternately with buttermilk, beating well after each addition.
2. Drop by rounded tablespoonfuls 2 in. apart onto greased baking sheets. Bake until the edges are lightly browned, 10-12 minutes. Remove to wire racks to cool.
3. For the frosting, combine the butter, confectioners' sugar, milk and vanilla; beat until smooth. Spread over cookies; if desired, sprinkle with chopped walnuts.
1 COOKIE: 135 cal., 4g fat (2g sat. fat), 15mg chol., 88mg sod., 24g carb. (17g sugars, 0 fiber), 1g pro.

5i

PECAN ROLL-UPS

Nut lovers' alert! Pecans tucked inside these delicate cookies make for especially luscious little bundles.
—Lee Roberts, Racine, WI

Prep: 45 min. + chilling
Bake: 15 min./batch + cooling
Makes: 8 dozen

- **1 cup butter, softened**
- **1 pkg. (8 oz.) cream cheese, softened**
- **¼ tsp. salt**
- **2 cups all-purpose flour**
- **1¼ cups confectioners' sugar, divided**
- **96 pecan halves (about 2 cups)**

1. In a large bowl, beat butter, cream cheese and salt until smooth. Gradually beat in flour. Divide dough in half; shape each into a disk. Wrap each disk in plastic; refrigerate 2 hours or until firm enough to roll.
2. Preheat oven to 350°. Dust a work surface with about 2 Tbsp. of confectioners' sugar. Roll one portion of dough into an 18x8-in. rectangle; cut crosswise into six 3-in.-wide sections. Cut each section crosswise into eight 1-in.-wide strips. Roll each strip around a pecan half; place rolls 1 in. apart on ungreased baking sheets. Dust work surface with an additional 2 Tbsp. confectioners' sugar and repeat with the remaining dough and pecans.
3. Bake 12-15 minutes or until the bottoms are lightly browned. Remove cookies to wire racks to cool completely.
4. Place the remaining confectioners' sugar in a shallow bowl. Roll the cookies in the sugar, coating well.
FREEZE OPTION: Bake and roll cookies in confectioners' sugar as directed. Place in freezer containers, separating layers with waxed paper; freeze for up to 3 months. Thaw before serving; dust with additional confectioners' sugar.
1 COOKIE: 51 cal., 4g fat (2g sat. fat), 8mg chol., 30mg sod., 4g carb. (2g sugars, 0 fiber), 1g pro.

LEE ROBERTS
Racine, WI

CHOCOLATE MINT DREAMS

My favorite flavor combination is chocolate and mint, so these frosted cookies are hard for me to resist. I always make sure to save some for my cookie trays so friends and family can enjoy them, too!
—Anne Revers, Omaha, NE

Prep: 30 min. • **Bake:** 5 min./batch + cooling
Makes: about 3 dozen

- **¾ cup butter, softened**
- **½ cup confectioners' sugar**
- **2 oz. unsweetened chocolate, melted and cooled**
- **¼ tsp. peppermint extract**
- **1½ cups all-purpose flour**
- **1 cup miniature semisweet chocolate chips**

ICING

- **2 Tbsp. butter, softened**
- **1 cup confectioners' sugar**
- **¼ tsp. peppermint extract**
- **1 to 2 Tbsp. 2% milk**
- **1 to 2 drops green food coloring, optional**

DRIZZLE

- **½ cup semisweet chocolate chips**
- **½ tsp. shortening**

1. Preheat oven to 375°. Cream butter and confectioners' sugar until light and fluffy. Beat in the cooled chocolate and extract. Gradually beat in flour. Stir in chocolate chips. (The dough will be soft.)
2. Drop dough by tablespoonfuls 2 in. apart onto ungreased baking sheets. Bake until firm, 5-7 minutes. Cool on pans for 2 minutes, then remove to wire racks to cool completely.
3. For the icing, mix butter, confectioners' sugar, extract and enough milk to achieve the desired consistency. If desired, tint green with food coloring. Spoon over cookies.
4. In a microwave, melt chocolate chips and shortening; stir until smooth. Drizzle over tops of cookies.
1 COOKIE: 123 cal., 8g fat (5g sat. fat), 12mg chol., 37mg sod., 14g carb. (9g sugars, 1g fiber), 1g pro.

LEMON ZUCCHINI DROPS

When we lived on the East Coast, a local fruit and vegetable stand had a bakery that featured these soft cakelike cookies. We missed every bite when we moved to Arizona, so I developed this recipe.
—Barbara Franklin, Tucson, AZ

Prep: 20 min. • **Bake:** 10 min./batch + cooling
Makes: about 3½ dozen

- **½ cup butter, softened**
- **1 cup sugar**
- **1 large egg, room temperature**
- **1 cup finely shredded zucchini**
- **1 tsp. grated lemon zest**
- **2 cups all-purpose flour**
- **1 tsp. baking soda**
- **1 tsp. baking powder**
- **1 tsp. ground cinnamon**
- **½ tsp. salt**
- **½ cup raisins**
- **½ cup chopped walnuts**

LEMON GLAZE

- **2 cups confectioners' sugar**
- **2 to 3 Tbsp. lemon juice**

1. Preheat oven to 375°. Cream the butter and granulated sugar until light and fluffy. Beat in egg, zucchini and lemon zest. Combine flour, baking soda, baking powder, cinnamon and salt; gradually add to the creamed mixture and mix well. Stir in raisins and walnuts.
2. Drop dough by tablespoonfuls 3 in. apart onto lightly greased baking sheets. Bake for 8-10 minutes or until lightly browned. Remove to wire racks to cool.
3. For glaze, combine confectioners' sugar and enough lemon juice to achieve a thin spreading consistency. Spread or drizzle over cooled cookies.
1 COOKIE: 99 cal., 3g fat (2g sat. fat), 10mg chol., 89mg sod., 17g carb. (12g sugars, 0 fiber), 1g pro.

STRAWBERRY PILLOWS

Make cookie trays extra special with these mini pie look-alikes stuffed with sweet strawberry preserves. Yum!
—Amy Sauerwalt, Columbia, MD

Prep: 30 min. + chilling
Bake: 10 min./batch + cooling
Makes: 5 dozen

- **1 cup butter, softened**
- **1 pkg. (8 oz.) cream cheese, softened**
- **1 cup sugar**
- **1½ tsp. vanilla extract**
- **2¾ cups all-purpose flour**
- **⅔ cup strawberry preserves**

1. Cream the butter, cream cheese and sugar until light and fluffy. Beat in vanilla. Gradually beat in flour. Divide the dough into four portions. Shape each into a disk; wrap in plastic. Refrigerate until firm enough to roll, about 2 hours.
2. Preheat oven to 375°. On a floured surface, roll out each disk of dough to ⅛-in. thickness. Cut with a floured 2-in. round cookie cutter. Place half the circles on ungreased baking sheets; place ½ tsp. preserves in the center of each. Top with the remaining circles and press edges lightly with a fork to seal. Cut slits in the top of each cookie. Bake until the edges are light brown, 7-9 minutes. Remove from pans to wire racks to cool.
1 COOKIE: 83 cal., 4g fat (3g sat. fat), 12mg chol., 36mg sod., 10g carb. (6g sugars, 0 fiber), 1g pro.

CARAMEL PECAN SHORTBREAD

My grandchildren look for Grandma's candy bar cookies every Christmas. I recommend doubling the recipe for these sweet treats because they go so fast.
—Dorothy Buiter, Worth, IL

Prep: 30 min. + chilling
Bake: 15 min./batch + cooling
Makes: about 4 dozen

- **¾ cup butter, softened**
- **¾ cup confectioners' sugar**
- **2 Tbsp. evaporated milk**
- **1 tsp. vanilla extract**
- **2 cups all-purpose flour**
- **¼ tsp. salt**

FILLING

- **28 caramels**
- **6 Tbsp. evaporated milk**
- **2 Tbsp. butter**
- **½ cup confectioners' sugar**
- **¾ cup finely chopped pecans**

ICING

- **1 cup (6 oz.) semisweet chocolate chips**
- **3 Tbsp. evaporated milk**
- **2 Tbsp. butter**
- **½ cup confectioners' sugar**
- **½ tsp. vanilla extract**
- **Pecan halves**

1. Cream the butter and confectioners' sugar until light and fluffy. Beat in milk and vanilla. Combine flour and salt; gradually add to the creamed mixture. Cover and refrigerate for 1 hour or until easy to handle.
2. Preheat oven to 325°. On a lightly floured surface, roll out the dough to ¼-in. thickness. Cut into 2x1-in. strips. Place 1 in. apart on greased baking sheets.
3. Bake 12-14 minutes or until lightly browned. Remove to wire racks to cool.
4. For the filling, combine caramels and milk in a large saucepan. Cook and stir over medium-low heat until the caramels are melted and smooth. Remove from the heat; stir in the butter, sugar and pecans. Cool for 5 minutes. Spread 1 tsp. over each cookie.
5. For the icing, in a microwave-safe bowl, melt chips and milk; stir until smooth. Stir in the butter, sugar and vanilla until smooth. Cool for 5 minutes.
6. Spread 1 tsp. icing on each cookie; top each with a pecan half. Let stand until set. Store in an airtight container.
1 COOKIE: 126 cal., 7g fat (3g sat. fat), 12mg chol., 61mg sod., 16g carb. (10g sugars, 1g fiber), 1g pro.

CHOCOLATE MACADAMIA SNOWBALLS

I came up with this recipe by accident one day when I wanted to make some cookies. I decided to use some ingredients that were already in my cupboard—these were the delicious result.
—Barbara Sepcich, Galt, CA

Prep: 20 min. + chilling • **Bake:** 15 min.
Makes: 2½ dozen

- **½ cup butter, softened**
- **¼ cup confectioners' sugar**
- **½ tsp. vanilla extract**
- **1¼ cups all-purpose flour**
- **1 jar (3½ oz.) macadamia nuts, finely chopped**
- **1 cup (6 oz.) semisweet chocolate chips**
- **½ cup coarsely chopped macadamia nuts**
- **Additional confectioners' sugar**

1. In a small bowl, cream butter and sugar until light and fluffy. Beat in vanilla. Gradually add flour and mix well. Stir in nuts (dough will be stiff); set aside.
2. For the filling, in a microwave-safe bowl, melt chocolate chips; stir until smooth. Stir in nuts; cool slightly. Drop by ½ teaspoonfuls onto a waxed paper-lined baking sheet; cover and refrigerate for 30 minutes.
3. Preheat oven to 375°. Shape teaspoonfuls of dough around each piece of chocolate-nut mixture so the filling is completely covered. Place 2 in. apart on ungreased baking sheets.
4. Bake until lightly browned, 12-14 minutes. Roll warm cookies in confectioners' sugar; cool on wire racks.
1 COOKIE: 117 cal., 9g fat (4g sat. fat), 8mg chol., 45mg sod., 9g carb. (4g sugars, 1g fiber), 1g pro.

CHEWY APPLE OATMEAL COOKIES

My family has always loved oatmeal raisin cookies, but I wanted to try something new with the classic recipe. We enjoy apples, and I thought the dried fruit would make a good cookie. I was right!
—Jan Marshall, Fenton, MO

Prep: 20 min. • **Bake:** 10 min./batch
Makes: 4 dozen

- **1 cup butter, softened**
- **1 cup packed brown sugar**
- **½ cup sugar**
- **2 large eggs, room temperature**
- **1 tsp. vanilla extract**
- **1½ cups all-purpose flour**
- **2 tsp. ground cinnamon**
- **1 tsp. baking soda**
- **¼ tsp. salt**
- **3 cups old-fashioned oats**
- **½ cup chopped dried apples**

1. Preheat oven to 350°. In a large bowl, cream butter and sugars until light and fluffy. Beat in eggs and vanilla. Combine flour, cinnamon, baking soda and salt; gradually add to the creamed mixture and mix well. Stir in oats and apples.
2. Drop by rounded tablespoonfuls 2 in. apart onto ungreased baking sheets. Bake until golden brown, 10-12 minutes. Let stand for 1 minute before removing to wire racks.
1 COOKIE: 97 cal., 4g fat (3g sat. fat), 19mg chol., 71mg sod., 14g carb. (7g sugars, 1g fiber), 1g pro. **DIABETIC EXCHANGES:** 1 starch, 1 fat.

5i

BROWNIE CRACKLES

Chocolate chips and a convenient brownie mix provide the rich chocolate flavor in these irresistible cookies. Rolling the dough in powdered sugar gives them their inviting crackled appearance.
—Ellen Govertsen, Wheaton, IL

Prep: 15 min. + standing • **Bake:** 10 min./batch
Makes: 3 dozen

- **1 pkg. fudge brownie mix (13x9-in. pan size)**
- **1 cup all-purpose flour**
- **1 large egg**
- **½ cup water**
- **¼ cup canola oil**
- **1 cup (6 oz.) semisweet chocolate chips**
- **Confectioners' sugar**

1. Preheat oven to 350°. In a large bowl, beat the brownie mix, flour, egg, water and oil until well blended. Stir in chocolate chips. Let stand for 30 minutes.
2. Place confectioners' sugar in a shallow dish. Drop dough by tablespoonfuls into sugar; gently roll to coat. Place 2 in. apart on greased baking sheets. Bake 8-10 minutes or until set. Remove from pans to wire racks to cool.
2 COOKIES: 154 cal., 6 g fat (2 g sat. fat), 8 mg chol., 84 mg sod., 24 g carb., 1 g fiber, 2 g pro.

LARA'S TENDER GINGERSNAPS

Soft gingersnaps embody the tastes and smells of the Christmas season, but are perfect for any fall or winter gathering. I enjoy the flavors of cloves, cinnamon and ginger blended into one delicious cookie.
—Lara Pennell, Mauldin, SC

Prep: 15 min. + chilling • **Bake:** 10 min./batch
Makes: 3 dozen

- 1 **cup packed brown sugar**
- ¾ **cup butter, melted**
- 1 **large egg, room temperature**
- ¼ **cup molasses**
- 2¼ **cups all-purpose flour**
- 1½ **tsp. ground ginger**
- 1 **tsp. baking soda**
- 1 **tsp. ground cinnamon**
- ½ **tsp. ground cloves**
- ¼ **cup sugar**

1. In a large bowl, beat brown sugar and butter until blended. Beat in egg and molasses. Combine the flour, ginger, baking soda, cinnamon and cloves; gradually add to brown sugar mixture and mix well (dough will be stiff). Cover and refrigerate for at least 2 hours.
2. Shape dough into 1 in. balls. Roll in sugar. Place 2 in. apart on greased baking sheets.
3. Bake at 350° for 9-11 minutes or until set. Cool for 1 minute before removing from pans to wire racks.
1 COOKIE: 99 cal., 4g fat (2g sat. fat), 16mg chol., 67mg sod., 15g carb. (9g sugars, 0 fiber), 1g pro. **DIABETIC EXCHANGES:** 1 starch, ½ fat.

READER REVIEW

"These are the best! I made a huge batch and froze the dough balls so I can just pull a few out and stick in the oven (less temptation to eat the whole batch). I even dipped them in white candy coating for an event we went to—yum-yum!"
SNOWMOSS, TASTEOFHOME.COM

CHERRY CHOCOLATE CHUNK COOKIES

These rich, fudgy cookies are chewy and studded with tangy dried cherries. It's a good thing the recipe makes only a small batch, because we eat them all in one night!
—Trisha Kruse, Eagle, ID

Prep: 15 min. • **Bake:** 15 min./batch
Makes: about 1½ dozen

- ½ **cup butter, softened**
- ¾ **cup sugar**
- 1 **large egg, room temperature**
- 2 **Tbsp. 2% milk**
- ½ **tsp. vanilla extract**
- 1 **cup all-purpose flour**
- 6 **Tbsp. baking cocoa**
- ¼ **tsp. baking soda**
- ¼ **tsp. salt**
- 1 **cup semisweet chocolate chunks**
- ½ **cup dried cherries**

1. Preheat oven to 350°. Cream butter and sugar until light and fluffy. Beat in egg, milk and vanilla. In a separate bowl, whisk flour, cocoa, baking soda and salt; gradually beat into the creamed mixture. Stir in chocolate and cherries.
2. Drop by rounded tablespoonfuls 2 in. apart onto baking sheets lightly coated with cooking spray. Bake until firm, 12-14 minutes. Cool for 1 minute before removing to a wire rack.
1 COOKIE: 159 cal., 8g fat (5g sat. fat), 22mg chol., 88mg sod., 22g carb. (15g sugars, 1g fiber), 2g pro.

CUCCIDATI

These cookies are a little bit of work, but it's well worth it for the compliments that will roll in—it's the best cookie recipe I've found!
—Carolyn Fafinski, Dunkirk, NY

Prep: 30 min. + chilling
Bake: 10 min./batch + cooling
Makes: about 5 dozen

- 2 **cups raisins**
- ¾ **lb. pitted dates**
- ¾ **cup sugar**
- 2 **small navel oranges, peeled and quartered**
- ⅓ **lb. dried figs**
- ⅓ **cup chopped walnuts**
- ¼ **cup water**

DOUGH

- 1 **cup shortening**
- 1 **cup sugar**
- 2 **large eggs, room temperature**
- ¼ **cup 2% milk**
- 2 **tsp. vanilla extract**
- 3½ **cups all-purpose flour**
- 1 **tsp. salt**
- 1 **tsp. baking powder**
- 1 **tsp. baking soda**

GLAZE

- 2 **cups confectioners' sugar**
- 2 **to 3 Tbsp. 2% milk**

1. Place the first seven ingredients in a food processor; cover and process until finely chopped. Set aside.
2. In a large bowl, cream shortening and sugar until light and fluffy. Beat in the eggs, milk and vanilla. Combine the flour, salt, baking powder and baking soda; gradually add to the creamed mixture and mix well. Divide dough into four portions; cover and refrigerate for 1 hour.
3. Preheat oven to 400°. Roll out each portion of dough between two sheets of waxed paper into a 16x6-in. rectangle. Spread 1 cup of filling lengthwise down the center of each rectangle. Starting at a long side, fold the dough over the filling; fold the other side over top. Pinch the seams and edges to seal. Cut each rectangle diagonally into 1-in strips. Place strips seam side down on parchment-lined baking sheets.
4. Bake 10-14 minutes or until the edges are golden brown. Cool for 10 minutes before removing from pans to wire racks to cool completely. Combine confectioners' sugar and enough milk to achieve the desired consistency; drizzle over cookies. Store in an airtight container.
1 COOKIE: 132 cal., 4g fat (1g sat. fat), 7mg chol., 67mg sod., 24g carb. (17g sugars, 1g fiber), 1g pro.

PUMPKIN CHIP COOKIES

These golden cakelike cookies are my favorite, especially around the holidays. They disappear quickly from the dessert trays. The subtle pumpkin and cinnamon flavors pair nicely with chocolate chips.
—Tami Burroughs, Salem, OR

Prep: 10 min. • **Bake:** 10 min./batch
Makes: about 10 dozen

- **1½ cups butter, softened**
- **2 cups packed brown sugar**
- **1 cup sugar**
- **1 large egg, room temperature**
- **1 tsp. vanilla extract**
- **1 can (15 oz.) pumpkin**
- **4 cups all-purpose flour**
- **2 tsp. baking soda**
- **2 tsp. ground cinnamon**
- **1 tsp. salt**
- **2 cups quick-cooking oats**
- **2 cups semisweet chocolate chips**

1. Preheat oven to 350°. Cream butter and sugars until light and fluffy. Beat in egg and vanilla. Beat in pumpkin. In another bowl, whisk together flour, baking soda, cinnamon and salt; gradually beat into the creamed mixture. Stir in oats and chocolate chips.
2. Drop by tablespoonfuls 2 in. apart onto ungreased baking sheets. Bake until lightly browned, 10-12 minutes. Remove cookies from pans to wire racks to cool.
1 COOKIE: 76 cal., 3g fat (2g sat. fat), 8mg chol., 61mg sod., 12g carb. (7g sugars, 1g fiber), 1g pro.

CANDY BAR FUDGE

My manager at work knows I like to try new treat recipes, and shared this one. I've made this chewy and chocolaty fudge many times since. It's like a candy bar. Everyone loves it.
—Lois Freeman, Oxford, MI

Takes: 20 min. + chilling
Makes: 2¾ lbs. (64 pieces)

- **½ cup butter**
- **⅓ cup baking cocoa**
- **¼ cup packed brown sugar**
- **¼ cup whole milk**
- **3½ cups confectioners' sugar**
- **1 tsp. vanilla extract**
- **30 caramels, unwrapped**
- **1 Tbsp. water**
- **2 cups salted peanuts**
- **½ cup semisweet chocolate chips**
- **½ cup milk chocolate chips**

1. In a microwave-safe bowl, combine butter, cocoa, brown sugar and milk. Microwave on high until the mixture boils, about 2 minutes. Stir in the confectioners' sugar and vanilla. Pour into a greased 8-in. square dish.
2. In another microwave-safe bowl, heat the caramels and water on high for 1¼ minutes or until melted. Stir in peanuts; spread over chocolate layer. Microwave chocolate chips on high for 30 seconds or until melted; spread over the caramel layer. Chill until firm.
1 PIECE: 101 cal., 5g fat (2g sat. fat), 5mg chol., 48mg sod., 14g carb. (12g sugars, 1g fiber), 2g pro.

BUTTERSCOTCH-RUM RAISIN TREATS

I love making rum raisin rice pudding around the holidays. Those flavors inspired this recipe. Crispy rice cereal adds crunch, but nuts, toasted coconut, or candied pineapple could do the job, too.
—Crystal Schlueter, Babbitt, MN

Takes: 20 min. • **Makes:** about 4½ dozen

- **1 pkg. (10 to 11 oz.) butterscotch chips**
- **1 pkg. (10 to 12 oz.) white baking chips**
- **½ tsp. rum extract**
- **3 cups Rice Krispies**
- **1 cup raisins**

1. Line 56 mini muffin cups with paper liners. In a large bowl, combine butterscotch and white chips. Microwave, uncovered, on high for 30 seconds; stir. Microwave in additional 30-second intervals, stirring until smooth.
2. Stir in extract, Rice Krispies and raisins. Drop by rounded tablespoonfuls into the prepared mini muffin cups. Chill until set.
FREEZE OPTION: Freeze cookies in freezer containers, separating layers with waxed paper. Thaw before serving.
1 TREAT: 76 cal., 4g fat (3g sat. fat), 1mg chol., 21mg sod., 11g carb. (9g sugars, 0 fiber), 0 pro.

COCONUT CLOUDS

A big dollop of buttercream and a sprinkle of toasted coconut make these soft cookies the first to disappear from cookie trays. Be sure to toast the coconut! The flavor it adds is absolutely heavenly.
—Donna Scofield, Yakima, WA

Prep: 45 min. • **Bake:** 10 min./batch + cooling
Makes: about 5½ dozen

- **¼ cup butter, softened**
- **¼ cup shortening**
- **1 cup sugar**
- **½ cup packed brown sugar**
- **2 large eggs, room temperature**
- **1 tsp. coconut extract**
- **1 tsp. vanilla extract**
- **1 cup sour cream**
- **2¾ cups all-purpose flour**
- **1 tsp. salt**
- **½ tsp. baking soda**
- **1 cup sweetened shredded coconut, toasted**

BROWNED BUTTER FROSTING

- **⅓ cup butter, cubed**
- **3 cups confectioners' sugar**
- **3 Tbsp. evaporated milk**
- **1 tsp. coconut extract**
- **1 tsp. vanilla extract**
- **2 cups sweetened shredded coconut, toasted**

1. Preheat oven to 375°. Cream butter, shortening and sugars until light and fluffy; beat in eggs and extracts. Stir in sour cream. In another bowl, whisk together the flour, salt and baking soda; gradually beat into the creamed mixture. Stir in coconut.
2. Drop dough by tablespoonfuls 2 in. apart onto lightly greased baking sheets. Bake until set, 8-10 minutes. Remove to wire racks to cool completely.
3. For the frosting, in a small heavy saucepan, heat butter over medium heat until golden brown, 5-7 minutes, stirring constantly. Transfer to a small bowl; gradually beat in the confectioners' sugar, milk and extracts. Spread over cookies. Dip in coconut; let stand until set. Store in an airtight container.
NOTE: To toast coconut, bake in a shallow pan in a 350° oven for 5-10 minutes or cook in a skillet over low heat until golden brown, stirring occasionally.
1 COOKIE: 110 cal., 5g fat (3g sat. fat), 13mg chol., 72mg sod., 16g carb. (11g sugars, 0 fiber), 1g pro.

5i

BUTTERY 3-INGREDIENT SHORTBREAD COOKIES

These buttery cookies are so simple to prepare, with only a few ingredients. To give them extra visual flair, use a doily or a stencil to dust a confectioners' sugar pattern on top.
—Patricia Prescott, Manchester, NH

Prep: 10 min. • **Bake:** 30 min. + cooling
Makes: 16 cookies

- **1 cup unsalted butter, softened**
- **½ cup sugar**
- **2 cups all-purpose flour**
- **Confectioners' sugar, optional**

1. Preheat oven to 325°. Cream butter and sugar until light and fluffy. Gradually beat in flour. Press dough into an ungreased 9-in. square baking pan. Prick with a fork.
2. Bake until light brown, 30-35 minutes. Cut into squares while still warm. Cool completely on a wire rack. If desired, dust cookies with confectioners' sugar.
1 COOKIE: 183 cal., 12g fat (7g sat. fat), 31mg chol., 2mg sod., 18g carb. (6g sugars, 0 fiber), 2g pro.

5i

BUCKEYES

These buckeyes are always popular at my church's annual fundraiser. They resemble chestnuts or buckeyes—hence the name.
—Merry Kay Opitz, Elkhorn, WI

Takes: 30 min. + chilling
Makes: about 5½ dozen

- **5½ cups confectioners' sugar**
- **1⅔ cups peanut butter**
- **1 cup butter, melted**
- **4 cups semisweet chocolate chips**
- **1 tsp. shortening**

1. In a large bowl, beat the sugar, peanut butter and butter until smooth. Shape into 1-in. balls; set aside.
2. Microwave chocolate chips and shortening on high until melted; stir until smooth. Dip balls in chocolate, allowing excess to drip off. Place on a wire rack over waxed paper; refrigerate for 15 minutes or until firm. Cover and store in the refrigerator.
2 CANDIES: 302 cal., 18g fat (8g sat. fat), 15mg chol., 119mg sod., 35g carb. (31g sugars, 2g fiber), 4g pro.

5i

ALMOND CHERRY FUDGE

Cooked in the microwave, this fast fudge is a sweet addition to any holiday gathering. I make it when I need a quick treat for a school party or to take to a neighbor.

—Shellie Tucker, Hendersonvlle, TN

Prep: 20 min. + chilling
Makes: about 1 lb. (64 pieces)

- **2 cups semisweet chocolate chips**
- **1 can (14 oz.) sweetened condensed milk**
- **½ cup chopped almonds**
- **½ cup red candied cherries, chopped**
- **1 tsp. almond extract**

1. Line an 8-in. square pan with foil and grease the foil; set aside. In a microwave, heat the chocolate chips and milk on high for about 1 minute; stir. Microwave in additional 10- to 20-second intervals until chocolate is melted; stir until smooth. Stir in the almonds, cherries and extract. Spread into prepared pan. Cover and chill for 2 hours or until set.

2. Using foil, lift fudge out of pan. Discard the foil; cut the fudge into 1-in. squares. Store in the refrigerator.

1 PIECE: 55 cal., 3g fat (1g sat. fat), 2mg chol., 9mg sod., 8g carb. (7g sugars, 0 fiber), 1g pro.

CRANBERRY COOKIES WITH BROWNED BUTTER GLAZE

I won a baking contest with these chunky glazed cookies that are so easy, even novice bakers can pull them off. What makes them special? Fresh cranberries.

—Laurie Cornett, Charlevoix, MI

Prep: 40 min. • **Bake:** 10 min./batch + cooling
Makes: about 4½ dozen

- **½ cup butter, softened**
- **1 cup sugar**
- **¾ cup packed brown sugar**
- **1 large egg, room temperature**
- **2 Tbsp. orange juice**
- **3 cups all-purpose flour**
- **1 tsp. baking powder**
- **½ tsp. salt**
- **¼ tsp. baking soda**
- **¼ cup 2% milk**
- **2½ cups coarsely chopped fresh cranberries**
- **1 cup white baking chips**
- **1 cup chopped pecans or walnuts**

GLAZE

- **⅓ cup butter, cubed**
- **2 cups confectioners' sugar**
- **1½ tsp. vanilla extract**
- **3 to 4 Tbsp. water**

1. Preheat oven to 375°. In a large bowl, cream butter and sugars until light and fluffy. Beat in egg and orange juice. In another bowl, whisk flour, baking powder, salt and baking soda; add to creamed mixture alternately with milk. Stir in cranberries, baking chips and pecans.

2. Drop dough by level tablespoonfuls 1 in. apart onto greased baking sheets. Bake for 10-12 minutes or until light brown. Remove from pans to wire racks to cool completely.

3. For the glaze, in a small heavy saucepan, melt butter over medium heat. Heat for 5-7 minutes or until golden brown, stirring constantly. Remove from heat. Stir in the confectioners' sugar, vanilla and enough water to reach a drizzling consistency. Drizzle over cookies. Let stand until set.

1 COOKIE: 130 cal., 5g fat (3g sat. fat), 12mg chol., 66mg sod., 19g carb. (13g sugars, 1g fiber), 1g pro.

LAURIE CORNETT
Charlevoix, MI

MINI CINNAMON ROLL COOKIES

Intense cinnamon flavor fills this yummy cross between a snickerdoodle and a cinnamon roll. These are at their absolute best with a cup of freshly brewed coffee.
—Mary Gauntt, Denton, TX

Prep: 1 hour • **Bake:** 10 min./batch + cooling
Makes: about 2½ dozen

- **1 cup butter, softened**
- **1¾ cups sugar, divided**
- **3 large egg yolks, room temperature**
- **1 Tbsp. plus 1 tsp. honey, divided**
- **1 tsp. vanilla extract**
- **2½ cups all-purpose flour**
- **1 tsp. baking powder**
- **½ tsp. salt**
- **½ tsp. cream of tartar**
- **1 Tbsp. ground cinnamon**
- **8 oz. white baking chocolate, chopped**

1. Preheat oven to 350°. In a large bowl, cream the butter and 1¼ cups of sugar until light and fluffy. Beat in the egg yolks, 1 Tbsp. honey and vanilla. Combine the flour, baking powder, salt and cream of tartar; gradually add to creamed mixture and mix well.
2. Shape a heaping tablespoonful of dough into a 6-in. log. In a shallow bowl, combine cinnamon and the remaining sugar; roll log in the cinnamon sugar. Loosely coil log into a spiral; place on a greased baking sheet. Repeat, placing cookies 1 in. apart. Sprinkle with remaining cinnamon sugar.
3. Bake for 8-10 minutes or until set. Remove to wire racks to cool completely. In a small bowl, melt the baking chocolate with the remaining honey; stir until smooth. Drizzle over cookies. Let stand until set. Store in an airtight container.
1 COOKIE: 189 cal., 9g fat (6g sat. fat), 38mg chol., 105mg sod., 25g carb. (17g sugars, 0 fiber), 2g pro. **DIABETIC EXCHANGES:** 1½ starch, 1½ fat.

DID YOU KNOW?
We test our recipes with double-acting baking powder, which contains two different acids that react at different times. The first creates gases when mixed with the liquid in the recipe; the second creates gases when exposed to oven heat. Most baking powders sold today are double-acting.

RED VELVET WHOOPIE PIES

Everyone gets a kick out of this fun take on the red velvet cake. If you like, take a shortcut by using packaged cream cheese frosting for the filling.
—Judi Dexheimer, Sturgeon Bay, WI

Prep: 40 min. • **Bake:** 10 min./batch + cooling
Makes: 2 dozen

- **¾ cup butter, softened**
- **1 cup sugar**
- **2 large eggs, room temperature**
- **½ cup sour cream**
- **1 Tbsp. red food coloring**
- **1½ tsp. white vinegar**
- **1 tsp. clear vanilla extract**
- **2¼ cups all-purpose flour**
- **¼ cup baking cocoa**
- **2 tsp. baking powder**
- **½ tsp. salt**
- **¼ tsp. baking soda**
- **2 oz. semisweet chocolate, melted and cooled**

FILLING

- **1 pkg. (8 oz.) cream cheese, softened**
- **½ cup butter, softened**
- **2½ cups confectioners' sugar**
- **2 tsp. clear vanilla extract**

TOPPINGS

- **White baking chips, melted**
- **Finely chopped pecans**

1. Preheat oven to 375°. In a large bowl, cream butter and sugar until light and fluffy. Beat in eggs, sour cream, food coloring, vinegar and vanilla. In another bowl, whisk flour, cocoa, baking powder, salt and baking soda; gradually beat into creamed mixture. Stir in the cooled chocolate.
2. Drop dough by tablespoonfuls 2 in. apart onto parchment-lined baking sheets. Bake for 8-10 minutes or until the edges are set. Cool on pans 2 minutes, then remove to wire racks to cool completely.
3. For the filling, in a large bowl, beat cream cheese and butter until fluffy. Beat in the confectioners' sugar and vanilla until smooth. Spread the filling on the bottom of half of the cookies; cover with the remaining cookies.
4. Drizzle with melted baking chips; sprinkle with pecans. Refrigerate until serving.
FREEZE OPTION: Freeze baked, unassembled cookies in freezer containers. Thaw in covered containers. Fill and decorate as directed.
1 WHOOPIE PIE: 272 cal., 15g fat (9g sat. fat), 56mg chol., 199mg sod., 32g carb. (22g sugars, 1g fiber), 3g pro.

Seasonal Specialties

No matter what the season, you'll find so many reasons to celebrate! From summer's fresh bounty to winter's coziest comfort foods and everything in between, these recipes will turn your gatherings into memorable occasions.

CHRISTMAS CUTOUTS

Making and decorating these tender sugar cookies left a lasting impression on our four children. Now that they're grown, they've all asked for my recipe so they can make the same memories with their own children.
—Shirley Kidd, New London, MN

Prep: 25 min. + chilling
Bake: 10 min./batch
Makes: about 3½ dozen

- **1 cup butter, softened**
- **1½ cups confectioners' sugar**
- **1 large egg, room temperature**
- **1 tsp. vanilla extract**
- **½ tsp. almond extract**
- **2½ cups all-purpose flour**
- **1 tsp. baking soda**
- **1 tsp. cream of tartar**

FROSTING

- **3¾ cups confectioners' sugar**
- **3 Tbsp. butter, softened**
- **1 tsp. vanilla extract**
- **2 to 4 Tbsp. 2% milk**
- **Liquid or paste food coloring and assorted sprinkles, optional**

1. Cream butter and confectioners' sugar until light and fluffy. Beat in egg and extracts. In another bowl, whisk together flour, baking soda and cream of tartar; gradually beat into creamed mixture. Shape into a disk; wrap in plastic. Refrigerate until firm enough to roll, 2-3 hours.
2. Preheat oven to 375°. On a lightly floured surface, roll dough to ⅛-in. thickness. Cut with floured 2-in. cookie cutters. Place on ungreased baking sheets.
3. Bake until the edges begin to brown, about 7-8 minutes. Remove from pan to wire racks; cool completely.
4. For frosting, beat confectioners' sugar, butter, vanilla and enough milk to reach the desired consistency; tint with food coloring if desired. Spread over cookies. Decorate cookies as desired.
1 COOKIE: 134 cal., 5g fat (3g sat. fat), 18mg chol., 74mg sod., 21g carb. (15g sugars, 0 fiber), 1g pro.

VALENTINE'S DAY

STRAWBERRIES & CHAMPAGNE CHEESECAKE

Hosting a Galentine's Day with the girls or celebrating a traditional Valentine's Day with your sweetie? Here's how to show some love.
—*Kathryn Work, Louisville, KY*

Prep: 45 min. • **Bake:** 55 min+ chilling
Makes: 12 servings

- 1 **cup champagne or other sparkling wine**
- 2 **cups chocolate graham cracker crumbs (about 14 whole crackers)**
- 2 **cups sugar, divided**
- ½ **cup butter, melted**
- 1 **cup sliced fresh strawberries**
- 3 **pkg. (8 oz. each) cream cheese, softened**
- ½ **cup sweetened condensed milk**
- 2 **Tbsp. cornstarch**
- 2 **large eggs, lightly beaten**
- 2 **large egg yolks**

TOPPING

- 20 **fresh strawberries, hulled**
- ⅓ **cup milk chocolate chips**
- 1 **tsp. shortening, divided**
- ⅓ **cup white baking chips**
- 1 **cup heavy whipping cream**
- ¼ **cup confectioners' sugar**

1. Place champagne in a small saucepan. Bring to a boil; cook until liquid is reduced to ¼ cup, about 8 minutes. Set aside to cool.
2. In a small bowl, combine graham cracker crumbs, ½ cup sugar and butter. Press onto bottom and 1½ in. up the sides of a greased 9-in. springform pan; set aside. Arrange sliced strawberries over the bottom.
3. In a bowl, beat cream cheese and remaining sugar until smooth. Beat in the sweetened condensed milk, cornstarch and reduced champagne. Add eggs and egg yolks; beat on low speed just until combined. Pour over strawberries. Place pan on a baking sheet.
4. Bake at 325° until center is almost set, 55-60 minutes. Cool cake on a wire rack for 10 minutes. Carefully run a knife around edge of the pan to loosen; cool cheesecake 1 hour longer. Cover and refrigerate overnight.
5. Remove sides of the springform pan. For topping, wash strawberries and gently pat with paper towels until completely dry. Slice and arrange over cheesecake. In a microwave, melt chocolate chips and ½ tsp. shortening; stir until smooth. Drizzle over strawberries. Repeat melting and drizzling with white baking chips and remaining shortening.
6. In a small bowl, beat cream until it begins to thicken; add the confectioners' sugar; beat until soft peaks form. Serve cheesecake with whipped cream.

1 SLICE: 684 cal., 42g fat (25g sat. fat), 185mg chol., 378mg sod., 68g carb. (55g sugars, 1g fiber), 9g pro.

CHAMPAGNE COCKTAIL

This amber drink is a champagne twist on the traditional old-fashioned. Try it with extra-dry champagne and don't skip the bitters.
—Taste of Home *Test Kitchen*

Takes: 5 min. • **Makes:** 1 serving

- 1 **sugar cube or ½ tsp. sugar**
- 6 **dashes bitters**
- ½ **oz. brandy**
- ½ **cup chilled champagne**
- **Fresh rosemary sprig and fresh or frozen cranberries, optional**

Place sugar in a champagne flute or cocktail glass; sprinkle with bitters. Add brandy; top with champagne. If desired, top with rosemary and cranberries.

1 SERVING: 130 cal., 0 fat (0 sat.fat), 0 chol., 0 sod., 5g carb. (2g sugars, 0 fiber), 0 pro.

2 tsp. grated lemon zest
½ tsp. salt
¼ tsp. pepper
⅛ tsp. cayenne pepper
½ cup butter, softened
1 cup soft bread crumbs
¼ cup butter, melted
4 lobster tails (8 to 10 oz. each)
4 beef tenderloin steaks (4 oz. each)
4 tsp. coarsely ground pepper

1. In a small skillet, saute garlic in 2 tsp. oil until tender; remove from the heat. In a small bowl, combine parsley, green onions, thyme, lemon zest, salt, pepper, cayenne and the reserved garlic. Set aside ½ cup of mixture for crumb topping.
2. Add softened butter to remaining herb mixture; mix well. Shape into a 1-in.-thick log; wrap and refrigerate until firm, 30 minutes.
3. For crumb topping, combine the bread crumbs, melted butter and reserved herb mixture; set aside.
4. Split lobster tails in half lengthwise. With cut side up and using scissors, cut along the edge of shell to loosen the cartilage covering the tail meat from the shell; remove and discard cartilage.
5. Place lobster tails on a baking sheet; top with the reserved crumb topping. Bake, uncovered, at 375° until meat is firm and opaque and crumbs are golden brown, 15-20 minutes.
6. Meanwhile, sprinkle steaks with coarse pepper. In a large skillet over medium heat, cook steaks in remaining oil for 4-5 minutes on each side or until meat reaches desired doneness (for medium-rare, a thermometer should read 135°; medium, 140°; medium-well, 145°).
7. Unwrap herb butter; cut four ¼-in.-slices from log. Place one slice on each steak. Serve with lobster. Rewrap the remaining butter; refrigerate for 1 week or freeze for up to 3 months.
1 SERVING: 793 cal., 52g fat (26g sat. fat), 355mg chol., 1289mg sod., 10g carb. (1g sugars, 1g fiber), 69g pro.

LINZER HEART COOKIES

This specialty cookie takes a little extra effort, but the delectable results are well-worth it. I bake the tender jam-filled hearts when I need something fancy to serve for special occasions.
—Jane Pearcy, Verona, WI

Prep: 20 min. + chilling • **Bake:** 10 min./batch
Makes: 3 dozen

1¼ cups butter, softened
1 cup sugar
2 large eggs, room temperature
3 cups all-purpose flour
1 Tbsp. baking cocoa
½ tsp. salt
¼ tsp. ground cinnamon
¼ tsp. ground nutmeg
⅛ tsp. ground cloves
2 cups ground almonds
Raspberry jam
Confectioners' sugar

1. In a large bowl, cream the butter and sugar until light and fluffy. Add eggs, one at a time, beating well after each addition. Combine the flour, cocoa, salt, cinnamon, nutmeg and cloves; gradually add to the creamed mixture and mix well. Stir in almonds. Refrigerate for 1 hour or until easy to handle.
2. On a lightly floured surface, roll out dough to ⅛-in. thickness. Cut with a 3-in. heart-shaped cookie cutter. From the center of half the cookies, cut out a heart or round shape with a 1½-in. cookie cutter.
3. Place on ungreased baking sheets. Bake at 350° for 10-12 minutes or until the edges are golden brown. Remove to wire racks to cool.
4. Spread ½ tsp. jam over the bottom of the solid cookies. Sprinkle cutout cookies with confectioners' sugar; carefully place over jam.
1 COOKIE: 163 cal., 9g fat (4g sat. fat), 29mg chol., 101mg sod., 18g carb. (9g sugars, 1g fiber), 3g pro.

SURF & TURF

For an intimate dinner with close friends, serve this stunning dinner of tenderloin steaks and lobster tail. Your guests just might think they are dining at a fine restaurant.
—Taste of Home *Test Kitchen*

Prep: 25 min. + chilling • **Bake:** 15 min.
Makes: 4 servings

2 garlic cloves, minced
2 tsp. plus 2 Tbsp. olive oil, divided
¼ cup minced fresh parsley
3 Tbsp. chopped green onions
2 Tbsp. minced fresh thyme

ST. PATRICK'S DAY

MARY SHENK
DeKalb, IL

IRISH SPICED BEEF

My Irish ancestors brought this recipe along when they immigrated to the United States. Start it at least five days ahead of time to spice and tenderize the meat; the flavor's worth the time it takes to develop.
—Mary Shenk, DeKalb, IL

Prep: 20 min. + chilling • **Bake:** 4 hours
Makes: 14 servings

- **1 fresh beef brisket (6 lbs.)**
- **⅓ cup packed brown sugar**
- **¾ cup coarse sea salt**
- **¼ cup chopped onion**
- **4 bay leaves, crushed**
- **3 tsp. pepper**
- **2 tsp. dried rosemary, crushed**
- **2 tsp. dried thyme**
- **1½ tsp. ground allspice**
- **1½ tsp. ground cloves**
- **4 medium onions, sliced**
- **4 medium carrots, sliced**
- **2 celery ribs, sliced**
- **2 cups stout or beef broth**
- **Rye bread, Swiss cheese slices and Dijon mustard, optional**

1. Place beef in a 15x10x1-in. baking pan; rub with brown sugar. Refrigerate, covered, for 24 hours.
2. In a small bowl, mix salt, chopped onion, bay leaves and seasonings; rub over beef. Refrigerate, covered, 3 days, turning and rubbing salt mixture into beef once each day.
3. Preheat oven to 325°. Remove and discard the salt mixture. Place beef, onions, carrots, celery and stout in a roasting pan. Add water to come halfway up the brisket. Roast, covered, 4-4½ hours or until meat is tender. Cool meat in cooking juices for 1 hour.
4. Remove beef; discard the vegetables and cooking juices. Transfer beef to a 13x9-in. baking dish. Refrigerate, covered, overnight.
5. Cut diagonally across the grain into thin slices. If desired, serve with spiced beef with rye bread, cheese and mustard.
NOTE: This is a fresh beef brisket, not corned beef.
4 OZ. COOKED BEEF: 268 cal., 8g fat (3g sat. fat), 83mg chol., 560mg sod., 6g carb. (5g sugars, 0 fiber), 40g pro.

THIN MINT MILK SHAKE

Save a sleeve of those yummy chocolate-mint Girl Scout cookies to use in creamy milkshakes. They go over big with kids and adults alike. Top each with a maraschino cherry.
—Shauna Sever, San Francisco, CA

Takes: 5 min. • **Makes:** 2 servings

- **3 Tbsp. creme de menthe or 3 Tbsp. 2% milk plus a dash of peppermint extract**
- **1¼ to 1½ cups vanilla ice cream**
- **7 Girl Scout Thin Mint cookies**
- **Green food coloring, optional**

Place all ingredients in a blender in the order listed; cover and process until blended. Serve milkshakes immediately.
⅔ CUP: 363 cal., 12g fat (7g sat. fat), 36mg chol., 70mg sod., 49g carb. (47g sugars, 1g fiber), 3g pro.

HOMEMADE IRISH CREAM

Add some creamy goodness to your cup of joe with a splash of this alcohol-free version of the Irish favorite.
—Marcia Severson, Hallock, MN

Takes: 10 min. • **Makes:** 3⅓ cups

- **1 can (12 oz.) evaporated milk**
- **1 cup heavy whipping cream**
- **½ cup 2% milk**
- **¼ cup sugar**
- **2 Tbsp. chocolate syrup**
- **1 Tbsp. instant coffee granules**
- **2 tsp. vanilla extract**
- **¼ tsp. almond extract**

EACH SERVING

- **½ cup brewed coffee**

In a blender, combine first eight ingredients; cover and process until smooth. Store in the refrigerator. For each serving, place coffee in a mug. Stir in ⅓ cup Irish cream. Heat mixture in a microwave if desired. Irish whiskey may be added to this recipe if desired.
1 CUP: 165 cal., 11g fat (7g sat. fat), 44mg chol., 53mg sod., 12g carb. (11g sugars, 0 fiber), 3g pro.

REUBEN WAFFLE POTATO APPETIZERS

I love Reubens, so I turned this classic sammie into a fun appetizer. Just put some corned beef, sauce and sauerkraut on waffle fries.
—Gloria Bradley, Naperville, IL

Prep: 30 min. • **Bake:** 10 min./batch
Makes: about 4 dozen

- **1 pkg. (22 oz.) frozen waffle-cut fries**
- **4 oz. cream cheese, softened**
- **2 cups shredded fontina cheese, divided**
- **⅓ cup Thousand Island salad dressing**
- **3 Tbsp. chopped sweet onion**
- **1½ tsp. prepared horseradish**
- **12 oz. sliced deli corned beef, coarsely chopped**
- **1 cup sauerkraut, rinsed, well drained and chopped**
- **2 Tbsp. minced fresh chives**

1. Prepare waffle fries according to package directions for baking. Meanwhile, in a small bowl, beat the cream cheese, 1 cup fontina cheese, salad dressing, onion and horseradish until blended.
2. Remove fries from the oven; reduce oven setting to 400°. Top each waffle fry with about ¼ oz. of corned beef and 1 tsp. each of the cream cheese mixture, sauerkraut and remaining fontina cheese. Bake until cheese is melted, 8-10 minutes. Sprinkle with chives.
1 APPETIZER: 62 cal., 4g fat (2g sat. fat), 12mg chol., 168mg sod., 4g carb. (0 sugars, 0 fiber), 3g pro.

EASTER

BACON & EGG LASAGNA

My sister-in-law served this special dish for Easter breakfast one year, and our whole family loved the mix of bacon, eggs, noodles and cheese. Now I sometimes assemble it the night before and bake it in the morning for a terrific hassle-free brunch entree.
—Dianne Meyer, Graniteville, VT

Prep: 45 min. • **Bake:** 35 min. + standing
Makes: 12 servings

- 1 **lb. bacon strips, diced**
- 1 **large onion, chopped**
- ⅓ **cup all-purpose flour**
- ½ **to 1 tsp. salt**
- ¼ **tsp. pepper**
- 4 **cups 2% milk**
- 12 **lasagna noodles, cooked and drained**
- 12 **hard-boiled large eggs, sliced**
- 2 **cups shredded Swiss cheese**
- ⅓ **cup grated Parmesan cheese**
- 2 **Tbsp. minced fresh parsley, optional**

1. In a large skillet, cook the bacon until crisp. Remove with a slotted spoon to paper towels. Drain, reserving ⅓ cup of drippings. In the drippings, saute the onion until tender. Stir in flour, salt and pepper until blended. Gradually stir in milk. Bring to a boil; cook and stir for 2 minutes or until thickened. Remove mixture from the heat.
2. Spread ½ cup sauce in a greased 13x9-in. baking dish. Layer with four noodles, a third of the eggs and bacon, Swiss cheese and white sauce. Repeat the layers twice. Sprinkle with Parmesan cheese.
3. Bake, uncovered, at 350° until bubbly, for 35-40 minutes. If desired, sprinkle with parsley. Let casserole stand for 15 minutes before cutting.
1 PIECE: 386 cal., 20g fat (9g sat. fat), 252mg chol., 489mg sod., 28g carb. (7g sugars, 1g fiber), 23g pro.

5i

MAPLE-PEACH GLAZED HAM

This is one of my husband's favorite recipes. He makes it regularly for his group of friends on the weekends because it's so good and easy.
—Bonnie Hawkins, Elkhorn, WI

Prep: 5 min. • **Bake:** 2 hours
Makes: 16 servings (about 2 cups sauce)

- 1 **fully cooked bone-in ham (7 to 9 lbs.)**
- 2 **cups peach preserves or orange marmalade**
- ½ **cup maple syrup**
- ⅓ **cup orange juice**
- 2 **Tbsp. ground ancho chili pepper, optional**

1. Preheat oven to 325°. Place ham on a rack in a shallow roasting pan. Cover and bake until a thermometer reads 130°, 1¾-2¼ hours.
2. Meanwhile, in a small saucepan, mix the preserves, syrup, orange juice and, if desired, chili pepper until blended. Remove ¾ cup mixture for glaze.
3. Remove ham from oven; brush with some of the glaze. Bake, uncovered, 15-20 minutes longer or until a thermometer reads 140°, brushing occasionally with remaining glaze.
4. Bring preserves mixture in saucepan to a boil over medium heat, stirring occasionally. Cook and stir for 1-2 minutes or until slightly thickened. Serve as a sauce with ham.
4 OZ. COOKED HAM WITH 2 TBSP. SAUCE: 294 cal., 5g fat (2g sat. fat), 87mg chol., 1040mg sod., 34g carb. (31g sugars, 0 fiber), 29g pro.

READER REVIEW

"Great tasting ham that's both simple and versatile. Since I have loads of homemade preserves from our apricots this year, I used that in place of the peach preserves."

RINSHIN, TASTEOFHOME.COM

SPRING ASPARAGUS

This fresh and colorful side dish is delicious served warm or cold. I get lots of compliments on the homemade dressing.
—Millie Vickery, Lena, IL

Takes: 25 min. • **Makes:** 8 servings

- **1½ lbs. fresh asparagus, trimmed and cut into 2-in. pieces**
- **2 small tomatoes, cut into wedges**
- **3 Tbsp. cider vinegar**
- **¾ tsp. Worcestershire sauce**
- **⅓ cup sugar**
- **1 Tbsp. grated onion**
- **½ tsp. salt**
- **½ tsp. paprika**
- **⅓ cup canola oil**
- **⅓ cup sliced almonds, toasted**
- **⅓ cup crumbled blue cheese, optional**

1. In a large saucepan, bring 1 cup water to a boil. Add asparagus; cook, covered, until crisp-tender, 3-5 minutes. Drain; place in a large bowl. Add tomatoes; cover vegetables and keep warm.
2. Place vinegar, Worcestershire sauce, sugar, onion, salt and paprika in a blender; cover and process until smooth. While processing, add oil gradually in a steady stream. Toss with the asparagus mixture. Top with almonds and, if desired, cheese.
¾ CUP: 154 cal., 11g fat (1g sat. fat), 0 chol., 159mg sod., 12g carb. (10g sugars, 1g fiber), 2g pro. **DIABETIC EXCHANGES:** 2 fat, 1 vegetable, ½ starch.

ITALIAN RICOTTA EASTER BREAD

I tweaked our family's traditional Easter bread by adding ricotta and a few other ingredients. The almond extract yields an amazing flavor!
—Tina Mirilovich, Johnstown, PA

Prep: 30 min. • **Bake:** 45 min.
Makes: 18 servings

- **¾ cup plain or butter-flavored shortening, room temperature**
- **1½ cups sugar**
- **3 large eggs, room temperature**
- **3 large egg yolks, room temperature**
- **1 cup whole-milk ricotta cheese**
- **1 tsp. almond extract (or flavor of choice)**
- **6 cups all-purpose flour**
- **1 Tbsp. baking powder**
- **1 tsp. salt**
- **½ cup 2% milk**

GLAZE

- **1½ cups confectioners' sugar**
- **3 Tbsp. 2% milk**
- **½ tsp. almond extract (or flavor of choice)**
- **Sliced toasted almonds or assorted sprinkles**

1. Preheat oven to 350°. Cream shortening and sugar until light and fluffy. Add eggs and egg yolks, one at a time, beating well after each addition. Beat in ricotta and extract. In another bowl, whisk flour, baking powder and salt; add to creamed mixture alternately with milk, beating well after each addition, stirring in final 1 cup flour by hand.
2. Turn onto a lightly floured surface; divide into thirds. Roll each into an 18-in. rope. Place ropes on a parchment-lined baking sheet and braid. Pinch ends to seal; tuck under the braid. Bake bread until a toothpick inserted in center comes out clean, for 45-55 minutes (do not overbake). Remove to wire racks to cool.
3. Meanwhile, beat confectioners' sugar, milk and extract until smooth. Brush on the bread while still warm; top glaze with sliced toasted almonds or sprinkles.
1 PIECE: 376 cal., 11g fat (4g sat. fat), 68mg chol., 247mg sod., 60g carb. (28g sugars, 1g fiber), 8g pro.

CINCO DE MAYO

STEAK FAJITAS

Zesty salsa and tender strips of steak make these traditional fajitas extra good, and the whole wheat tortillas are a nice touch.
—Rebecca Baird, Salt Lake City, UT

Takes: 30 min. • **Makes:** 6 servings

- **2 large tomatoes, seeded and chopped**
- **½ cup diced red onion**
- **¼ cup lime juice**
- **1 jalapeno pepper, seeded and minced**
- **3 Tbsp. minced fresh cilantro**
- **2 tsp. ground cumin, divided**
- **¾ tsp. salt, divided**
- **1 beef flank steak (about 1½ lbs.)**
- **1 Tbsp. canola oil**
- **1 large onion, halved and sliced**
- **6 whole wheat tortillas (8 in.), warmed**
- **Sliced avocado and lime wedges, optional**

1. For salsa, place the first five ingredients in a small bowl; stir in 1 tsp. cumin and ¼ tsp. salt. Let stand until serving.
2. Sprinkle steak with the remaining cumin and salt. Grill, covered, over medium heat or broil 4 in. from heat until meat reaches desired doneness (for medium-rare, a thermometer should read 135°), 6-8 minutes. Let stand 5 minutes.
3. Meanwhile, in a skillet, heat the oil over medium-high heat; saute the onion until crisp-tender. Slice the steak thinly across the grain; serve in tortillas with onion and salsa. If desired, serve with avocado and lime wedges.

NOTE: Wear disposable gloves when cutting hot peppers; the oils can burn skin. Avoid touching your face.
1 FAJITA: 329 cal., 12g fat (4g sat. fat), 54mg chol., 498mg sod., 29g carb. (3g sugars, 5g fiber), 27g pro. **DIABETIC EXCHANGES:** 3 lean meat, 2 starch, ½ fat.

SPICY CORN KABOBS

Corn on the cob becomes a tangy delight when grilled, sauced, and zinged with a splash of lime.
—Leah Lenz, Los Angeles, CA

Prep: 10 min. • **Grill:** 25 min.
Makes: 6 servings

- **6 medium ears sweet corn, husked and halved**
- **¼ cup sour cream**
- **¼ cup mayonnaise**
- **½ cup grated cotija cheese or Parmesan cheese**
- **2 tsp. chili powder**
- **¼ tsp. cayenne pepper, optional**
- **6 lime wedges**

1. Insert a metal or soaked wooden skewer into the cut end of each piece of corn. Grill, covered, over medium heat until tender, for 25-30 minutes, turning often.
2. In a small bowl, combine sour cream and mayonnaise; spread over corn. Sprinkle with cheese, chili powder and, if desired, cayenne. Serve with lime wedges.
2 KABOBS: 205 cal., 13g fat (4g sat. fat), 20mg chol., 222mg sod., 19g carb. (3g sugars, 3g fiber), 6g pro.

SPICY REFRIED BEANS

Jazz up a can of refried beans with jalapeno pepper, seasonings and cheese. Serve with tortilla chips on the side for scooping.
—Taste of Home *Test Kitchen*

Takes: 15 min. • **Makes:** 2 cups

- **1 small onion, chopped**
- **1 jalapeno pepper, seeded and chopped**
- **1 garlic clove, minced**
- **2 tsp. vegetable oil**
- **1 can (16 oz.) refried beans**
- **2 Tbsp. water**
- **1 tsp. hot pepper sauce**
- **¼ tsp. ground cumin**
- **¼ tsp. chili powder**
- **⅛ tsp. cayenne pepper**
- **½ cup shredded Monterey Jack cheese**

In a large skillet, saute the onion, jalapeno and garlic in oil for 2-3 minutes or until tender. Stir in the beans, water, hot pepper sauce, cumin, chili powder and cayenne pepper. Cook and stir over medium-low heat until the beans are heated through. Transfer to a serving bowl; sprinkle with cheese.

NOTE: Wear disposable gloves when cutting hot peppers; the oils can burn skin. Avoid touching your face.

¼ CUP: 95 cal., 4g fat (2g sat. fat), 11mg chol., 212mg sod., 10g carb. (2g sugars, 3g fiber), 5g pro. **DIABETIC EXCHANGES:** 1 fat, ½ starch.

MEXICAN CHOCOLATE SUGAR CRISPS

My grandma loved these cookies so much, she would hide them from my grandpa! I think of her every time I make a batch. Stir in a little chili powder if you like Mexican spice.
—Michele Lovio, Thousand Oaks, CA

Prep: 30 min. • **Bake:** 10 min./batch
Makes: 4½ dozen

- **¾ cup shortening**
- **1¼ cups sugar, divided**
- **1 large egg, room temperature**
- **¼ cup light corn syrup**
- **2 oz. unsweetened chocolate, melted and cooled**
- **1¾ cups all-purpose flour**
- **1½ tsp. ground cinnamon**
- **1 tsp. baking soda**
- **¼ tsp. salt**
- **1 cup (6 oz.) semisweet chocolate chips**

1. Preheat oven to 350°. In a large bowl, cream shortening and 1 cup sugar until fluffy. Beat in the egg, corn syrup and the melted chocolate. In another bowl, whisk flour, cinnamon, baking soda and salt; gradually beat into the creamed mixture. Stir in chocolate chips.

2. Shape dough into 1-in. balls; roll in balls in remaining sugar. Place cookies 2 in. apart on ungreased baking sheets (do not flatten). Bake 8-10 minutes or until tops are puffed and cracked. Cool on pans 2 minutes. Remove to wire racks to cool.

FREEZE OPTION: Freeze shaped balls of dough on baking sheets until firm. Transfer to resealable plastic freezer bags; return to freezer. To use, bake cookies as directed.

TO MAKE AHEAD: Dough can be made 2 days in advance. Wrap in plastic and place in a resealable bag. Store in the refrigerator.

1 COOKIE: 85 cal., 4g fat (2g sat. fat), 3mg chol., 37mg sod., 11g carb. (8g sugars, 1g fiber), 1g pro.

SUMMER HARVEST

WINNING RHUBARB-STRAWBERRY PIE

I was raised on a farm and I often ate rhubarb, so it's natural for me to use it in a pie. I prefer to use lard for the flaky pie crust and thin, red rhubarb stalks for the filling. These two little secrets helped this recipe win top honors at the 2013 Iowa State Fair.
—Marianne Carlson, Jefferson, IA

Prep: 50 min. + chilling • **Bake:** 65 min.
Makes: 8 servings

- 1 **large egg**
- 4 **to 5 Tbsp. ice water, divided**
- ¾ **tsp. white vinegar**
- 2¼ **cups all-purpose flour**
- ¾ **tsp. salt**
- ¾ **cup cold lard**

FILLING

- 1¼ **cups sugar**
- 6 **Tbsp. quick-cooking tapioca**
- 3 **cups sliced fresh or frozen rhubarb, thawed**
- 3 **cups halved fresh strawberries**
- 3 **Tbsp. butter**
- 1 **Tbsp. 2% milk**
- **Coarse sugar**

1. In a small bowl, whisk egg, 4 Tbsp. ice water and vinegar until blended. In a large bowl, mix flour and salt; cut in the lard until crumbly. Gradually add egg mixture, tossing with a fork, until dough holds together when pressed. If mixture is too dry, slowly add additional ice water, a teaspoon at a time, just until mixture comes together.
2. Divide dough in half. Shape each into a disk; wrap in plastic. Refrigerate for at least 1 hour or overnight.
3. Preheat oven to 400°. In a large bowl, mix the sugar and tapioca. Add the rhubarb and strawberries; toss to coat evenly. Let stand 15 minutes.
4. On a lightly floured surface, roll one half of dough to a ⅛-in.-thick circle; transfer to a 9-in. pie plate. Trim pastry even with rim.
5. Add filling; dot with butter. Roll remaining dough to a ⅛-in.-thick circle. Place over filling. Trim, seal and flute the edge. Cut slits in top. Brush milk over pastry; sprinkle with coarse sugar. Place the pie on a baking sheet; bake for 20 minutes.
6. Reduce oven setting to 350°. Bake until crust is golden brown and filling is bubbly, 45-55 minutes. Cool pie on a wire rack.

NOTE: If using frozen rhubarb, measure the rhubarb while still frozen, then thaw completely. Drain in a colander, but do not press liquid out.

1 PIECE: 531 cal., 25g fat (11g sat. fat), 53mg chol., 269mg sod., 73g carb. (35g sugars, 3g fiber), 5g pro.

FIRE & ICE TOMATOES

You won't miss the salt in this refreshing tomato salad. It's well-seasoned with cayenne pepper, mustard seed and vinegar, but it's not the least bit spicy. This dish is always a hit at picnics and potlucks.
—Nan Rickey, Yuma, AZ

Prep: 10 min. • **Cook:** 5 min. + chilling
Makes: 8 servings

- 5 **large tomatoes, cut into wedges**
- 1 **medium onion, sliced**
- ¾ **cup white vinegar**
- 6 **Tbsp. sugar**
- ¼ **cup water**
- 3 **tsp. mustard seed**
- ¼ **tsp. cayenne pepper**
- 1 **large cucumber, sliced**

1. Place the tomatoes and onion in a large heatproof nonreactive bowl. In a small saucepan, combine vinegar, sugar, water, mustard seed and cayenne; bring to a boil. Cook 1 minute, stirring to dissolve sugar; pour carefully over the tomato mixture. Cool completely.
2. Stir in cucumber. Refrigerate mixture, covered, overnight.

¾ CUP: 72 cal., 1g fat (0 sat. fat), 0 chol., 11mg sod., 17g carb. (0 sugars, 2g fiber), 2g pro.
DIABETIC EXCHANGES: 2 vegetable, ½ starch.

CORN & SQUASH QUESADILLAS

Grilled vegetables give these quesadillas their distinctive flair, while cumin and jalapeno peppers add a little zip.
—Mildred Sherrer, Fort Worth, TX

Prep: 40 min. • **Cook:** 10 min.
Makes: 6 servings

- **2 medium ears sweet corn, husks removed**
- **2 medium yellow summer squash, halved lengthwise**
- **½ small sweet onion, cut into ¼-in. slices**
- **1 to 2 jalapeno peppers**
- **1 Tbsp. minced fresh basil**
- **1½ tsp. minced fresh oregano**
- **1 garlic clove, minced**
- **¼ tsp. salt**
- **¼ tsp. ground cumin**
- **6 flour tortillas (8 in.), warmed**
- **1 cup shredded Monterey Jack cheese**
- **1 Tbsp. canola oil**

1. Grill corn, covered, over medium heat for 10 minutes; turn. Place the squash, onion and jalapenos on grill; cover and cook for 5-6 minutes on each side. When vegetables are cool enough to handle, remove corn from the cobs, chop the squash and onion, and seed and chop the jalapenos. Place in a large bowl.
2. Stir in the basil, oregano, garlic, salt and cumin. Place ½ cup filling on one side of each tortilla; sprinkle with cheese. Fold tortillas over filling. On a griddle or large skillet, cook the quesadillas in oil over medium heat until heated through, 1-2 minutes on each side. Cut into wedges.

NOTE: Wear disposable gloves when cutting hot peppers; the oils can burn skin. Avoid touching your face.

1 QUESADILLA: 301 cal., 12g fat (5g sat. fat), 17mg chol., 454mg sod., 38g carb. (5g sugars, 3g fiber), 11g pro. **DIABETIC EXCHANGES:** 2 starch, 1 medium-fat meat, 1 vegetable, ½ fat.

RUSTIC SUMMER VEGETABLE PASTA

My veggie pasta proves that you can't have too much of a good thing. Feel free to change it up with whatever fresh veggies are in the garden or at the farmers market. It's a super way to try things you haven't used before.
—Bryn Namavari, Chicago, IL

Prep: 15 min. • **Cook:** 30 min.
Makes: 8 servings

- **3 Tbsp. olive oil, divided**
- **1 medium zucchini, cut into ¾-in. pieces**
- **1 medium yellow summer squash, cut into ¾-in. pieces**
- **1 medium onion, chopped**
- **1 medium eggplant, peeled and cut into ¾-in. pieces**
- **2 cups sliced fresh mushrooms**
- **2 garlic cloves, minced**
- **¾ tsp. crushed red pepper flakes**
- **1 can (28 oz.) crushed tomatoes**
- **½ tsp. salt**
- **½ tsp. pepper**
- **1 Tbsp. minced fresh oregano or 1 tsp. dried oregano**
- **1 Tbsp. minced fresh parsley**
- **3 Tbsp. minced fresh basil or 1 Tbsp. dried basil, divided**
- **1 pkg. (14½ oz.) uncooked multigrain spaghetti**
- **½ cup shredded Parmesan cheese**

1. In a 6-qt. stockpot, heat 1 Tbsp. oil over medium-high heat. Add zucchini and yellow squash; cook and stir until tender. Remove from pan.
2. In same pot, heat 1 Tbsp. oil over medium-high heat. Add the onion, eggplant and mushrooms; cook and stir until tender. Add garlic and pepper flakes; cook 1 minute longer. Add tomatoes, salt and pepper. Stir in the oregano, parsley and half of the basil; bring to a boil. Reduce heat; simmer, uncovered, 15 minutes, stirring occasionally.
3. Meanwhile, cook spaghetti according to package directions. Drain; add spaghetti and squash to vegetable mixture. Drizzle with the remaining oil; toss to combine. Top pasta with cheese and remaining basil.

2 CUPS: 315 cal., 8g fat (2g sat. fat), 4mg chol., 445mg sod., 50g carb. (9g sugars, 8g fiber), 15g pro.

4TH OF JULY PICNIC

HONEY-MELON SALAD WITH BASIL

Put the sweet taste of summer in your salad. Loaded with juicy cantaloupe and honeydew and glazed with a honey dressing, this will be gone in minutes. Watermelon is a colorful addition, too.
—Khurshid Shaik, Omaha, NE

Takes: 20 min.
Makes: 12 servings

- **6 cups cubed cantaloupe (about 1 medium)**
- **6 cups cubed honeydew melon (about 1 medium)**
- **¼ cup honey**
- **3 Tbsp. lemon juice**
- **½ tsp. paprika**
- **¼ tsp. salt**
- **¼ tsp. coarsely ground pepper**
- **¼ cup minced fresh basil or mint**
- **¾ cup dried cranberries, optional**

In a large bowl, combine the cantaloupe and honeydew. Refrigerate, covered, until serving. In a small bowl, whisk the honey, lemon juice, paprika, salt and pepper. Pour over melons just before serving; toss to coat. Stir in basil and, if desired, dried cranberries. Serve with a slotted spoon.

1 CUP: 68 cal., 0 fat (0 sat. fat), 0 chol., 72mg sod., 17g carb. (16g sugars, 1g fiber), 1g pro.

SUMMER STEAK KABOBS

These meaty skewers not only satisfy my love of warm-weather outdoor cooking, they feature a mouthwatering marinade, too. It's terrific with chicken and pork, but I prefer beef because it becomes remarkably tender.
—Christi Ross, Guthrie, TX

Prep: 20 min. + marinating • **Grill:** 10 min.
Makes: 6 servings

- **½ cup canola oil**
- **¼ cup soy sauce**
- **3 Tbsp. honey**
- **2 Tbsp. white vinegar**
- **½ tsp. ground ginger**
- **½ tsp. garlic powder**
- **1½ lbs. beef top sirloin steak, cut into 1-in. cubes**
- **½ lb. whole fresh mushrooms**
- **2 medium onions, cut into wedges**
- **1 medium sweet red pepper, cut into 1-in. pieces**
- **1 medium green pepper, cut into 1-in. pieces**
- **1 medium yellow summer squash, cut into ½-in. slices**
- **Hot cooked rice**

1. In a large bowl, combine the first six ingredients. Add beef; turn to coat. Cover; refrigerate 8 hours or overnight.

2. On 12 metal or soaked wooden skewers, alternately thread the beef and vegetables; discard marinade. Grill kabobs, covered, over medium heat until the beef reaches desired doneness, 10-12 minutes, turning occasionally. Serve with rice.

2 KABOBS: 257 cal., 12g fat (2g sat. fat), 46mg chol., 277mg sod., 11g carb. (7g sugars, 2g fiber), 27g pro. **DIABETIC EXCHANGES:** 3 lean meat, 1½ fat, 1 vegetable.

RED, WHITE & BLUE DESSERT

I tweaked a recipe I found and ended up with this rich, fresh-tasting dessert. Decorated to resemble a flag, it's perfect for the Fourth of July or any other patriotic occasion. A glass bowl really shows it off.
—Sue Gronholz, Beaver Dam, WI

Takes: 20 min. • **Makes:** 18 servings

- **2 pkg. (8 oz. each) cream cheese, softened**
- **½ cup sugar**
- **½ tsp. vanilla extract**
- **½ tsp. almond extract**
- **2 cups heavy whipping cream, whipped**
- **2 qt. strawberries, halved, divided**
- **2 qt. blueberries, divided**

1. In a large bowl, beat cream cheese, sugar and extracts until fluffy. Fold in the whipped cream. Place a third of the mixture in a 4-qt. bowl. Reserve 20 strawberry halves and ½ cup blueberries for garnish.
2. Layer half of the remaining strawberries and blueberries over cream mixture. Top with another third of the cream mixture and the remaining berries. Spread remaining cream mixture on top. Use the reserved berries to make a flag on top.
1 CUP: 168 cal., 10g fat (6g sat. fat), 32mg chol., 44mg sod., 20g carb. (15g sugars, 3g fiber), 2g pro.

CLEO'S POTATO SALAD

My mom, Cleo Lightfoot, loved cooking all kinds of different recipes, but her favorite meal was one she served when hosting backyard barbecues in the summer. She would make her famous ribs, baked beans and this delicious potato salad.
—Joan Hallford, North Richland Hills, TX

Prep: 25 min. • **Cook:** 20 min.
Makes: 12 servings

- **3½ lbs. red potatoes (about 12 medium), cut into 1-in. cubes**
- **6 bacon strips, chopped**
- **¼ cup sugar**
- **1 Tbsp. all-purpose flour**
- **½ cup water**
- **1 large egg, lightly beaten**
- **3 Tbsp. cider vinegar**
- **1 Tbsp. grated onion**
- **1 tsp. celery seed**
- **1 tsp. salt**
- **½ tsp. pepper**
- **1 cup heavy whipping cream, whipped**
- **4 hard-boiled large eggs, chopped**
- **2 medium celery ribs, chopped**

1. Place potatoes in a large saucepan; cover with water. Bring to a boil. Reduce heat; cook, uncovered, until tender, 10-15 minutes. Drain; cool completely.
2. Meanwhile, in a saucepan, cook the bacon over medium heat until crisp. Remove with a slotted spoon; drain on paper towels. Remove all but 1 Tbsp. drippings from pan.
3. Stir sugar and flour into the drippings until smooth. Gradually stir in water; cook and stir over medium-high heat until thickened and bubbly. Remove from the heat. Stir a small amount of hot mixture into beaten egg; return all to pan, stirring constantly. Slowly bring to a boil, stirring constantly; remove from heat. Transfer to a large bowl; cool completely.
4. Gently stir in vinegar, onion and seasonings. Fold in whipped cream. Stir in the eggs, celery, potatoes and bacon. Refrigerate potato salad, covered, until serving.
¾ CUP: 211 cal., 11g fat (5g sat. fat), 90mg chol., 272mg sod., 23g carb. (5g sugars, 2g fiber), 6g pro.

CAMPFIRE CLASSICS

ALISSA KEITH
Forest, VA

POTATO-SAUSAGE FOIL PACKS

We first tried these smoky campfire bundles at a friend's house and loved the simplicity of this great meal. Now we often make them for our summer weeknight dinners.
—Alissa Keith, Forest, VA

Prep: 20 min. • **Grill:** 30 min.
Makes: 4 servings

- **1 medium green pepper**
- **1 medium sweet red pepper**
- **1 medium sweet yellow pepper**
- **1 pkg. (14 oz.) smoked turkey kielbasa, sliced**
- **2 large potatoes, cut into wedges**
- **1 medium onion, chopped**
- **4 tsp. lemon juice**
- **4 tsp. olive oil**
- **½ tsp. garlic powder**
- **½ tsp. pepper**
- **Lemon wedges, optional**

1. Cut the peppers into 1-in. pieces; place in a large bowl. Toss with next seven ingredients. Divide mixture among four double thicknesses of heavy-duty foil (about 18x12 in.). Fold foil around mixture, sealing tightly.

2. Grill, covered, over medium heat until the potatoes are tender, 30-35 minutes. Open foil carefully to allow steam to escape. If desired, serve with lemon wedges.

1 SERVING: 344 cal., 10g fat (2g sat. fat), 62mg chol., 990mg sod., 42g carb. (8g sugars, 6g fiber), 21g pro.

CAMPFIRE PANCAKES WITH PEANUT MAPLE SYRUP

My family loves eating s'mores around the campfire when we vacation at the lake. These campfire pancakes are my special tribute to those happy times.
—Cheryl Snavely, Hagerstown, MD

Takes: 20 min.
Makes: 8 pancakes (¼ cup syrup)

- **1 pkg. (6½ oz.) chocolate chip muffin mix**
- **⅔ cup 2% milk**
- **1 large egg, lightly beaten**
- **½ cup miniature marshmallows**
- **¼ cup butterscotch chips**
- **¼ cup maple syrup**
- **1 Tbsp. chunky peanut butter**

1. In a large bowl, combine muffin mix, milk and egg; stir just until moistened. Fold in marshmallows and chips.

2. Lightly grease a griddle; heat over medium heat. Pour batter by ¼ cupfuls onto griddle. Cook until bubbles on top begin to pop and bottoms are golden brown. Turn; cook until second side is golden brown.

3. Meanwhile, microwave maple syrup and peanut butter in 10- to 20-second intervals until heated through. Serve with pancakes.

2 PANCAKES WITH 1 TBSP. SYRUP MIXTURE: 407 cal., 13g fat (7g sat. fat), 50mg chol., 386mg sod., 63g carb. (43g sugars, 2g fiber), 8g pro.

INDIVIDUAL CAMPFIRE STEW

These handy packets are perfect for grilling or whipping up over a campfire. I can get several outdoor chores done while they're cooking.
—Margaret Riley, Tallahassee, FL

Prep: 15 min. • **Grill:** 25 min.
Makes: 4 servings

- **1 large egg, lightly beaten**
- **¾ cup dry bread crumbs**
- **¼ cup ketchup**
- **1 Tbsp. Worcestershire sauce**
- **1 tsp. seasoned salt**
- **1 lb. lean ground beef (90% lean)**
- **2 cups frozen shredded hash brown potatoes, thawed**
- **1 cup diced carrots**
- **1 cup condensed cream of chicken soup, undiluted**
- **¼ cup milk**

1. Prepare grill for indirect heat. In a large bowl, combine the first five ingredients. Crumble beef over mixture and mix well. Shape into four patties. Place each patty on a greased double thickness of heavy-duty foil (about a 12-in. square); sprinkle each with potatoes and carrots.
2. Combine soup and milk; spoon over meat and vegetables. Fold foil around the mixture and seal tightly. Grill, covered, over indirect medium heat for 25-30 minutes or until meat is no longer pink and potatoes are tender. Open foil carefully to allow steam to escape.
1 SERVING: 397 cal., 15g fat (6g sat. fat), 129mg chol., 1333mg sod., 34g carb. (6g sugars, 3g fiber), 29g pro.

TEST KITCHEN TIP
For some added convenience when making Individual Campfire Stew, replace the diced carrots with 1 cup of thawed frozen carrots or mixed vegetables. If you want to take the flavor up a notch, add a few herbs such as rosemary or marjoram.

CHERRY-CHOCOLATE PUDGY PIE

Here's an ooey-gooey treat that's just right for campfires and cookouts.
—Josh Carter, Birmingham, AL

Takes: 10 min. • **Makes:** 1 serving

- **2 slices white bread**
- **3 Tbsp. cherry pie filling**
- **1 Tbsp. chopped almonds**
- **1 Tbsp. semisweet chocolate chips**

1. Place one slice of white bread in a greased sandwich iron. Spread with pie filling; top with almonds, chocolate chips and remaining bread slice. Close iron.
2. Cook over a hot campfire until sandwiches are golden brown and heated through, about 3-6 minutes, turning occasionally.
1 SANDWICH: 309 cal., 9g fat (3g sat. fat), 0 chol., 294mg sod., 51g carb. (9g sugars, 3g fiber), 7g pro.

HOT QUICK BANANA BOATS

These delicious, warm bananas are great on camp-outs or in the backyard. You can eat them right out of the foil bowl. That makes cleanup a breeze, too.
—Sheila Parker, Reno, NV

Takes: 20 min. • **Makes:** 4 servings

- **4 large unpeeled bananas**
- **8 tsp. semisweet chocolate chips**
- **8 tsp. trail mix**
- **¼ cup miniature marshmallows**

1. Place each banana on a 12-in. square of foil; crimp and shape foil around the bananas so they sit flat; do not close over bananas.
2. Cut each banana lengthwise about ½ in. deep, leaving ½ in. uncut at both ends. Gently pull each banana peel open, forming a pocket. Fill pockets with the chocolate chips, trail mix and marshmallows.
3. Grill bananas, covered, over medium heat for 4-5 minutes or until marshmallows are melted and golden brown.
1 SERVING: 196 cal., 5g fat (2g sat. fat), 0 chol., 7mg sod., 41g carb. (24g sugars, 4g fiber), 2g pro.

SLOW-COOKER REUBEN SPREAD

My daughter shared this recipe with me for a hearty spread that tastes just like a Reuben sandwich. Serve it from the slow cooker so it stays tasty and warm.
—Rosalie Fuchs, Paynesville, MN

Prep: 5 min. • **Cook:** 2 hours • **Makes:** 3½ cups

- 1 **can (14 oz.) sauerkraut, rinsed and well drained**
- 1 **pkg. (8 oz.) cream cheese, cubed**
- 2 **cups shredded Swiss cheese**
- 1 **pkg. (3 oz.) deli corned beef, chopped**
- 3 **Tbsp. prepared Thousand Island salad dressing**
- **Snack rye bread or crackers**

In a 1½-qt. slow cooker, combine the first five ingredients. Cover and cook on low until cheeses are melted, 2-3 hours; stir to blend. Serve warm with bread or crackers.

2 TBSP.: 69 cal., 6g fat (3g sat. fat), 18mg chol., 203mg sod., 1g carb. (1g sugars, 0 fiber), 3g pro.

5i

SAUSAGE & SAUERKRAUT

Three young children involved in different activities keep me running year-round. I created this tasty, quick-and-easy dish so I can throw it together in no time on those extra-busy nights. Add a green salad on the side and you're done.
—Mary Lyon, Spotsylvania, VA

Takes: 30 min. • **Makes:** 4 servings

- 6 **medium red potatoes, cubed**
- 2 **Tbsp. canola oil**
- 1 **small onion, halved and sliced**
- 1 **lb. smoked sausage, cut into ¼-in. pieces**
- 1 **pkg. (16 oz.) sauerkraut, rinsed and well drained**
- ¼ **tsp. pepper**

In a large skillet, saute the potatoes in oil for 5-6 minutes or until lightly browned. Stir in onion; saute for 3-4 minutes or until tender. Add the sausage, sauerkraut and pepper. Cook, uncovered, over medium heat for 4-5 minutes or until heated through, stirring the mixture occasionally.

1½ CUPS: 611 cal., 38g fat (14g sat. fat), 76mg chol., 2119mg sod., 47g carb. (8g sugars, 7g fiber), 22g pro.

RED CABBAGE WITH APPLE

This delicious combination has a sweet and tart flavor with a hint of bacon and apple that goes perfectly with sauerbraten or any pork dish.
—Patricia Rutherford, Winchester, IL

Prep: 15 min. • **Cook:** 40 min.
Makes: 6 servings

- 3 **bacon strips, diced**
- 1 **medium onion, chopped**
- 1 **medium apple, peeled and chopped**
- 1 **small head red cabbage, chopped**
- 1 **cup water**
- ¼ **cup white wine vinegar**
- 1 **Tbsp. sugar**
- ½ **tsp. salt**

1. In a large saucepan, cook the bacon over medium heat until crisp. Using a slotted spoon, remove to paper towels to drain.
2. In the drippings, saute onion and apple until tender. Stir in the remaining ingredients. Bring to a boil. Reduce heat; cover and simmer the mixture for 30 minutes or until tender. Stir in reserved bacon.

¾ CUP: 131 cal., 5g fat (2g sat. fat), 8mg chol., 333mg sod., 19g carb. (12g sugars, 4g fiber), 4g pro. **DIABETIC EXCHANGES:** 2 vegetable, 1 fat, ½ starch.

TEST KITCHEN TIP
When buying heads of cabbage, look for those with crisp, firmly packed leaves. The head should feel heavy for its size. You can store cabbage tightly wrapped in a plastic bag in the refrigerator for up to 2 weeks. Remove the core, rinse and blot dry just before using.

SLOW-COOKER SAUERBRATEN

My family is of German Lutheran descent, and although we enjoy traditional sauerbraten, I never liked the amount of time and fuss it takes to make it. This recipe is so good and so easy. It's lovely with dumplings, spaetzle, vegetables or a salad.
—Norma English, Baden, PA

Prep: 20 min. • **Cook:** 6 hours
Makes: 8 servings

- **1 bottle (14 oz.) ketchup**
- **1 large onion, chopped**
- **¾ cup packed brown sugar**
- **¾ cup cider vinegar**
- **1 Tbsp. mixed pickling spices**
- **3 bay leaves**
- **1 boneless beef chuck roast or rump roast (3 to 4 lbs.)**
- **4 cups water**
- **1½ cups crushed gingersnap cookies (about 30 cookies)**
- **2 Tbsp. cornstarch**
- **¼ cup cold water**

1. Mix first six ingredients. Place roast in a 5-qt. slow cooker; add water. Pour ketchup mixture over top. Add cookie crumbs. Cook, covered, on low until meat is tender, for 6-8 hours.
2. Remove roast from slow cooker; keep warm. Strain cooking juices; skim fat. Transfer 4 cups juices to a saucepan; bring to a boil. Mix cornstarch and water until smooth; stir into cooking juices. Return to a boil; cook and stir until thickened, 1-2 minutes. Serve with roast.
1 SERVING: 475 cal., 11g fat (3g sat. fat), 101mg chol., 858mg sod., 58g carb. (40g sugars, 1g fiber), 35g pro.

OLD-WORLD RICOTTA CHEESECAKE

I reconstructed this dessert based on an old recipe that was never written down. Zwieback crust reminds me of the cheesecake I enjoyed as a child, but sub other crumbs if you want.
—Mary Beth Jung, Hendersonville, NC

Prep: 20 min. • **Bake:** 1 hour + chilling
Makes: 12 servings

- **1⅔ cups zwieback, rusk or plain biscotti crumbs**
- **3 Tbsp. sugar**
- **½ tsp. ground cinnamon**
- **⅓ cup butter, softened**

FILLING

- **2 cartons (15 oz. each) ricotta cheese**
- **½ cup sugar**
- **½ cup half-and-half cream**
- **2 Tbsp. all-purpose flour**
- **1 Tbsp. lemon juice**
- **1 tsp. finely grated lemon zest**
- **¼ tsp. salt**
- **2 large eggs, room temperature, lightly beaten**

TOPPING

- **1 cup sour cream**
- **2 Tbsp. sugar**
- **1 tsp. vanilla extract**

1. Combine the zwieback crumbs, sugar and cinnamon; mix in butter until the mixture is crumbled. Press onto the bottom and 1½ in. up sides of a greased 9-in. springform pan. Refrigerate until chilled.
2. Preheat the oven to 350°. Beat all filling ingredients except eggs until smooth. Add eggs; beat on low until combined. Pour into crust. Place pan on a baking sheet.
3. Bake until center is set, about 50 minutes. Remove from oven; let stand 15 minutes, leaving oven on. Combine topping ingredients; spoon around edge of cheesecake. Carefully spread over filling. Bake 10 minutes longer. Loosen sides from the pan with a knife; cool 1 hour. Refrigerate 3 hours or overnight, covering when completely cooled. Remove rim from pan. Refrigerate leftovers.
1 SLICE: 260 cal., 14g fat (9g sat. fat), 83mg chol., 191mg sod., 25g carb. (16g sugars, 0 fiber), 7g pro.

HALLOWEEN

CRYSTAL SCHLUETER
Babbitt, MN

SO-EASY-IT'S-SPOOKY BAT CAKE

This gorgeous dessert starts with a boxed cake mix. Then it's an easy and magical trick to make the bat, sprinkled with cocoa.
—*Crystal Schlueter, Babbitt, MN*

Prep: 25 min. + chilling
Bake: 25 min.
Makes: 16 servings

- 1 **devil's food or orange cake mix (regular size)**
- 1 **tsp. orange food coloring, optional**

ORANGE FROSTING
- 4⅔ **cups confectioners' sugar**
- 1 **cup butter, softened**
- 2 **tsp. vanilla extract**
- **Orange food coloring**
- 6 **to 7 Tbsp. 2% milk**

CHOCOLATE FROSTING
- 4 **cups confectioners' sugar**
- ⅔ **cup baking cocoa, sifted**
- 1 **cup butter, softened**
- 2 **tsp. vanilla extract**
- 6 **to 7 Tbsp. 2% milk**
- 10 **peanut butter cups, finely chopped**
- **Dutch-processed cocoa or confectioners' sugar**

1. Prepare and bake cake mix according to package directions, using two 9-in. round baking pans. If preparing orange cake, add orange food coloring. Cool as package directs.
2. For bat design, cut a bat pattern from card stock. Wrap with foil.
3. For devil's food cake, prepare the orange frosting by beating confectioners' sugar, butter, vanilla, food coloring and enough milk to reach a spreading consistency. For orange cake, prepare chocolate frosting by beating confectioners' sugar, cocoa, butter, vanilla and enough milk for spreading.
4. Using a long serrated knife, trim tops of the cakes if domed. Place one cake layer on a serving plate. Spread with 1 cup of frosting; sprinkle with chopped candies. Top with the remaining cake layer, bottom side up. Spread the remaining frosting over top and sides of cake. Refrigerate until set, about 30 minutes.
5. Lay bat pattern on top of cake. Using a fine-mesh strainer, sift Dutch-processed cocoa or confectioners' sugar over frosting. Lift pattern carefully to remove.

FREEZE OPTION: Wrap cooled cake layers in plastic wrap, then cover securely in foil; freeze. To use, thaw the cakes before unwrapping. Assemble as directed.

1 SLICE: 470 cal., 23g fat (10g sat. fat), 67mg chol., 424mg sod., 63g carb. (48g sugars, 2g fiber), 5g pro.

BUBBLIN' SWAMP JUICE

Here's a thick, creamy beverage that reminds kids of marshmallow-topped hot cocoa—only it's Halloween green! Garnish each mug with gummy insects for extra creepy-crawly appeal.
—Taste of Home *Test Kitchen*

Takes: 10 min. • **Makes:** 4 servings

- 4 **cups whole milk**
- 1 **cup vanilla or white chips**
- 12 **drops green food coloring**
- 8 **drops yellow food coloring**
- ¼ **cup miniature marshmallows**
- 4 **centipede gummies**

In a large saucepan, heat milk and chips over medium heat. Whisk until chips are melted and mixture is blended (do not boil). Remove from the heat; stir in food coloring. Garnish with marshmallows and candy.

1 CUP: 417 cal., 22g fat (13g sat. fat), 33mg chol., 149mg sod., 47g carb. (43g sugars, 0 fiber), 10g pro.

JACK-O'-LANTERN PIZZAS

Set out a variety of toppings and let the kids decorate their own pumpkin-head pizzas.
—Rachel DeVault, Grove City, OH

Takes: 30 min. • **Makes:** 1 dozen

- **1 lb. ground beef**
- **½ tsp. salt**
- **¼ tsp. pepper**
- **1 pkg. (12 oz.) English muffins, split and toasted**
- **1 jar (14 oz.) pizza sauce**
- **2 cups shredded part-skim mozzarella cheese**
- **Sliced ripe olives**
- **Chopped and slivered sweet red, yellow and green peppers**

1. Preheat oven to 425°. In a large skillet, cook and crumble beef over medium heat until no longer pink, 5-7 minutes; drain. Stir in the salt and pepper.

2. Place muffins in 15x10x1-in pans. Spread tops with pizza sauce; top with beef. Sprinkle with the cheese.

3. Bake until the cheese is melted, for about 5 minutes. Add olives and peppers to make jack-o'-lantern faces.

1 MINI PIZZA: 216 cal., 9g fat (4g sat. fat), 35mg chol., 511mg sod., 19g carb. (3g sugars, 1g fiber), 15g pro.

MERINGUE BONES

This unique treatment for meringue will delight all your little ghosts and ghouls, and it travels well, too. You will get requests for the recipe, and folks will be surprised by how simple it is.
—Taste of Home *Test Kitchen*

Prep: 30 min. • **Bake:** 1½ hours + cooling
Makes: 1 dozen

- **2 large egg whites, room temperature**
- **⅛ tsp. cream of tartar**
- **½ cup sugar**

1. In a small bowl, beat egg whites and cream of tartar on medium speed until soft peaks form. Gradually add sugar, 1 Tbsp. at a time, beating on high until stiff peaks form. Place mixture in a heavy-duty resealable plastic bag; cut a small hole in a corner of bag.

2. On parchment-lined baking sheets, pipe meringue into a 3-in. log. Pipe two 1-in. balls on the opposite sides of each end of the log. Repeat with remaining meringue. Bake at 225° for 1½ hours or until firm. Remove to wire racks. Store in an airtight container.

1 SERVING: 35 cal., 0 fat (0 sat. fat), 0 chol., 9mg sod., 8g carb. (8g sugars, 0 fiber), 1g pro.

READER REVIEW

"These are a must-have at Halloween parties. So easy, and delicious. The great thing about meringue is you can flavor it with just about anything."

SUEFALK, TASTEOFHOME.COM

SOUTHERN GREEN BEANS WITH APRICOTS

Green beans and apricots have become a family tradition. Enhanced with balsamic vinegar, the flavors in this southern side will make your taste buds pop.
—Ashley Davis, Easley, SC

Prep: 15 min. • **Cook:** 20 min.
Makes: 8 servings

- **2 lbs. fresh green beans, trimmed**
- **1 can (14½ oz.) chicken broth**
- **½ lb. bacon strips, chopped**
- **1 cup dried apricots, chopped**
- **¼ cup balsamic vinegar**
- **¾ tsp. salt**
- **¾ tsp. garlic powder**
- **¾ tsp. pepper**

1. Place beans and broth in a large saucepan. Bring to a boil. Cook, covered, 4-7 minutes or until beans are crisp-tender; drain.
2. In a large skillet, cook bacon over medium heat until crisp, stirring occasionally. Remove with a slotted spoon; drain on paper towels. Discard drippings, reserving 1 Tbsp. of the drippings in pan.
3. Add apricots to drippings; cook and stir over medium heat until softened. Stir in the vinegar, salt, garlic powder, pepper and beans; cook and stir 2-3 minutes longer or until the beans are coated. Sprinkle with bacon.
¾ CUP: 149 cal., 6g fat (2g sat. fat), 12mg chol., 464mg sod., 21g carb. (14g sugars, 5g fiber), 6g pro.

DILLY BARBECUED TURKEY

This is one of my brother-in-law's special cookout recipes. The onions, garlic and herbs in the marinade make a tasty, tender turkey, and the aroma prompts the family to gather around the grill.
—Sue Walker, Greentown, IN

Prep: 10 min. + marinating • **Grill:** 1 hour
Makes: 6 servings

- **1 cup plain yogurt**
- **½ cup lemon juice**
- **⅓ cup canola oil**
- **½ cup minced fresh parsley**
- **½ cup chopped green onions**
- **4 garlic cloves, minced**
- **4 Tbsp. fresh minced dill or 4 tsp. dill weed**
- **1 tsp. dried rosemary, crushed**
- **1 tsp. salt**
- **½ tsp. pepper**
- **1 turkey breast half with bone (2½ to 3 lbs.)**

1. In a large bowl, combine the first 10 ingredients. Pour half into a large resealable plastic bag; add turkey. Seal bag and turn to coat. Cover and refrigerate for 6-8 hours or overnight. Cover and refrigerate remaining yogurt mixture.
2. Drain and discard marinade from turkey. Grill turkey, covered, over medium-hot heat, basting often with reserved marinade, for 1-1¼ hours or until a thermometer reads 180°.
3 OZ. COOKED TURKEY: 245 cal., 12g fat (0 sat. fat), 40mg chol., 127mg sod., 5g carb. (0 sugars, 0 fiber), 28g pro. **DIABETIC EXCHANGES:** 3 lean meat, 1 vegetable, 1 fat.

4. In a large bowl, beat the egg, egg white, sugars, salt and spices until smooth. Beat in pumpkin. Gradually beat in milk. Pour into pastry shell. Bake at 375° until a knife inserted in the center comes out clean, 45-50 minutes. Cool on a wire rack. Garnish with leaf cutouts. If desired, top the pumpkin pie with whipped cream. Refrigerate leftovers.

1 SLICE: 249 cal., 8g fat (2g sat. fat), 32mg chol., 295mg sod., 40g carb. (26g sugars, 3g fiber), 6g pro.

SLOW-COOKER MASHED POTATOES

Sour cream and cream cheese give richness to these smooth make-ahead potatoes. They're wonderful for your Thanksgiving or Christmas dinner. There's no last-minute mashing, so meal prep is even easier.

—*Trudy Vincent, Valles Mines, MO*

Prep: 20 min. • **Cook:** 2 hours
Makes: 10 servings

- **3 oz. cream cheese, softened**
- **½ cup sour cream**
- **¼ cup plus 1 Tbsp. softened butter, divided**
- **1 envelope ranch salad dressing mix**
- **1 Tbsp. minced fresh parsley**
- **6 cups warm mashed potatoes (without added milk or butter)**

In a large bowl, combine the cream cheese, sour cream, ¼ cup butter, salad dressing mix and parsley; stir in mashed potatoes. Transfer to a 3-qt. slow cooker. Cover and cook on low for 2-3 hours. Top with remaining butter.

¾ CUP: 210 cal., 11g fat (7g sat. fat), 27mg chol., 670mg sod., 23g carb. (1g sugars, 4g fiber), 3g pro.

CLASSIC PUMPKIN PIE

Nothing says Thanksgiving better than a slice of pumpkin pie. And you can relish every luscious bite of this version because the tender crust is made with a mere hint of canola oil and butter.

—Taste of Home *Test Kitchen*

Prep: 20 min. • **Bake:** 45 min. + cooling
Makes: 8 servings

- **1 cup all-purpose flour**
- **1 tsp. sugar**
- **¼ tsp. salt**
- **3 Tbsp. canola oil**
- **1 Tbsp. butter, melted**
- **2 to 3 Tbsp. cold water**

FILLING

- **1 large egg**
- **1 large egg white**
- **½ cup packed brown sugar**
- **¼ cup sugar**
- **½ tsp. salt**
- **½ tsp. ground cinnamon**
- **⅛ tsp. each ground allspice, nutmeg and cloves**
- **1 can (15 oz.) solid-pack pumpkin**
- **1 cup fat-free evaporated milk**
- **Whipped cream, optional**

1. In a small bowl, combine the flour, sugar and salt. Using a fork, stir in oil and butter until dough is crumbly. Gradually add enough water until dough holds together. Roll out between sheets of plastic wrap or waxed paper into an 11-in. circle. Freeze for 10 minutes.

2. Remove top sheet of wrap; invert pastry into a 9-in. pie plate. Remove the remaining wrap. Trim and flute edges. Chill.

3. Roll pastry scraps to ⅛-in. thickness. Cut with a 1-in. leaf-shaped cookie cutter. Place on an ungreased baking sheet. Bake at 375° until edges are very lightly browned, 6-8 minutes. Cool on a wire rack.

HANUKKAH

TENDER BEEF BRISKET

A touch of sugar mellows the flavorful sauce that's drizzled over this brisket. The original recipe came to me from a friend. I revised it for the slow cooker.

—Sondra Morrow, Mesa, AZ

Prep: 20 min. • **Cook:** 6 hours
Makes: 8 servings

- **1 fresh beef brisket (3 to 4 lbs.), trimmed and cut in half**
- **1 cup ketchup**
- **1 small onion, chopped**
- **2 Tbsp. cider vinegar**
- **1 Tbsp. prepared horseradish**
- **1 Tbsp. prepared mustard**
- **1 tsp. sugar**
- **½ tsp. pepper**

1. Place the brisket in a 3-qt. slow cooker. In a bowl, combine the remaining ingredients. Pour over brisket. Cover and cook on low for 6 hours or until tender.
2. Remove the beef; set aside. Pour the sauce into a saucepan; cook, uncovered, over low heat for 13-15 minutes or until reduced and thickened, stirring occasionally. Slice the meat across the grain; serve with sauce.
NOTE: This is a fresh beef brisket, not corned beef.
1 SERVING: 253 cal., 7g fat (3g sat. fat), 72mg chol., 464mg sod., 10g carb. (9g sugars, 0 fiber), 35g pro. **DIABETIC EXCHANGES:** 5 lean meat, ½ starch.

VANILLA & CINNAMON-KISSED APPLE LATKES

Apples replace potatoes, and orange juice, cinnamon and vanilla helping to take this version to the dessert realm.

—Candace McMenamin, Lexington, SC

Prep: 20 min. • **Cook:** 5 min./batch
Makes: 3 dozen

- **2 Tbsp. confectioners' sugar**
- **2 Tbsp. ground cinnamon**
- **4 cups all-purpose flour**
- **⅔ cup sugar**
- **2 tsp. baking powder**
- **½ tsp. salt**
- **2 cups orange juice**
- **1 cup 2% milk**
- **4 large eggs, lightly beaten**
- **1 tsp. vanilla extract**
- **2¾ lbs. apples (about 6 large apples), peeled and shredded**
- **¾ cup canola oil**

1. In a small bowl, combine confectioners' sugar and cinnamon; set aside.
2. In a large bowl, combine the flour, sugar, baking powder and salt. Stir in the orange juice, milk, eggs and vanilla until blended; fold in apples.
3. Heat 2 Tbsp. oil in a large cast-iron or other heavy skillet over medium heat. Drop batter by ¼ cupfuls into oil; press lightly to flatten. Fry in batches until golden brown on both sides, using remaining oil as needed. Drain on paper towels. Sprinkle with cinnamon-sugar.
3 LATKES WITH 1 TSP. CINNAMON-SUGAR: 422 cal., 17g fat (2g sat. fat), 72mg chol., 200mg sod., 62g carb. (27g sugars, 3g fiber), 8g pro.

1 SLICE: 452 cal., 9g fat (3g sat. fat), 54mg chol., 350mg sod., 89g carb. (61g sugars, 1g fiber), 6g pro.

RASPBERRY CHOCOLATE RUGELACH

We celebrate both Hanukkah and Christmas, and these treats are always on the menu. The fruit-and-chocolate filling is a real delight. You can cover and refrigerate unbaked cookies overnight or freeze them for up to two months.
—GP Busarow, Whitehall, MT

Prep: 40 min. + chilling
Bake: 20 min./batch
Makes: 32 cookies

- ½ **cup butter, softened**
- 4 **oz. cream cheese, softened**
- 1 **cup all-purpose flour**
- ¼ **tsp. salt**

FILLING

- ¼ **cup dried currants**
- 2 **Tbsp. sugar**
- ½ **tsp. ground cinnamon**
- ¼ **cup seedless raspberry jam**
- ⅔ **cup finely chopped pecans**
- ¼ **cup miniature semisweet chocolate chips**

1. In a large bowl, beat butter and cream cheese until smooth. Combine the flour and salt; gradually add to the creamed mixture and mix well.
2. Divide dough in half; form into two balls. Flatten to 5-in. circles; wrap in plastic wrap. Refrigerate for 8 hours or overnight.
3. Place currants in a small bowl. Cover with boiling water; let stand for 5 minutes. Drain well and set aside. Combine the sugar and cinnamon; set aside.
4. On a lightly floured surface or pastry mat, roll one portion of dough into an 11-in. circle. Brush with half of the jam. Sprinkle with half of the cinnamon-sugar, pecans, chocolate chips and currants; press down gently.
5. Cut into 16 wedges. Roll up wedges from the wide end and place point side down 2 in. apart on a parchment-lined baking sheet. Curve ends to form a crescent. Cover and refrigerate for 30 minutes before baking. Repeat with remaining dough and filling.
6. Bake at 350° for 18-22 minutes or until golden brown. Remove to wire racks to cool.
1 COOKIE: 90 cal., 6g fat (3g sat. fat), 11mg chol., 49mg sod., 8g carb. (4g sugars, 1g fiber), 1g pro. **DIABETIC EXCHANGES:** 1 fat, ½ starch.

HOLIDAY HONEY CAKE

One year I gave a friend a platter of my assorted home-baked Christmas cookies. The next day, she brought over slices of this delicious cake, which she made for Hanukkah. We exchanged recipes, and my family and I have been enjoying this moist and flavorful honey cake ever since. I top mine with a creamy caramel glaze.
—Kristine Chayes, Smithtown, NY

Prep: 20 min. + standing • **Bake:** 50 min.
Makes: 12 servings

- 3 **large eggs, separated**
- 3½ **cups all-purpose flour**
- 1 **cup sugar**
- 2½ **tsp. baking powder**
- 1 **tsp. baking soda**
- 1 **tsp. ground cinnamon**
- ½ **tsp. salt**
- ½ **tsp. ground cloves**
- ¼ **tsp. ground ginger**
- 1⅓ **cups brewed coffee**
- 1⅓ **cups honey**
- ¼ **cup canola oil**
- ¼ **tsp. cream of tartar**

CARAMEL GLAZE

- 3 **Tbsp. butter**
- ⅓ **cup packed brown sugar**
- 2 **Tbsp. 2% milk**
- ¾ **cup confectioners' sugar**
- 1 **tsp. vanilla extract**

1. Place egg whites in a large bowl; let stand at room temperature 30 minutes.
2. Meanwhile, preheat oven to 350°. Sift flour, sugar, baking powder, baking soda, cinnamon, salt, cloves and ginger together twice; place in another large bowl.
3. In a small bowl, whisk the egg yolks, coffee, honey and oil until smooth. Add to the flour mixture; beat until well blended.
4. Add cream of tartar to the egg whites; with clean beaters, beat on high speed just until stiff but not dry. Fold a fourth of the egg whites into batter, then fold in the remaining egg whites.
5. Gently transfer to an ungreased 10-in. tube pan. Bake on lowest oven rack 50-60 minutes or until top springs back when lightly touched. Immediately invert pan; cool cake completely, about 1½ hours.
6. In a small heavy saucepan, melt butter. Stir in brown sugar and milk. Bring to a boil; cook over medium heat until sugar is dissolved. Stir in confectioners' sugar and vanilla; cook until thickened, about 5 minutes.
7. Run a knife around sides and center tube of pan. Remove honey cake to a serving plate and add glaze.

CHRISTMAS

CONTEST-WINNING BRAISED SHORT RIBS

I've been relying on this recipe ever since I bought my first slow cooker many years ago. The fall-off-the-bone-tender ribs are so good to come home to after a busy day.
—Peggy Edwards, Heber City, UT

Prep: 20 min. • **Cook:** 6 hours
Makes: 7 servings

- **½ cup all-purpose flour**
- **1½ tsp. salt**
- **1½ tsp. paprika**
- **½ tsp. ground mustard**
- **4 lbs. bone-in beef short ribs**
- **2 Tbsp. canola oil**
- **2 medium onions, sliced**
- **1 cup beer or beef broth**
- **1 garlic clove, minced**

GRAVY

- **2 tsp. all-purpose flour**
- **1 Tbsp. cold water**

1. In a shallow dish, combine the flour, salt, paprika and mustard. Add ribs in batches and turn to coat. In a large skillet, brown the ribs in oil; drain.

2. Place onions in a 5-qt. slow cooker; add ribs. Top with beer and garlic. Cover and cook on low until meat is tender, for 6-7 hours.

3. Remove short ribs and onions to a serving platter; keep warm. Skim fat from cooking juices; transfer to a small saucepan. Bring to a boil. Combine flour and water until smooth; gradually stir into the pan. Bring to a boil; cook and stir for 2 minutes or until thickened. Serve with ribs.

1 SERVING: 281 cal., 14g fat (5g sat. fat), 62mg chol., 547mg sod., 12g carb. (4g sugars, 1g fiber), 22g pro.

AUNT GRACE'S EGGNOG

When I was growing up, I couldn't get enough of the nonalcoholic eggnog my aunt prepared for us kids. Now I enjoy the adult version. It's great with a platter of holiday cookies.
—Susan Hein, Burlington, WI

Prep: 15 min. • **Cook:** 15 min. + chilling
Makes: 20 servings

- **8 cups 2% milk, divided**
- **6 large eggs**
- **1 cup plus 2 Tbsp. sugar, divided**
- **½ cup rum**
- **½ cup brandy**
- **½ tsp. ground nutmeg**
- **3 cups heavy whipping cream**
- **Cinnamon sticks and additional ground nutmeg, optional**

1. In a large saucepan, heat 4 cups milk until bubbles form around sides of pan. Meanwhile, in a large bowl, whisk eggs and 1 cup of sugar until blended. Slowly stir in hot milk; return all to saucepan.

2. Cook over medium-low heat 6-8 minutes or until slightly thickened and a thermometer reads at least 160°, stirring constantly (do not allow to boil). Immediately transfer mixture to a large bowl.

3. Stir in rum, brandy, nutmeg and remaining milk. Refrigerate, covered, several hours or until cold.

4. In a large bowl, beat cream until it begins to thicken. Add remaining sugar; beat until soft peaks form. Fold into egg mixture. (Mixture may separate; stir before serving.) If desired, serve the eggnog with cinnamon sticks and additional nutmeg.

¾ CUP: 263 cal., 16g fat (10g sat. fat), 104mg chol., 77mg sod., 17g carb. (17g sugars, 0 fiber), 6g pro.

BACON CHEESE WREATH

My grandmother makes this smoky bacon and Parmesan spread for special occasions and holidays. For a pretty yuletide presentation, accent the cream cheese wreath with parsley and pimientos.

—Lisa Carter, Warren, IN

Prep: 10 min. + chilling • **Makes:** about 3 cups

- **2 pkg. (8 oz. each) cream cheese, softened**
- **½ cup mayonnaise**
- **⅓ cup grated Parmesan cheese**
- **¼ cup sliced green onions, optional**
- **10 bacon strips, cooked and crumbled**
- **Parsley sprigs and diced pimientos, optional**
- **Assorted crackers**

1. In a small bowl, beat the cream cheese, mayonnaise, Parmesan cheese and onions if desired. Stir in bacon. Cover and refrigerate for 1-2 hours.

2. Invert a small bowl in the center of a serving platter. Drop the cream cheese mixture by rounded tablespoonfuls around edge of bowl. Remove bowl. Smooth cream cheese mixture, forming a wreath. Garnish with parsley and pimientos if desired. Serve with crackers.

2 TBSP.: 87 cal., 9g fat (3g sat. fat), 15mg chol., 116mg sod., 0 carb. (0 sugars, 0 fiber), 2g pro.

HOME-FOR-CHRISTMAS FRUIT BAKE

Pop this special dish in the oven and mouths will water in anticipation— the cinnamony aroma is tantalizing! The fruit comes out slightly tart and tender while the pecan halves add a delightful crunch. And the colors are so festive the fruit holds a place of honor at the table.

—Bonnie Baumgardner, Sylva, NC

Prep: 15 min. • **Bake:** 45 min.
Makes: 12 servings

- **1 medium apple, peeled and thinly sliced**
- **1 tsp. lemon juice**
- **1 can (20 oz.) pineapple chunks**
- **1 can (29 oz.) peach halves, drained**
- **1 can (29 oz.) pear halves, drained**
- **1 jar (6 to 8 oz.) maraschino cherries**
- **½ cup pecan halves**
- **⅓ cup packed brown sugar**
- **1 Tbsp. butter, melted**
- **1 tsp. ground cinnamon**

1. Preheat oven to 325°. Toss apple slices with lemon juice. Arrange fruit in a greased 2½-qt. baking dish. Drain pineapple, reserving ¼ cup juice. Combine pineapple, peaches and pears; spoon over apples. Top with the cherries and pecans; set aside.

2. In a small saucepan, combine brown sugar, butter, cinnamon and reserved pineapple juice. Cook and stir over low heat until sugar is dissolved and butter is melted. Pour over fruit. Bake, uncovered, until the apples are tender, about 45 minutes. Serve warm.

¾ CUP: 220 cal., 4g fat (1g sat. fat), 3mg chol., 21mg sod., 49g carb. (44g sugars, 3g fiber), 1g pro.

HOLLY BERRY COOKIES

What would Christmas be without overflowing trays of treats? We begin baking these festive cookies early and freeze them until December.
—Audrey Thibodeau, Gilbert, AZ

Prep: 30 min. + chilling • **Bake:** 10 min./batch
Makes: 2 dozen

- 2 **cups all-purpose flour**
- 1 **cup sugar**
- 1 **tsp. ground cinnamon**
- ¾ **tsp. baking powder**
- ¼ **tsp. salt**
- ½ **cup cold butter, cubed**
- 1 **large egg**
- ¼ **cup 2% milk**
- ⅔ **cup seedless raspberry jam**

GLAZE

- 2 **cups confectioners' sugar**
- 2 **Tbsp. 2% milk**
- ½ **tsp. vanilla extract**
- **Red Hots**
- **Green food coloring**

1. In a large bowl, combine the first five ingredients. Cut in the butter until mixture resembles coarse crumbs. In a small bowl, beat egg and milk. Add to crumb mixture just until moistened. Cover and refrigerate for 1 hour or until dough is easy to handle.

2. On a lightly floured surface, roll out dough to ⅛-in. thickness. Cut with a 2-in. round cookie cutter. Place on ungreased baking sheets. Bake at 375° for 8-10 minutes or until edges are lightly browned. Cool on wire racks. Spread jam on half of the cookies; top each with another cookie.

3. In a small bowl, combine the sugar, milk and vanilla until smooth; spread over cookies. Decorate with Red Hots before glaze is set. Let dry. With small new paintbrush and green food coloring, paint holly leaves on cookies.

1 COOKIE: 171 cal., 4g fat (3g sat. fat), 20mg chol., 81mg sod., 32g carb. (23g sugars, 0 fiber), 2g pro.

MACADAMIA & COCONUT CARAMELS

I collect cookbooks from all over the world, and I use them to create new and different dishes. These smooth caramels have a scrumptious and exotic flavor. Individually wrapped, they are easy to put in festive boxes or tins for gifts.
—Sharon Delaney-Chronis, South Milwaukee, WI

Prep: 25 min. • **Cook:** 25 min. + chilling
Makes: 64 pieces (1½ lbs.)

- 1 **tsp. plus ½ cup butter, divided**
- 1 **cup packed light brown sugar**
- ½ **cup light corn syrup**
- ¼ **tsp. cream of tartar**
- ¾ **cup sweetened condensed milk**
- ½ **cup sweetened shredded coconut**
- ½ **cup chopped macadamia nuts**
- ½ **tsp. vanilla extract**

1. Line an 8-in. square baking dish with foil and grease the foil with 1 tsp. butter; set aside.

2. In a large heavy saucepan, combine the brown sugar, corn syrup, cream of tartar and remaining butter; bring to a boil over medium heat, stirring constantly. Remove from the heat; gradually stir in milk. Cook and stir over medium-low heat until a candy thermometer reads 244° (firm-ball stage).

3. Remove from the heat; stir in remaining ingredients. Pour mixture into prepared dish. Refrigerate until set, at least 2 hours.

4. Using foil, lift candy out of dish. Gently peel off foil; cut caramel into 1-in. squares. Wrap individually in waxed paper; twist ends. Store in an airtight container.

NOTE: We recommend that you test your candy thermometer before each use by bringing water to a boil; the thermometer should read 212°. Adjust recipe temperature up or down based on your test.

1 PIECE: 56 cal., 3g fat (1g sat. fat), 5mg chol., 23mg sod., 8g carb. (6g sugars, 0 fiber), 0 pro.

GRETA KIRBY
Carthage, TN

PINEAPPLE & MACADAMIA NUT CAKE

This delicious cake with a tropical twist is my own invention. It's a huge hit among family and friends, and it even inspired fierce bidding at a local charity auction! Using a cake mix saves a little time so you can splurge on the filling.
—Greta Kirby, Carthage, TN

Prep: 20 min. • **Bake:** 25 min. + cooling
Makes: 16 servings

- **1 pkg. white or yellow cake mix, regular size**
- **1¼ cups unsweetened pineapple juice**
- **½ cup canola oil**
- **3 large eggs, room temperature**

FILLING

- **¾ cup sugar**
- **4 tsp. all-purpose flour**
- **2 large egg yolks**
- **¼ cup butter, melted**
- **1 can (8 oz.) unsweetened crushed pineapple, undrained**
- **¼ cup chopped macadamia nuts, toasted**

FROSTING

- **½ cup butter, softened**
- **4 cups confectioners' sugar**
- **2 to 4 Tbsp. 2% milk**
- **Additional chopped macadamia nuts, optional**

1. Preheat oven to 350°. Combine cake mix, pineapple juice, oil and eggs; beat on low speed for 30 seconds. Beat on medium for 2 minutes. Pour batter into three greased and floured 8-in. round baking pans.

2. Bake until a toothpick inserted in center comes out clean, 25-30 minutes. Cool cake for 10 minutes before removing from pans to wire racks to cool completely.

3. For filling, combine sugar and flour in a large saucepan. Whisk in egg yolks, butter and pineapple until blended. Bring to a boil over medium heat; cook and stir until thickened and bubbly, about 2 minutes. Remove from heat; cool to room temperature. Reserve ⅓ cup pineapple mixture for frosting; gently stir nuts into remaining pineapple mixture.

4. Place one cake layer on a serving plate; spread with half of the filling. Repeat. Top with remaining cake layer.

5. For frosting, cream butter, confectioners' sugar, reserved pineapple mixture and enough milk to reach a spreading consistency. Spread over top and sides of cake. If desired, chop and toast additional nuts; sprinkle on top and around bottom of cake.

1 SLICE: 457 cal., 20g fat (7g sat. fat), 81mg chol., 296mg sod., 69g carb. (55g sugars, 1g fiber), 3g pro.

5i

PEPPERMINT PUFF PASTRY STICKS

I wanted to impress my husband's family with a holiday treat reminiscent of something they'd find in a European bakery, and these chocolaty treats are the fine result. The flaky pastry melts in your mouth.
—Darlene Brenden, Salem, OR

Prep: 15 min. • **Bake:** 15 min./batch
Makes: 3 dozen

- **1 sheet frozen puff pastry, thawed**
- **1½ cups crushed peppermint candies**
- **10 oz. milk chocolate candy coating, coarsely chopped**

1. Preheat oven to 400°. Unfold pastry sheet. Cut in half to form two rectangles. Cut each rectangle crosswise into 18 strips, about ½ in. wide. Place on ungreased baking sheets. Bake until golden brown, 12-15 minutes. Remove from pans to wire racks to cool completely.
2. Place crushed candies in a shallow bowl. In a microwave, melt candy coating; stir until smooth. Dip each cookie halfway in coating; allow excess to drip off. Sprinkle cookies with peppermint candies. Place on waxed paper; let stand until set. Store puff pastry sticks in an airtight container.
1 COOKIE: 89 cal., 4g fat (2g sat. fat), 0 chol., 24mg sod., 13g carb. (7g sugars, 1g fiber), 1g pro.

READER REVIEW

"These are so simple and delicious! I brushed the puff pastry with an egg wash before putting it in the oven for golden color."

DEBORAH, TASTEOFHOME.COM

MINT CHOCOLATE WAFERS

My grandmother gave me a cookbook stuffed with recipes. This is a slight twist on one of the first—and best—recipes I made from the book. It's best to store these in the refrigerator.
—Mary Murphy, Evansville, IN

Prep: 1 hour + chilling
Bake: 10 min./batch
Makes: 10 dozen

- **1 large egg**
- **⅓ cup water**
- **3 Tbsp. canola oil**
- **1 pkg. chocolate fudge cake mix (regular size)**
- **½ cup cake flour**

COATING

- **4 cups (24 oz.) semisweet chocolate chips**
- **¼ cup shortening**
- **½ tsp. peppermint extract**
- **Sprinkles**

1. In a large bowl, beat egg, water and oil until blended. Gradually beat in cake mix and flour.
2. Divide dough in half. Shape each into a disk; wrap in plastic. Refrigerate 2 hours or until firm enough to roll.
3. Preheat oven to 350°. On a lightly floured surface, roll each portion of dough to ⅛-in. thickness. Cut with a floured 1½-in. round cookie cutter. Place 1 in. apart on greased baking sheets.
4. Bake 8-10 minutes or until firm. Remove from pans to wire racks to cool completely.
5. In top of a double boiler or a metal bowl over hot water, melt chocolate chips and shortening; stir until smooth. Stir in extract. Spread cookies with chocolate mixture. Place on waxed paper-lined baking sheets. Decorate with sprinkles. Refrigerate until set.
NOTE: This recipe was tested with Betty Crocker chocolate fudge cake mix.
1 COOKIE: 52 cal., 3g fat (1g sat. fat), 2mg chol., 32mg sod., 7g carb. (5g sugars, 0 fiber), 1g pro.

ALPHABETICAL INDEX

SUBSTITUTIONS & EQUIVALENTS

EQUIVALENT MEASURES

3 teaspoons	= 1 tablespoon	**16 tablespoons**	= 1 cup
4 tablespoons	= ¼ cup	**2 cups**	= 1 pint
5⅓ tablespoons	= ⅓ cup	**4 cups**	= 1 quart
8 tablespoons	= ½ cup	**4 quarts**	= 1 gallon

FOOD EQUIVALENTS

Macaroni	1 cup (3½ ounces) uncooked	= 2½ cups cooked
Noodles, Medium	3 cups (4 ounces) uncooked	= 4 cups cooked
Popcorn	⅓-½ cup unpopped	= 8 cups popped
Rice, Long Grain	1 cup uncooked	= 3 cups cooked
Rice, Quick-Cooking	1 cup uncooked	= 2 cups cooked
Spaghetti	8 ounces uncooked	= 4 cups cooked

Bread	1 slice	= ¾ cup soft crumbs, ¼ cup fine dry crumbs
Graham Crackers	7 squares	= ½ cup finely crushed
Buttery Round Crackers	12 crackers	= ½ cup finely crushed
Saltine Crackers	14 crackers	= ½ cup finely crushed

Bananas	1 medium	= ⅓ cup mashed
Lemons	1 medium	= 3 tablespoons juice, 2 teaspoons grated zest
Limes	1 medium	= 2 tablespoons juice, 1½ teaspoons grated zest
Oranges	1 medium	= ¼-⅓ cup juice, 4 teaspoons grated zest

Cabbage	1 head = 5 cups shredded	**Green Pepper**	1 large = 1 cup chopped
Carrots	1 pound = 3 cups shredded	**Mushrooms**	½ pound = 3 cups sliced
Celery	1 rib = ½ cup chopped	**Onions**	1 medium = ½ cup chopped
Corn	1 ear fresh = ⅔ cup kernels	**Potatoes**	3 medium = 2 cups cubed

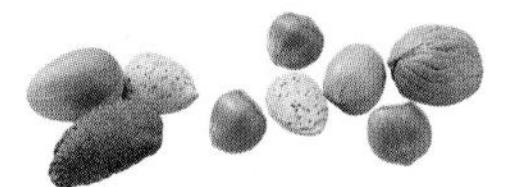

Almonds	1 pound = 3 cups chopped	**Pecan Halves**	1 pound = 4½ cups chopped
Ground Nuts	3¾ ounces = 1 cup	**Walnuts**	1 pound = 3¾ cups chopped

EASY SUBSTITUTIONS

WHEN YOU NEED...		USE...
Baking Powder	1 teaspoon	½ teaspoon cream of tartar + ¼ teaspoon baking soda
Buttermilk	1 cup	1 tablespoon lemon juice or vinegar + enough milk to measure 1 cup (let stand 5 minutes before using)
Cornstarch	1 tablespoon	2 tablespoons all-purpose flour
Honey	1 cup	1¼ cups sugar + ¼ cup water
Half-and-Half Cream	1 cup	1 tablespoon melted butter + enough whole milk to measure 1 cup
Onion	1 small, chopped (⅓ cup)	1 teaspoon onion powder or 1 tablespoon dried minced onion
Tomato Juice	1 cup	½ cup tomato sauce + ½ cup water
Tomato Sauce	2 cups	¾ cup tomato paste + 1 cup water
Unsweetened Chocolate	1 square (1 ounce)	3 tablespoons baking cocoa + 1 tablespoon shortening or oil
Whole Milk	1 cup	½ cup evaporated milk + ½ cup water

GET COOKING WITH A WELL-STOCKED KITCHEN

In a perfect world, you plan weekly or even monthly menus and have all the ingredients on hand to make each night's dinner. The reality, however, is that you may not get to think about dinner until you walk through the door.

With a reasonably stocked pantry, refrigerator and freezer, you'll still be able to serve a satisfying meal in short order. Consider these tips:

QUICK-COOKING MEATS—such as boneless chicken breasts, chicken thighs, pork tenderloin, pork chops, ground meats, Italian sausage, sirloin and flank steaks, fish fillets and shrimp—should be stocked in the freezer. Wrap individual pieces and portions, so you can remove only the amount you need. For the quickest defrosting, wrap meats for freezing in small, thin packages.

FROZEN VEGETABLES are a real time-saver. Simply pour out the amount needed—no additional preparation is required.

PASTAS, RICE, RICE MIXES AND COUSCOUS are great staples to have in the pantry—and they generally have a long shelf life. Remember that thinner pastas, such as angel hair, cook faster than thicker pastas, and fresh (refrigerated) pasta cooks faster than dried.

DAIRY PRODUCTS like milk, sour cream, cheeses (shredded, cubed or crumbled), eggs, yogurt, butter and margarine are perishable, so check the use-by date on packages and replace as needed.

CONDIMENTS like ketchup, mustard, mayonnaise, salad dressings, salsa, taco sauce, soy sauce, stir-fry sauce, hot sauce, lemon juice and lime juice add flavor to many dishes. Personalize the list to suit your family's tastes.

FRESH FRUIT AND VEGETABLES can make a satisfying pre-dinner snack. Oranges and apples are not as perishable as bananas. Ready-to-use salad greens are perfect for an instant salad.

DRIED HERBS, SPICES, VINEGARS and seasoning mixes add lots of flavor and keep for months.

PASTA SAUCES, OLIVES, BEANS, broths, canned tomatoes, canned vegetables and canned or dried soups are ideal to have on hand for a quick meal—and many of these items are common recipe ingredients.

GET YOUR FAMILY INTO THE HABIT of posting a grocery list. When an item is used up or is almost gone, just add it to the list for your next shopping trip. This way you're less likely to run completely out of an item, and you'll also save time when writing your grocery list.

MAKE THE MOST OF YOUR TIME EVERY NIGHT

With recipes in hand and the kitchen stocked, you're well on the way to a relaxing family meal. Here are some pointers to help get dinner on the table fast:

PREHEAT THE OVEN OR GRILL before starting on the recipe.

PULL OUT THE REQUIRED INGREDIENTS, mixing tools and cooking tools before beginning any prep work.

USE CONVENIENCE ITEMS whenever possible. Think pre-chopped garlic, onion and peppers, shredded or cubed cheese, seasoning mixes and jarred sauces.

MULTITASK! While the meat is simmering for a main dish, toss a salad together, cook a side dish or start on dessert.

ENCOURAGE HELPERS. Have younger children set the table. Older ones can help with ingredient preparation or can even assemble the recipes themselves.

TAKE CARE OF TWO MEALS IN ONE NIGHT by planning main-dish leftovers or making a double batch of favorite sides.

TRICKS TO TAME HUNGER WHEN IT STRIKES

Are the kids begging for a pre-supper snack? Calm their rumbling tummies with nutritious, not-too-filling noshes.

START WITH A SMALL TOSSED SALAD. Try a ready-to-serve salad mix, and add their favorite salad dressing and a little protein, like cubed cheese or julienned slices of deli meat.

CUT UP AN APPLE and smear a little peanut butter on each slice, or offer other fruits such as seedless grapes, cantaloupe, oranges or bananas. For variety, give kids vanilla yogurt or reduced-fat ranch dressing as a dipper, or combine a little reduced-fat sour cream with a sprinkling of brown sugar. Too busy to cut up the fruit? A fruit snack cup will also do the trick.

DURING THE COLD MONTHS, a small mug of soup with a few oyster crackers on top can really hit the spot.

RAW VEGGIES such as carrots, cucumbers, mushrooms, broccoli and cauliflower are tasty treats, especially when served with a little hummus for dipping. Many of these vegetables can be purchased already cut.

OFFER A SMALL SERVING of cheese and crackers. Look for sliced cheese, and cut the slices into smaller squares to fit the crackers. Choose a cracker that's made from whole wheat, such as an all-natural seven-grain cracker.